Storied Ground

People have always attached meaning to the landscape that surrounds them. In *Storied ground* Paul Readman uncovers why landscape matters so much to the English people, exploring its particular importance in shaping English national identity amid the transformations of modernity. The book takes us from the white cliffs of Dover to the fells of the Lake District; from the streetscapes of industrial Manchester to the heart of London. This panoramic journey reveals the significance, not only of the physical characteristics of landscapes, but also of the sense of the past, collective memories and cultural traditions that give these places their meaning. Between the late eighteenth and early twentieth centuries, Englishness extended far beyond the pastoral idyll of chocolate-box thatched cottages, waving fields of corn and quaint country churches. It was found in diverse locations – urban as well as rural, north as well as south – and it took strikingly diverse forms.

Paul Readman is Professor of Modern British History at King's College London. He is author of *Land and nation in England: Patriotism, national identity and the politics of land* (2008). His other publications include, as co-editor, *The land question in Britain, 1750–1950* (2010), *Borderlands in world history, 1700–1914* (2014) and *Walking histories, 1800–1914* (2016), as well as many articles and essays. As a keen walker and perpetual tourist, he has a longstanding interest in the diverse ways that human experience shapes, and is shaped by, landscape and place. *Storied ground* explores these questions against the backdrop of ideas about history, national identity and the environment.

Storied Ground

Landscape and the Shaping of English National Identity

Paul Readman
King's College London

CAMBRIDGE
UNIVERSITY PRESS

CAMBRIDGE
UNIVERSITY PRESS

University Printing House, Cambridge CB2 8BS, United Kingdom

One Liberty Plaza, 20th Floor, New York, NY 10006, USA

477 Williamstown Road, Port Melbourne, VIC 3207, Australia

314–321, 3rd Floor, Plot 3, Splendor Forum, Jasola District Centre,
New Delhi – 110025, India

79 Anson Road, #06-04/06, Singapore 079906

Cambridge University Press is part of the University of Cambridge.

It furthers the University's mission by disseminating knowledge in the pursuit of
education, learning and research at the highest international levels of excellence.

www.cambridge.org
Information on this title: www.cambridge.org/9781108424738
DOI: 10.1017/9781108344043

First published 2018

Printed in the United Kingdom by TJ International Ltd. Padstow Cornwall

A catalogue record for this publication is available from the British Library.

ISBN 978-1-108-42473-8 Hardback

For Martha Vandrei

CONTENTS

FIGURES

ACKNOWLEDGEMENTS

This book has taken a long time to complete. The origins of some of the research presented here lie in my 2002 Ph.D. dissertation, which was supervised by Jon Parry and examined by David Cannadine and Peter Mandler. In various ways, these three scholars have had a major influence on my thinking; my debt to them is deep. I have, of course, other debts to acknowledge and many of them are associated with King's College London, which has been my academic home for more than fifteen years. I'm particularly grateful to the college for the award of research leave in the academic years 2012/13 and 2013/14, at the end of my term as Head of the Department of History. Without this leave, I might never have finished this book. But without the advice, encouragement and friendship of my departmental colleagues at King's I might never have attempted it at all. One conversation in the late afternoon of Monday 4 June 2007 was especially consequential. As it happened, this conversation was a formal one – my annual appraisal by a senior colleague. On this occasion my interlocutor was David Carpenter, a medievalist, and to him I presented a dilemma: should I write a book about the politics of late Victorian and Edwardian patriotism, or should I embark on a study of landscape and national identity in English culture, over a much longer chronological period? These were the two ideas for projects I had at the time; I could see the pros and cons of each; I was torn between them. David, however, had no doubt that the book on landscape was the one to write, and his enthusiastic conviction put an end to my dithering; my gratefulness to him for this intervention has only increased over time.

Other departmental colleagues at King's, too, were a great source of advice, wisdom and moral support. I'd particularly like to thank Marie Berry, Jim Bjork, Arthur Burns, Laura Clayton, David Edgerton, Alana Harris, Ian McBride, Niall O'Flaherty, Simon Sleight, Sarah Stockwell, Adam Sutcliffe, Richard Vinen and Abigail Woods; but really I could name the whole department. Indeed, I am lucky to be a member of a department that combines a high degree of intellectual seriousness with a deep-rooted commitment to convivial collegiality: evening forays with Ian, Niall, Marie and others to such important enablers of scholarship as the Seven Stars on Carey Street and the Harp on Chandos Place were and remain a great solace to me.

King's students as well as King's staff have helped me with this book, many of the ideas herein being shaped in seminar discussions associated with a long-running master's-level course on 'Patriotism and national identities in Britain', and – more recently – a final-year undergraduate Thematic Special Subject on 'Nations'. My thanks, also, go to my current and former Ph.D. students, who have done so much to widen the range of my historical knowledge, and enrich my understanding – not least via the meetings and other activities of the Modern British History Reading Group. I am certain that I have learnt more from them than they have from me.

Beyond the Department of History, but still within King's, I'd like to thank Clare Brant, David Green, Sonia Massai, Clare Pettitt, Max Saunders and Keith White (whose copy of John Urry's *The tourist gaze* is still in my possession: sorry Keith!). I am also very appreciative of my colleagues in the Arts and Humanities Faculty Office: combining a vice-decanal role with completing a major project presents some challenges, and I give heartfelt thanks to Ian Barrett, Russell Goulbourne, Nicola Rankin, Katrin Tiedau and the other current and former denizens of Room 2.19 of the Virginia Woolf Building for putting up with my book-induced lapses and distractedness over the past few years. Still further up the King's administrative hierarchy, I'm enormously grateful to Chris Mottershead, who found just the right words at just the right time to spur me on towards the finish line.

Outwith King's, but still within the wider University of London (reports of its death remain exaggerated), I gained much from my involvement in the Modern British History seminar at the Institute of Historical Research, and indeed some of the research for this book was presented at that forum. Further afield (though also during her time at King's), Ludmilla Jordanova helped me in many ways: with this project, with my work, and indeed with much else besides. So too did my old friend William Mulligan; in a variety of congenial contexts in Dublin, Glasgow, London and Berlin I have been enlightened and enriched by his conversation, and sustained by his camaraderie. I must also thank Rona Cran and Martin Spychal for sybaritic nocturnal escapades; the occasional company of their marvellous cats; and life-enhancing exchanges about history, literature, films and music (including some memorable debates about the artistic merits of Bob Dylan and the Beach Boys). In a similar vein, I thank Julie Hipperson and Dan Browne for their conversation, revelry and enthusiasm for gastronomic adventure – and for persuading me that there are some shreds of silver lining in the cloud that is the Hipster takeover of large parts of central London.

I owe much to Mark Freeman, from whom I have learnt a great deal – and not just about history – over the course of many years. Mark's generosity of spirit, sense of the absurd and enthusiasm for wholesome non-academic pursuits are a shining example to a profession that can sometimes take itself far too seriously. Mark, moreover, was one of a number of people who worked closely with me on 'The redress of the past: Historical pageants in Britain, 1905–2016', an Arts and Humanities Research Council-funded project (AH/K0003887/1) that overlapped with the later stages of my work on this book. Historical pageantry is a different subject from landscape, but the two projects address cognate themes, and my debt to the 'Redress of the past' team is profound. For their winning combination of scholarly rigour, professionalism and *joie de vivre* I thank Angela Bartie, Paul Caton, Ginestra Ferraro, Luis Figueira, Linda Fleming, Mark Freeman (again), Tom Hulme, Alex Hutton, David Little, Geoffroy Noël, Charlotte Tupman, Paul Vetch and Miguel Vieira.

Many other people helped in different ways. For pointers, references and support of various kinds I am grateful to: Sally Alexander, Ben Anderson, Elizabeth Baigent, Nicola Bishop, Rob Colls, Ben Cowell, Matthew Cragoe, Melanie Hall, Tony Howe, Michael Hulme, Ann Poulson, Roland Quinault, Kathryn Rix, Kristina Spohr, Astrid Swenson, Tony Taylor, James Thompson, Robert Whelan and William Whyte. My friend and academic collaborator Chad Bryant of the University of North Carolina at Chapel Hill has been a particular source of insight and stimulating discussion, especially on wider methodological issues. Indeed, in recent years I've spent a good deal of time in the chipmunk-enhanced campus of Chapel Hill, working on projects that – while quite separate from the present one – helped shape some of the thinking behind it: aside from Chad, my thanks also to his UNC colleagues, especially Lloyd Kramer, Susan Pennybacker and Cynthia Radding.

A version of Chapter 1 was first published in the journal *History*, 99 (2014) as '"The cliffs are not cliffs": The cliffs of Dover and national identities in Britain, *c.* 1750–1914'; I am grateful to John Wiley & Sons Ltd and the Historical Association for permission to reproduce this material. I wish also to acknowledge the following people and institutions for permission to reproduce images to which they hold the copyright: Beaulieu Estate Archive; Bridgeman Images; British Library; Cambridge University Library; Christie's Images; Fitzwilliam Museum, Cambridge; Getty Images; Hampshire Cultural Trust; Hampshire Record Office; Manchester Art Gallery; National Museums Liverpool; New Forest Ninth Centenary Trust; Northumberland Archives; Towneley Hall Art Gallery & Museum, Burnley.

This book was commissioned by Michael Watson of Cambridge University Press, and I am most grateful to him for his encouragement and patience over the course of the project's long gestation. Michael's advice over the years did much to influence the overall shape of the book. Indeed, his periodic enquiries as to how the project was going served as useful reminders that I had obligations to scholarship as well as to university administration, thereby reinforcing the wise counsel Ian McBride had given me soon after I arrived at King's (delivered while dodging buses on the Aldwych, en route to lunch): always – always – 'make time for research'. Also at Cambridge University Press, Melissa Shivers and Lisa Carter provided invaluable help with the publication process, and Robert Whitelock did much to spot and eliminate mistakes at copy-editing stage. I was lucky, too, that the Press sent the draft typescript to excellent readers. Indeed, the final stages of writing were given a great boost by the enormously useful, generous and learned comments of these two anonymous reviewers. Their input saved me from a number of errors and omissions, and helped strengthen the arguments and claims that I make in the book. The mistakes and weaknesses that remain are my responsibility alone.

Nearly all of this book was written in my office in King's College London, but nearly all of the research behind it was done in libraries and archives, and to these institutions and their staff I owe an enormous debt of gratitude: the British Library; Cambridge University Library; the Bodleian Library; Senate House Library, London; the Maughan Library, King's College London; Hampshire Record Office; Northumberland Archives; Surrey History Centre; Cumbria Archive Service; National Trust Archives; Westminster City Archives. The business of doing research and writing using the resources of these places was further eased through grants to defray various expenses, and I am most grateful to King's College London and the Isobel Thornley Bequest to the University of London for their generosity in making such funding available to me.

Not all my debts are to universities, libraries, archives and academic friends and colleagues, of course. My parents Anita and Peter and my brothers Ben and Dan continue to take a kindly interest in what I do, and have offered much encouragement over the years. So too has Sue Drew ('Auntie Sue'), whose home in Sheffield has been the scene of much stress-relieving lounging around, conversation and drinking of gins and tonic, as well as a base for revivifying excursions into the Peak District (a landscape that, perhaps unforgivably, does not feature in this book).

My greatest debt of all is to Martha Vandrei, whose love and intellectual comradeship have shaped this project in innumerable ways. Martha kept me going, kept the demons at bay when things got tough, and brought me fully to appreciate – not least by the example of her own work – that historians of real merit are always good *writers*: history, as somebody once said, is a literary art. But history is also a discipline that should take its practitioners away from writing-desk and library from time to time – especially when it comes to a subject like mine here. Martha encouraged me to put this point of view into practice, accompanying me in on-foot explorations of a great many English landscapes over the last few years. Some of these landscapes feature in this book; others do not. But wherever we went – whether down the Thames from Richmond to Wandsworth or along the gritstone crags of Stanage Edge – our walks and talks helped me work out what it was I wanted to say. I can only hope that my efforts to say it do justice to the dedication.

INTRODUCTION

> Landscape associates people and place … landscape is not a mere visible surface, static composition, or passive backdrop to human theatre … Landscape connotes a sense of the purposefully shaped, the sensual and aesthetic, the embeddedness in culture … Landscape has meaning.[1]

People have always attached meaning to the world around them, and these meanings have changed over time. In European societies from the later eighteenth century, the surface of the earth was increasingly seen not only in material terms, as an economic resource to be exploited, but also as 'landscape', as an object of aesthetic and moral value. Landscape was understood to incorporate human engagement with the physical environment over time. Although areas of 'wilderness' still existed, landscape was generally seen not as 'natural', but as something created in dialogue with men and women. In the words of John Stilgoe,

> Once in a while landscape is new, fresh, almost virginal. South Georgia, the Falkland Islands, Kerguelen, the Crozets, Macquarie, Elephant, Pitcairn, and other islands … proved bereft of humans when Europeans discovered them. Unknown to humankind, not just Europeans, they existed only as wilderness when found … But typically landscape is mature, often hoary, sometimes ancient, part prehistoric. Wilderness appears timeless.[2]

[1] A. W. Spirn, *The language of landscape* (New Haven and London, 1998), pp. 16–18.
[2] J. R. Stilgoe, *What is landscape?* (Cambridge, MA, 2015), p. 83.

As an historical product of humanity in all its diversity, landscape has attracted a great variety of aesthetic and moral responses. Different landscape features have been valued for different reasons by different cultures, and interpreted in different ways.[3] Human responses to landscape are necessarily subjective.[4] Yet, as with human responses to countless other things, generalisations remain possible: most obviously, perhaps, landscape has been valued on account of being seen as distinctively beautiful, picturesque or otherwise visually impressive.[5]

That said, assessments of the visual appeal of any given landscape feature do not derive from its (perceived) physical characteristics alone; because landscape is a human construct, exogenous factors inevitably come into play. Since Kant, philosophers have understood that evaluations of aesthetic worth depend on the quality of authenticity.[6] Like forged art, landscape known to be 'fake' – to use Robert Elliot's term – does not exert the same appeal as that deemed to be 'original'. Thus, knowledge that an apparently 'unspoilt' hillside had previously been quarried limits one's appreciation of it, even if no traces remain of the quarry, the landscape having been 'restored' to the appearance it had before the works were undertaken.[7] The value of landscape depends on factors other than its perceived physical properties. Many visually inconspicuous landscape features are after all of considerable cultural significance: examples include sources of rivers, birthplaces of famous figures, and sites of battles and other historical events.[8] Crucial here is what may be termed associational value, the value placed on

---

[3] Y.-F. Tuan, *Space and place* (Minneapolis, 2008 [1977]), esp. p. 162; and, for the particular point on culture affecting perception, Y.-F. Tuan, *Passing strange and wonderful: Aesthetics, nature, and culture* (Washington, DC, 1993), p. 101.

[4] T. W. Adorno, *Aesthetic theory* (London, 1984 [1970]), p. 104; D. W. Meinig (ed.), *The interpretation of ordinary landscapes* (Oxford, 1979), pp. 3, 33–4.

[5] D. Lowenthal, 'Finding valued landscapes', *Progress in Human Geography*, 2 (1978), 373–418.

[6] '[W]ere we to play a trick on our lover of the beautiful, and plant in the ground artificial flowers … and perch artfully carved birds on the branches of trees, and were he to find out how he had been deceived, the immediate interest which these things previously had for him would at once vanish … The fact is that our intuition and reflection must have as their concomitant the thought that the beauty in question is nature's handiwork; and this is the sole basis of the immediate interest that is taken in it'; I. Kant, *Critique of judgement* (Oxford, 2007 [1790]), pp. 128–9.

[7] R. Elliot, 'Faking nature', *Inquiry*, 25 (1982), 81–93. Elliot's arguments are extended further in his *Faking nature: The ethics of environmental restoration* (London, 1997).

[8] Tuan, *Space and place*, pp. 161–2.

those connections and interactions between the environment and human experience that both create landscape qua landscape, and supply the basis for the ascription of meanings to it.

Especially important vectors of the spread and valence of associations attaching to landscape have been artistic and literary productions, their impact being aided by the commercialisation of culture and the development of modern tourism and leisure practices. In the British context one might think, for instance, of the 'Constable country' of Suffolk and Essex, made so famous by the paintings of the eponymous artist that the travel agents Thomas Cook were offering coach tours of the locality by the 1890s.[9] Similarly, in relation to poets and novelists, 'Dickens Land', 'Thackeray-land', 'Wordsworthshire', 'Hardy's Wessex', 'The Land of Scott', 'The Brontë Country' and 'The Country of George Eliot' had all emerged before the end of the nineteenth century.[10] Writing in the *Quarterly Review* in 1881, one commentator noted that

> it is English scenery, with its historical associations, which has inspired our poets, artists, and novelists. There are spots everywhere that evoke the shade of Shakespeare, from the cliff at Dover to the blasted heath of Forres … Who can look on the windings of the Severn without thinking of Milton's 'Comus'; and what prettier pictures can we have of cottage life and country superstitions than those he gives with such exquisite grace and delicacy in 'L'Allegro'?[11]

The role of art and literature in so contributing to the appeal of landscape was part of a wider-felt sense of connection between landscape and the past: as the *Quarterly* reviewer observed, it was the 'historical associations' inscribed in the landscape that had so drawn the attention of English painters and writers. The landscape was storied. Indeed, it might be said that landscape is by definition storied. Recall the words of Stilgoe, quoted above: 'typically landscape is mature,

---

9 S. Daniels, *Fields of vision: Landscape imagery and national identity in England and the United States* (Cambridge, 1994), pp. 210–13. For the late-nineteenth-century enthusiasm for Constable, see I. Fleming-Williams and L. Parris, *The discovery of Constable* (London, 1984).

10 N. J. Watson, *The literary tourist* (Basingstoke, 2006), p. 5.

11 [A. I. Shand], 'Walks in England', *Quarterly Review*, 152 (July 1881), 146.

often hoary, sometimes ancient, part prehistoric'. Since the early modern period, if not before, societies have understood time to confer value on place. European (and non-European) landscapes evocative of past ages, significant events, the great figures of old, have come to be esteemed precisely because of these associations. Many of the more resonantly evocative of these became, to use a term now worn somewhat threadbare, 'sites of memory' – focal points for mobilising a collective consciousness of the past.[12] In large part because of its associations with human history, landscape was thus transformed into heritage, the impulse driving this shift in sensibility fuelling, among other things, the modern-day preservation and conservation movements.

The process by which landscape became heritage was inextricably bound up with contemporaneous constructions of collective identity. Before the eighteenth century, the heritage embodied in landscape tended to be related to local and confessional identities, as Alexandra Walsham's work on the Reformation-era environment has demonstrated.[13] Over time, however, this heritage was increasingly understood to be national in character, despite the persistence of associations between landscape and locality (which, as we shall see, were by no means antithetical to the newer languages of landscape and nation). Just as a particular landscape might have special value for an individual on account of its being evocative of events in that individual's past (connected, for instance, with happy experiences in childhood), so did national communities come to ascribe value to landscapes evocative of the imagined pasts of those communities. On account of its historical associations, landscape became a powerful means by which a people's sense of self and identity might be maintained and celebrated, its utility in this respect growing stronger in the context of industrialisation, urbanisation, rapid technological and societal change, and other transformations of modernity.[14]

This is a point worth emphasising. Nations are by definition territorial entities, laying claim to defined portions of the earth's surface as rightfully their own. As the sociologist Michael Billig has written,

---

[12] P. Nora, *Realms of memory: Rethinking the French past*, 3 vols. (New York, 1996–8).

[13] A. Walsham, *The reformation of the landscape: Religion, identity, and memory in early modern Britain and Ireland* (Oxford, 2011).

[14] For an especially valuable discussion of the dislocating effects of the technological and other changes associated with the experience of modernity, see S. Kern, *The culture of time and space, 1880–1918*, 2nd edn (Cambridge, MA, 2003).

nationalism is never 'beyond geography', the 'imagining of a "country"' necessarily involving 'the imagining of a bounded totality beyond
immediate experience of place'; while for the philosopher David Miller
a key 'aspect of national identity is that it connects a group of people to
a particular geographical place … A nation … must have a homeland.'[15]
Historians agree. In his recent survey of nationalism in Europe and
America since the late eighteenth century, Lloyd Kramer has pointed
out that 'All nations and nationalisms claim a homeland or bounded
territory … Nationhood can scarcely be imagined without reference to
specific lands, just as selfhood cannot be understood without reference
to specific human bodies.'[16] For Kramer, as for many other scholars,
European intellectuals such as Herder, Fichte and Mazzini played a
vital role in establishing the importance of geography to conceptualisations of the nation, the homeland being imagined as continuing
undiluted up to its borders, there being separated from the similarly
undiluted domains of other nations.[17]

Yet the imbrication of geography and nationhood goes beyond
the definition, assertion and political control of territorial homelands.
While bounded space is certainly important, specific places – landscapes – are no less so. Indeed, when it comes to the cultural as opposed
to the political imagining of nations, they are crucial. As Stephen
Daniels observed in his path-breaking *Fields of vision*, 'Landscapes,
whether focusing on single monuments or framing stretches of scenery, provide visible shape; they picture the nation.'[18] Across the world
in the modern period, landscapes, and distinctive landscapes in particular, have functioned as powerful symbols of national identity. The
American 'Wild West', the Swiss Alps and the Norwegian Fjords are
obvious examples here. One recent study has highlighted the importance of river landscapes to national identities, using case studies from
France, the United States, Ireland and elsewhere; another has explored
the potent appeal of the Russian Steppe to the nationalist sensibilities
of that country; and there are of course many other examples, the work

[15] M. Billig, *Banal nationalism* (London, 1995), p. 74; D. Miller, *On nationality*
(Oxford, 1995), p. 24.
[16] L. Kramer, *Nationalism in Europe and America: Politics, cultures, and identities since
1775* (Chapel Hill, NC, 2011), p. 57.
[17] *Ibid.*, pp. 58–9.
[18] Daniels, *Fields of vision*, p. 5.

in this vein produced by art historians being especially notable and extensive.[19]

Despite this literature, however, the significance of the *historical* associations of nationally valued landscapes has been insufficiently appreciated. This is surprising, not least because of the acknowledged significance of understandings of the past to nationalist discourse more generally. Indeed, building on the work of theorists of nations and nationalism such as Anthony D. Smith, who have insisted on the importance of history as an agent of nationalist mobilisation,[20] historians have shown an increasing interest in the part it played in the shaping of modern-day national cultures and identities. In the British context, one might point to the work of Billie Melman on nineteenth-century understandings of history as 'a chamber of horrors', Stephanie Barczewski on the myths of Robin Hood and King Arthur, or Martha Vandrei on the long continuities of British historical culture.[21] In addition, the ever-burgeoning work on memory and commemoration has also deepened our understanding of the ways in which the past can be brought to bear on contemporary ideas of national belonging, most notably in relation to the experience of the First and Second World Wars.[22] And a further well-ploughed furrow of enquiry has been

---

[19] T. Cusack, *Riverscapes and national identities* (Syracuse, NY, 2010); C. Ely, *This meager nature: Landscape and national identity in imperial Russia* (DeKalb, IL, 2002); A. R. H. Baker, 'Forging a national identity for France after 1789: The role of landscape symbols', *Geography*, 97 (2012), 22–8; D. Hooson (ed.), *Geography and national identity* (Oxford, 1994); P. Bishop, *An archetypal Constable: National identity and the geography of nostalgia* (London, 1995).

[20] This argument is clear throughout Smith's work as a whole, but an especially succinct expression of it can be found in his debate with Ernest Gellner in the pages of *Nations and Nationalism*: see A. D. Smith, 'Nations and their pasts', *Nations and Nationalism*, 2 (1996), 358–65; and A. D. Smith, 'Memory and modernity: Reflections on Ernest Gellner's theory of nationalism', *Nations and Nationalism*, 2 (1996), 371–88.

[21] B. Melman, *The culture of history: English uses of the past 1800–1953* (Oxford, 2006); S. L. Barczewski, *Myth and national identity in nineteenth-century Britain: The legends of King Arthur and Robin Hood* (Oxford, 2000); M. Vandrei, *Queen Boudica and historical culture in Britain since 1600: An image of truth* (Oxford, 2018); and M. Vandrei, 'A Victorian invention? Thomas Thornycroft's "Boudicea" group and the idea of historical culture in Britain', *Historical Journal*, 57 (2014), 485–508.

[22] The literature on this is vast. See, e.g., J. Winter, *Sites of memory, sites of mourning: The Great War in European cultural history*, 2nd edn (Cambridge, 2014 [1995]); S. Goebel, *The Great War and medieval memory: War, remembrance and medievalism in Britain and Germany, 1914–1940* (Cambridge, 2007); M. Connelly, *We can take it! Britain and the memory of the Second World War* (London, 2004);

history writing itself. It may be that historians – perhaps motivated by professional narcissism – are naturally drawn to study the work of their forebears, but whatever the reason, considerable attention has been paid to the ways in which the work of nineteenth- and twentieth-century historians intersected with, and helped to construct, patriotic discourse and understandings of the nation.[23] In particular, and following the lead of J. W. Burrow, British intellectual and cultural historians have had much to say about the Anglo-Saxonism of Stubbs, Freeman and other Victorian historians, and the teleologies of national progress that informed and found expression in their work.[24] In the wider European context, a major research project led by Stefan Berger on 'Representations of the past: National histories in Europe' has generated considerable interest in national historiographies and their nationalist significance, not least by means of its associated book series on 'Writing the nation', seven volumes of which have appeared at time of writing since 2008.[25] Yet for all that this work has elucidated the importance of the relationship between the past and the nation, it has had relatively little to say about landscape in this connection.[26] The

L. Noakes and J. Pattinson (eds.), *British cultural memory and the Second World War* (London, 2013).

[23] See, e.g., P. Mandler, *History and national life* (London, 2002); T. Lang, *The Victorians and the Stuart heritage* (Cambridge, 1995); J. Stapleton, *Sir Arthur Bryant and national history in twentieth-century Britain* (Lanham, MD, 2005). Many of the essays collected in S. Collini, *English pasts: Essays in history and culture* (Oxford 1999) and S. Collini, *Common reading: Critics, historians, publics* (Oxford, 2008) are also relevant here.

[24] J. W. Burrow, *A liberal descent: Victorian historians and the English past* (Cambridge, 1981); C. Parker, *The English historical tradition since 1850* (Edinburgh, 1990), esp. Chapter 1; M. Bentley, *Modernizing England's past: English historiography in the age of modernism, 1870–1970* (Cambridge, 2005), esp. Chapters 1–3; G. A. Bremner and J. Conlin (eds.), *Making history: Edward Augustus Freeman and Victorian cultural politics* (Oxford, 2015).

[25] See, e.g., S. Berger and C. Lorenz (eds.), *The contested nation: Ethnicity, class, religion, and gender in national histories* (Basingstoke, 2008); S. Berger and C. Conrad, *The past as history: National identity and historical consciousness in modern Europe* (Basingstoke, 2015); S. Berger and C. Lorenz (eds.), *Nationalizing the past: Historians as nation builders in modern Europe* (Basingstoke, 2015).

[26] There are, of course, some exceptions, perhaps the most notable of which is provided by the work done on the German idea of *Heimat* and its relationship with local, regional and national identities. See, e.g., C. Applegate, *A nation of provincials: The German idea of Heimat* (Berkeley, 1990); A. Confino, *The nation as a local metaphor: Württemberg, imperial Germany and national memory, 1871–1918* (Chapel Hill, NC, 1997).

same can be said of the work of historians of national identity more generally, and even those treatments that have emphasised the importance of the past, or of memory. Kramer's study, cited above, is an example. While cognisant of the territorial determinants of nationhood, it pays less attention to landscape than to history writing and language, stressing the 'crucial' role historians played in 'describing the national meaning of the past and … showing how the living generations were always connected to the dead'.[27]

This relative neglect of the patriotic force of valued landscapes reflects a more general privileging of the textual on the part of professional historians: 'modern conditions of research', Raphael Samuel pointed out some time ago, 'seem to dictate an almost complete detachment from the material environment'.[28] Yet, as Samuel's own work on memory, heritage and British identity demonstrated so eloquently, history manifests itself in a wide plurality of contexts: its 'subject matter is promiscuous', encompassing far more than the written word, let alone the 'chronological past of the documentary record' or the recondite interpretations of university-based scholars.[29] History, Samuel insisted, is present in fiction, myth, folk traditions, ritual, art, photography and material culture.[30] It is also deeply inscribed in landscape – indeed, it is intimately connected to the cultural value assigned to landscape, and more specifically to its patriotic significance.

The failure of historians fully to appreciate this is especially striking given what we know from social theorists about the historical associations typically attaching to valued landscapes, as well as their importance as sources of national symbolism and – at a more fundamental level – the fact that nations exist in space as well as time. Geographers in particular have understood that in the valued landscapes of a nation, space and time are powerfully conjoined. As Jan Penrose has put it, 'Every society has stories about its origins and its past. These stories … always occur in space and are usually associated with specific sites and/or landscapes.'[31] Indeed, a now quite considerable

---

[27] Kramer, *Nationalism in Europe and America*, Chapter 3, p. 73.

[28] R. Samuel, *Theatres of memory*, Vol. I: *Past and present in contemporary culture* (London, 1994), p. 269.

[29] *Ibid.*, pp. x, 443.

[30] *Ibid.*, esp. pp. 3–48; and see also R. Samuel, *Theatres of memory*, Vol. II: *Island stories: Unravelling Britain* (London, 1998).

[31] J. Penrose, 'Nations, states and homelands: Territory and territoriality in nationalist thought', *Nations and Nationalism*, 8 (2002), 277–97 (p. 282).

number of geographers have explored the relationship between landscape and national identities – one might mention Stephen Daniels, David Lowenthal, Peter Bishop, Denis Cosgrove, David Matless and Catherine Brace, among others.[32] Of these, David Lowenthal, one of the pioneers in the area, stands out as particularly important on account of the emphasis he has placed on the landscape–past nexus. In a series of books and articles across the space of several decades, Lowenthal has insisted that the English see their landscape not simply as beautiful or otherwise visually distinctive, but as 'both admirable and ancestral'.[33] The value placed on English landscape, he has argued, has been to a large degree determined by its association with the past of the national community, and in this respect England stands out as distinctive: 'Nowhere else is landscape so freighted as legacy.'[34] In articulating this argument, Lowenthal has stressed the importance of the countryside: the landscape most valued by the English is largely rural in character. This is no wilderness of untamed nature, but a landscape suggestive of many centuries of human occupation and cultivation, and thus the antiquity of the English nation.[35]

---

[32] See, e.g., Daniels, *Fields of vision*; D. Cosgrove and S. Daniels (eds.), *The iconography of landscape: Essays on the symbolic representation, design, and use of past environments* (Cambridge, 1988); D. Matless, *Landscape and Englishness* (London, 1998); Bishop, *Archetypal Constable*; D. Lowenthal, 'British national identity and the English landscape', *Rural History*, 2 (1991), 205–30; C. Brace, 'Looking back: The Cotswolds and English national identity, c. 1890–1950', *Journal of Historical Geography*, 25 (1999), 502–16; C. Brace, 'Finding England everywhere: Regional identity and the construction of national identity, 1890–1940', *Ecumene*, 6 (1998), 90–109.

[33] Lowenthal, 'British national identity and the English landscape', p. 215. See also D. Lowenthal and H. E. Prince, 'English landscape tastes', *Geographical Review*, 55 (1965), 186–222; D. Lowenthal, *The past is a foreign country* (Cambridge, 2015 [1986]), esp. pp. 104–5, 183–4; D. Lowenthal, *The heritage crusade and the spoils of history* (London, 1996), esp. pp. 7, 185–6.

[34] D. Lowenthal, 'Landscape as heritage: National scenes and global changes', in J. M. Fladmark (ed.), *Heritage: Conservation, interpretation and enterprise* (Aberdeen, 1993), pp. 3–15 (p. 9). See also D. Lowenthal, 'European and English landscapes and national symbols', in Hooson, *Geography and national identity*, pp. 15–38 (pp. 20–1).

[35] 'Beloved rural England is trebly historical. Its features are compages of datable cultural acts, mostly ascribable to ancestral precursors. The past that permeates this landscape is not the primordial wild, but a nearer history infused with memorable human processes, desires, decisions, and tastes'; Lowenthal, 'British national identity and the English landscape', 216.

It is of course England and the English nation that form the focus of the present book, and the importance of the countryside to constructions of English national identity is now quite generally recognised. In his wide-ranging synoptic study, *The making of English national identity*, Krishan Kumar concluded that by the late Victorian period, 'the essential England was rural', and many other scholars have made similar pronouncements.[36] In this perspective, although ideologues of the nation since Herder had promoted the idea of a return to nature and the countryside, away from the artificiality and corruption of towns, the impulse took particularly strong hold in England, and assumed distinctively conservative forms. Rooted in the rural, the discourse of Englishness was opposed to modernity and its works, extolling instead a pastoral south country of picturesque cottages, gently rolling farmland and stable social hierarchies, with squire and parson at the top. Given the actual lived experience of modern-day Englishmen and women – rich or poor, villager or city-dweller – much of this was a mirage, but it nonetheless offered a seductive vision of peace and order, permeating English culture and having a real influence on elite and popular attitudes. Some scholars – most notably Martin Wiener – have even suggested that this reactionary ruralism undermined the British 'industrial spirit', retarding economic development and contributing to the eventual ruin of the once-mighty workshop of the world.[37] Many more, however, have been content to identify and elucidate the phenomenon, without seeking to connect it to economic performance. Often drawing heavily on Wiener and his claim that the Industrial Revolution was increasingly seen as 'an unEnglish aberration, "A spread over a green and pleasant land of dark satanic mills that ground down their inmates"',[38] they have done so in a bewildering variety of contexts. These include art and literature,[39] architecture

[36] K. Kumar, *The making of English national identity* (Cambridge, 2003), p. 211.
[37] M. J. Wiener, *English culture and the decline of the industrial spirit, 1850–1980* (Cambridge, 1981).
[38] Daniels, *Fields of vision*, pp. 214–15, citing Wiener, *English culture*.
[39] See, e.g., P. Street, 'Painting deepest England: The late landscapes of John Linnell and the uses of nostalgia', in C. Shaw and M. Chase (eds.), *The imagined past: History and nostalgia* (Manchester, 1989), pp. 68–80; C. Payne, *Toil and plenty: Images of the agricultural landscape in England, 1780–1890* (New Haven and London, 1993). Many art historians have suggested that in the second half of the nineteenth century a concept of Englishness was developed that excluded the industrial north, was focused on 'south country' pastoralism, and was culturally reactionary and conservative. In

and garden design,[40] the folk song and dance revival,[41] the history of landscape preservation and the National Trust,[42] and the garden city movement. Thus, for example, Standish Meacham tells us that proponents of the garden city – facing 'the realities of class division and the threat of class conflict' – sought to return to a 'conservative English past', one that was paternalistic, undemocratic and pre-industrial,[43] and so reached for a mythical rural Englishness that 'replaced grim realities with the cosy village where all lived healthy lives, cultivated

this interpretation, even radical ruralism – such as that espoused by William Morris – contributed to the 'rural mythology' that worked to 'bolster the cultural hegemony of the class that owned, or had owned, the land' (Payne, *Toil and plenty*, pp. 40–2).

[40] A. Helmreich, *The English garden and national identity: The competing styles of garden design, 1870–1914* (Cambridge, 2002); R. Strong, *Country life, 1897–1997* (London, 1996).

[41] G. Boyes, *The imagined village: Culture, ideology and the English folk revival* (Manchester, 1993).

[42] For John Walton, to take one example, the early preservationist movement was animated by what he terms the 'noblesse oblige' and 'authoritarian paternalism' of 'high tory Ruskinianism', the National Trust to which it led celebrating and sustaining the 'preserved enclaves' of 'a deeply conservative vision of England': J. K. Walton, 'The National Trust: Preservation or provision?', in M. Wheeler (ed.), *Ruskin and the environment* (Manchester, 1995), pp. 158–62; J. K. Walton, 'The National Trust centenary: Official and unofficial histories', *The Local Historian*, 26 (1996), 80–8 (p. 86). For similar, see for example P. C. Gould, *Early green politics: Back to nature, back to the land, and socialism in Britain 1880–1914* (Brighton, 1988), pp. 88ff.; M. Bunce, *The countryside ideal: Anglo-American images of landscape* (London, 1994), pp. 182–4 and *passim* for a reading of the English countryside ideal as profoundly conservative. See also the journalistic accounts of Paula Weideger and Jeremy Paxman (P. Weideger, *Gilding the acorn: Behind the façade of the National Trust* (London, 1994), esp. p. 36; J. Paxman, *The English*, 2nd edn (London, 1999)). In Paxman's view, the original purpose of the National Trust was 'to protect those picturesque areas of countryside the landed gentry didn't want for their field sports' (p. 152).

[43] S. Meacham, *Regaining paradise: Englishness and the early garden city movement* (New Haven and London, 1998), pp. 2, 183. On the whole, Meacham's conclusions have been well received. See, for instance, S. Heathorn, 'An English paradise to regain? Ebenezer Howard, the Town and Country Planning Association and English ruralism', *Rural History*, 11 (2000), 113–28. As Heathorn has commented, Meacham's work shows how 'The movement that Howard helped to begin had as its only binding element a shared idealization of English rusticity. The village green, the quaint artisan cottage and the benevolent paternalistic squire featured in this romantic view of the pre-industrial past: a seemingly simpler and better past that represented all that was worthy of the appellation "English"' (p. 119). For a more critical review, see P. Mandler, 'Visions of merrie Letchworth', *Times Literary Supplement*, 18 February 2000, p. 21.

their gardens, and accepted their place within a hierarchy governed by an elite that understood its obligations to those whom it both ruled and served'.[44]

Such interpretations, however, have not quite swept all before them. In a spirited rejoinder, Peter Mandler has argued that the rural Englishness identified by many scholars was in fact culturally marginal, better seen more as a protest against prevailing trends than representative of mainstream perspectives. With approximately three-quarters of its population living in towns and cities by 1900, England was 'a nation that had come to terms with its urbanity'.[45] The culture of the dominant classes was 'aggressively urban and materialist',[46] while phenomena such as the folk-song revival reflected 'the values of some *bien-pensant* Bohemians and would-be squires, but nothing like the British Establishment or even the average upper-middle-class family'.[47] As for preservationist organisations such as the National Trust, they had small, unrepresentative memberships and were 'distrusted by government as wet and faddish'.[48] There is much to be said for this critique. As Mandler shows very clearly, a reactionary language of protest was not absent from the discourse of rural Englishness, finding expression in, for example, the writings of the Poet Laureate Alfred Austin (1835–1913), who had a good deal to say in praise of 'hamlets snug', 'proud demesnes', 'blue spires of cottage smoke mong woodlands green' and 'authority' being 'loved in every vale'.[49] It is also the case, moreover, that organisations devoted to the preservation of rural landscape and culture – the Commons Preservation Society, the National Trust, the Lake District Defence Society, the English Folk Song and Dance Society – did not, before the First World War, have anything approaching mass memberships. Yet for all that, the scale and variety of nineteenth- and early-twentieth-century engagement with land, landscape and the rural is too extensive to be regarded as culturally marginal. This engagement was apparent not only in art and literature, but also in activities

[44] Meacham, *Regaining paradise*, p. 183; and see also, e.g., pp. 68–9.
[45] P. Mandler, 'Against "Englishness": English culture and the limits to rural nostalgia, 1850–1940', *Transactions of the Royal Historical Society*, 6th series, 7 (1997), 155–75 (p. 160).
[46] *Ibid.*, p. 170.
[47] *Ibid.*, p. 169.
[48] *Ibid.*, p. 170.
[49] A. Austin, 'Why I am a Conservative', *National Review*, 6 (December 1885), 564–5.

as diverse as amateur botany and geology, gardening, antiquarian and heritage tourism, photography, cycling, rambling, and mountain climbing.[50] And to take the particular example of landscape preservation, while the bodies giving institutional expression to this impulse may not have had mass memberships, such was not the aim of their leaders, whose focus was rather on acquiring the support of public figures and thus influencing public opinion.[51] In this they achieved considerable success: to give one index of it, between 1865 and 1897 more than 13 square miles of open space were preserved in and around the Greater London area (not counting 5,531 acres saved in Epping Forest), while at least 15,000 acres in provincial towns and cities were preserved over the same period.[52] Moreover, the fruits of such campaigning by middle-class activists were congruent – to a large degree – with the autonomous preferences of working-class people themselves, many of

[50] See, for example, D. Gervais, *Literary Englands: Versions of Englishness in modern writing* (Cambridge, 1993); C. Wood, *Paradise lost: Paintings of English country life and landscape 1850–1914* (London, 1988); P. Howard, 'Painters' preferred places', *Journal of Historical Geography*, 11 (1985), 138–54; P. Howard, *Landscapes: The artists' vision* (London, 1991); A. Secord, 'Science in the pub: Artisan botanists in nineteenth-century Lancashire', *History of Science*, 32 (1994), 269–315; D. E. Allen, *The naturalist in Britain: A social history,* 2nd edn (Princeton, 1994 [London, 1976]), 67–70; Watson, *Literary tourist*; P. Readman, 'The place of the past in English culture, *c.* 1890–1914', *Past & Present*, 186 (2005), 147–99; J. Taylor, *A dream of England: Landscape, photography and the tourist's imagination* (Manchester, 1995); H. Taylor, *A claim on the countryside: A history of the British outdoor movement* (London, 1997); C. Bryant, A. Burns and P. Readman (eds.), *Walking histories, 1800–1914* (Basingstoke, 2016); J. Marsh, *Back to the land: The pastoral impulse in England, from 1880 to 1914* (London, 1982); J. Burchardt, *Paradise lost: Rural idyll and social change in England since 1800* (London, 2002); Helmreich, *English garden*; M. Tebbutt, 'Rambling and manly identity in Derbyshire's Dark Peak, 1880s–1920s', *Historical Journal*, 49 (2006), 1125–53; R. W. Clark, *The Victorian mountaineers* (London, 1953); S. Thompson, *Unjustifiable risk? The story of British climbing* (Milnthorpe, 2010).

[51] P. Readman, 'Preserving the English landscape, 1870–1914', *Cultural and Social History*, 5 (2008), 197–218.

[52] R. Hunter, 'The movements for the inclosure and preservation of open lands', *Journal of the Royal Statistical Society*, 60 (1897), 400–2. For Epping Forest, see E. Baigent, 'A "Splendid pleasure ground [for] the elevation and refinement of the people of London": Geographical aspects of the history of Epping Forest', in E. Baigent and R. J. Mayhew (eds.), *English Geographies 1600–1950: Historical essays on English customs, cultures, and communities in honour of Jack Langton* (Oxford, 2009), pp. 104–26.

whom had been and continued to be active participants in protests over commons and rights of way.[53]

It seems, then, that while engagement with landscape and the rural can certainly be exaggerated, it was nevertheless a central element of English cultural life (for all that its more alienated and nostalgic manifestations were unrepresentative of prevailing attitudes, as Mandler has demonstrated). The lived environment of modern Britain was increasingly urban and industrial, but this only served further to elevate the cultural significance of the non-urban and non-industrial. As Raymond Williams pointed out many years ago,

> So much of the past of the country, its feelings and its literature, was involved with rural experience, and so many of its ideas of how to live well ... persisted and even were strengthened [from the later nineteenth century], that there is almost an inverse proportion ... between the relative importance of the working rural economy and the cultural importance of rural ideas.[54]

Thus, while most Englishmen and women lived in towns and cities from the mid nineteenth century on, discourses of rural Englishness remained integral to their experience of modernity. Embodying continuity with the past, these discourses constituted an important means by which a recognisable, historically rooted understanding of national identity was articulated at a time of significant social, economic and technological change. Although in some of their manifestations these rural expressions of Englishness may have been founded on myth, consciously or unconsciously eliding the squalor that could lurk in the most picturesque of rose-embowered cottages, they nonetheless had a powerful real-world effect. Their influence was evident in a range of areas, including the preservation of landscape and open spaces, 'back-to-the-land' and agrarian reform initiatives, tourism and recreation, changing trends in art and architecture, and of course fictional and

---

[53] Readman, 'Preserving'; P. Readman, 'Octavia Hill and the English landscape', in E. Baigent and B. Cowell (eds.), *'Nobler imaginings and mightier struggles': Octavia Hill, social activism and the remaking of British society* (London, 2016), pp. 163–84; E. Baigent, 'Octavia Hill, nature and open space: Crowning success or campaigning "utterly without result"', in Baigent and Cowell, *'Nobler imaginings'*, pp. 141–61.

[54] R. Williams, *The country and the city* (London, 1973), p. 248.

factual rural writing.[55] Yet their prevalence should not lead us to conclude that English culture was somehow anti-modern, permeated by a reactionary, conservative-nostalgic mindset. On the contrary, the conceptualisation of rural landscape as national heritage was compatible with a wide range of ideological perspectives – not least those avowedly progressive in complexion – and was accommodated within, and indeed supportive of, the English experience of modernity.

This is one of the central contentions of the present book. In pursuing it I seek to demonstrate the ideological heterogeneity of patriotic concerns with rural landscapes, and – more particularly – to build on the work of scholarship that has emphasised the plurality of British meanings of modernity. As Martin Daunton and Bernhard Rieger have pointed out, nineteenth- and early twentieth-century British responses to social, economic, technological and cultural change did not necessarily imply an acceptance of a sharp break between past and present. Indeed, as they note, 'casting the present as uniquely distinct from the past was by no means the only mode of interpreting temporal relations in debates about modernity'.[56] More often than not, in fact, the accent was less on fundamental transformation or rupture than on continuous development: both in culture and politics, the idea of continuity between the past, present and future was a prominent element of the British experience of modernity.[57] This rootedness of modernity in the past, in history, was notably evident in cultural engagement with the landscape, particularly the rural landscape – redolent as it was of an older, pre-industrial England. This engagement took various forms, but taken as a whole was powerfully expressive of a desire to maintain a sense of continuity with the national past. The English countryside was prized for its aesthetic qualities, its visual distinctiveness, and this doubtless contributed to its significance in constructions of national identity. But more important still to the nationalist significance of the

---

[55] See works cited in n. 50, above, and in addition P. Readman, *Land and nation in England: Patriotism, national identity and the politics of land, 1880–1914* (Woodbridge, 2008).

[56] B. Rieger and M. Daunton, 'Introduction', in M. Daunton and B. Rieger (eds.), *Meanings of modernity: Britain from the late-Victorian era to World War II* (Oxford and New York, 2001), pp. 1–21 (p. 5).

[57] *Ibid.*, esp. pp. 8ff. On this theme, see also G. K. Behlmer and F. M. Leventhal (eds.), *Singular continuities: Tradition, nostalgia, and identity in modern British culture* (Stanford, 2000), esp. introduction; and Readman, 'Place of the past'.

English rural landscape was the fact that its features were endowed with potent associational value through their connection with the past, being seen as witnesses to the history of the nation and its continuity over time.

My argument as to the nationalistic significance of landscape in the context of the English experience of nineteenth-century modernity is not, however, confined to discussion of the 'natural' environment or the countryside. Acknowledging the falsity of any sharp dichotomy between 'natural' and 'non-natural' landscape,[58] this book moves beyond much of the focus of existing scholarship, taking due account of the importance of the rural while insisting that other landscapes also played a key part in the construction of English national identity. The 'essential England', to use Kumar's formulation, could certainly be found in the shires of the home counties, but it could also be found in other places, in urban as well as rural contexts – from the bleak moorlands of the Northumbrian borders to the dirty, awesome and thoroughly man-made landscapes of industry in Manchester and its environs. The common denominator here was the associational value that attached to such environments, and in particular the felt presence of the past. And even if this presence was perhaps not felt as strongly in urban as it was in rural contexts, it was nonetheless there in some force: as Lynda Nead has shown, even in the context of the breakneck pace of improvement in mid Victorian London – the new streets and buildings, the slum clearance schemes, the Underground – 'modernity leans upon and is haunted by the figure of the past'.[59] For too long it has been assumed that the epitome of Englishness was the pastoral south country – all chocolate-box thatched cottages, waving fields of corn and quaint country churches. For sure, such idealisations were (and are) powerful, and powerfully supportive of some conceptions of Englishness, but the locations of English identity were more various, more congenial to a range of ideological positions, and thus more effective as a vehicle of nationalist discourse, in all its complexity, than such an incomplete picture might suggest.

[58] As W. G. Hoskins emphasised long ago, 'Not much of England, even in its more withdrawn, inhuman places, has escaped being altered by men in some subtle way or other, however untouched we may fancy it is at first sight': W. G. Hoskins, *The making of the English landscape* (London, 2005 [1955]), p. 3.
[59] L. Nead, *Victorian Babylon: People, streets and images in Victorian London* (New Haven and London, 2000), p. 32.

Much scholarship on landscape and national identity has a contemporary or twentieth-century focus. The chronological focus of this book, by contrast, is the nineteenth century – or more precisely the period between the last few decades of the eighteenth century and the outbreak of the First World War. Although it is undoubtedly a hackneyed observation, it is worth pointing out that this period – what might be termed the very long nineteenth century – was a time of great and trans-formative change. Industrialisation, democratisation (or at any rate the emergence of a politics less dominated by crown and aristocracy), the growth of the newspaper press and the development of new technolo-gies of communication – the penny post, the railway, the telegraph – all had profound cultural as well as social and economic effects. One of the most significant of these was the impetus given to the construc-tion of national identity. The spread of what Benedict Anderson has called 'print capitalism', the increased mobility of the population and other processes of modernisation made possible, as never before, the imagining of an English national community.[60] It was in this period that modern-day understandings of Englishness came into being and were diffused across a wide cross-section of society. It may well be that conceptualisations of an English 'nation' existed before the end of the eighteenth century: there is certainly a case to be made for tracing the origins of a sense of English nationhood to the medieval period.[61] But for all that some members of a literate, intellectual minority may have discerned the existence of an English nation, and made generalisa-tions about the common characteristics of the English people – Bede or Henry of Huntingdon are exemplary figures here – it seems undeni-able that a widely felt sense of English identity was a distinctive fea-ture of post-Enlightenment modernity. Nations have little reality before relatively large numbers of people come to see themselves as sharing a

---

[60] See B. Anderson, *Imagined communities: Reflections on the origin and spread of nationalism* (London, 2006 [1991]).

[61] See, e.g., A. Hastings, *The construction of nationhood: Ethnicity, religion and nation-alism* (Cambridge, 1997), esp. Chapters 1–2; J. Gillingham, 'Henry of Huntingdon and the twelfth-century revival of the English nation', in J. Gillingham (ed.), *The English in the twelfth century: Imperialism, national identity, and political val-ues* (Woodbridge, 2000), pp. 123–44; R. R. Davies, 'The peoples of Britain and Ireland 1100–1400, I: identities', *Transactions of the Royal Historical Society*, 6th series, 4 (1994), 1–20.

common national identity.⁶² This is not to say that nationalist ideologies did not draw upon medieval and early modern myths, traditions and histories, but it is to insist, as Smith has put it, that

> Nations are modern, as is nationalism, even when their members think they are very old and even when they are in part created out of pre-modern cultures and memories. They have not been there all the time. It is possible that something like modern nations emerged here and there in the ancient and medieval worlds … But, in general, nations are modern.⁶³

As elsewhere in Europe, it was the period from the later eighteenth century that saw the forging of modern British identities, including the identity of the English. And in England, landscape was of central and critical importance to this process – particularly insofar as it was associated with the past and with the imagined continuities of the nation. Bearing in mind Daniels's point that it is specific places, not territory in general, that do most to 'give shape to the imagined community of the nation',⁶⁴ this argument is developed through a series of detailed case studies of individual, quite different, landscapes: the cliffs of Dover, the Northumbrian borderland, the Lake District, the New Forest, the city of Manchester, and the River Thames. Taken together, these case studies illustrate the depth and significance of the relationship between landscape and English national identity, in its crucial formative period between the late eighteenth and early twentieth centuries.

Part 1 of the book explores the relationship between national identity and two English border landscapes. In a wide range of contexts, borders and borderlands have long been recognised as doing important work in the construction, affirmation and definition of identities, and those of the British Isles are no exception. It is at borders that national territories begin and end, and partly as a consequence of this they have often formed the focus of especially overt articulations of nationalist discourse and ideas. The cliffs of Dover, which are the focus of the first chapter, are one such landscape. Although the cliffs had not attracted very significant cultural comment before the late eighteenth

---

⁶² See W. Connor, 'When is a nation?', *Ethnic and Racial Studies*, 13 (1990), 92–103.
⁶³ Smith, 'Memory and modernity', 385.
⁶⁴ Daniels, *Fields of vision*, p. 5.

century, they subsequently became closely associated with historically constructed conceptions of the national homeland and its defence: the landscape of the cliffs came to symbolise the continuous integrity of the nation over centuries. Moreover, the patriotic associations with which the cliffs were bound up spoke to British as well as English sentiments of belonging, illustrating how the Englishness of English landscapes could support not only an English sense of identity, but a wider sense of Britishness.

The interdependence of the relationship between English and British identities was even more apparent in the landscape of the English border with Scotland, which is discussed in Chapter 2. Here, the history of cross-border enmity between the two nations was indelibly inscribed in the landscape. With its blood-soaked battlefields, ruined castles and martial ballad culture, it was a place closely associated with inter-community conflict and division. Yet these associations came to support a distinctive expression of Englishness, one that fed into wider discourses of Unionist-nationalism present on both sides of the border. They also supported a version of Englishness quite different from that of the shires of the south country, which is so often thought to be dominant. Austere and rugged, the windswept moorlands and remote valleys of the Northumberland borderland were nothing like the pastoral home counties, yet this landscape was an important element of the topography of Englishness – a topography that, as this book argues throughout, was more variously and pluralistically located than is often assumed.

The strong relationship between landscape, the past and national identity had important implications. Perhaps most notably, the growing tendency to value landscape on account of its associations with the past was a key factor behind the emergence of the movement for landscape preservation, early institutional expressions of this development being the establishment of the Commons Preservation Society (1865) and the National Trust (1894), as well as the formation of a plethora of smaller organisations. In an increasingly democratic political context, a new idea of amenity emerged. This was founded on a patriotic appreciation of landscape as national for two interrelated reasons. First, because of its association with the English past, and second, because of its being perceived as an inheritance to which the whole people – the nation – now had a rightful claim. Landscape was increasingly understood to be 'national property'.

Two key sites for the development of this understanding are explored in the pair of chapters that make up Part II of the book, which has as its focus the development of the movement for landscape preservation. Chapter 3 examines patriotic readings of the Lake District landscape and its associations, showing how these readings were instrumental in motivating the agenda of preservationists. Predicated on the idea of valued landscape as belonging to the nation in a moral if not strictly proprietorial sense, the patriotism of preservation came into conflict with other conceptions of the public/national interest in landscape. Chapter 4 offers a case study of a landscape, the New Forest, over which just such a conflict developed. Here, an understanding of the forest – which was crown land – as of national value as a source of timber (and state revenue) collided with the interests both of forest commoners and of those who saw the place as of great amenity value as an historic cultural landscape. The outcome of this debate reveals much about the character of the patriotic ideas animating the preservationist dispensation as it developed in the late Victorian and Edwardian periods. Oriented towards the past, it was nevertheless expressive of a distinctively English modernity. Indeed, preoccupation with the past, as it was inscribed in a landscape such as the New Forest, was no repudiation of the 'industrial spirit'; it was a positive, accommodative response to the contemporary experience of social, cultural and technological change.

The modernity of nineteenth-century patriotic concern with landscape is not only evident from case studies of rural or mainly rural places, however. Part III of the book, 'Beyond the South Country', seeks to extend the preoccupations of much existing scholarship on landscape and nation by emphasising the very important connections between national identity and urban – as well as rural – landscapes. As shown in Chapter 5, such connections were discerned and celebrated even in Manchester, 'shock city' of the Industrial Revolution. For all that it was a focus of concern over the 'condition of England' and the negative effects of industrialisation, 'Cottonopolis' – like the New Forest and the Lake District – was a fully integrated element of the geography of Englishness. Indeed, the assertiveness of the patriotic language associated with Manchester reveals the extent to which modern Englishness, as it developed over the course of the long nineteenth century, had local and regional roots. These roots were spread throughout the country; they were not just confined to the south. This is not to say, however, that the landscape of southern England was unimportant in constructions of national identity. But even here the essence of Englishness was not only to be found in picturesque villages and rolling farmland. Through a study of the River Thames and its hinterland, Chapter 6 acknowledges the appeal of an older, peaceable rural England as embodied in the scenery of the upper river, with its tranquil backwaters, rustic-vernacular cottages and mills, and pervading atmosphere of repose. Yet patriotic appreciation of the Thames was not confined to such scenes. Throughout the period, the river was associated with the nation's long history of commercial prosperity, as well as with the history of the capital city itself: its course from source to sea linked the rural with the urban, the past with the present and future.

PART I

Borders

1 THE CLIFFS OF DOVER

British identities have long been inextricably connected to the sea. Nineteenth-century historians such as E. A. Freeman, J. A. Froude and J. R. Seeley had no compunction in describing the inhabitants of the British Isles as 'folk of the sea' for whom the sea was their 'natural home', while Robert Louis Stevenson described the sea as 'our approach and bulwark … the scene of our greatest triumphs and dangers, and we are accustomed in lyrical strains to claim it as our own'.[1] The sea was British: it carried the trade that sustained the workshop of the world, it helped provide the means of exploration and colonial expansion; it was seen as the happy hunting-ground of the Royal Navy and nursery of the national character.[2] Yet while it may have promoted outward-looking sensibilities in some – not least in relation to imperialism – there was another side to the nation's maritime identity, and this was arguably more important. The relationship with the sea promoted what might be termed a discrete sense of islandhood, a constellation of patriotic sentiment that focused on an English homeland.

One key focus of this sentiment was the English Channel. Described in 1870 by Prime Minister William Gladstone as a 'wise

---

[1] J. A. Froude, *Oceana*, new edn (London, 1886), p. 16; E. A. Freeman, 'Latest theories on the origin of the English', *Contemporary Review*, 57 (January 1890), 36–51 (p. 45); R. L. Stevenson, 'The English admirals', in *'Virginibus puerisque' and other papers* (London, 1881), p. 193. See also J. R. Seeley, *The expansion of England* (London, 1883).

[2] See C. F. Behrman, *Victorian myths of the sea* (Athens, OH, 1977).

dispensation of Providence',[3] its existence seemed to suggest that the territorial integrity of the nation was part of the natural order of things, perhaps even divinely ordained. But the Channel was not simply valued as a moat usefully separating the country from the Continent. Its significance went deeper, as evident from the cultural work done by one of its most prominent landscape features, the examination of which forms the subject of this chapter – the port of Dover, and more particularly the white chalk cliffs that frame the town. Situated at the narrowest point of the Channel, just over 20 miles from France and easily visible from there on a clear day, the locale was saturated with patriotic meaning. Some idea of the strength of this is given by *John Heywood's illustrated guide to Dover*, a cheap, popular guidebook published in 1894. Having noted the rivalry among the seaside towns on the Channel coast, the writer concludes that Dover and its environs were *sui generis*:

> Arriving at Dover, and standing on the Admiralty Pier and contrasting the view commanded from that position with the aspect of other places, one feels constrained to declare that, after all, there's no town on the coast so fit to stand face to face with foreign lands, so fit to be the first view of British soil, as historic, cliff-guarded, castle-crowned Dover. There are a breadth, a majesty, a grandeur about the cliffs and castle that make the gazer feel they are worthy of the honour they have so long enjoyed, the honour of being the great outposts of British power. No Englishman can view them without pride and satisfaction – pride in their history, their strength, and their beauty … Even the man of 'peace at any price' must grow proud and martial within sight of Dover Castle and Cliffs.[4]

'Ancient and picturesque, warlike and graceful',[5] Dover and its cliffs symbolised the nation and its history, and were thus a worthy focus of patriotic pride.

What follows will explore the ways in which the cliffs of Dover came to stand for insular ideas of English nationhood.

---

[3] [W. E. Gladstone], 'Germany, France, and England', *Edinburgh Review*, 132 (October 1870), 554–93 (p. 588).
[4] John Heywood, *John Heywood's illustrated guide to Dover* (London [1894]), pp. 9–10.
[5] *Ibid.*, p. 12.

Notwithstanding the tub-thumping tone of *Heywood's guide*, these ideas – for all that they could be made compatible with jingo senti-ment – were significantly disconnected from imperial ties of belonging, or at any rate operated independently of them. Yet at the same time, they were closely associated with and supportive of a wider sense of British identity. Understood as historical witnesses to past time, the cliffs represented the continuity of the national homeland, acting as powerful symbols of defence, defiance and difference across the long nineteenth century. Furthermore, it was not so much the physical appearance of the white cliffs that conduced to their potent nation-alistic significance, but the associations they triggered in the minds of contemporaries. After all, in terms of natural physical properties, there were – and are – many similarities between the cliffs of Dover and their similarly white counterparts at Cap Blanc Nez in northeast France, on the other side of the Channel.

The cliffs of Dover attracted relatively scant attention in contemporary discourse before the middle of the eighteenth century. That they were an important landmark was beyond doubt, as is evident from the map of Britain produced in Italy in 1546. This, the first engraved map of British Isles apart from those in editions of Ptolemy's *Geographia*, fea-tured a naturalistic depiction of the white cliffs, in miniature, integrated into its overall design.[6] But in the written record, fleeting allusion was the norm even in works that otherwise had much to say about the town of Dover or the county of Kent. In his famous *Britannia*, a 'choro-graphicall description' of Britain published in English in 1610, William Camden alluded to 'a mighty ridge of steepe high Cliffs, *Cicero* termeth them *moles magnificas*, that is, *Stately* cliffes bringing forth *Sampier* in great plenty', but said little more.[7] It appears likely that while the cliffs made a visual impression, they did not attract much in the way of posi-tive value judgments. Writing in the 1720s, Daniel Defoe felt the Dover 'coast affords nothing of Note'.[8] Typically, the town and particularly its castle were considered worthy of more comment (not all of this, of

---

[6] E. Lynam, *The map of the British Isles of 1546* (Jenkintown, PA, 1934), pp. 1–3.

[7] W. Camden, *Britannia* (London, 1610 [1586]), p. 344.

[8] D. Defoe, *A tour thro' the whole island of Great Britain*, 2 vols. (London, 1968 [1724–6]), Vol. I, p. 123.

course, was approbatory, Dover having a long-established reputation as an expensive and unpleasant place for travellers).[9]

By Defoe's time, however, attitudes were changing. Previously, most cultivated commentators had found the sea and its shores disagreeable, with sea cliffs – like mountains – much more likely to provoke sentiments of horror than pleasure: landscapes of danger, they were to be avoided rather than sought out, let alone celebrated. But from the early-to-mid eighteenth century onwards, the rising attraction of the sublime saw increased cultural interest in coastal landscapes, particularly those wild or rocky in character. Indeed, for Alain Corbin, at this time 'the white cliffs of the Channel' emerged as one of the 'ideal hunting-grounds for lovers of the picturesque', being much prized by artists such as Paul Sandby, Alexander Cozens and William Daniell.[10] There is some truth in this, but the shift in attitudes was not as sudden or as early as is sometimes made out, especially when it came to landscapes of exposed chalk such as the cliffs of Dover, the picturesque attitudes to which Corbin's account perhaps oversimplifies somewhat. Widely acknowledged as one of the leading popularisers of the picturesque, William Gilpin found much to admire in the verdant, hill-framed view of Dover Castle from the Folkestone road, but found the chalk cliffs 'disagreeable' and 'unpleasing', comprising 'a blank glaring surface with little beauty, either of form or colour'.[11] Gilpin even included in his censure the famous 'Shakespeare's Cliff', a promontory just outside Dover so called on account of its associations with a scene in *King Lear*. For the picturesque Gilpin, his eye primed to admire asymmetry and variety in nature, the uniform whiteness and regular wall-like form of the cliffs were problematic. Indeed, it was only where the otherwise exposed chalk had been 'tinted with vegetation' that he considered the cliffs to have any aesthetic value at all: 'chalk', he felt, 'disfigures any landscape'.[12]

---

[9] Defoe's dismissive comments about the coastline extended to the town, about which he felt that neither it nor its 'old, useless, decay'd' castle had 'any Thing of Note to be said of them' (*ibid.*, p. 122).

[10] A. Corbin, *The lure of the sea: The discovery of the seaside 1750–1840* (London, 1995 [1988]), pp. 121–8, 140–5 (p. 143).

[11] W. Gilpin, *Observations on the coasts of Hampshire, Sussex, and Kent, relative chiefly to picturesque beauty: Made in the summer of the year 1774* (London, 1804), pp. 77–8.

[12] *Ibid.*, pp. 85, 92, 45.

However, whatever Gilpin's general impact on the picturesque dispensation, his particular strictures on chalk cliffs did not have
any very lasting impact. Some late-eighteenth- and early-nineteenth-
century travellers recorded being disappointed by the sight of Dover
Cliffs: returning home from Scandinavia in 1796, Mary Wollstonecraft
'wondered how any body could term them grand; they appear so insig-
nificant to me, after those I had seen in Sweden and Norway'.[13] Yet
such disappointment was a function of the hold the cliffs had by then
taken on the popular imagination: sights that are supposed to impress
can disappoint; the reputedly humdrum or ugly cannot. More typical
than Wollstonecraft's were remarks lauding the 'striking appearance' of
the 'lofty white cliffs' at Dover.[14] Ann Radcliffe's account of her journey to Holland and Germany in 1794 contained similarly admiring
descriptions, with Shakespeare's Cliff being praised as 'sublime as the
eternal name it bears'.[15] And by 1818, the view of the Dover coast when
approached by sea from Walmer, to the north, was being commended
as 'one of the most striking prospects that imagination can conceive'.[16]

The effect of this shift in attitudes, uneven at first but decisive by
the turn of the nineteenth century, grew stronger and was more widely
disseminated as time passed. In the Victorian era improved communication, combined with the expansion of popular tourism, dramatically
increased the number of British men and women who actually saw the
white cliffs with their own eyes. Although Dover enjoyed a fleeting
early-to-mid-nineteenth-century popularity as a tourist destination in its
own right (see fig. 1), with the *Lady's Newspaper* commending its 'stupendous perpendicular cliffs' in 1847,[17] the expansion of cross-channel
traffic was the crucial factor here.[18] (Not the least reason for this was

[13] M. Wollstonecraft, *Letters written during a short residence in Sweden, Norway, and
Denmark* (London, 1796), letter XXV, p. 262.

[14] J. Aiken, *England delineated; or, A geographical description of every county in
England and Wales*, 2nd edn (London, 1790), p. 268.

[15] A. Radcliffe, *A journey made in the summer of 1794, through Holland and the western frontier of Germany, with a return down the Rhine: To which are added observations during a tour to the lakes of Lancashire, Westmoreland, and Cumberland*,
2 vols., 2nd edn (London, 1795), Vol. II, p. 174.

[16] L. Fussell, *A journey round the coast of Kent* (London, 1818), pp. 142–3.

[17] *Lady's Newspaper*, 28 August 1847, p. 207.

[18] In 1863, the number of passengers on the Dover–Calais route was 123,025; in the
1890s the annual total reached 300,000; in 1910 the combined total number of
travellers carried by the Dover–Calais and Dover–Ostend routes was over 590,000:
J. B. Jones, *Annals of Dover* (Dover, 1916), pp. 159–60, 167.

1 W. Westall, *Dover, from the beach*, engraved by E. Francis, *c.* 1830. Photo courtesy of The Print Collector/Print Collector/Getty Images.

the perception that the cliffs were shown to their best advantage when viewed from the seaward side: 'Dover can only be seen aright by one who comes to it from the sea', as Byron's Don Juan did as he was blown towards 'Albion's earliest beauties, / Thy cliffs, *dear Dover!*').[19]

But aside from the effects of transport and tourism, these years saw hugely important developments in technologies of image production, which served too to embed the cliffs in the emergent discourse of national heritage.[20] Innovations in engraving techniques made the mass production of lithographic prints possible from the 1830s on. As a consequence, artistic depictions of landscapes such as the white cliffs became much more available – and affordable – than previously, with J. M. W. Turner's work in particular reaching a wide audience in this way.[21] Later in the nineteenth century, photographs and other means of image reproduction furthered the process of commodification and dissemination. In December 1881, for example, the Kensington Fine

[19] A. D. Lewis, *The Kent coast* (London, 1911), pp. 266–7.
[20] For these technologies, see D. Brett, *The construction of heritage* (Cork, 1996), esp. pp. 65–8.
[21] See E. Helsinger, 'Turner and the representation of England', in W. J. T. Mitchell (ed.), *Landscape and power* (Chicago, 1994), pp. 103–25 (esp. pp. 105–6).

Art Association offered an oleograph reproduction of a painting by H. Hillier. Entitled *Dover pier and harbour by moonlight*, it depicted the port at night, sheltered by the white cliffs. Advertised in newspapers around the country – not only those of southern counties, but also in publications such as the *Manchester Times* – it was billed as a picture 'that will commend itself to all Englishmen, on account of the interest that is felt in the historic old town, watched as it is by the famous castle and the cliff which Shakespeare has described in language that will endure for all time'.[22]

The nineteenth-century popularisation – and nationalisation – of the image of Dover cliffs could simply be read as reflecting changing aesthetic tastes in landscape. But while it may be that the landscape came to be seen as compatible with mainstream Victorian ideas of the picturesque, this was not sufficient on its own. In order to explain the appeal and significance of the white cliffs over the course of the 200 years or so after the middle of the eighteenth century, it is necessary to consider additional factors. Beneath the adulatory descriptions of the cliffs' appearance as 'striking' (a word very frequently used) lurked influences other than the narrowly aesthetic, especially those connected to the associational value of landscape. It is this associational value to which we now turn.

To begin with, the white cliffs were associated with the nation, and the felt antiquity of the nation. This association was not new. 'Albion' had been used as a synonym for England or Britain for many centuries (not least in Camden's *Britannia*),[23] the word deriving from the Latin *albus*, meaning white: in a sense, then, the white cliffs of the south coast had already defined the nation. That said, the nineteenth and early twentieth centuries saw a marked strengthening of this association. Descanting on the 'fascination' of Dover cliffs, one guidebook remarked how 'in the white walls of this part of the coast the popular fancy sees something indefinable, indicative of Albion's glory'; while another claimed 'these strange white cliffs ... stand for England' perhaps even more than 'the very lion upon her standard' because '"Albion" was a name, at least in Europe, centuries before any

22 *Manchester Times*, 31 December 1881. See also, e.g., *Northampton Mercury*, 31 December 1881; *Sheffield Daily Telegraph*, 7 January 1882; *Manchester Courier and Lancashire General Advertiser*, 7 January 1882.
23 Camden, *Britannia*, p. 1.

2 J. M. W. Turner, *Straits of Dover*, engraved by William Miller, 1828. Photo courtesy of Culture Club/Getty Images.

national banner waved upon her shores.'[24] In 1908, the art historian and collector W. G. Rawlinson offered the opinion that Turner's *Straits of Dover* (fig. 2), which had appeared in the artist's still enormously popular *Picturesque views in England and Wales*, was a 'scene ... so *English*, so exactly what one sees on landing at Dover on a sunny, windy day'.[25]

As reflected in this reading of Turner's picture, the developing association between the cliffs, the sea and nationality was congruent with the strengthening of the conceptualisation of Britain – and England – as an 'island nation' in contemporary cultural discourse.[26] The final

---

[24] *A guide-book and itinerary of Dover* (Dover, 1896), p. 30; A. G. Bradley, *England's outpost: The country of the Kentish Cinque Ports* (London, [1921]), pp. 317–18.

[25] W. G. Rawlinson, *The engraved work of J. M. W. Turner*, 2 vols. (London, 1908), Vol. I, pp. 125–6.

[26] The comparative scholarly neglect of this phenomenon is worth remarking upon. While the connections between pastoral landscapes and Englishness have been extensively discussed, it remains the case – as Jan Rüger has pointed out – that relatively little attention has been given to the relationship between coastal landscapes and discourses of national identity: J. Rüger, *The great naval game: Britain and Germany in the age of empire* (Cambridge, 2007), pp. 170–4. That discussion which does exist tends to be rather fleeting, or very general: see, for example,

surrender of Calais to France in 1558 had laid the foundations of the view that the Channel was the border, and this view was further bolstered by the spread of Enlightenment-generated ideas that nation-statehood was properly defined by natural boundaries such as seas, rivers and mountains.[27] By the nineteenth century, with the strength and successes of the Royal Navy increasingly a source of self-congratulation for the British, the connections between the sea, insularity and national greatness were axiomatic.[28] Notoriously, Britain's geographical separateness from the Continent was a matter of celebration and, when combined with increasingly secure geological knowledge, helped reinforce the longstanding idea that English nationhood was naturally (or providentially) ordained. In 1801, the well-known actor, composer and writer Charles Dibdin 'rejoiced' in the thought that the country had been separated from the Continent 'either by an earthquake or a partial deluge', as 'it is self-evident that whatever gave us our insular situation laid the foundation of our glory'.[29] It was a message that was much repeated over the course of the century and beyond, not least in educational books aimed at the young.[30] Indeed, its strength and persistence do much to explain why proposals to construct a tunnel under the English Channel met with the hostility they did. Early efforts in the 1880s and 1890s foundered on the objection, in the words of E. A. Freeman, a prominent opponent of the tunnel, that it would

R. Colls, *Identity of England* (Oxford, 2002), pp. 237–42; K. Lunn and A. Day, 'Britain as island: National identity and the sea', in H. Brocklehurst and R. Phillips (eds.), *History, nationhood and the question of Britain* (Basingstoke, 2004), pp. 124–36; R. S. Peckham, 'The uncertain state of islands: National identity and the discourse of islands in nineteenth-century Britain and Greece', *Journal of Historical Geography*, 29 (2003), 499–515.

[27] See P. Readman, C. Radding and C. Bryant, 'Introduction: Borderlands in a global perspective', in P. Readman, C. Radding and C. Bryant (eds.), *Borderlands in world history, 1700–1914* (Basingstoke, 2014), pp. 7–8.

[28] Behrman, *Victorian myths of the sea*. See also G. Quilley, '"All ocean is her own": The image of the sea and the identity of the maritime nation in eighteenth-century British art', in G. Cubitt (ed.), *Imagining nations* (Manchester, 1998), pp. 132–52.

[29] C. Dibdin, *Observations on a tour through almost the whole of England*, 2 vols. (London, 1801), Vol. 1, p. 21.

[30] One children's publication of 1858 celebrated the day 'when the sea broke through with a roar and a bound' as one that had given Britain 'a distinct place among the nations of the world': I. Wilson, *Our native land* (London, 1858), p. 72.

make the inhabitants of Britain 'cease to be islanders, and become continentals'.[31]

This patriotic solicitude for Britain remaining *virgo intacta* – as the Conservative politician Lord Randolph Churchill had phrased it in opposing Channel tunnel legislation in June 1888 – was sharpened by the fact that the proposals for a tunnel envisaged it beginning at or near the white cliffs. (Indeed, Sir Edward Watkin's schemes of the 1880s and 1890s called for the submarine link to begin near Shakespeare's Cliff itself, exploratory works beginning in the early 1880s.[32]) The cliffs had emerged as a powerful emblem of an insular, maritime national identity, one that was shaped less by the expanding overseas empire than by Britain's place in Europe, particularly as affected by historical rivalries with continental powers, especially France. It was this identity that the tunnel threatened to subvert. To a significant extent, from the nineteenth century onwards the cliffs came to stand as a synecdoche of separateness from the Continent, of Britain's status as an island apart from the rest of Europe, functioning as a landscape of difference for the inhabitants of an island kingdom.

The nationalistic deployment of the white cliffs reflected their association not only with insularity, but also with the defence of the British Isles against foreign military threats, particularly invasion. The association between Dover and defence was of longstanding, with the medieval monk and historian Matthew Paris's thirteenth-century description of the town as 'the lock and key' of the kingdom being much quoted.[33] Dover's great castle, and its antiquity as a fortified site, did much to contribute to this; but as powerful a symbol of defence and defiance as

[31] E. A. Freeman, 'Alter orbis', *Contemporary Review*, 41 (June 1882), 1042. It would be the same story with later attempts made in the interwar period, and even in 1975 the Labour Cabinet minister Barbara Castle could confess her relief that Tony Crosland had shelved the plans then being considered, her sentiments being founded on 'a kind of earthy feeling that an island is an island and should not be violated' (K. Wilson, *Channel tunnel visions 1850–1945: Dreams and nightmares* (London, 1994), 188–92; B. Castle, *The Castle diaries 1964–1976* (London, 1990), p. 545).

[32] For Randolph Churchill, see *Hansard*, 3rd series, 327 (27 June 1888), 1500. For the history of the channel tunnel, see Wilson, *Channel tunnel*.

[33] See, for example, Camden, *Britannia*, p. 344; *Handbook for travellers in Kent*, 5th edn (London, 1892), p. 50; F. M. Hueffer [Ford Madox Ford], *The Cinque Ports: A historical and descriptive record* (Edinburgh, 1900), p. 242; *The Dover official guide and souvenir* (Dover, 1930), p. 13.

3 J. M. W. Turner, *Dover from Shakespeare's Cliff*, in *Picturesque views on the southern coast of England*, from *Drawings made principally by J. M. W. Turner, and engraved by W. B. Cooke, George Cooke, and other eminent engravers* (London, 1826). Reproduced by kind permission of the Syndics of Cambridge University Library: LE.2.39.

the castle undoubtedly was, it was rarely considered in isolation from the cliffs upon which it perched, and from which it derived much of its iconographic force. Turner's *Dover from Shakespeare's Cliff* (1826; fig. 3) is a classic rendition of the scene, showing the guns of the modern fortifications engaged in practice-firing (in the direction of France), with the medieval castle prominent in the background.

In fact, the cliffs of Dover were themselves potent emblems of national defence, with or without the castle: metaphorically as well as physically, they functioned as ramparts. In nineteenth- and early-twentieth-century publications, they were described as 'white walls', as 'natural defences of the most impregnable character'.[34] A great deal was made of the story that when Julius Caesar arrived at the Kentish

---

[34] *Dover: The gateway to England* (Dover, 1931), p. 6; *A guide-book and itinerary of Dover* (Dover, 1896), p. 30; *A pictorial and descriptive guide to Dover*, 6th edn (London, [1924–5]), p. ix; S. T. Davies, *Dover* (London, 1869), p. 3.

coast, the sight of heavily armed Britons thronging the white cliffs had encouraged him to seek a landing place elsewhere, but they were as much natural fortifications of the mind than anything else. In 1878, *Black's guide to Kent* commended Dover 'with its walls of glittering chalk, majestic and impregnable' as 'a fitting symbol of English Power'.[35]

The symbolic significance of the cliffs in this regard – their status as monuments to a long and continuing history of resistance to foreign adversaries – is borne out by the fact that artistic depictions often exaggerated their height, so emphasising their status as bulwarks or battlements. Those of Turner provide a good case in point. The artist first visited Dover in 1792, and returned on several occasions in later years, the town and its environs being a frequent subject for his later topographical watercolours.[36] Featuring the fortifications of the Western Heights in the foreground, along with a soldier looking out to sea and the practice-firing of guns, *Dover from Shakespeare's Cliff* presents one example, representing the cliffs as being significantly higher than they were in reality, as does the artist's *Dover Castle* (1822).[37] And in his painting *Dover* (*c.*1825), so great was Turner's artistic licence that John Ruskin was moved to object that he had 'lost the real character of Dover Cliffs by making the town at their feet three times lower in proportionate height than it really is'.[38]

The representation of the cliffs as towering natural battlements reflected perceptions of their military significance, the heights around the town having been extensively fortified in the late eighteenth and early nineteenth centuries (William Cobbett famously complained of the expense incurred in making 'a great chalk-hill a honey-comb' in which 'to hide Englishmen from Frenchmen').[39] But it also reflected more generalised anxieties about the threat of invasion, with the experience of the Napoleonic Wars being important here. Yet the fears persisted long after 1815, deep into the Victorian period and

[35] *Black's guide to Kent* (Edinburgh, 1878), p. 213.
[36] E. Joll, M. Butlin and L. Herrmann (eds.), *The Oxford companion to J. M. W. Turner* (Oxford, 2001), p. 79.
[37] E. Shanes, *Turner's rivers, harbours and coasts* (London, 1981), pp. 28–9, 33–4, and Plates 46, 67.
[38] J. Ruskin, *The harbours of England* (Orpington, 1895), pp. 63–4.
[39] W. Cobbett, *Rural rides*, ed. I. Dyck (Harmondsworth, 2001 [1830]), pp. 156–8 (pp. 158, 157).

beyond. Louis Napoleon's *coup d'état* in 1851 was followed by a slew of invasion scares. Concerns about the designs of a resurgent France led to the further fortification of England's southern coastline and, in 1859, the creation of the Volunteer Force – a locally organised precursor to the twentieth-century Territorial Army and Home Guard.[40] France's defeat by Prussia in 1870–1 did not end such anxieties, partly because distrust of the French was so deep-seated (witness the controversies surrounding the early Channel tunnel proposals), but mainly because an assertive imperial Germany prompted renewed fears of invasion – as manifested in the outcry provoked by publications such as George Tomkyns Chesney's *Battle of Dorking* (1871), to give an early example, and William Le Queux's *Daily Mail*-serialised *Invasion of 1910*, to give a rather later one.[41]

For all their xenophobia and sensationalism, these Victorian and Edwardian scare stories were not entirely irrational, nor were they dismissed as such by contemporary opinion. Advances in technology had made invasion seem all the more possible. Steam power meant ships could operate at much higher speeds than previously, making the threat of a surprise attack – or 'bolt from the blue' – loom larger. It also meant ships could operate independently of tides and winds: the unpredictability of the weather could no longer thwart a determined enemy, as, arguably, it had done in 1588 with the Spanish Armada. In 1845, Lord Palmerston told the House of Commons that 'the Channel is no longer a barrier. Steam navigation has rendered that which was before impassable by a military force nothing more than a river passable by a steam bridge.'[42] This was hyperbole, certainly, but the fear was strongly felt, and it intensified as ships became still faster and more manoeuvrable as the century wore on.

Advances in aviation made matters yet worse. The 1783 balloon ascent by the Montgolfier brothers may have triggered some prognostications of airborne assault, not least after the first balloon crossing of the English Channel in January 1785, but the slow speed and ready combustibility of hot-air balloons ensured that such speculations remained on the wilder fringes of alarmist discourse for the

---

[40] See H. Cunningham, *The Volunteer Force: A social and political history, 1859–1908* (London, 1975).
[41] For invasion-scare literature, see I. F. Clarke, *Voices prophesying war 1763–1984* (London, 1966).
[42] *Hansard*, 3rd series, 82 (30 July 1845), 1223–4.

next hundred years or so. Winged and motor-powered flight changed things dramatically, however, as it soon became apparent that these were technologies with far more military potential. In his *War in the air* of 1908, H. G. Wells observed that 'with the flying machine war alters its character: it ceases to be an affair of "fronts" and becomes an affair of "areas"; neither side, victor or loser, remains immune from the gravest injuries'.[43] The following year, a dramatic demonstration of Wells's prescience was given by Louis Blériot, who succeeded in flying his monoplane across the English Channel, landing near the cliffs of Dover on 25 July 1909 – a feat that the *Daily Express* greeted with the headline that 'Britain is no longer an island.'[44] In the event, the experience of the First World War would do relatively little to blur the boundaries of the battlefield, notwithstanding the German air raids on southern and eastern England (which in the event caused relatively few casualties). At war's end, Field Marshal Sir Douglas Haig was welcomed home in an elaborately choreographed ceremony at Dover, the iconographic significance of his landing site being readily apparent to contemporary commentators as well as the commander-in-chief himself, who in his speech on disembarkation described the town as 'keeper of the eastern gate of England' and 'guardian of the Narrow Seas'.[45]

If the white cliffs functioned as an emblem of national security and defiance, and as a marker of difference projected against continental adversaries, then they also functioned as a symbol of the national home and of homecoming. This is significant not least because of the importance of the idea of home in the construction of British national identities: as the author of one elementary school textbook saw fit to declare, the 'chief characteristic of English men and women is their love of "home"'.[46] Guarding the historical 'gateway to England', the cliffs framed the port that for many centuries was the main route in and out of the country, a town that in the sixteenth century William Camden had judged to be 'a place of passage of all other most haunted', of which 'it was provided in old time by a speciall Statute, that no man

---

[43] Cited in Clarke, *Voices prophesying war*, pp. 100–1.

[44] B. A. Elliot, *Blériot: Herald of an age* (Stroud, 2000), pp. 125–6.

[45] *Manchester Guardian*, 20 December 1918, p. 7; J. B. Firth, *Dover and the Great War* (Dover, [1920]), pp. 118–21.

[46] S. Heathorn, *For home, country, and race: Constructing gender, class and Englishness in the elementary school, 1880–1914* (Toronto, 2000), p. 151.

going forth of the realme in pilgrimage, should els where embark and take sea'.[47] The traffic handled by Dover port increased steadily from the mid eighteenth century on, with the introduction of a regular steam-packet service to Calais in 1818 and the arrival of the railway at Dover in 1844 greatly facilitating access to and from the Continent. These developments, combined with the growth of international trade and tourism, meant that by the 1890s the number of travellers on the Dover–Calais route totalled around 300,000 per year – a figure that would increase still further in the twentieth century.

As more people gained first-hand experience of the white cliffs through journeying to and from Dover, the association with home gained greater strength. It is of course the case that 'home' has had wildly varying meanings for inhabitants of the British Isles, not least because in the English language the word can stand for many different things – house, neighbourhood, village, county, town, city, country, nation.[48] In all cases, however, the concept of home is inseparable from the idea of travelling or – speaking more abstractly – movement in space. Implicitly or explicitly, all individuals define their relationship to their personal homes (however imagined) in spatial terms: one is at home, away from home, near home and so on.[49] Following from this, it can readily be seen how the white cliffs of Dover, as a much-viewed and physically distinctive marker of homecoming for people whose more particular homes were inevitably scattered all over England, came to function as a powerful symbol of a larger national homeland, and specifically a homeland conceptualised as (part of) an island, as inextricably linked to the sea. In doing so, it acted as the externally orientated complement to the ruralised, more inwardly focused idealisations of home, centred in large part on the idyllic country village and its cottages.[50]

Unsurprisingly, therefore, references to the white cliffs as emblems of 'The sever'd land of home'[51] saturated nineteenth- and

---

[47] Camden, *Britannia*, p. 344.

[48] In the Romance languages, by contrast, 'home' is more typically used simply as a synonym for 'house'. See D. E. Sopher, 'The landscape of home', in Meinig, *Interpretation of ordinary landscapes*, pp. 130–1.

[49] As one geographer has put it, 'Home … cannot be understood except in terms of journey': J. D. Porteous, 'Home: The territorial core', *Geographical Review*, 66 (1976), 383–90 (p. 387).

[50] Heathorn, *For home, country, and race*, pp. 141–51.

[51] *Bow Bells*, 25 (November 1876), 490.

early-twentieth-century cultural discourse, with many poems and novels making much of the connection. Popular songs frequently deployed
the image of the cliffs as a symbol of 'old England' for emigrants, sailors, soldiers fighting overseas and returning travellers.[52] It was also a
staple of tourist guidebooks. To the weary traveller coming back from
abroad, the cliffs were presented as standing for the nation as a whole.
Used in this way as an emblem of home, the white cliffs were felicitously capacious. As an idealised marker of the national home, the cliffs
complemented and sometimes encompassed more specific and personal
patrias. In words for a song of 1904, W. A. Mackenzie described how,
for the homecoming traveller, the image of the mother or wife waiting
in the 'little English nook, where a nestling village sleeps' is recalled 'In
the fairest and the rarest sight that glads our eyes, / In the tall white
cliffs of England, glimm'ring o'er the Channel foam'.[53]

Embedded in the collective national consciousness, the cliffs
were also carried about the world by the British. Voyaging down the
Congo River in the 1870s, Henry Stanley came upon a riparian swell-
ing 2,500 yards wide – which he named Stanley Pool – on the right of
which 'towered a long row of cliffs, white and glistening, so like the
cliffs of Dover that Frank [Francis John Pocock, son of a sailor from
Kent] at once exclaimed that it was a bit of England'. The explorers
then named the cliffs 'Dover Cliffs' in an attempt, replicated *mutatis
mutandis* by Europeans elsewhere, to domesticate the otherwise alien-
ating landscape of the colonised, transforming it into the landscape of
empire.[54]

The nationalistic potency of the white cliffs was due in large
part to their associations with national history. As Anthony D. Smith

[52] Examples of musical scores held in the British Library include G. Linley and
W. Neuland, *The white cliffs of England* (1833); J. F. Duke, *Farewell white cliffs of
old England* (1899); A. Johnstone and W. A. Mackenzie, *The white cliffs of England*
(1904); P. Edgar and H. E. Pether, *The white cliffs of England (are the white cliffs of
home)* (1916).

[53] 'In some little English nook, where a nestling village sleeps, / There's a mother sits
and waits, or a wife that weeps, or a wife that weeps. / Ah! we hear their loving call,
and we see them one and all / In the fairest and the rarest sight that glads our eyes, /
In the tall white cliffs of England, glimm'ring o'er the Channel foam, / From our dear
ones sending welcome to the wand'rers nearing home'; Johnstone and Mackenzie,
White cliffs.

[54] H. M. Stanley, *Through the dark continent*, 2 vols. (New York, 1988 [London,
1878]), Vol. II, pp. 254–5.

4 Albert Henry Payne, *Dover*, *c.* 1850: a view from Shakespeare's Cliff. Engraving. Photo courtesy of Science and Society Picture Library/Getty Images.

has argued, homelands are imagined as historic territories, their landscapes those of national ancestors and national heritage.[55] As a potent symbol of the homeland over centuries, the cliffs of Dover were closely connected to the national past, its vicissitudes and worthies. This is well shown by the white cliffs' relationship with William Shakespeare. In Act IV of *King Lear* the blinded Gloucester asks Edgar to lead him the edge of 'a cliff whose high and bending head / Looks fearfully in the confined deep'.[56] Gloucester's intended place of suicide – to which Edgar does not in the end lead him – was evidently a well-known landmark in Tudor and Stuart England; identified as the prominent headland to the southwest of Dover town, it was subsequently named 'Shakespeare's Cliff' in honour of the connection. It had lost a good deal of height

[55] A. D. Smith, *Myths and memories of the nation* (Oxford, 1999), pp. 149–59.
[56] W. Shakespeare, *The tragedy of King Lear*, in W. Shakespeare, *The complete works: Compact edition*, ed. S. Wells and G. Taylor (Oxford, 1988), Act IV, Scene 1 (p. 964), and Act IV, Scene 5 (pp. 966–7).

because of landslips over the years, which only served to increase the propensity of literal-minded commentators to remark on how much lower in altitude and precipitousness it seemed in comparison to the Bard's description.[57] Yet in truth, the physical character of Shakespeare's Cliff was only a small part of its appeal; notwithstanding the fact that Edgar did not take Gloucester there, it was the literary association with *King Lear* that mattered. This provided a means by which the educated of the metropolis and elsewhere could claim ownership of the landscape and its meaning, even from the inhabitants of Dover itself, who could not necessarily be counted upon to appreciate great literature. In 1848, the year of revolutions, one contributor to the *London Journal* wrote of the contrast between the 'dull and ignorant' coastguard posted on the summit of the eponymous cliff, 'who neither thinks nor knows any thing of Shakespeare', and the earnest 'strangers … every day bending their steps, recalling at each some line of the tragic scene while labour-ing up the steep ascent, in the expectation of the extensive and glori-ous view they are to enjoy from the dizzy height, with some nervous apprehension that they may "topple down headlong"'. Such sentiments, however, can be read as defensive reactions, being a function of the increasing hold of Shakespeare over not just the educated elite, but the public at large – including the proletarian public.[58] And with the ripen-ing and broadening of the cult of Shakespeare from the mid nineteenth century on, few British guidebooks or commentaries on Dover and its environs failed to draw attention to the associations with *King Lear*.[59] For the ordinary visitor as much as the connoisseur, associations such as these were vital to the appeal and significance of the landscape, not-withstanding its purely visual impact: '[h]owever fine, as an object, the Shakspeare [*sic*] Cliff may be, there is nothing about it so remarkable as to exercise the particular interest of the topographer and the tourist, in an island like this, which, on its western shores especially, is so famous

---

[57] See, for example, Aiken, *England*, p. 276.

[58] For radical bardolatry, see A. Taylor, 'Shakespeare and radicalism: The uses and abuses of Shakespeare in nineteenth-century popular politics', *Historical Journal*, 45 (2002), 357–79.

[59] For good examples, see *Black's guide to Kent*, pp. 207–9; M. Walcott, *A guide to the coast of Kent* (London, 1859), pp. 14, 88; Heywood, *Illustrated guide*, pp. 7–9.

for rock-scenery were it not for the halo which the genius of Shakspeare has shed over it'.[60]

But the Shakespearean associations of the white cliffs were just one dimension of a wider relationship with national history and heritage. The longstanding associations with defence and past resistance to invasion have already been remarked upon. Yet the cliffs were also seen to bear more general witness to the story of the nation. Crowned by their ancient castle, in whose precincts stood a Roman watchtower (widely believed to be the oldest building in the country), the cliffs brought to life 'a series of vivid pictures that have made European history'.[61] These included the ceremonial comings and goings of various monarchs, from Edward I to Queen Victoria; the defeat of the French under Eustace the Monk in 1295; the Spanish Armada; and much else besides: 'On what grand historic scenes – on what memorable festivals – have yonder cliffs looked down!', exclaimed one guidebook in the 1870s.[62] Lapidary statements signalling how the cliffs were 'grandly associated with nearly every page of British history' featured prominently in the discourse throughout.[63]

Perceived as witnesses to national history, the cliffs were also seen as ancient, constituent parts of the nation's heritage and comforting markers of continuity. Perhaps ignorant of the fact that the man-made Admiralty Pier at Dover had done much to limit the effects of erosion, tourist guidebooks asserted that the 'chalky heights' of the white cliffs, 'strong in their natural strength, seem to defy both age, decay, and the fiercest onslaughts of Father Time'[64] – this claimed rocky asperity also reinforcing their established associations with resistance to foreign threats. The cliffs were a bright and unchanging marker of national identity – and national persistence – down through the centuries. White when the Romans came, and still white today, they functioned as powerful symbols of the continuity of the homeland across more than 1,000 years:

> In history's dawn we see the ancient Britons in battle array on the Dover cliffs, differing greatly in many respects from Dovorians

---

[60] *Saturday Magazine*, 10 (April 1837), 138.
[61] *The Dover official guide and souvenir* (Dover, 1930), p. 9.
[62] *Black's guide to Kent*, p. 213.
[63] Heywood, *Illustrated guide*, pp. 6–7, 10–12 (p. 10).
[64] Davies, *Dover*, p. 2.

of to-day, yet as true and patriotic as those of the Twentieth Century ... Dover, from the earliest times, margined a charming bay, and although Saxons, Normans and English have slightly modified its features, the Town and Port still nestles between the tall, white cliffs, the addition of forty thousand more people to the population having altered but little the physical features.[65]

Whatever the ebb and flow of human history, the cliffs were imagined as continuing to testify to the persistence of the nation.

In this way, the cliffs of Dover played a significant role in what Smith has called 'the territorialisation of memory', acting as witnesses to the survival of the English people over time, and symbolising the continuity of the national home.[66] The cliffs' function in this respect grew more important from the late nineteenth century on, in the context of the accelerating pace of urbanisation and technological change, and the speeding-up of life generally that was experienced across European societies at this time.[67] While these developments generated great excitement and conferred palpable benefits, they could also stimulate fears of degeneration and national decline, and impose new pressures and anxieties on individuals. Against this backdrop, the continuity represented by the cliffs served to bolster national identity, the underpinnings of which seemed increasingly assailed by the dislocating effects of urban-industrial modernity. It is worth recalling here Raymond Williams's observation that the cultural value a society typically places on the 'natural' environment and its landscapes is directly related to the urban-industrial development of that society: increased idealisation of land, landscape and the rural was a function of the experience of nineteenth- and twentieth-century modernity, not its antithesis.[68] England was no exception. In the context of the (real and perceived) rapidity of economic, social and cultural change after the mid eighteenth century, landscapes such as the white cliffs provided reassurance that despite the changes and challenges of the contemporary world, the homeland persisted still. As represented by the cliffs, this homeland was insular; it was defined by its being surrounded by the

---

[65] Jones, *Annals of Dover*, pp. 430–1; also Heywood, *Illustrated guide*, pp. 5–6.
[66] A. D. Smith, *Chosen peoples: Sacred sources of national identity* (Oxford, 2003), pp. 134ff; and Smith, *Myths*, esp. pp. 150–2.
[67] For this context, see Kern, *Culture of time and space*.
[68] Williams, *Country and the city*, p. 248.

sea. Despite Blériot and what he portended, insularity remained a crucial component of English identity, and the imagining of the white cliffs
as national landscape provides compelling evidence of this. Finally,
although this national landscape was inextricably linked to the sea,
it was focused on the island homeland rather than on the overseas
empire. Indeed, it may be that historians have exaggerated the connections between the sea, the empire and English/British identities[69] – at
any rate for the people of the British Isles (for some of the inhabitants of
the empire, it may have been a different story).[70] Throughout the modern period, the bulk of the Royal Navy was stationed in home waters.
Ironically, the progressively heated late Victorian and Edwardian claims
about the Navy being essential for imperial defence correlated almost
perfectly with its progressive concentration in Europe.[71] The continued
valorisation of the white cliffs as markers of an identity based on insularity was the cultural counterpart to this.

Various idealised and generalised views of the English countryside also performed this function, one example being the powerful
symbolism of the English 'south country' and its signature landscape
of tranquil villages, verdant fields and rolling downland.[72] But this
function was also performed by particular, individual landscapes: as
in other European countries, national identities in Britain were importantly predicated on local identities, local and national patriotisms
being in a symbiotic and mutually supportive relationship across most
of the modern period.[73] Particularity, of course, could be a source of
local pride: in Dover's case, the town was jealous of its cliffs, and fully

[69] For some suggestive remarks on this, see S. Conway, 'Empire, Europe and British
naval power', in D. Cannadine (ed.), *Empire, the sea and global history* (Basingstoke,
2007), pp. 22–40.

[70] The Australian politician and post-war Prime Minister R. G. Menzies (1894–1978)
is one later example of such an individual. Menzies 'idealised England' and its landscape, culture and institutions – not least the white cliffs – combining this with an
understanding that 'Australians were simply Britons in another part of the world',
and as such were integral to a larger imperial unity. See J. Brett, *Robert Menzies'
forgotten people,* 2nd edn (Carlton, 2007), pp. 114–23, 190–2 (pp. 190, 192).

[71] P. P. O'Brien, 'The titan refreshed: Imperial overstretch and the British Navy before
the First World War', *Past & Present,* 172 (2001), 146–69.

[72] A. Howkins, 'The discovery of rural England', in R. Colls and P. Dodd (eds.),
Englishness: Politics and culture 1880–1920, 2nd edn (London, 2014 [1986]), pp.
85–111.

[73] Readman, 'Place of the past', pp. 176–9. Germany provides perhaps the most useful
comparator: see esp. Confino, *Nation as a local metaphor.*

5 *An advertisement on Dover Cliffs*, from Clarence Moran, *The business of advertising* (London, 1905). Reproduced by kind permission of the Syndics of Cambridge University Library: misc.7.90.1529.

conscious of their symbolic importance. It was for this reason that the turn-of-the-century town council, prompted by a local petition, took steps to remove a large advertisement for Quaker Oats that had been affixed to the cliff face above the harbour. Local opinion condemned the prominently placed hoarding, all too visible from the sea, as an affront to 'the welfare and reputation and picturesqueness of Dover', the 'traditions' and 'ancient features' of the place.[74] But the offence to locality was also, and primarily, an offence to nationality: the local patriotism of Dovorians was based on outrage that 'the historic front of "Old Albion"' had been 'disfigured only to proclaim the virtues of Yankee Oats'.[75] In the case of the white cliffs (unlike some other valued landscapes), the national was prior, dominating the local. Perhaps

---

[74] *A Beautiful World*, 9 (1900–3), pp. 9–10, 18; *Dover Observer*, 24 August 1901, p. 7.
[75] *Dover Observer*, 7 September 1901, p. 7; *Dover and County Chronicle*, 12 October 1901, p. 3.

the quintessential national landscape, the cliffs figured and limned the homeland, emphasising its insular character.

To an extent the nation represented by the cliffs was distinctively English: although difficult to demonstrate conclusively, it is almost certainly the case that the cliffs were more meaningful markers of home for inhabitants of England, particularly southern England, than for the Welsh or the Scots. This was in part a simple function of geography. The white cliffs were located in the southeast corner of England, and fronted the English Channel. They were also composed of chalk, which carried very strong associations with the English landscape, especially the downlands of the south. One book on the Kent coast published in 1914 even asserted – quite incorrectly – that 'we in England have a world-monopoly of chalk'.[76] But despite these felt connections between the white cliffs and Englishness, their importance as markers of a larger British homeland should not be underestimated. The port of Dover's long-established position as the key place of passage to and from continental Europe played a key role here. From the eighteenth century on, people from all parts of the British Isles could identify the cliffs with home. In 1772, one Yorkshireman described how catching just a glimpse of the cliffs of Dover from Calais town walls 'gave me such satisfactory sensations as are only to be felt by such who have been absent from their native land, and on the point of returning to it'.[77] Fifty years later, another north-countryman – son of the proprietor of the *Leeds Mercury* – described the cliffs as 'giant ramparts to our happy land', welcoming to the returning traveller; and 100 years later again the Nottinghamshire-born Arthur Mee thought the white cliffs 'the gladdest sight the Englishman [away] from home can wish to see'.[78] And for all that inhabitants of Scotland had recourse to alternative national landscapes that exerted a stronger appeal at least so far as Scottishness was concerned, it would seem that the white cliffs could even exert a patriotic pull on them as Britons, also. Arriving in Boulogne in 1765 after two years of continental travel, the writer Tobias Smollett – a British as well as a Scottish patriot, though certainly no lover of the

---

[76] C. G. Harper, *The Kentish coast* (London, 1914), pp. 271–2.

[77] C. Cayley, *A Tour thorough [sic] Holland, Flanders, and part of France: In the year 1772* (Leeds, 1773), p. 104.

[78] E. Baines, jun., 'Letters from the continent (no. 1)', *Leeds Mercury*, 5 January 1833; A. Mee, *Kent* (London, 1936), p. 144.

town of Dover – nevertheless experienced intense pleasure on seeing the white cliffs, the sight reminding him of all the reasons why he was so 'attached to his country'.[79] Later on, the daughter of the duke of Argyll – having just departed Dover for France in July 1814 – recorded in her diary how the view of the cliffs 'recall[s] a sensation of pride to every British heart'.[80] Later still, after the carnage of the Great War, the Scottish General Haig lauded the significance of the white cliffs as a marker of homecoming, going so far as to call them 'a most inspiring spectacle [that] in itself repays us for all that we have been privileged to do in the discharge of our duty to King and country'.[81]

Such personal views of the cliffs were bound up with the dissemination and consumption of their image – across the British Isles – in artworks, lithographic prints, photography and film. This helped further entrench their position as fixtures in national topographies, and aided in the imagining of these topographies and in the territorialisation of national memories. The cliffs supported an idea of England that was closely related to a larger, though still insular, sense of Britishness.

---

[79] Letter XLI from Boulogne, 13 June 1765, in T. Smollett, *Travels through France and Italy* (Oxford, 1981 [1766]), p. 327. For Smollett's views on Dover, see *ibid.*, pp. 4–6; for his 'sympathetic Britishness', see E. Gottlieb, *Feeling British: Sympathy and national identity in Scottish and English writing, 1707–1832* (Lewisburg, PA, 2007), pp. 61–98.

[80] 'Diary of Lady Charlotte Susan Maria Campbell Bury, July, 1814', in *Diary illustrative of the times of George the fourth interspersed with original letters from … Queen Caroline*, Vol. II (Philadelphia, PA, 1838), p. 18.

[81] *Manchester Guardian*, 20 December 1918, p. 7. Even in the twenty-first century, the cliffs retain strong associations with Britain and Britishness in the popular mindset. This was nicely illustrated by the enormously enthusiastic and patriotic public response to the National Trust's 2012 'White Cliffs of Dover Appeal', which – in the teeth of a global recession – raised £1.2 million from over 16,500 people in just 133 days, the money going towards the purchase of 0.8 miles of coastline. Examination of the hundreds of messages of support posted by donors on the appeal's webpage suggests that about as many described the cliffs as a British as they did an English landmark. 'Leanne, Mark and Aidan' donated 'Because we're proud to be British and the White Cliffs just say "British"!'; Stella Wood gave because they were 'an iconic feature of Great Britain'; while Karen White's generosity sprang from their being 'A true Great British treasure'. For another donor ('GE'), 'This is one area that … everyone associates with the UK.' www.nationaltrust.org.uk/get-involved/donate/current-appeals/white-cliffs-of-dover-appeal/?id=298; www.nationaltrust.org.uk/get-involved/donate/current-appeals/white-cliffs-of-dover-appeal/?id=318; www.nationaltrust.org.uk/get-involved/donate/current-appeals/white-cliffs-of-dover-appeal/?id=253; www.nationaltrust.org.uk/get-involved/donate/how-youve-helped/white-cliffs-of-dover-appeal/ (all accessed 14 December 2012).

While the inland landscape of Kent was emphatically and exclusively an English landscape, being celebrated as the 'garden of England' and the natural habitat of that archetypal rural patriot, the sturdy yeoman, its coastline could be invested with different national meanings: its Englishness was inseparable from the common British experience of islandhood. Founded on the idea of the cliffs as a symbol of the historic homeland and its continuity over centuries, this insular, British-inflected Englishness proved surprisingly robust and enduring. Its beginnings correlated with the late-eighteenth- and early-nineteenth-century beginnings of Britishness more generally, and as with this wider phenomenon, the conflict with Revolutionary and Napoleonic France was the crucial catalyst.[82] In the context of war with an enemy directly across the Channel, and one that presented a real threat of invasion, the cliffs proved a very effective delineator of the British – as well as English – homeland against the menace of the continental Other.

Finally, the white cliffs also provide evidence of the strength, in the age of empire, of conceptualisations of national identity centred on the historic island homeland rather than more recently acquired territories outside Europe. For inhabitants of Britain, at any rate, the cliffs were only indirectly connected with the imperial mission as it was variously conceived between the eighteenth and twentieth centuries. That said, the island-focused patriotic charge carried by the cliffs was not incompatible with the imperialist project, nor was it uncongenial to the agents of this project. Memories of the white cliffs and what they signified were carried to colonial borderlands in the imaginations of explorers, servicemen and emigrants. But typically, the connotations of the white cliffs were insular in character; the associations they triggered were inward- rather than outward-facing in orientation.

Visually, the cliffs of Dover are a relatively unusual landscape feature, and high-flown claims of their distinctiveness resounded down through the centuries. Writing in 1914, Charles G. Harper felt confident that there was 'nothing in the rest of the whole wide world in the least resembling' the 'bastioned chalky heights' of 'the "white cliffs of Albion"'.[83] Unsurprisingly, claims of their superiority to the

---

[82] See L. Colley, *Britons: Forging the nation, 1707–1837*, 2nd edn (New Haven and London, 2009 [1994]).

[83] Harper, *Kentish coast*, pp. 271–2.

landscape on the other side of the Channel were often heard, one ultra-patriotic writer of the 1820s reckoning that the 'beauty' and 'power' of the Dover coastline, with its 'romantic and lofty' cliffs, was such that a 'stranger … who lands in Dover for the first time, and compares the delightful Picturesque scenery before him with the opposite shore near Calais, will naturally imagine that he is treading on enchanted Ground'.[84] Other eyes saw things rather differently. One early example of such a person was the Linnaean naturalist Pehr Kalm, who in 1747 had been commissioned by the Swedish government to travel to North America on a botanical fact-finding mission. Departing from the Kentish port of Deal a few miles north of the white cliffs, Kalm soon found himself in the notoriously choppy waters of the Straits of Dover. Laboriously trying to make its way south and west, the ship on which he was travelling was buffeted back and forth between the French and English coasts. In the course of this ordeal, Kalm managed to make some naturalistic observations. '[T]he land on both sides has the same *facies* and appearance', he wrote, 'so that if one who had seen the coast of England should get to see the coast of France here, and did not know it was such, he would certainly believe that it was the English coast … and English hills'.[85]

That so many English men and women saw things so differently over the course of the next two centuries is mainly due to patriotism. The cliffs of Dover were valued as an iconic symbol of the national homeland in part because of their appearance, since to function as any sort of widely recognisable landmark a landscape needs to be visually memorable. More significant than this, however, were the associations with which the landscape was bound up. It is worth recalling that judgments about the value of any landscape – even aesthetic judgments – are never reliant on physical characteristics alone. Thus for the British the physical appearance of the white cliffs may have been sufficient to establish them as landmarks and make more plausible claims of distinctiveness, but this alone does not account for the weight of the patriotic load carried by the landscape. Had it been otherwise, the chalk cliffs of the Seven Sisters on the Sussex coast – which, it could be said, are visually more impressive than those at Dover – would have played a

---

[84] T. Lowndes, *Tracts in poems and verse* (Dover, 1825), pp. 14–15.
[85] [P. Kalm], *Kalm's account of his visit to England on his way to America in 1748* (London and New York, 1892), p. 455.

more prominent role in constructions of national identity. Any explanation of the nationalistic significance of the white cliffs of Dover must give due weight to the determining role played by exogenous factors. The cliffs' historical associations with national defence, homecoming and homeland, and national culture – with an island past and island experiences – mattered more than their physical characteristics taken in isolation. That this was so illustrates one of the central contentions of this book: it is only through considering the associational value of landscape that we can fully understand its role and significance in the construction of national identities. In the next chapter, this point is further developed with reference to another English border landscape, one found more than 300 miles to the north of the coast of Kent.

2 THE NORTHUMBRIAN BORDERLAND

Until the afforestation schemes of the mid-to-late twentieth century, much of the landscape of northern Northumberland was characterised by extensive tracts of open moor, isolated river valleys, bare grasslands dotted with sheep and breezy heather-clad hills. Wild, remote and in large part uncultivated, it presented a stern and austere appearance, in sharp contrast to the smiling, felicitous rurality of the south-country ideal, with its waving fields of corn, thatched cottages and flower gardens (see fig. 6). It might be said, indeed, that the bleak and apparently inhospitable environment of the Northumbrian border is a poor candidate for consideration as a valued landscape, when set against the quaint villages and undulating farmland of the home counties – let alone, for example, the mountain grandeur of the Lake District, or the picturesque appeal of the Wye Valley and the Cornish coast. Yet any such assessment would be mistaken. While it is not the case that the remote valleys of North Tynedale, Coquetdale or Redesdale exerted the same kind of attraction as such places as Grasmere or the New Forest, the appeal of the Northumbrian borderland was far greater, and of far more cultural significance, than might at first sight be apparent. As with the border landscape of the cliffs of Dover, but in different ways, that of Northumberland illustrates the imbrication of English and British identities. For all its asperity, the English–Scottish borderland came to be valued as an important cultural landscape, one rich in associations with the past and powerfully expressive of a particular

6 Photograph of a small burn, with Simonside in the distance: Coquetdale, Northumberland, *c.* 1910. Northumberland Archives: NRO 01449/537.

Unionist-British variety of Englishness. What follows discusses the development of this phenomenon.

Indications of the growing stature of the Northumberland borderland as a cultural landscape were apparent from the second quarter of the nineteenth century, by which time it had become established as a tourist destination. As early as April 1826, the *Literary Gazette* remarked on the 'multitudes' of visitors being drawn there every year.[1] The publication of guidebooks and travelogues testified to its touristic appeal, early examples including John Mason's *The border tour*, published in two editions in 1826, and Stephen Oliver's *Rambles in Northumberland* (1835).[2] Works such as these were followed by others, such as Walter

[1] *Literary Gazette*, 483 (April 1826), 248.
[2] [J. Mason], *The border tour throughout the most important and interesting places in the counties of Northumberland, Berwick, Roxburgh and Selkirk*, 3rd edn (Edinburgh, 1833 [1826]); S. Oliver, *Rambles in Northumberland, and on the Scottish border* (London, 1835).

White's *Northumberland and the border* (two editions, 1859), with an important milestone being reached in 1864 when Murray's brought out a Durham and Northumberland volume in its counties series of handbooks.[3] From then on, the quantity of tourist literature increased markedly, with the publication of cheaper volumes – including W. W. Tomlinson's important *Comprehensive guide of the county of Northumberland* – being indicative of a further expansion of interest.[4]

Changing tastes in landscape scenery do something to explain this growing appeal. Bleak moorlands and bare, rounded hillsides offered little to late-eighteenth- and early-nineteenth-century eyes, especially those influenced by the aesthetics of the picturesque. In 1778, the antiquarian William Hutchinson might have been fascinated by the historic remains to be found in the countryside around places such as Rothbury and Wooler, but the scenery thereabouts was 'dreary and desolate'.[5] More condemnatory still was the Revd Richard Warner, whose turn-of-the-century tour through northern England and Scotland dismissed the countryside of Northumberland as generally 'naked and unpicturesque', in unhappy harmony with the county's disagreeable climate. Around Berwick-on-Tweed, for example, he found the hills 'uniform and lumpish' and the vales 'wide and unwooded', the scenery being everywhere 'unadorned with those indispensable features in agreeable landscapes, lofty trees and spreading shrubs'.[6] Later commentators, however, were less critical. By the last few decades of the nineteenth century, landscapes hitherto denigrated as 'barren' or 'bleak' came to be valued for a range of reasons. Their spaciousness, and the sense of freedom and wild liberty thus conferred, were increasingly seen as an attractive feature, at least by those – G. M. Trevelyan being one famous example – who championed the benefits of rambling across the open country.[7] In part, of

[3] W. White, *Northumberland and the border* (London, 1859); J. Murray (publisher), *A handbook for travellers in Durham and Northumberland*, 3rd edn (London, 1890 [1864]).

[4] W. W. Tomlinson, *Comprehensive guide to the county of Northumberland*, 10th edn (London, 1923 [1889]). See also, e.g., *Dawson's illustrated guide to the borderland* (Berwick-on-Tweed, 1885).

[5] W. Hutchinson, *A view of Northumberland*, 2 vols. (Newcastle-upon-Tyne, 1778), Vol. I, pp. 179–80, 227, 240.

[6] R. Warner, *A tour through the northern counties of England, and the borders of Scotland*, 2 vols. (Bath, 1802), Vol. II, pp. 10–12, 42–3.

[7] See G. M. Trevelyan, 'Walking', in G. M. Trevelyan (ed.), *'Clio, a muse', and other essays literary and pedestrian* (London, 1913), pp. 56–81; and – for his appreciation

course, these new perspectives on wild, open landscapes were connected to the growing appreciation of the amenity value of common land, which found institutional expression in the foundation of the Commons Preservation Society and the activities with which it and its supporters were associated.[8] But they were also connected to a more general aesthetic concern with upland and moorland scenery – Dartmoor being another example – which was reflected in contemporary landscape art. As Peter Howard has shown, the late Victorian and Edwardian periods saw painterly interest in 'sombre pictures of the moors' co-exist alongside 'rustically pretty scenes of cottages, villages, [and] farms'.[9] For some artists and their publics, moorland exerted a pure visual appeal; for others, however, its attraction as subject-matter reflected a preoccupation with social problems: 'dreary landscapes' could provide appropriate settings for depictions of the hardships of rural life and labour at a time of agricultural depression.[10]

This last point is significant. However much places such as those of north Northumberland might have been rehabilitated in purely visual terms, their representation as hard and austere landscapes remained remarkably persistent, even as they gained popularity and cultural significance. As Tomlinson acknowledged in his guidebook of 1888, Redesdale might well appear 'a wild and monotonous stretch of dreary moorland', barren and treeless, and for this reason might disappoint some tourists – even if others would thrill to the revivifying and liberating effects of contact with its expanses of open space. But, he continued, whatever differences of opinion there might be on these issues, they were – or ought to be – trumped by the associations the landscape stimulated in the mind of the visitor, as 'the wild waste of heather and bracken … forms a fitting background to the dark history

of the Northumberland borderland in particular – G. M. Trevelyan, 'The Middle Marches', *Independent Review*, 5 (1905), 336–51.

[8] Readman, 'Preserving'; Readman, 'Octavia Hill'; M. J. D. Roberts, 'Gladstonian liberalism and environment protection, 1865–76', *English Historical Review*, 128 (2013), 292–322.

[9] P. J. Howard, 'Changing taste in landscape art: An analysis based on works exhibited at the Royal Academy, 1769–1980, and depictions of Devonshire landscape', Ph.D. dissertation (University of Exeter, 1983), p. 500. See also Howard, *Landscapes*; and Howard, 'Painters' preferred places'. For Dartmoor, see M. Kelly, *Quartz and feldspar. Dartmoor: A British landscape in modern times* (London, 2016).

[10] See H. D. Rodee, 'The "dreary landscape" as a background to scenes of rural poverty in Victorian paintings', *Art Journal*, 36 (1977), 307–13.

of Redesdale, and owes much to the fascination it may exert over the tourist to its tragic memories of feud and foray, alas! too numerous'.[11] In this way, the bleak and forbidding wilderness of Redesdale exerted a felicitously melancholy appeal as a site of history, romance and conflict: its associational value made it a cultural landscape of considerable power.

What was true of Redesdale was true of the northern and middle part of Northumberland more generally. The whole area, from the Roman wall to the Scottish border, could be seen as embodying past history, and specifically a long history of wars, raiding and national animosities. Writing in his *Romance of Northumberland* (1908), A. G. Bradley put it succinctly: 'Northumberland shows its stormy past all over its surface. There is much that is ancient, but almost every bit of this, whether entire or fragmentary, breathes of bygone war.'[12]

Among those places, of course, that breathed most heavily of war were the many castles, towers and other fortified dwellings with which the countryside was littered. The ubiquity of the fortified remains, lovingly recorded in antiquarian literature such as Sir Walter Scott's *Border antiquities* (1814) and Cadwallader Bates's *Border holds of Northumberland* (1891), testified to the intensity and persistence of conflict over centuries. Nobles built castles, such as the magnificent Alnwick, seat of the dukes of Northumberland, or the atmospheric, now semi-ruinous Warkworth (see fig. 7); the gentry and clergy built pele towers, such as that inhabited by the historian and future bishop of London Mandell Creighton when he became vicar of Embleton in 1875; smaller proprietors built bastle-houses, with their doors several feet off the ground to deter the ingress of marauders. There were even fortified barns for cattle.[13] The consequence was an architectural inheritance of martial simplicity, the 'many-gabled, picturesque timber-houses of the south' being non-existent here. As Creighton explained,

> the chief features of Northumberland at the present day tell a
> tale of constant struggles. The villages and towns in the northern
> part of the country strike the stranger as singularly cold and

[11] Tomlinson, *Comprehensive guide*, pp. 296–7.
[12] A. G. Bradley, *The romance of Northumberland* (London, 1908), p. 13.
[13] C. J. Bates, *The border holds of Northumberland*, Vol. I (Newcastle-upon-Tyne, 1891).

7 John Greig, *Warkworth Castle, Northumberland*. Engraving, from Sir Walter Scott, *The border antiquities of England and Scotland*, 2 vols. (London, 1814), Vol. II. Photo courtesy of Print Collector/Getty Images.

> bare. There are no picturesque houses of any antiquity. The architecture is severe, simple, and solid. There are scanty traces of ornament even in the few ancient churches which have any pretensions to architectural beauty. The reason is, that for centuries the dwellers in Northumberland encamped rather than dwelt on their land.[14]

The history of conflict, as written into the built environment, was often inseparably intertwined with the natural landscape, as in the case of Norham Castle. Immortalised in Sir Walter Scott's epic poem *Marmion* and painted by Turner and Landseer, Norham was situated on the River Tweed, on a physical embodiment of the border line, and had been the scene of many battles and skirmishes with the Scots. These historical associations meant that by the late nineteenth century it had become a significant attraction for heritage-minded tourists, who visited in sufficient numbers for there to be a tea-shop in the castle

[14] M. Creighton, *The story of some English shires* (London, 1897), pp. 13ff. (p. 22).

grounds by 1889.[15] However, the troublous past was also immanent in landscapes that lacked built memorials to conflict. Battlefields were an obvious case in point, with that of Flodden Field near Branxton being the pre-eminent example of such a site of memory. Scene of the great English victory of 1513, which saw the death of James IV of Scotland and many of his nobles, this otherwise unprepossessing tract of moor and farmland drew numerous visitors and a great deal of literary and historical attention across the nineteenth and into the twentieth century, and we will have more to say about Flodden presently. Yet the past was felt to pervade less remarkable landscapes still: it was ubiquitous. One writer in 1887 reckoned the 'wild, desolate region' of the Northumbrian borders to be 'the Cock-Pit of England; as about every hill, and valley, and stream linger tales of the old days, when Englishman and Scot rarely met but to exchange blows';[16] another, around the same time, thought 'Every acre of this country is linked with some historical, legendary, and romantic association.'[17] This was particularly true of the Cheviot Hills. Largely uninhabited, remote and seen as having relatively little scenic merit, especially on the English side, this massive, rounded upland range was seen – like the River Tweed – as a 'natural frontier' dividing the two countries. Marking the border and thus centuries of Anglo-Scottish conflict, the Cheviots were suffused with historical associations and largely celebrated for this reason. On 'look[ing] up from Belford or Wooler to the lowering brown masses of the Cheviots',[18] it was impossible not to think of the 'Ballad of Chevy Chase' and the Battle of Otterburn; approaching Scotland via the 'unsurpassable solitude' of the Carter Bar, 'we do not walk unaccompanied, for fierce altercation and Border cries come down with the wind from Peel Fell and Carter Fell'.[19] As William Howitt recognised in the 1840s, despite all the changes wrought by modernity – the demolition of old fortresses, for example[20] – the Cheviot landscape was

---

[15] 'Norham Castle', *Monthly Chronicle of North-Country Lore and Legend*, April 1889, pp. 151–4.

[16] F. Abell, 'A tramp in Northumberland', *London Society*, 51 (February 1887), 161.

[17] 'Some famous border fights', *Temple Bar*, 93 (November 1891), 387.

[18] [A. I. Shand], 'The borders and their ballads', *Blackwood's Edinburgh Magazine*, 131 (April 1882), 469.

[19] P. A. Graham, *Highways and byways in Northumbria* (London, 1920), pp. 278–9.

[20] Of the thirty-seven castles inhabited by major nobles in 1460, only about one-quarter were still intact by the 1860s: 'From the Tyne to the Tweed', *Gentleman's Magazine*, July 1861, 21.

irreducibly historicised: 'the hills and the rivers art could not remove if it would', and 'many a wide dark waste of heath yet lies here and there amid these regions of modern fertility, where tradition still stalks in all its ancient strength, and says, here fought the Briton and the Scot, and here the Douglas or the Percy fell'.[21]

This, then, was imagined as a blood-soaked landscape, one powerfully evocative of centuries of conflict – both in its built and in its natural environment. The persistence of its status as wilderness, at least in more remote parts, assisted in this respect. As one commentator remarked in 1891, while parts of the county might now enjoy a relatively high state of cultivation, still 'Nature, in that grand, wild, too little known part of Northumberland lying under the western march line … to a great extent answers to the description given generally by old Froissart, five hundred years ago. He calls it "a savage and wylde country, full of desarts and mountaignes, and a ryghte poore country of everything saving of beestis".'[22] This helped make it, to an extent, a landscape of horror, suggestive of dark and bloody deeds on bleak moorlands, of isolated, wind-blasted castles and their dungeons (the forbidding ruined keep of the Hermitage, just over the Scottish border, was especially evocative in this respect, being the place where the evil Lord Soulis was supposed to have sold himself to the devil).[23] It was a place where war, violence and lawlessness had been a way of life. As Hutchinson remarked in his influential 1778 *View of Northumberland*, 'the wild American never devised more shocking barbarities than stained these borders'. The 'common charnel of the two nations', Hutchinson went on, this was a landscape that had seen much plunder and devastation, with towns and villages being laid waste by rampaging groups whose 'heroes … walked forth … spreading desolation in the most savage manner, for the reward of savages: reciprocal slaughters, devastations, and cruelties marked both people'.[24]

---

[21] W. Howitt, *Visits to remarkable places* (London, 1840), pp. 506–7.

[22] 'Some famous border fights', 386.

[23] The castle was still being described as 'the wickedest place on the Border' in the 1930s, as a chilling reminder of a crueller past: 'Gaunt, grim, defiant, the wicked castle stands in friendless isolation. No ivy clings to its walls, no trees grow beside it, no flowers bloom to lessen its austerity. It seems as if the kindly plants refuse either to forgive or forget': P. Brown, *The second Friday book of north country sketches* (Newcastle-upon-Tyne, 1935), pp. 49–50.

[24] Hutchinson, *View of Northumberland*, Vol. II, pp. 67, 99–101.

Hutchinson was a man of refined taste and sensibilities, and in his remarks we feel the shudder of Enlightenment disgust at the barbarity of the uncivilised border past. The shudder of later years, however, was a rather more complex response, the bloody deeds of former times now exerting a darkly Gothic attraction. As Billie Melman's work has shown, Victorians imagined the past in various ways, and the happily comforting or placidly nostalgic by no means dominated the discourse.[25] The past could unsettle, and was sometimes valued for its unsettling qualities; indeed, as with the Tower of London or Madame Tussaud's, it could be fascinatingly horrific. Representations of the Northumbrian border landscape could correlate with this perspective. 'What would history be without its crimes and its horrors?', asked one contributor to the *St James's Magazine* in the course of an article on the Cheviot Hills published in the 1860s:

> The truth seems to be ... that there exists, in every one of us, an intuitive sympathy with the lawless and the daring; and, if consent to crime amounts to complicity, I fear that most of us must be considered as accessories after the fact to every deed of murder and violence recorded in history, from the Conquest downward. Madame Tussaud was a sage: there is a private chamber of horrors in every one of us! ... what makes every hill and dale in the Cheviots so attractive, but the very fact that the district was one of the most thoroughly disreputable and lawless in the three kingdoms, and that almost every valley, rock, and ruin bear the record of some bygone deed of violence and atrocity?[26]

The perceived horror of the borderland past presented an agreeable contrast with the peaceable and productive present, thus supporting teleologies of national progress (of which more later), but it was also connected to – and lightened by – nineteenth-century romantic and medievalist sensibilities. In the context of the Northumberland border, these sensibilities were perhaps best embodied in the ballad literature with which the landscape and its people were associated, and also by the enormous popularity of this literature. A native of Northumbria

[25] Melman, *Culture of history*.
[26] 'A knapsack and fishing-rod tour on the Cheviots', *St James's Magazine*, February 1862, 301–2.

himself, the historian G. M. Trevelyan had no doubt as to the reason why 'our cultured and commercial society' had grown enamoured of the rude landscape of the border and its 'cut-throat' history. The answer was simple: 'the Border people wrote the Border Ballads'.[27] Genuine products of the oral culture of the borderland, and quite precisely located in its landscape, the ballads told stories of daring deeds of valour and adventure, brave and tragic deaths, great battles and great loves, all set against the backdrop of cross-border conflict and familial feuding. Although often associated more with the Scottish side of the Cheviot Hills, the ballad tradition was equally well rooted in the countryside of the Northumbrian frontier, being sustained throughout the eighteenth and nineteenth centuries by wandering pedlars, tinkers and pipers (such as the famously roguish Jimmy Allan), whose songs and tunes recalled 'the bloody and admired deeds of their ancestors'.[28] It was also a real presence in settled folk culture, in the quotidian life of the isolated villages, farmhouses and shepherds' cottages that dotted the north Northumberland landscape. Having grown up on the banks of the Tyne in Cherryburn near Eltringham in the 1750s and 1760s, the celebrated wood-engraver Thomas Bewick recalled how

> the Winter evenings were often spent in listening to the traditionary Tales & songs, relating to Men who had been eminent for their prowess & bravery in the Border Wars, and of others who had been esteemed for better & milder qualities … I used to be particularly struck or affected with the warlike music & the Songs relative to the former description of characters.[29]

This oral tradition was translated into written record. Bishop Thomas Percy's *Reliques of ancient English poetry* (1765) included a good number of Northumbrian ballads (notably 'Chevy Chase', which Joseph Addison of the *Spectator* had identified in 1711 as 'the favourite

[27] Trevelyan, 'Middle Marches', 346. For Trevelyan on ballads, see also G. M. Trevelyan, *A layman's love of letters* (London, 1954), pp. 85ff.
[28] *A historical and descriptive view of the county of Northumberland*, 2 vols. (Newcastle-upon-Tyne, 1811), Vol. 1, p. 230. For Allan (1734–1810), see J. Thompson, *A new, improved, and authentic life of James Allan* (London, 1828), and, for his continuing cultural presence into the late nineteenth century, see R. Welford, 'James Allan, piper and adventurer', *Monthly Chronicle of North-Country Lore and Legend*, 4 (June 1887), 145–6.
[29] T. Bewick, *A memoir*, ed. I. Bain (Oxford, 1979 [London, 1862]), p. 8.

ballad of the common people of England').[30] It did much to generate both popular and elite interest in ballad literature, and was republished a great many times.[31] Still more significant, however, was the contribution of Sir Walter Scott, who did more than anyone to draw attention to the distinctive landscape and culture of the border – Northumbrian as well as Scottish.[32] There is no doubt that Scott himself was much influenced by the landscape, one crucial formative experience being his stay in a farmhouse near Wooler in Northumberland in 1791, while on holiday with his uncle, Robert Scott. As he wrote to William Clerk, not only was he 'in one of the wildest and most romantic situations' imaginable;

> To add to my satisfaction, we are amidst places renowned by the feats of former days; each hill is crowned with a tower, or camp, or cairn, and in no situation can you be near more fields of battle: Flodden, Otterburn, Chevy Chase, Ford Castle, Chillingham Castle, Copland Castle, and many another scene of blood, are within the compass of a forenoon's ride.[33]

The rich historical associations of the border landscape inspired Scott in his own writing – pre-eminently *Marmion*, his hugely popular epic poem on the Battle of Flodden,[34] but also his well-known novel *Rob Roy*, the first half of which is set in Northumberland, and which contains very accurate and evocative descriptions of, *inter alia*, the remote valleys of the Upper Coquet and even the local vernacular architecture.[35] In addition to its contribution to such fictional works, however, the storied landscape of the borders stimulated Scott's antiquarian activities. From 1792, following a second excursion with his uncle,

[30] T. Percy, *Reliques of ancient English poetry: Consisting of old heroic ballads, songs, and other pieces of our earlier poets, (chiefly of the lyric kind) together with some few of a later date* (London, 1765); Trevelyan, *Layman's love of letters*, p. 86; *Spectator*, 21 May 1711.

[31] J. Reed, *The border ballads* (Stocksfield, 1991) pp. 2–3, 124–8.

[32] 'There is, in fact, no real prose of the Northumberland selfhood, or of the experience of living in Northumberland, before the advent of Sir Walter Scott': W. Ruddick, 'Sir Walter's Scott's Northumberland', in J. H. Alexander and D. Hewitt (eds.), *Scott and his influence* (Aberdeen, 1983), pp. 22–30 (p. 22).

[33] Letter to William Clerk, 26 August 1791, in W. Scott, *The letters of Sir Walter Scott 1787–1807*, ed. H. J. C. Grierson, 12 vols. (London, 1932), Vol. i, pp. 18–19.

[34] W. Scott, *Marmion: A tale of Flodden Field* (Edinburgh, 1808).

[35] Ruddick, 'Scott's Northumberland', pp. 27–8.

Scott began to collect ballads and other folkloric material from the crofters and shepherds of Liddesdale and elsewhere (his most notable informant being James Hogg, the 'Ettrick Shepherd'), an anthology of which he published as *Minstrelsy of the Scottish border* (1802–3).[36] Although the accent here was on the Scottish borderland, the ballads were common to popular culture on both sides of the national line, and – not least because of their focus on cross-border conflict, raiding and reiving – addressed events and themes that were common to both. They were, moreover, set in landscapes on either side of the border, the deeds they commemorated often being done on English ground. The battles of Flodden, Otterburn and Homildon, for example, may have loomed large in the border ballads sung in Berwickshire and Roxburghshire, yet they were all fought in Northumberland.

Popularised by Percy and Scott, the border ballads occupied an important place in nineteenth-century culture. Replete with images of men fighting to often grisly deaths on bleak moorland landscapes, they presented a bloody picture of the past, one that was in many ways compatible with the view of history as a chamber of horrors: as one broadside version of the 'Ballad of Chevy Chase' related, after his legs were hacked off in the battle of Otterburn, Sir Thomas Widdrington fought 'upon his stumpes' to the bitter end.[37] But the ballads' sanguinary content was relieved by their grandly dramatic and often tragic emphasis on the great, everlasting themes of human experience (those of life, death and love), and on the qualities of valour and honour displayed on and off the field of battle. They were in some respects seen as equivalent to classical Greek poetry. Introducing the 1908 edition of Scott's *Minstrelsy*, the poet Alfred Noyes felt that in the ballads 'we feel the large Homeric air again',[38] and those of whose deeds they sang were often cast in a heroic light, irrespective of whether their allegiance was to England or Scotland. Guidebook and topographical

---

[36] W. Scott, *Minstrelsy of the Scottish border: Consisting of historical and romantic ballads, collected in the southern counties of Scotland*, 3 vols. (Kelso, 1802–3); Mark Girouard, *Return to Camelot: Chivalry and the English gentleman* (New Haven and London, 1981), p. 34; J. Sutherland, *The life of Walter Scott* (Oxford, 1995), pp. 46–7, 69–87.

[37] 'For Witherington needs must I wayle / as one in dolefull dumps, / For when his leggs were smitten of, / he fought upon his stumpes': Reed, *Border ballads*, p. 125.

[38] W. Scott, *The minstrelsy of the Scottish border*, ed. A. Noyes (London, 1908), p. xi.

literature routinely depicted the battles that featured in the ballads as gallant struggles, marked by bravery and chivalry on both sides.[39]

The ballads' emphasis on the positive qualities of the warring moss-troopers was important; while they might have been savage in battle and prey to destructive passions such as revenge, they also behaved according to a moral code, one that correlated with Victorian and Edwardian ideas of the chivalry thought to have characterised medieval society.[40] In the ballads and their associated commentaries, the warriors of the marches were routinely portrayed as loyal to their friends, chary of attacks on women, and rarely deliberately or wantonly cruel. They were cast as men of honour and nobility, the latter quality being reinforced by the involvement of the scions of great families on both sides of the border – the Percies, the Douglases and their like – and of course, given the borderland's status as the battleground of two nations, the crowned heads of these nations as well.[41] Moreover, these noble qualities were, at least by the nineteenth century, regarded as having been present on both sides, English and Scots alike – even by commentators who might otherwise be considered nationalistic or partisan.[42] In this way, the history of the border landscape was transformed from the grim, desolate killing ground, identified in Hutchinson and other eighteenth-century commentators, to a landscape of storied romance – not without its horror and tragedy, to be sure, but also strongly associated with nobility of thought and deed, chivalry, bravery, and honour. This perspective is nicely caught in the opening sentence of Andrew and John Lang's *Highways and byways in the border* (1913): 'The "Border" is a magical word, and on either side of a line that constantly varied in the course of English and Scottish victories and defeats, all is enchanted ground, the home

[39] See, e.g., J. F. Terry, *Northumberland yesterday and to-day* (Newcastle-upon-Tyne, 1913), pp. 179–84, 187ff.

[40] For which, see Girouard, *Return to Camelot*.

[41] See, e.g., [Shand], 'Borders and their ballads'; 'Some famous border fights', esp. 385–6; 'History and poetry of the Scottish border', *Blackwood's Magazine*, 153 (June 1893), 866; E. Bogg, *A thousand miles of wandering in the border country* (Newcastle-upon-Tyne and York, 1898), p. 197; Graham, *Highways and byways in Northumbria*, pp. 282–4.

[42] See, e.g., M. A. B. Hamilton, 'The border ballads', *National Review*, 5 (May 1885), 349.

of memories of forays and fairies, of raids and recoveries, of loves and battles long ago.'[43]

The popularity of the ballads and the modern poetry they inspired helped rehabilitate the border's history and landscape. This rehabilitation was permanent. On the occasion of the opening of a London exhibition of watercolours illustrating scenes from Scott's border ballads in 1887, the *Saturday Review* noted the persisting popularity of 'the Wizard of the North' and the landscape that his work brought to life. 'Every spot which he has described – be it abbey, hall, old manor, moated grange, heath, battlefield, plain, or mountain pass – he has immortalized and converted into a place of pilgrimage for his innumerable admirers.'[44] Of course, while Scott's popularity as a writer waned as time went on, it did not do so significantly until at least the 1890s,[45] and the re-reading of the landscape and history of the borders, which he was so influential in shaping, endured to inform tourist and wider cultural sensibilities on into the twentieth century. As one commentator averred in 1893, thanks to Scott 'the Border country has become enchanted ground, and … the names of its hills, its glens, and its streams are household words wherever English is spoken'.[46]

The emphasis on the noble qualities displayed on both Scottish and English sides reveals what might be termed a British agenda – one wholly compatible with Scott's personal perspective, the role he played in articulating what Graeme Morton has called 'unionist-nationalism' having been much remarked on by historians.[47] Indeed, in the nineteenth century, the border – on both Scottish and English sides – was re-conceptualised as a Unionist landscape. Perhaps the *locus classicus* in this Unionist landscape imaginary was Flodden Field. Site of the bloody battle in 1513, this was certainly a place replete with associations of horror and tragedy. But by the nineteenth century, far from functioning as a divisive landmark of fraternal strife between two uneasily united nations, it was a landscape of romance and valour.

---

[43] A. Lang and J. Lang, *Highways and byways in the border* (London, 1913), p. 1.

[44] 'Borderland scenery exhibition', *Saturday Review*, 23 April 1887, p. 586.

[45] D. Hewitt, 'Scott, Sir Walter (1771–1832)', *Oxford dictionary of national biography* (Oxford, 2004).

[46] 'History and poetry of the Scottish border', 865.

[47] See G. Morton, *Unionist-nationalism: Governing urban Scotland, 1830–1860* (East Linton, 1999); C. Kidd, 'The canon of patriotic landmarks in Scottish history', *Scotlands*, 1 (1994), 1–17.

Scott's *Marmion* was of course crucial here, its enduring appeal helping to ensure that the battlefield remained an important cultural-historical landmark – one, indeed, that was increasingly visited by tourists, their sensibilities stimulated by coverage of the site in popular as well as elite periodicals, not to speak of guidebooks.[48] As rector of the nearby village of Ford, H. M. Neville was well placed to assess levels of interest in the place and, as he explained in 1896

> Sir Walter Scott has done wonders in throwing a romantic interest over a battle scene which before had breathed chiefly of pathos and sadness, and inspired in Scottish hearts such plaintive notes as we hear in the 'Flowers of the Forest', and so now that the national animosities are at rest between the two countries, and time has healed those deep wounds, and history explained the mistakes of ancient strife … Flodden has its tale to tell of Marmion, De Wilton, and Lady Clare, and the quest for the well of Sybil Grey is often as keen as that of those who would study the battle ground.[49]

Marmion and the readings of the past with which it was associated helped allow the landscape of Flodden to be consumed as myth-history, its horror offset by the romance and glamour of balladry. Increasing temporal distance also played its part, especially when amplified by the vagueness of much belletrist and fictional literature (the battle and its context being a subject for poetry, plays and prose of varying quality, the nadir probably being reached with Alfred Austin's inevitably dire poetical drama *Flodden Field*, which was performed at Her Majesty's Theatre, London, in June 1903).[50] Linked to

---

[48] See, e.g., G. Eyre-Todd, 'Flodden's fatal field', *Gentleman's Magazine*, 268 (February 1890), 171–6; A. G. Bradley, 'Flodden field', *Macmillan's Magazine*, 24 (October 1907), 951–9; W. S. Dalgleish, 'Flodden or Branxton?', *Good Words*, 34 (December 1893), 669–77; Revd Canon Butler, 'Flodden field and the vale of till', *Leisure Hour*, November 1882, 677–81. The young Beatrix Potter was among those fascinated by Flodden, making several trips to the battlefield while on holiday near Coldstream in the summer of 1894: L. Linder (ed.), *The journal of Beatrix Potter 1881–1897*, new edn (London, 1989), pp. 329, 334, 341, 344, 349–50, 352, 355, 360.

[49] H. M. Neville, *Under a border tower: Sketches and memories of Ford Castle, Northumberland* (Newcastle-upon-Tyne, 1896), p. 258.

[50] A. Austin, *Flodden field* (London, 1903). 'It would be wanton hyperbole to call *Flodden Field* a strong play', was the restrained verdict of *The Times*, 9 June 1903, p. 9.

this, however, there was another factor: the changing visual appearance of the battlefield. In 1513, Flodden had been uncultivated moorland, an appropriately bleak setting for the melancholy and tragic drama that had unfolded. But the union of the crowns – and more particularly the agricultural improvements of the later eighteenth century – had wrought great changes to the landscape, here as elsewhere in Northumberland, effecting a transformation from what the rural writer Richard Heath called 'almost a state of nature'.[51] Peace, technological innovation and enclosure meant that the dreary waste had given way to sheep pasture, and sometimes even waving fields of corn. This was appreciated in rather straightforward terms by early commentators such as Hutchinson, who unambiguously celebrated how the constant and brutal conflict of the past had been replaced by agriculture and relative prosperity, largely thanks to the effects of union.[52] Later readings, however, were more complex. Writing in the early Victorian period, William Howitt had no doubt of the transformative impact of union on the landscape of Flodden. Recounting his own visit to the battlefield, published in *Visits to remarkable places*, he presented the site as an embodiment of 'the signal effects of the Union'. While '[t]he name of the field itself is one of gloom and desolation',

> [o]ur astonishment was therefore proportionate to find the 'dark Flodden' of the poets, so fair and so cultivated; a scene of plentiful corn-fields and comfortable farms ... Where the 'rank reivers and moss-troopers' used to gallop over moss and moorland, there now stretch the richest meadows, the fairest fields. The track which used to lie between the two countries – a blasted and desolate region, ravaged with fire and sword,

---

[51] R. Heath, 'Northumbrian hinds and Cheviot shepherds' [1871], in R. Heath, *The English peasant* (London, 1893), pp. 207–15.

[52] 'What blessings have flowed in upon this land from the union of the kingdoms ...?', he asked. 'The ferocity of the inhabitants is subdued ... Cultivation, with all the comeliness of Plenty laughs in the valleys; the streams are taught to labour in mechanic systems, to aid the manufacturer; every Creek and Bay is thronged with ships; the gloomy Tower, that frowned defiance from each Eminence, sinks in the dust, whilst a Palace receives the descendants of her Lord, with all the bounties of Opulence and Peace. Desert plains stained with slaughter, and track'd with the progress of Rapine and Violence, formerly spread forth an extensive scene of desolation, where now rising woods, inclosed farms, villages, and hamlets are disposed under the smiles of prosperity': Hutchinson, *View of Northumberland*, Vol. 1, pp. 130–4.

drenched with blood, and peopled only with horrible memories –
is now turned into a garden.

Fittingly for a landscape that had seen such valour displayed on both
sides, the two countries had, Howitt concluded, now 'blended' into each
other.[53]

Yet the unionising of the Flodden landscape brought dangers,
too. In particular, there was the risk that the passage of time, the course
of the plough and all the other benefits of modern agriculture would alter
the landscape beyond recognition, and with it obliterate the associations
with history and literature that made it so evocative of a bloody if romantic past. Howitt was sensible of this, even worrying that the inroads of
'improvement' were going too far at Flodden, imperilling what remained
of the physical traces of the battlefield, as described both in history writing and *Marmion*, and also denying access to the site to the heritage-
minded visitor. The quarrying on the hill from which King James IV
surveyed the disposition of the troops before the battle was one concern;
the enclosure of hitherto freely accessible moorland was another.[54] Some
later commentators were still more forthright, one English visitor in the
1880s suggesting that 'the face of the country has so changed that it is
almost impossible to picture the scene as it was presented to the English
and Scottish Warriors three hundred and seventy years ago'.[55]

This threatened loss of connection to the past led to a memo-
rialising reaction, one which pressed the battlefield into the service of
an explicitly Unionist project. In 1907, the Berwickshire Naturalists'
Club, whose members were drawn almost equally from both sides of
the border, discussed a proposal to commission a monument to be
erected at Flodden in commemoration of the battle. The brainchild
of Francis Norman, naval officer, former mayor of Berwick-on-Tweed
and noted local historian, the proposal was approved and a fundraising campaign mounted under the direction of an Anglo-Scots committee chaired by the poet, writer and native of Kelso in the Scottish
borders, Sir George Douglas.[56] This resulted in the erection of a large
cross of Aberdeen granite where King James was said to have fallen,

[53] Howitt, *Visits to remarkable places*, pp. 189–90.
[54] *Ibid.*, pp. 191–3.
[55] Abell, 'Tramp in Northumberland', 167.
[56] P. Usherwood, J. Beach and C. Morris, *Public sculpture of north-east England*
(Liverpool, 2000), pp. 21–2; *History of the Berwickshire Naturalists' Club*, 20

on Piper's Hill, Branxton Moor, which was unveiled on 27 September
1910 before a crowd of at least 1,000 people. A simple plaque, affixed
to the north face of the monument, read: 'Flodden / 1513 / To the
brave of both nations'. This inscription was a succinct expression of
the organisers' Unionist agenda: the battle had been a clash of equals,
and the soldiers on each side had displayed equal valour in the heat
of the fight. It was thus appropriate that English and Scots should
combine together in mutual recognition of the gallantry of their ancestors, and preserve the connections that the Flodden landscape – now
much changed – had with this common heritage. In the course of his
address at the unveiling, Douglas gave voice to this theme of unity in
commemoration, stressing how the 'Rivals of old' had come together,
'our hands to-day join[ed] in one common enterprise – our hearts in
one emotion'.[57] The memorial was designed to stand as a reminder of
the ancient enmity between England and Scotland, an enmity between
two great nations, but also one that had passed – having been eclipsed
by union and the benefits of peace. By all accounts it achieved its
objective. One 1916 guidebook recommended it to tourists as 'a fitting
memorial to splendid past bravery and present unity'.[58] It was also
integrated in local ceremonial traditions on both sides of the border.
As the Northumbrian writer Nancy Ridley reported in the 1960s, a
wreath was placed at the cross in August every year to coincide with
Coldstream's civic week, with an associated sermon and address being
held on Branxton Hill 'to pay tribute to Scots and English who fought
and died so long ago on Flodden Field'.[59]

  In this way the landscape of Flodden was reconceptualised for
Unionist ends. Its cultivated aspect emphasised the progress achieved
since the cessation of border strife, yet the linkages with the past these
improvements threatened to sever were sustained by memorialisation. Preservation of the historical associations of the (changed) landscape thus caused past conflict to stand in sharp contrast to present
peace: Flodden became a landscape of British national progress. The
same might be said for the Northumbrian border landscape as a whole,
whether the preservation of these associations was accomplished

(1906–8), 273–4, 307; 'The Flodden memorial', *History of the Berwickshire
Naturalists' Club*, 21 (1909–11), 165–8.
[57] 'The Flodden memorial', 167.
[58] E. Morris, *Northumberland* (London, 1916), p. 162.
[59] N. Ridley, *Portrait of Northumberland*, 4th edn (London, 1973 [1965]), pp. 128–9.

through memorialisation, historical and antiquarian writing, literature, or a combination of different methods. Other battlefields also offered peaceful scenes of rural prosperity while at the same time affording access to the romantic past of moss-trooping days. Otterburn (1388) was one such example, being a site that, like Flodden, had been transformed by agricultural improvements – including enclosure – yet whose historical associations were preserved nevertheless. Not the least reason for this was the existence of a monument (Percy's Cross – rather older than the cross on Branxton Hill), situated near the battlefield.[60]

In many other places on the Northumberland border, the impress of modernity was felt still less strongly than at Flodden or Otterburn: castles and other fortified buildings survived in abundance, and much moorland and hillside – as at Carter Bar, the ancient route into Scotland and scene of numerous skirmishes – was untouched by the plough or enclosure.[61] But even so, many of the castles and pele towers were ruined, which not only accentuated their picturesque appeal but also emphasised the pastness of the past. The days of border strife were now long gone; they belonged to the realms of balladry and Scott-inspired myth-history. Their imaginative reconstruction thus threatened no dangerous recrudescence of old enmities, but offered agreeable opportunity for romantic reverie and reflection on the continuities of history amidst tangible evidence of progress and improvement. Writing in the 1890s, H. M. Neville had no doubt that the Northumbrian landscape as a whole was replete with 'the glamour of romance' and historical associations. Littered with ruined castles and towers, ancient chapels, battlefields, and suggestively bleak tracts of moorland and hillside, the landscape could readily be 're-peopled' through imaginative reconstruction, and the 'stormy past' of chivalry, feud and fray brought back to life once more. By engaging with the landscape in this way, Neville continued, we come

to see the present more truly and pleasantly than we might otherwise regard it, in the very matter of fact days in which we live. And then when we look around us, and at first feel inclined to ask: where is the romance in the life of our people now? we

---

[60] Abell, 'Tramp in Northumberland', 163.
[61] [Shand], 'Borders and their ballads', 468–9.

shall be able to adjust our sight to what we look upon, and in spite of the hard facts we see, there will be still something of the sweet blue mist clinging about the lives and ways of our Border folk, and we shall conclude, after all, that the knights, and warriors, and ladies, and monks, and nuns, of the old days, have not monopolized and used up all the romance of life, and that there may be as much heroism and virtue in a one-roomed cottage and the turnip field of to-day as ever there was in the towers and battles of the days of yore.[62]

The historical associations of the border landscape offered continuity with a romanticised past, one whose connotations with national conflict had been re-fashioned for unionist purposes. So successful was this re-fashioning that it was sometimes hard to discern the line of the border, or indeed perceive differences in the topography on either side. To an extent, the Northumbrian border, with its historical associations with Scottish as well as English national history, was a shared landscape, over which it was difficult to assert very confident claims of exclusive ownership. This uncertainty was especially marked at Berwick-on-Tweed, a town in which the late-nineteenth- and early-twentieth-century traveller still discovered a 'great confusion of tongues', Scots and English intermingled, just as Tobias Smollett had done in the 1760s.[63] Detached by the border from the county that bore its name, its geographical position appeared at variance with the logic that the River Tweed marked the national boundary line on the eastern marches, before giving way to the ridge of the Cheviots further west. This logic was deeply entrenched, finding expression in A. G. Bradley's youthful misapprehension that 'I was entering Scotland' as the train in which he was a passenger rumbled over Robert Stephenson's Royal Border Bridge across the Tweed at Berwick – a bridge whose opening in 1850 was celebrated, significantly enough, as 'The last act of the Union'.[64] Scottish minds were perhaps especially susceptible to

[62] Neville, *Under a border tower*, pp. 272–4.
[63] Bradley, *Romance of Northumberland*, pp. 134–5; Cf. T. Smollett, *The present state of all nations*, 8 vols. (London, [1768]–69), Vol. II, p. 274.
[64] *The Times*, 31 August 1850; *Newcastle Courant*, 30 August 1850; S. Smiles, *Lives of the engineers. The locomotive: George and Robert Stephenson*, new edn (London, 1879), pp. 310–12; A. G. Bradley, *When squires and farmers thrived* (London, 1927), pp. 63–4.

this (mis)reading of the Berwick landscape. Travelling across the same bridge later in life, Bradley overheard a Scotsman exclaiming to a friend that 'it's guid to be in Auld Scotland again!', a remark that earned the censure of Commander Norman (of Flodden Memorial fame), who happened to be seated in the same carriage, and who 'rubbed into those homing Scots a lesson in geography that was not likely ever to fade'.[65] Yet for all that Norman was formally correct, the impression that Berwick was only very uncertainly English proved impossible to eradicate. Bradley – an Englishman – reckoned the town and its bounds to be in character 'obviously part of Berwickshire' and by extension Scotland,[66] while other commentators thought it presented what Arthur Mee would later call a uniquely 'rugged air of individuality', somehow independent of both nations.[67] Very rarely was it characterised as English in an exclusive or homogeneous way.

This was true of other parts of the Northumbrian border landscape. Writing about the moorland countryside around Kielder in 1835, Stephen Oliver found that 'the precise boundaries of each kingdom [were] rather "*ill to red*"',[68] a judgement with which Bradley would concur three-quarters of a century later when he visited the same district.[69] Moreover, even when topography did appear to present a clearly defined boundary line, as was the case along the Tweed west of Berwick, experience of the landscape often blurred the sense of national division. In an account of a visit to Coldstream in the 1920s, the Scottish writer Agnes Herbert recounted how

> From the top of the rise where you leave Coldstream behind I was endeavouring to find a line of demarcation. And there was none. What did I expect, I wonder? I had thought that Scotland must give way to a recognizable Northumberland. But no, the difference was not apparent! The sheep grazing alongside the roads ... were the comfortable, well-fed beasts of the Lowlands ... there were the same small, round, haystacks.[70]

[65] Bradley, *When squires and farmers thrived*, pp. 63–4.
[66] *Ibid.*, p. 65.
[67] A. Mee (ed.), *The king's England. Northumberland: England's farthest north* (London, 1952), pp. 5, 40–1.
[68] Oliver, *Rambles*, p. 163.
[69] Bradley, *Romance of Northumberland*, p. 293.
[70] A. H. Cooper and A. Herbert, *Northumberland* (London, 1923), pp. 3–4.

8 J. M. W. Turner, *Norham Castle on the River Tweed*, c.1822–3. Watercolour on paper. Reproduced in W.G. Rawlinson and A. J. Finberg, *The water-colours of J. M. W. Turner* (London, 1909). Photo by Print Collector/Getty Images.

This is not to suggest that all readings of the border landscape eschewed reference to difference and division. Turner's *Norham Castle on the River Tweed* (c. 1822–3) is a case in point. Here, the line of demarcation is very far from being 'ill to red'; indeed, in this painting Turner appears to be making an explicitly English nationalist statement. As David Hill has pointed out, it is very clear which is the English and which is the Scottish side of the river, the former being depicted as more advanced and prosperous than the latter, as dominant and superior. Turner, Hill writes, 'seems to intend that we remember this is the border for the most prominent figure at the left wears plaid … On the English side is the imposing bulk of Norham, but on the left a mere bothy. The Scots work with rowboats but the English with sail. The cattle are on the right. The contrast in wealth is obvious, and this contrast has been the source of conflict that had required the castle.'[71]

[71] D. Hill, *Turner in the north: A tour through Derbyshire, Yorkshire, Durham, Northumberland, the Scottish borders, the Lake District, Lancashire and Lincolnshire* (New Haven and London, 1996), pp. 88–92.

But in general, however, such readings of the border landscape became rarer as time passed, not least because of the integration of the Scots, and of Scotland, into dominant ideologies of common Britishness.[72] Turner's painting may have cast the landscape and inhabitants of the north bank of the Tweed as alien and inferior, but by the early nineteenth century this was a minority perspective. For the English patriot, the Other was increasingly to be found outwith the British Isles, beyond the white cliffs of Dover.[73]

Yet if this was the case, what did it imply for the relationship between the Northumbrian border landscape and Englishness? In one interpretation, proximity to Scotland had served to dilute rather than stimulate English nationalist sentiment: what Howitt had called the 'blending' of the boundary line had denationalised the landscape, perhaps even making it more Scottish than English in character, at least to some eyes.[74] Written by a Hertfordshire man, the first edition of Methuen's *Little guide to Northumberland*, published in 1916, described an encounter with the county's landscape as being an experience in which 'one is everywhere confronted with a Caledonian character'. In the desolate hilly country of the border, the guide continued, this Scottishness was especially pronounced. 'The moor is Scottish moor, the burns are Scottish burns, the artificial wood, the native saugh trees in the bogs, the hard-faced little villages that nestle in the hills – all are strangely reminiscent of something observed, or felt elsewhere.' The landscape was, the author concluded, 'essentially Scottish'.[75] This was a rather unusual perspective, however; while Scottish influences of various sorts might have been acknowledged, the north Northumbrian landscape was generally consumed as English. Indeed, assertive claims of Englishness are not hard to find: Hexham, just forty or so miles from Scotland, rejoiced in a town motto featuring the boast that the place was 'the heart o' England'.[76] That said, the Englishness of the Northumbrian border was of a distinctive sort,

---

[72] Colley, *Britons*, remains the classic account of this process.

[73] *Ibid.*, and see also L. Colley, 'Britishness and otherness: An argument', *Journal of British Studies*, 31 (1992), 309–29.

[74] Howitt, *Visits to remarkable places*, pp. 189–90.

[75] Morris, *Northumberland*, pp. 4–6.

[76] A. B. Hind, in Northumberland County History Committee, *A History of Northumberland*, 15 vols. (Newcastle-upon-Tyne, 1893–1940), Vol. III [1896]: *Hexhamshire*, Part I, p. 19.

standing in marked contrast to that presented in the pastoral 'south country' discourse identified by Howkins and other writers.[77] The English border landscape was connected to a specific sense of regional and national belonging, one that calls into question totalising generalisations – or assumptions, spoken or unspoken – about the unitary nature of English national identity. We have for some years been comfortable with the idea of Britain as 'a union of multiple identities';[78] it is time the multiplicity of *English* identities was similarly well recognised, and the meanings and readings attached to the Northumbrian border is suggestive in this respect.

In the English border context, landscape was both seen as representative of identities, and as a factor behind their shaping over time. The second point is important. For many centuries, the dialect of north Northumbrians had drawn comment – not least in Shakespeare's *Henry IV, Part II*, in which Lady Percy says of her dead husband Hotspur, son of the earl of Northumberland, 'And speaking thick, which nature made his blemish, / Became the accents of the valiant.'[79] A particular feature of this accent, and one particularly noted, was the unusual pronunciation – or perhaps non-pronunciation – of the letter 'r'. This was the 'Northumbrian burr', well exemplified in a Hexham labourer's reported response to one visitor's praise of his gooseberries in the 1850s: 'Yes, the baw-ies aw fine this yeaw'.[80] Some commentators, particularly those writing in the eighteenth and early nineteenth centuries, were scathing, regarding the burr as an uncivilised imperfection of speech: Defoe in the 1720s and Smollett in the 1760s called it a 'Shibboleth', the latter likening its sound to that of 'the cawing of rooks'.[81] Yet as Defoe and others also recognised, the burr was a source of pride to the inhabitants of the region, and was common to all classes of the community, rich as well as poor, until quite late on.[82]

---

[77] Howkins, 'Discovery of rural England'.

[78] L. Brockliss and D. Eastwood (eds.), *A union of multiple identities: The British Isles c. 1750–c. 1850* (Manchester, 1997).

[79] W. Shakespeare, *Henry IV, Part II*, Act II, Scene 3.

[80] W. White, *Northumberland and the border* (London, 1859), p. 60. '"What do they burn in that kiln?", I inquired of a woman at Ovington; and she, though meaning bricks, said "B-hick".'

[81] Defoe, *Tour*, Vol. II, p. 662; Smollett, *Present state of all nations*, Vol. II, p. 266.

[82] Defoe, *Tour*, Vol. II, p. 662. Having married into the Charltons of Hesleyside Hall near Bellingham, Barbara Charlton was surprised by the accent of the eighty-three-year old Catherine Fenwick, great-aunt of her husband, when she arrived at her

And whether denigrated or valued, the burr was seen as a product of the particular environment and landscape of the Northumbrian border, a judgement with which linguistic studies of the phenomenon concur.[83] Certainly, the isolation and poor communications of the region helped ensure its survival, its later twentieth-century decline being a function of decreasing remoteness and increasing accessibility. Associated with the scattered rural populations of hills and moors, the burr did not feature in the speech of the industrialised and urbanised south of the county: as one commentator noted in 1893, at an election petition in Newcastle-upon-Tyne, two judges had difficulty with the dialects of witnesses from the border.[84] Its northern boundaries demarcated by the Cheviot Hills and the River Tweed,[85] the burr was not found in Scotland, where the trilled 'r' was common even just across the border. As P. Anderson Graham reported in 1920, at Ladykirk on the Scottish side of the border the 'English wayfarer … coming from the pleasant burr of the Norham villagers, meets … the broad accent of the Scottish hind.'[86]

Distinctively a feature of north Northumberland and closely associated with its landscape, the burr functioned as an important marker of belonging and difference. As linguistic studies have pointed out, its strength and persistence over time, and its intimate connection with place, could well be an expression of a desire – conscious or unconscious – 'to maintain difference in identity in the border region'.[87] But other markers of north Northumbrian identity existed too, and as with the burr, these were closely associated with landscape. The character of the people was a case in point. Many commentators made much of the idea that the physical environment

new home in 1839. As Barbara reported, Catherine was a well-attired, 'comely' lady; however, 'To my great astonishment, she spoke the broadest Northumbrian, this being the first occasion on which I had heard that peculiar, sing-song accent, and it seemed so strange hearing it for the first time from a lady looking like a duchess and speaking like a cook! But it was not long before I learnt to love that historical burr, immortalized by Shakespeare in Henry IV': B. Charlton, *Recollections of a Northumbrian lady 1815–1866* (Stocksfield, 1989 [1949]), p. 123.

[83] C. Påhlsson, *The Northumbrian burr: A sociolinguistic study* (Lund, 1972).

[84] Revd J. Christie, *Northumberland: Its history, its features, and its people* (Carlisle, Newcastle-upon-Tyne and London, 1893), pp. 125–6.

[85] Påhlsson, *Northumbrian burr*, p. 24.

[86] Graham, *Highways and byways in Northumbria*, p. 43.

[87] K. Wales, *Northern English: A social and cultural history* (Cambridge, 2006), pp. 100–2, 170 (p. 100); Påhlsson, *Northumbrian burr*.

of the borderland had been instrumental in shaping the traits of its inhabitants. For early writers, often far from enamoured of the bleak moorland scenery, the moral to be drawn was an obvious one: a savage environment had bred a savage people, whose rapacious habits in past centuries were to an important extent a function of topography.[88] The uncultivated wilderness and its remoteness from civilisation and state power had combined with national and clan animosities to encourage a pervasive lawlessness, traces of which were still to be found amongst the people of the region. As a 'historical and descriptive view' of Northumberland opined in 1811, the inhabitants of the hilly border districts of the county were quite different in character, still, from people living elsewhere. Their manners were akin to the rough country in which they lived, being marked by 'coarseness and simplicity', and – isolated in remote villages and hillside cottages – they retained 'the vulgar opinions and local prejudices of their forefathers'.[89]

As time passed, however, attitudes shifted. The re-imagining of the historic landscape of the borders as evocative of a sanguinary yet romantic past played an important part, allowing the present-day inhabitants of the region to take on the status of inheritors of the virtues of the heroes celebrated in balladry. The asperity of the landscape was now seen to have produced a hardy and upright class of people, whose attributes – which in the past might have encouraged lawlessness and roguery – could now be directed towards more wholesome patterns of behaviour. This wholesomeness was vividly caught by Howard Pease, who in 1899 described the Northumbrian borderer as 'a bare-headed gipsy lass, freckled with sun and wind, who "fends" for her living with strategies of hand and head', an individual who stood in marked contrast to 'the well-dowered matron' of the south, secure in her more placid pastoral comforts. The stern virtues of the former, Pease explained, were a product of her historic environment. 'Still', he went on, 'in the northern blood, the heritage of the "raid" and the "fray" abides, and still, as of old, are the children of the Borderland nursed by the keen wind of the moorland and the sea. "Hard and heather-bred" ran the ancient North-Tyne slogan; "hard and heather-bred – yet – yet – yet".'[90]

[88] E. Mackenzie, *A historical and descriptive view of the county of Northumberland*, 2nd edn (Newcastle-upon-Tyne, 1825), p. 57.
[89] *A historical and descriptive view* (1811), Vol. I, p. 230.
[90] H. Pease, *Tales of Northumbria* (London, 1899), p. 5.

And while the instinct for fighting might not have gone away entirely,[91] the man who in former times would have been a marauding moss-trooper could now put his martial energies to the services of the British Army, the performance of Northumbrian regiments in the Boer and Great Wars being generally regarded as creditable.[92]

Thus the distinctive landscape of the Northumbrian border was felt to have preserved a distinctive pattern of speech (the burr), and distinctive traits of character – the latter now tamed and put to better use than in the more turbulent past. This helped sustain a sense of regional identity, an Englishness wreathed in the glamour of a martial past, one immanent in a storied landscape of breezy moors and ruined castles. It was quite different from that found in southern counties – what Bradley called 'Blankshire' – where a limpidly domesticated Englishness exuded an atmosphere that suggested 'nothing but ages of tranquillity'.[93] Pointing to and revelling in such contrasts was a means of celebrating Englishness more generally. Cultural engagement with the Northumbrian border landscape shows how patriotic discourse located Englishness everywhere, on the windswept Northumbrian border as well as quaint Cotswold villages.[94] Moreover, it also demonstrates the important role played by regional identities in supporting broader ideas of patriotic belonging. A strong sense of Northumbrian or border identity was not incompatible with – indeed, it served to bolster – a vigorous sense of Englishness.

The patriotic celebration of a distinctive Northumbrian identity can be traced back centuries, of course, but owed its modern form to the late-eighteenth- and early-nineteenth-century growth in antiquarian interest in the region, a development that Hutchinson's *View of Northumberland*, first published in 1778, played an important part in stimulating.[95] This interest came more from within than without, from

---

[91] 'Manly strength is prized among the Northumbrian shepherd families at the present day. In the district between the Cheviot Hills and the head of the Coquet, a young man was, not a great many years since, courting a lass named Hedley, whom he wished to marry. "Let him in among us", said the mother when the proposal came to be deliberated; "he's a grand fighter"': J. Hardy (ed.), *The Denham tracts* (London, 1892), Vol. 1, pp. 27–8.

[92] H. Pease, *Northumbria's Decameron* (London, 1927), pp. 110, 173–4.

[93] Bradley, *Romance of Northumberland*, pp. 291–2.

[94] Cf. Brace, 'Finding England everywhere'; and Brace, 'Looking back'.

[95] R. Sweet, '"Truly historical ground": Antiquarianism in the north', in R. Colls (ed.), *Northumbria: History and identity 547–2000* (Chichester, 2007), pp. 104–25.

the expanding professional and middle classes of the industrial north-east, as well as local clergymen and gentry. Its manifestations included the establishment of the Society of Antiquaries of Newcastle-upon-Tyne in 1813 and John Hodgson's monumental six-volume *History of Northumberland*, the first volume of which appeared in 1820.[96] It could also be seen in the enormous fascination with the archaeology of the Roman wall, and in the aesthetic tastes of the regional elite. This latter is perhaps worthy of further comment, not least because it can be conveniently tracked through examination of the architectural styles prevalent in the region.

Many aristocratic, gentry and industrialist families living in Northumberland, particularly in the north of the county, expressed an engagement with borderland heritage through the architecture of their houses. A desire for continuity with the imagined medieval moss-trooping past was much in evidence, right through the period. In some cases old houses, castles and pele towers were incorporated into new constructions, rather than being demolished and replaced, or rebuilt outright. Examples include Barmoor, where the old walls of a tower house were integrated into a new castellated design, and Belsay Hall, where a medieval castle was retained and connected to a new manor house extension.[97] Some architects, such as John Dobson of Newcastle, made a good living carrying out the restoration of old pele towers, with the aim of making these often draughty and impractical medieval buildings comfortable to live in, while retaining their historical features. At Chipchase Castle, for example, Dobson replaced the Georgian sash windows that had been installed in the eighteenth century with more historically accurate mullions and transoms.[98] Dobson and other architects were also responsible for modern houses in castellated styles deliberately evocative of the border past and its historic landscape, including Beaufront Castle near Hexham, built in 1836–42 in an 'assymetric Gothic' style with a tall tower (see fig. 9).[99]

---

[96] J. Hodgson, *A history of Northumberland, in three parts* (Newcastle-upon-Tyne, 1820–58). The first volume to be published was in fact the fifth volume in the series.

[97] N. Pevsner and I. Richmond, *Northumberland* (New Haven and London, 2002), pp. 158–9; F. Graham, *The old halls, houses and inns of Northumberland* (Newcastle-upon-Tyne, 1977), pp. 22–3, 30–3.

[98] M. J. Dobson, *Memoir of John Dobson* (London, 1885), pp. 31–2; Pevsner and Richmond, *Northumberland*, p. 231.

[99] M. Girouard, *The Victorian country house* (New Haven and London, 1979), pp. 396–7.

9 Postcard view of Beaufront Castle, Corbridge, Northumberland. Northumberland Record Office (n.d., early twentieth century). Northumberland Archives: NRO 05176/6.

Gothic, indeed, was a particularly prominent feature of the domestic architecture of the north Northumberland landscape, to the extent that J. Mordaunt Crook has even identified 'Northumbrian Gothick' as a sub-species of eighteenth- and nineteenth-century architectural style. Its prevalence in the county can easily be explained. The built expression of a romanticised medieval past, Gothic reflected dominant readings of borderland heritage and offered connections with the historic landscape: in this way, as Crook notes, 'the visual tradition of castle and pele-tower [was] posthumously extended in the construction of follies, eye-catchers and Gothick ruins'.[100] Early examples tended to be elaborate and fantastical, as in the cases of Twizell Castle,[101] Fowberry Tower,[102] Brizlee Tower on the Alnwick estate[103] and

---

[100] J. M. Crook, 'Northumbrian Gothick', *Journal of the Royal Society of Arts*, 121 (April 1973), 271–83 (p. 272).

[101] T. Faulkner and P. Lowery, *Lost houses of Newcastle and Northumberland* (York, 1996), pp. 63–4.

[102] Crook, 'Northumbrian Gothick', p. 273; Pevsner and Richmond, *Northumberland*, pp. 286–7.

[103] J. Macaulay, *The Gothic revival 1745–1845* (Glasgow and London, 1975), pp. 78–80.

10 *Alnwick Castle, seat of the duke of Northumberland, circa 1783.*
Engraving by William Watts after Lord Duncannon. From William Watts,
The seats of the nobility and gentry (London, 1779–86). Photo courtesy of
Hulton Archive/Getty Images.

indeed Alnwick Castle itself (fig. 10). The Gothickisation of Alnwick,
ancient seat of the Percys, was completed in 1786 by the first duke of
Northumberland and his wife Elizabeth, whose approach to the stew-
ardship of their estate recalled that of their feudal predecessors, a sense
of continuity with whom they displayed a heroic anxiety to preserve.[104]

And while Robert Adam and James Paine's elaborate Gothic
remodelling of their ancestral home might have borne little veri-
similitude to medieval fortified architecture, it did express a certain

[104] An admirer of medieval castles, ruins and rugged mountain scenery, the Duchess
Elizabeth recorded in her diary how HRH the duke of Cumberland had been
received on his visit to Alnwick in August 1770. Having been met by a twenty-one-
gun salute, the duke was given a banquet 'where the number of Dishes served up
was 177 exclusive of the Desert [*sic*] ... In short, the magnificence and Hospitality
display'd on this occasion at Alnwick Castle by its present illustrious possessors,
gave a striking picture of the state & Splendour of our ancient Barons & revived
the remembrance of their great progenitors the former Earls of Northumberland': J.
Greig (ed.), *The diaries of a duchess: Extracts from the diaries of the first duchess of
Northumberland, 1716–1776* (London, 1926), pp. 141–3. For the Gothickisation of
Alnwick, see Macaulay, *Gothic revival*, pp. 59–75.

form of engagement with the myth-history of border romance, then just moving into the cultural mainstream (it was no coincidence that Thomas Percy, of *Reliques* fame, had served as chaplain to the house of Northumberland for a time).[105] Later examples were rather more robust, as in the 'domestic castellated' Tudor-Gothic of Dobson, whose Beaufront Castle was a sort of 'border' version of Haddon Hall graciousness, its great hall embodying a desire on the part of its owner, William Cuthbert, a Newcastle industrialist, to 'create "instant history"' with hunting trophies, suits of armour, medieval weaponry and portraits of ancestors.[106]

By the mid Victorian period, the various forms of castellated Gothic that had once been popular were now unfashionable. The fourth duke of Northumberland carried out a further remodelling of Alnwick, sweeping away almost completely the Gothic features introduced in the late eighteenth century. Yet as had been the case with those of the first duke, these alterations – completed in 1864 – were once again carried out with a view to preserving continuity with an imagined past. To Victorian eyes, the fantastically elaborate Gothic of Adam and Paine seemed out of kilter with the robustly martial yet still romantic and chivalrous vision of border myth-history now in the ascendancy; and so the exterior of the castle was re-done in a simpler, feudal-fortress style by Anthony Salvin, while the interior benefited from a luxurious refurbishment, complete with modern conveniences such as hydraulically powered kitchen equipment. The reception rooms and bedrooms were done up in the then-popular Italian style of the fifteenth and sixteenth centuries. This was the duke's wish, and Salvin had his misgivings, but there was some consistency in the contrast. Facing outwards to the border landscape, and indeed part of that landscape, the exterior was appropriately fortress-like and romantic; facing inwards to fashionable society, the interior conformed to the taste in decor prevailing among the wealthy elite.[107]

---

[105] Crook, 'Northumbrian Gothick', 274–7.

[106] T. Faulkner and A. Greg, *John Dobson: Architect of the north east* (Newcastle-upon-Tyne, 2001), pp. 61–4; Pevsner and Richmond, *Northumberland*, pp. 202, 161.

[107] J. Allibone, *Anthony Salvin: Pioneer of Gothic revival architecture* (Cambridge 1988), pp. 79–85. Similar contrasts could be found in other grand architectural commissions, one notable local example being Cragside, the Gothic-Tudor mansion designed by Norman Shaw for the arms-manufacturer William Armstrong. Completed in 1884, the house was set on a 300-foot crag near Rothbury, and

11 Photograph of Ford Castle, *c.* 1900. Northumberland Archives: SANT/ PHO/ALB/12/40.

Around the same time as the remodelling of Alnwick, something similar happened at Ford Castle, located at a strategic crossing-point on the River Till, about seven miles from the Scottish border (fig. 11). Originally of thirteenth-century construction and Gothickised twice in the eighteenth century, Ford was an historic site of some importance, having been visited by James IV before the Battle of Flodden, which had taken place nearby. Soon after arriving as chatelaine in 1859, the widowed marchioness of Waterford (who, appropriately enough, had met her husband in 1839 at that great festival of medievalism, the Eglinton Tournament) set upon an extensive programme of re-building. Waterford was very sensible of the historical associations of

appeared to contemporary observers as 'a romance in stone and mortar'. Yet for all the assertive – if eclectic – historicism of its external architecture (one of its towers was named for John Armstrong of Gilnockie, a famous sixteenth-century moss-trooper), Cragside was equipped with modern conveniences of the most advanced kind, including water-powered electric lighting. See D. Dougan, *The great gun-maker: The life of Lord Armstrong* (Warkworth, 1991 [1970]), at p. 118; also p. 120. Graham, *Old halls*, pp. 77–84; Pevsner and Richmond, *Northumberland*, pp. 244–6.

the place, even in its 'bastard Gothic' form, feeling that 'in the old towers of hoary stone, overlooking the beautiful valley and the field of
Flodden, you can still imagine something of the time of Marmion'.[108]
Seeking better to preserve these associations, and with them a sense of
continuity, Waterford had the architect James Bryce restore the castle to something more suggestive of a border fortress, stripping away
what she called 'the trumpery Gothic style of a hundred years [ago],
with a good deal of mock work, which was only screens, but intended
to look like walls'.[109] In this project, which was completed between
1861 and 1865, she was motivated by a Ruskinian desire for 'authenticity' in architecture, while at the same by a wish to recapture and
preserve some of the romance that attached to border myth-history as
imagined in ballad culture, and in the writings of Scott, of which she
was extremely fond. It can be seen, indeed, as a project that aimed at
the preservation of continuities between the castle and its historical
hinterland; the castle's restoration reconnected it to Flodden field (a
frequent conversation piece and day-trip destination for Waterford and
her house guests), as well as the historical-literary associations of the
border landscape more generally.

Friendly with John Ruskin, Waterford was herself an artist,
responsible for a series of impressive murals in Ford Schoolhouse,
among other things.[110] She can perhaps be bracketed with what Robert
Colls has called the 'New Northumbrian' movement, which got under
way in the later nineteenth century, building on the earlier antiquarian dispensation of Hutchinson, Hodgson and others.[111] This movement of artists, historians, and other writers and intellectuals was one
manifestation of a regional expression of English patriotism. Its *fons
et origo* can be said to have been Wallington Court, ancestral home of
the Trevelyan family, the central courtyard of which was – at Ruskin's
suggestion – covered with a roof and thereby transformed into a hall
in 1855. This hall was decorated with murals by the pre-Raphaelite

---

[108] Letters to Revd Canon T. F. Parker and Mrs Osborne, 30 July 1859 and 21 September
1859: A. J. C. Hare, *The story of two noble lives*, 3 vols. (London, 1893), Vol. III,
pp. 69, 74.

[109] Waterford to Mrs Bernal Osborne, 30 January 1865: Hare, *Story of two noble lives*,
Vol. III, p. 257. C. Hussey, 'Ford Castle, Northumberland – III', *Country Life*, 39
(25 January 1941), 78.

[110] C. Stuart, *Short sketch of the life of Louisa, marchioness of Waterford* (London,
1892); M. Joicey, *The Lady Waterford Hall and its murals* (Ford, *c.* 1983).

[111] R. Colls, 'The new Northumbrians', in Colls, *Northumbria*, pp. 151–77.

artist William Bell Scott, in which the landscape and history of the Northumbrian border loomed large. In addition to portraits of the Trevelyan family, Bell Scott's decorations featured a series of larger paintings, each depicting a scene from the history of Northumberland. Taken together, the story told was one of continuity, from the time of the Roman wall through the descent of the Danes, the age of Bede, the raiding and reiving of moss-trooping times, all the way to the present day – as illustrated by a scene of bustling activity on the quayside at Newcastle-upon-Tyne. The prominence of the border was emphasised by the 'Border Ballad of Chevy Chase', which was depicted on the upper spandrels all around the room.[112]

As reflected in the Wallington murals, the New Northumbrian dispensation involved celebration of the heritage and landscape of what the Liberal politician Robert Spence Watson – a prominent member of the movement – called 'this wild, free northern land of ours'.[113] It found expression in a plethora of locally produced guidebooks, flourishing naturalist and historical societies, and the pages of the county press. Poets such as James Armstrong achieved a certain fame for their evocations of the scenery and associations of their 'muirland hame', often – as in Armstrong's case – rendering their verse in the dialect of the borderland.[114]

Unsurprisingly, the leading lights of New Northumbrianism were middle-class and gentry figures, typically Liberal in political complexion (like the Trevelyans and Spence Watson), although undeniably part of the regional elite. Yet, as illustrated by its prevalence in the local press, New Northumbrian discourse had considerable popular purchase. In the assessment of Cadwallader Bates, writing in 1891, 'the unique devotion of the people of Northumberland to the history of their country is brought out in every local newspaper you take up'.[115] One such organ, the *Newcastle Weekly Chronicle*, was an

---

[112] For a description of the murals, see Sir C. Trevelyan, *Wallington: Its history and treasures* (Pelaw-on-Tyne, 1935), pp. 30–6.

[113] R. S. Watson, 'Northumbrian story and song', in T. Hodgkin, R. S. Watson, R. O. Heslop et al., *Lectures delivered to the Literary and Philosophical Society, Newcastle-upon-Tyne, on Northumbrian history, literature, and art* (Newcastle-upon-Tyne, 1898), pp. 25–172 (p. 26).

[114] J. Armstrong, *Wanny blossoms* (Carlisle, 1876); W. W. Tomlinson, 'James Armstrong', in W. Andrews (ed.), *North country poets*, 2 vols. (London, 1888–9), Vol. I, p. 109.

[115] Bates, *Border holds*, p. vii. Similar observations were made by metropolitan commentators. Concluding a discussion of 'some famous border fights' for *Temple Bar* in November of the same year, one writer noted that while 'more than one of

especially important outlet, publishing numerous articles on the history and folklore of the border – so many, indeed, that the paper even saw fit to bring out its own antiquarian journal in 1887, the *Monthly Chronicle of North-Country Lore and Legend*. Another notable outlet was the Berwickshire Naturalists' Club, which had been established for the purposes of examining 'the Natural History and Antiquities of the county and its adjacent districts'. Although dating back to 1831, the club's years of greatest importance correlated with the late-nineteenth- and early-twentieth-century highpoint of New Northumbrianism. It was, as we have seen, the prime mover behind the Flodden commemoration of 1910. And as this event suggested, the club was concerned with borderland heritage on both sides of the Anglo-Scottish divide; it held regular meetings in various places on either side of the border, as well as organising visits and fieldtrips for its not inconsiderable body of members, these being made alternately to Scottish and English destinations. With its membership drawn about equally from Northumberland and Berwickshire, and the president being elected from Scotland in one year and from England the next, the club was a powerful expression of a Unionist regional identity.[116] Predicated on a conceptualisation of the borderland as a transnational zone, this was an identity that involved but transcended English and Scots loyalties yet drew on a common British heritage, formerly conflictual but now re-imagined to serve the ends of unity. Similar perspectives were also found in other manifestations of New Northumbrian identity: the *Monthly Chronicle of North-Country Lore and Legend*, for example, carried many features on the Scots border and its heritage.

At the same time, however, the Unionist dimension to the New Northumbrian movement was not incompatible with a robust regional Englishness, one quite different – in part because of its Scottish inflections and connections – from its equivalents elsewhere. Yet while it

the events we have narrated' were 'remote history', belonging to the distant past, 'their memory still lingers in the country-side to an extent astonishing to the South Countryman, whose constant lament it is that, in his part of England, the present has so completely blotted out the past. Not only among the peasantry is this reverence for what has been remarkable. County feeling is nowhere so strong as in Northumberland: the gentry seem to cherish, almost as heirlooms, their native history, legends, manners, customs, and minstrelsy': 'Some famous border fights', 395.

[116] *History of the Berwickshire Naturalists' Club*, sesquicentenary volume with index, p. 2.

may have been different in form from other iterations of Englishness, being less exclusive or homogeneous, less inwardly English, it was no less forthright in pressing its patriotic claims. New Northumbrians sought to assert the importance of their region and its heritage by linking it with the great themes and events of national history, which, given the proximity of the border, they were well placed to do. It became, in some accounts, the cockpit of English history. In an article on Alnwick, published in 1888, W. W. Tomlinson remarked how 'The capture of William the Lion, the death of Malcolm Canmore, the march of the English armies northward and of the Scottish armies southward ... the movements of troops in the civil wars, Yorkists and Lancastrians, Royalists and Roundheads – these were the spectacles witnessed by the ancient burghers' of the town.[117]

As Colls has noted, all this reflected a patriotic desire on the part of the New Northumbrians to preserve a sense of continuity with their regional past. In doing so, they did not seek to repudiate industrial modernity, which after all formed the inescapable context of the daily lives of many of them (not least those who lived in Newcastle), but to 'affirm the modern world by re-charging it with historic meaning'.[118] This agenda is very much evident in the Wallington murals, with their telling of a story of progress through the ages from Roman antiquity to contemporary Tyneside. It was even evident in the activities of the marchioness of Waterford in her widowed seclusion at Ford, who combined enthusiasm for the world of medieval romance with a reluctance to turn back the clock. Frustrated by what she saw as the reactionary sensibilities of Augustus Hare, a regular visitor, she wrote of how

> He cares for everything that belongs to other times ... but this, I think, is a taste that wants mixing up with a more onward march. I love old things too, but I rejoice in the *providence* of progress, without which England would be such a country as Spain – a blank among nations – and I can see a desolate waste made frightful (its beauty lost) with a most utilitarian delight. I love *heads* that have done such great things for England as her engineers, and think that

---

[117] W. W. Tomlinson, 'Views in north Northumberland', *Monthly Chronicle of North-Country Lore and Legend*, 2 (March 1888), 128.

[118] Colls, 'New Northumbrians', p. 151.

romance of their useful lives greater than that of a knight-errant;
but then ... I am not a Conservative.[119]

The New Northumbrian desire to preserve continuities with
the past without renouncing modernity was consistent with the nationalistic uses to which history was put in England generally at the *fin de
siècle*, not least by those involved in the early preservationist movement.
Maintaining links with the past in turn helped maintain regional and
national identities, the dissolution of which would render the transformations of modernity more difficult to negotiate.[120] The landscape of
the Northumbrian border, with its historical associations, provided a
particular sort of connection with a particular sort of past, and supported a regional northern Englishness. For Colls, the articulation of
this Englishness – which reached its apogee in the discourse of the New
Northumbrians – was a defensive reaction to the dominance of conceptualisations of nationhood focused on 'college cloisters and south
country lanes'.[121] If this is right, it can be viewed as indicative of the
marginal, secondary and oppositional status of all versions of northern
Englishness – a point that Dave Russell has made in his book-length
treatment of the subject.[122] But as this chapter has suggested, a different interpretation is possible. On a-priori grounds, the far northeast
of England appears to be fertile soil for the nourishment of oppositional Englishness, not least because of its proximity to Scotland. Yet
while the Englishness of the Northumbrian border was based on a
distinctive sense of regional identity, it cast neither the Scots nor the
southern English as the 'Other' in any very antagonistic sense. It was in
some ways a Unionist-nationalist language, suffused with an intensely
English pride of place while at the same time acknowledging its close
connections with the Scottish past, now re-imagined – as at Flodden –
in ways calculated to express amity rather than enmity. In this way,
the landscape of the English border provides, *a fortiori*, an illustration
of the diversity of nineteenth- and twentieth-century English identities, and the role of landscape in the construction of those identities.

[119] Letter to Mrs Bernal Osborne, 28 August 1865: Hare, *Story of two noble lives*,
Vol. III, pp. 277–8.
[120] For this theme, see Readman, 'Place of the Past'.
[121] Colls, 'New Northumbrians', pp. 175–7.
[122] D. Russell, *Looking north: Northern England and the national imagination*
(Manchester, 2004), pp. 268–9.

Despite scholarly arguments for the hegemony of home county pastoralism, contemporaries were at ease with the variety of Englishness immanent in the various landscapes of England. In fact, the variety was a matter of celebration, an attribute of national greatness and a fit object of patriotic pride: beginning an address on the subject of the Northumbrian border in 1884, Mandell Creighton told his audience that 'English history is at bottom a provincial history'.[123] Within the wider unifying context of Great Britain, the diversity of English cultural landscapes could support mainstream understandings of nationhood. In the next chapter, we stay in the north of England, but turn to very different landscape: that of the Lake District.

[123] M. Creighton, *Historical essays and reviews*, ed. L. Creighton (London, 1902), p. 235; cf. M. Creighton, 'The Northumbrian border', *Macmillan's Magazine*, 50 (September 1884), 321.

PART II

Preservation

3 THE LAKE DISTRICT

The upland region of northwest England known as the Lake District, Lakeland or simply 'the Lakes' has long been among the most prized landscapes in Britain. Spread across 900 square miles of the historic counties of Cumberland, Westmorland and Lancashire, its scenery combines secluded valleys, verdant woodland, craggy mountains, dramatic waterfalls and – of course – impressive lakes. Its mountains are the highest in England, and its lakes the deepest and largest. By the Victorian period, it was well established as a tourist destination. As directed by their guidebooks, visitors admired the landscape of lake, dale and fell, such as the rugged heights of remote Wasdale, the grand expanse of Lake Windermere or the 'earthly paradise' of Gowbarrow Park on Ullswater.[1] In search of a more intense appreciation of the varied landscape of the Lake District, many climbed its hills and mountains, too. Described in one guidebook as 'perhaps … the grandest mountain in Great Britain' the hump-backed and easily accessible Skiddaw near Keswick was sufficiently popular by the 1870s for there to be refreshment huts on the path to the summit.[2]

It is often suggested that Victorian Lake District tourism was a middle- and upper-middle-class phenomenon, and remained so into the twentieth century. Certainly, there is no denying the appeal the Lakes

---

[1] J. Allison, *Allison's northern tourist's guide to the Lakes*, 7th edn (Penrith, 1837), p. 30.

[2] H. I. Jenkinson, *Jenkinson's practical guide to the English Lake District* (London, 1872), pp. 125, 183; 4th edn (London, 1879), p. 82; M. J. B. Baddeley, *Black's shilling guide to the English Lakes*, 20th edn (London, 1896), p. 114.

12 Roger Fenton, *Derwentwater, looking to Borrowdale*. Photograph, 1860. Photo courtesy of Science and Society Picture Library/Getty Images.

exerted over university-educated professionals in particular. Prominent among Lakeland's ardent admirers were doctors, lawyers, clerics and public schoolmasters, and the genteel villas, hotels and guesthouses that sprang up in the area reflected their predilections.[3] Yet, it is important not to underestimate the extent of the region's popularity. While the Lake District did not attract visitor numbers comparable to those of seaside resorts such as Blackpool, something approaching mass tourism had definitely arrived before the end of the nineteenth century. The extension of the railway network, first to Windermere (1847), and then to Coniston (1859) and Keswick (1865), was a crucial enabling

---

[3] For this, see, e.g., O. M. Westall, 'The retreat to Arcadia: Windermere as a select residential resort in the late-nineteenth century', in O. M. Westall (ed.), *Windermere in the nineteenth century* (Lancaster, 1991), pp. 34–48.

factor here.[4] In the first full year after opening in 1847, the Kendal and Windermere line carried 120,000 passengers, two-thirds travelling between May and October.[5] And if initially visits to the Lakes by train were only available to richer holidaymakers, who had the time and money to spare, later in the century matters changed considerably. Bank- and paid holidays, together with the increasing affordability of third-class and excursion fares, made the Lake District accessible to those of more modest means. Thus, while the Cockermouth, Keswick and Penrith Railway carried 75,000 third-class passengers in 1865, by 1882 this figure had jumped to a quarter of a million; and on Whit Monday the following year, about 10,000 day-trippers visited Windermere, most arriving by rail.[6] By the beginning of the twentieth century, half a million people came by train to the Lakes every year, nine-tenths travelling on third-class tickets.[7] Many of these would have been working-class visitors.

So, while the Lake District was not Blackpool, it was popular with English people generally. This popularity reflected its status as perhaps the most celebrated of all landscapes in the country. In ways quite different from seaside resorts, Lakeland was a place of unique and complex cultural significance. In the late nineteenth century, just as its appeal as a tourist destination was widening, it became the most important field of action for the emerging preservationist movement. It has even a claim to be the birthplace of modern environmentalism: in Harriet Ritvo's recent interpretation, it was over Lakeland fells and dales that the western world witnessed 'the dawn of green'.[8]

This chapter considers how the manifold cultural – and national – significance of the Lake District can be explained. One way of doing so is with reference to aesthetic taste: in this view, the importance of Lakeland was a consequence of the powerful visual appeal of the physical characteristics of its scenery – the form, texture, tone and

[4] D. Joy, *A regional history of the railways of Great Britain*, Vol. XIV: *The Lake Counties* (Newton Abbot, 1983), pp. 203–4, 206, 209–11.

[5] *Ibid.*, pp. 203–4.

[6] J. D. Marshall, *Old Lakeland* (Newton Abbot, 1971), p. 171; G. Berry and G. Beard, *The Lake District: A century of conservation* (Edinburgh, 1980), p. 2.

[7] L. Withey, *Grand tours and Cook's tours: A history of leisure travel, 1750 to 1915* (London, 1997), pp. 102–3.

[8] H. Ritvo, *The dawn of green: Manchester, Thirlmere, and modern environmentalism* (Chicago, 2009).

colour of its rocks, lakes, trees, mountains and so on. But any such interpretation is at best partial. Were it of use as a primary explanation, one might expect the Lake District to feature very prominently in British landscape art, but oddly enough, this has not generally been the case. Paintings of Lakeland were popular in the 1780s and 1790s, years that saw visits to the area by many leading artists – including Thomas Gainsborough, Paul Sandby, J. M. W. Turner and Joseph Wright of Derby – and that correlated with its 'discovery' by tourists and travel writers influenced by the picturesque sensibility propounded by Gilpin and others.[9] This artistic interest peaked early on, with the Lake District accounting for over 11 per cent of English landscapes shown at Royal Academy Summer Exhibitions in the 1780s.[10] As Peter Howard has demonstrated, however, the fashion for paintings of Lakeland scenes declined thereafter. By the 1830s and 1840s, not more than 3 or 4 per cent of pictures at the Summer Exhibitions featured the Lakes.[11] And while there was a revival in popularity in the 1850s and 1860s, there was no return to late-eighteenth-century levels of attention. By the turn of the twentieth century the two principal Lake counties together with the Furness district of Lancashire accounted for a smaller proportion of paintings shown than many single English counties (3 per cent, as compared to 9 per cent for Cornwall or 10 per cent for Sussex).[12] At least in terms of what Howard has called 'painters' preferred places',[13] Lakeland was something of a backwater.

This finding surprises, given the indubitable cultural significance of the landscape, its touristic popularity and, perhaps in particular, its connections with William Wordsworth and his fellow 'Lake Poets'. For Howard, the Royal Academy evidence suggests poetic associations were less important than often claimed, at least in terms of their influence on pictorial art; indeed, as he has pointed out, the brief late-eighteenth-century efflorescence of painterly attention predated the publication of Wordsworth's *Lyrical ballads* in 1798.[14] But that still leaves the problem of explaining the unique appeal exerted by the

[9] Victoria and Albert Museum, *The discovery of the Lake District: A northern Arcadia and its uses* (London, 1984), pp. 39–46.
[10] Howard, 'Changing taste in landscape art', p. 241.
[11] *Ibid.*, pp. 240–1.
[12] *Ibid.*, pp. 240, 300.
[13] Howard, 'Painters' preferred places'.
[14] Howard, 'Changing taste in landscape art', pp. 241, 323.

Lake District over the English cultural imaginary. It will be argued here that while the literary and other associations appertaining to the Lakes may have had a relatively limited influence on artistic preferences, they were crucial to the region's cultural and national significance more generally. As with the other valued landscapes discussed in this book, in the Lake District associations attaching to particular places counted for more than the physical characteristics of the terrain alone. Indeed, it was impossible, cognitively, to separate the physical landscape from the associations with which it was linked – the two were complexly imbricated. These associations, this chapter will suggest, were of various kinds. The literary connections with Wordsworth, Coleridge and others mattered, of course, but not as much as might be imagined; as it turned out, Wordsworth's verse counted less than his prose in establishing the Lake District in the collective national consciousness of the English. In what became known as his *Guide to the Lakes* Wordsworth presented the Lake District not so much in pictorial terms (for all that landscape beauty was important to him), but as a peopled landscape, a natural environment freighted with human history and experience. This account provided the basis for subsequent interpretations that amplified the idea of the Lake District as an historical landscape (the Vikings, as we shall see, were significant here), and increasingly one emblematic of popular, even democratic, conceptions of nationhood. By the late Victorian period, it had become the central focus of an emergent environmentalism based not simply on the preservation of 'wild' nature, but on the preservation of this nature as national property, free to the foot of all. As England entered the twentieth century, the Lake District had become perhaps the pre-eminent national landscape, one whose heritage and associations supported mainstream understandings of progress and modernity.

But the story must begin in the eighteenth century. Exponents of the picturesque aesthetic were quick to identify the special significance of the Lakes.[15] One early enthusiast was the poet Thomas Gray, whose account of his 1769 tour was published in 1775.[16] But the key moment

[15] M. Andrews, *The search for the picturesque: Landscape aesthetics and tourism in Britain, 1760–1800* (Aldershot, 1989), esp. pp. 153–95.
[16] Gray's journal of his tour first appeared in W. Mason, *The poems of Mr Gray: To which are prefixed memoirs of his life and writings* (York and London, 1775).

in establishing picturesque tourism in Lakeland came three years later, with Thomas West's *Guide to the Lakes*.[17] This was the first tourist handbook to the area; much republished, it remained very influential for at least half a century.[18] In its various editions, West directed his genteel readership to places that afforded visually rewarding viewpoints, or 'stations', from which picturesque vistas could be admired. His book was followed by others, notably William Gilpin's two-volume disquisition on Lakeland scenery, published in 1786 as part of his immensely popular series of 'Observations on Picturesque Beauty'.[19] With these works, the Lake District – like the Wye Valley – was firmly fixed as a place of distinctive aesthetic value in the minds of persons of taste, and first-hand experience of its landscape became a mark of a cultivated sensibility. Fashionable Hanoverians of means succumbed to what one such individual described as 'a *Rage for the Lakes*'.[20]

Schooled by the texts of West, Gilpin and others, victims of this rage – such as the gentlemanly tourist James Plumptre – set off in search of those favoured 'stations' that offered irregularity of form and variety of colour, going equipped with 'Claude' or 'Gray' glasses so as better to capture the picturesque effects.[21] But it was not just the strictly picturesque that appealed to these visitors, who by no means adhered to Burkean standards of rigour in discriminating between aesthetic categories.[22] Even after Uvedale Price's 1794 attempt to offer clearer definitions of the beautiful and the picturesque (Gilpin having conflated the two in extolling 'picturesque beauty'), a vague and capacious pictorialism remained the order of the day.[23] After all, one of the great draws of the Lake District was the variety of its scenery: the picturesque was conjoined with the beautiful, and alongside both could

---

[17] T. West, *A guide to the lakes in Cumberland, Westmorland and Lancashire* (London, 1778).

[18] Victoria and Albert Museum, *Discovery of the Lake District*, pp. 14–15.

[19] W. Gilpin, *Observations, relative chiefly to picturesque beauty, made in the year 1772, on several parts of England: Particularly the mountains, and lakes of Cumberland, and Westmoreland*, 2 vols. (London, 1786).

[20] Cited in Andrews, *Search for the picturesque*, p. 153.

[21] I. Ousby (ed.), *James Plumptre's Britain: The journals of a tourist in the 1790s* (London, 1992), pp. 142, 148–9, 153.

[22] Cf. E. Burke, *A philosophical enquiry into the origin of our ideas of the sublime and beautiful* (Oxford, 1990 [2nd edn, London, 1759 (1757)]).

[23] U. Price, *An essay on the picturesque* (London, 1794); cf. Gilpin, *Observations: Cumberland, and Westmoreland*.

be found the sublime. Indeed, the presence of the latter was important, allowing the experience of agreeable sensations of terror without
much in the way of intrepid adventuring. In 1792, Adam Walker wrote
enthusiastically of the 'many frightful precipices and roaring cascades'
easily to be found in the vicinity of Ambleside; while four years later,
in a similar vein, Ann Radcliffe described the not over-taxing approach
to Keswick from Penrith as 'sublime beyond the power of description',
and the gentle ascent of Skiddaw as 'dreadfully sublime', offering views
of 'a scenery to give ideas of the breaking up of a world'.[24] Even relatively low elevations, such as the 405-metre-high summit of Helm
Crag, could produce sensations of 'awful pleasure'.[25] Already before
Robert Southey wrote his famously onomatopoeic poem lauding the
'clattering and battering and shattering' Lodore Falls in Borrowdale,
the place could be described as 'the Niagara of Derwent Water' and,
on rainy days, 'a stupendous cataract'.[26] Bad weather, indeed, was a
significant source of the sublime, the experience of a thunderstorm on
lake or fell being a desideratum of many.[27] (For those unable or unwill-
ing to encounter real-life thunder, at Ullswater and elsewhere an aural
simulacrum could be created by the firing of cannon to cause what
Gilpin called 'exciting echoes', the 'variety of awful sounds' having 'a
wonderful effect on the mind; as if the very foundations of every rock
on the lake were giving way; and the whole scene, from some strange
convulsion, were falling into general ruin'.[28])

For English tourists seeking pleasurably terrifying landscape,
therefore, the Lake District was ideal. It was more accessible than the
faraway Swiss Alps, which had been made still less accessible by the
Revolutionary and Napoleonic Wars, and the sublimity of its mountain
summits was felicitously proximate to the picturesque and the beautiful: romantic lake, verdant woodland and pastoral dale were not over-
whelmed by rocky asperity, but complemented it. The much-admired

---

[24] A. [Adam] Walker, *Remarks made in a tour from London to the Lakes of Westmoreland
and Cumberland, in the summer of 1791* (London, 1792), p. 72; Radcliffe, *A journey
made in the summer of 1794*, Vol. II, pp. 263, 307, 328, 330, 333.

[25] 'A rambler' [J. Budworth], *A fortnight's ramble to the Lakes in Westmoreland,
Lancashire, and Cumberland* (London, 1792), p. 104.

[26] J. Robinson, *A guide to the lakes in Cumberland, Westmorland, and Lancashire*
(London, 1819), p. 127. Southey's poem 'The cataract of Lodore' was written
in 1820.

[27] [Budworth], *Fortnight's ramble*, p. 108.

[28] Gilpin, *Observations: Cumberland, and Westmoreland*, Vol. II, pp. 59–61.

13 Joseph Farington, *East side of Derwentwater, looking towards Lowdore Waterfall*. Engraving, from Thomas Hartwell Horne, *The Lakes delineated* (London, 1816). Reproduced by kind permission of the Syndics of Cambridge University Library: Ll.10.44.

landscape around Derwentwater, just south of Keswick, provided an epitome of this (see fig. 13). Fringed with attractive trees and dotted with picturesque islands, the lake was surrounded by steeply rising mountains, thereby offering scenery that presented what one commentator, writing of the view of the Lodore Falls on its eastern side, called 'a singularly harmonious assemblage of the sublime and beautiful'.[29] This was a place in which, as Walker put it in 1791, 'Beauty, Horror, and Magnificence, contend like the Three Goddesses for the Apple of Approbation!'[30]

As Walker's imagery suggests, late-eighteenth- and early-nineteenth-century 'Lakers' conceived themselves as judicious assessors of the aesthetic merits of what passed before their discerning eyes.

[29] T. H. Horne, *The lakes of Lancashire, Westmorland, and Cumberland: Delineated in forty-three engravings from drawings by Joseph Farington, R.A.* (London, 1816), p. 40.
[30] Walker, *Remarks made in a tour*, pp. 90–1.

This was a pictorialist rather than an environmentalist perspective; the value of any given landscape was a function of its appearance, of its capacity to make a visually satisfying impression – as a fine painting might – on the mind of its beholder. It followed that the inventory of pictures, or stations, presented by the Lake District could be improved upon through the agency of taste and money. Nature was not seen as good in itself; it was good insofar as it conduced to the looked-for visual effects, and where it did not, human intervention could supply the want. Tree planting was frequently urged as one means by which 'true taste' could do this, one Lakeland artist thinking Grasmere would be 'infinitely' more beautiful were its mountainsides more ornamented with timber.[31] Even the visual aspect of the lakes themselves was held susceptible of improvement. Visiting Ennerdale in the 1790s, Plumptre felt 'the beauty of this interesting lake' might be improved by the construction of artificial islands from the loose stones presently cluttering the shoreline, and the planting of trees on these islands – with perhaps also 'a stone hut … added for the accommodation of Fishers'.[32] Similarly, he thought the pictorial value of Skiddaw would be enhanced by placing a building on its summit, an improvement that would allow visitors to overnight there and so enjoy otherwise elusive sunrise and sunset vistas.[33]

More elaborate buildings than fishermen's huts and summit shelters came in for commendation. One consequence of the discovery of the Lakes was the erection of mansions and other genteel residences in the district, one of the first and most notable of these being the circular classical villa built on Belle Isle, Windermere, in 1774. As we shall see in the case of the Thames Valley, many commentators applauded such gentrifying developments, so long as the architecture and gardens conduced to good pictorial effect. As expanded by William Cockin in 1780, the second edition of West's *Guide* said much in praise of villas, seeing in the Belle Isle house and its grounds a possible augury of happily urbanising trends. 'I cannot but think them a considerable accession to the beauties of the lake', Cockin thought. 'And could one with a wish throw a bridge from shore to shore, place the uncommon

---

[31] W. Green, *A description of sixty studies from nature: Etched in the soft ground, by William Green, of Ambleside. After drawings made by himself in Cumberland, Westmoreland, and Lancashire* (London, 1810), pp. 33–5.

[32] Ousby, *James Plumptre's Britain*, p. 136.

[33] *Ibid.*, pp. 148–9.

row of houses near Shap across the island, or even conjure a city upon it … [Windermere] might then become a rival to the celebrated lake of Geneva, which owes its principal superiority over all other lakes to its having a city at one end, and being surrounded with palaces.'[34]

Reflecting eighteenth-century assumptions about cities being the only true nurseries of polite and civilised virtues, such flights of fancy had diminishing cultural purchase as time passed. Certainly, by the turn of the nineteenth century few would have welcomed the wholesale encroachment of bricks and mortar into Lake District beauty spots. Individual buildings that contributed appropriately Arcadian or picturesque effects to the landscape were a different matter, however, and continued to attract approbation. The modern houses that sprang up around Ullswater were 'handsome', one 1837 guidebook writing of how the land to the north side of the lake was 'studded and decorated with Gentlemen's seats, affording the most varied prospects, and giving additional beauty to the scene: being placed in the sweetest situations, they show beautifully off from the Lake, and can scarcely be appreciated in imagination, as they enhance the charms of nature by works of art'.[35]

Lyulph's Tower was one especially notable building on the north shore of Ullswater. A castellated Gothic-style hunting lodge, the building was constructed around 1780 for Charles Howard, eleventh duke of Norfolk, to entertain his visitors 'in all the magnificence of antient British hospitality'.[36] Named after a chieftain who according to tradition held sway in the locality in pre-Conquest times, Lyulph's Tower was admired as a visually appropriate addition to an already-romantic landscape (see fig. 14). In the words of one writer, the building was 'a judicious imitation of an antient edifice, and happily corresponds with the surrounding scenery'.[37] It continued to be so valued well into the nineteenth century, the 1837 edition of *Allison's northern tourist's guide* declaring the tower to be 'a most important and exceedingly beautiful object'.[38]

[34] [T. West], *A guide to the lakes, in Cumberland, Westmorland, and Lancashire,* [ed. and with additions by W. Cockin], 2nd edn (London, 1780), pp. 62–3.
[35] Allison, *Allison's northern tourist's guide,* p. 20.
[36] Horne, *Lakes of Lancashire, Westmorland, and Cumberland,* p. 71.
[37] P. Holland, *Select views of the lakes in Cumberland, Westmoreland and Lancashire* (Liverpool, 1792), n.p. See also, e.g., Robinson, *Guide to the Lakes,* p. 41.
[38] Allison, *Allison's northern tourist's guide,* pp. 22, 26.

14 Joseph Farington, *Ullswater and Liulph's Tower*. Engraving, from Thomas Hartwell Horne, *The Lakes delineated* (London, 1816). Reproduced by kind permission of the Syndics of Cambridge University Library: Ll.10.44.

It was just that, of course, an object – an element of a landscape viewed as one might view a painting: aesthetic considerations provided the benchmark of its value. Buildings falling short of this benchmark – that detracted from the pictorial value of their landscapes – were objects that drew condemnation from persons of taste.[39] Thus it was that the gentlemanly tourist William Gell, who visited the Lakes in 1797, could approve of Lyulph's Tower while expressing disgust at the developments on Vicar's Isle, Derwentwater.[40] There, the eccentric socialite Joseph Pocklington, scion of a Newark banking family, had thrown up a brightly whitewashed circular house on raised ground in the middle of the island. Gell and others thought it an eyesore, its visual offence being made worse by the church, boathouse, fort (with working cannon) and replica druid's circle that Pocklington also

[39] Despite his advocacy of island-creation on Ennerdale, James Plumptre criticised some of the new houses he saw in Grasmere and on the shores of Windermere, thinking them unpicturesque: Ousby, *James Plumptre's Britain*, p. 142.
[40] W. Gell, *A tour in the Lakes 1797* (Otley, 2000), pp. 22, 24–6, 28, 55–7.

installed in the grounds. The introduction of such 'miserable buildings' and 'fantastic gew gaws' was a 'disgrace' in so wonderful a setting, debasing the beautiful and picturesque qualities of the Derwentwater landscape.[41]

The despoliation of Vicar's Island was not Pocklington's only crime; he was also responsible for more follies, and a cottage, in the vicinity of the Bowder Stone, a huge boulder lying on land he owned in Borrowdale. Here, commentators complained, Pocklington had undermined the dignity of a landscape feature powerfully suggestive of awesome geological forces beyond the control of mankind. In his *Guide* of 1819, John Robinson described the Bowder Stone as 'a gigantic mass of rock, which from the similarity of its veins to those of the adjoining precipice, appears to have been detached from the latter by lightning, or some violent convulsion of nature'.[42] For arbiters of taste, Pocklington's interventions affronted the sublimity of the scene – and quite apart from the demerits of the 'little mock hermitage or chapel' and 'Druidical stone' that he erected nearby, he had reduced the place to a tawdry tourist attraction. As Robinson reported, Pocklington installed 'an old woman' in the cottage he had built in inappropriate proximity to the Stone, her job being 'to shew the rock' to tourists; he had also

> cleared away all the fragments round it; and, as it rests upon a narrow base, like a ship upon its keel, he has dug a hole underneath, through which the curious may gratify themselves, by shaking hands with the old woman. To add to these deformities, a crazy ladder has been erected against the Bowder Stone, to enable persons to see imperfectly from its top what they can behold to much better advantage from the summit of Castle Crag.[43]

For those schooled in the aesthetics of the picturesque and the sublime, Pocklington cheapened and lowered a landscape that ought to elevate and inspire: he vulgarised it.

---

[41] Warner, *A tour*, Vol. II, p. 98; Gell, *Tour*, pp. 24–8.
[42] Robinson, *Guide to the Lakes*, p. 134.
[43] *Ibid.*, pp. 135–6. The ladder – or a modern version of it – remains to this day.

The confidently voiced criticisms that Pocklington's activities attracted reflected the emergence of an idea of public aesthetic property in valued landscapes.[44] The popularity of aesthetically informed tourism and the guides and travelogues that promoted it established landscapes such as the Lake District as places of special merit whose distinctiveness made them objects of patriotic pride. These were places, it was increasingly felt, in which the public had some kind of moral stake (even if one that could not supersede the legal rights of property). As early as 1772, Gilpin had described a ruined abbey as 'a deposit, of which [the owner] is only the guardian, for the amusement and admiration of posterity'.[45] Other commentators followed with similar remarks, often made in relation to the Lake District. Reflecting on his visit there in 1802, Richard Warner described 'those scenes of Nature … which the general voice have [*sic*] pronounced to be beautiful' as 'the common property of the people'.[46] Eight years later, and most famously of all, Wordsworth termed the Lake District 'a sort of national property, in which every man has a right and interest who has an eye to perceive and a heart to enjoy'.[47] This was probably the most quoted statement in the poet's widely read *Guide*, and the sentiment it encapsulated had a huge influence on cultural understandings of the Lake District, not least in relation to preservationist campaigns.

Indeed, of all texts, Wordsworth's *Guide* was the most influential in shaping Lake District preservationism, and perhaps also cultural attitudes to the Lakes more generally. As Jonathan Bate has noted, it was 'without question the most widely read work of the most admired English poet of the first half of the nineteenth century', and was much republished thereafter, the 1842 edition going through five further

---

[44] For this development generally, see Helsinger, 'Turner and the representation of England', p. 106.

[45] Gilpin, *Observations: Cumberland, and Westmoreland*, Vol. II, p. 188.

[46] Warner, *A Tour*, Vol. II, p. 99.

[47] W. Wordsworth, *A description of the scenery of the lakes in the north of England*, 3rd edn (London, 1822), p. 101. Wordsworth's *Guide* had a complicated publication history. It was first published anonymously, as an introduction to the Revd Joseph Wilkinson's *Select views in Cumberland, Westmoreland, and Lancashire* (London, 1810); a revised version appeared as an annex to Wordsworth's own *The River Duddon: A series of Sonnets* (London, 1820) before it was published as a stand-alone volume in 1822. The fifth edition, published in 1835, was the first to use 'Guide' in its title.

editions in seventeen years.[48] The *Guide* broke new ground, in a quiet way revolutionising attitudes. Informed by the aesthetics of the picturesque and the sublime, and drawing heavily on Gilpin, West, Gray and the like, previous guidebook- and belletrist writing had taken a squarely pictorialist approach: Lake District landscapes were appraised on the grounds of their visual appearance alone. This had been the basis of cultural appreciation of Lakeland; Wordsworth overturned it. Abandoning the emphasis on 'stations' and aesthetics, and writing from the point of view of a resident, he offered a holistic account dealing not only with the physical landscape, but also with human society and its interrelationship with nature. Wordsworth's Lake District was peopled, and his guide showed an unprecedented sensitivity to how local inhabitants engaged with their environment. Above all he valued the traditional cottage economy of the area, presenting it as being in harmony with nature.[49] In his eyes, Lakeland had for many years been

> a perfect Republic of Shepherds and Agriculturalists, among whom the plough of each man was confined to the maintenance of his own family, or to the occasional accommodation of his neighbour ... The Chapel was the only edifice that presided over these dwellings ... Neither highborn Nobleman, Knight, nor Esquire, was here; but many of these humble sons of the hills had a consciousness that the land, which they walked over and tilled, had for more than five hundred years been possessed by men of their name and blood.[50]

Yet, as Wordsworth pointed out, the Lake District environment was under threat from new developments. While the overall tone of the *Guide* was not defensive or elegiac,[51] its text made clear that the popularity of the Lakes among persons of wealth presented certain problems. Wordsworth was not opposed to these people building houses in the area, but he felt it important that in doing so they should work with, rather than against, nature – and it was a cause of regret to him that some did not. To Wordsworth's mind 'ornamental gardening'

[48] J. Bate, *Romantic ecology: Wordsworth and the environmental tradition* (London, 1991), pp. 41–4 (p. 41).
[49] *Ibid.*, esp. pp. 45–52.
[50] Wordsworth, *Description of the scenery of the lakes*, pp. 63–5.
[51] A point made in S. Gill, *Wordsworth and the Victorians* (Oxford, 1998), p. 248.

and elaborate new buildings imposed a 'formality and harsh contrast' that was wholly out of keeping with the natural environment. Unlike the old farmsteads and small churches, which nestled unobtrusively in the landscape and in so doing reflected a respect for their surroundings, these opulent new houses – often exposed on hillsides and vantage points – embodied a spirit of 'ostentation' and contempt for theirs; such mansions were 'eminently unnatural and out of place' in mountainous contexts.[52] By extolling the nature-respecting vernacular culture of the Lake District, and contrasting it with the disrespect for nature caused by misapplied wealth, Wordsworth was adopting a perspective that can be described as environmental in character; indeed, it would perhaps not be too much to call it environmental*ist* – one predicated on the importance of harmonious interaction between ordinary people and the natural world.

To be sure, there was some fancifulness in Wordsworth's panegyric to the happy rustics of old-time Lakeland, and as he aged, moreover, his politics became increasingly reactionary. But what Bate has termed Wordsworth's 'romantic ecology' never left him, and can perhaps even be detected in his opposition to the Windermere railway scheme in the 1840s, which he voiced in a series of letters to the *Morning Post* in 1844. This opposition, Bate suggests, did not reflect any desire to prevent the artisan from visiting the Lakes; it was instead an objection to the organised mass tourism Wordsworth felt might ensue (particularly if the railway promoters were unable to resist the temptation further to extend the line over Dunmail Raise to Keswick, and thus deep into the heart of Lakeland).[53] Bate probably goes too far in his defence of Wordsworth here, but whatever we make of the poet's opposition to the Windermere railway in the 1840s, it was not this but his earlier *Guide* that had the most lasting impact. However much Wordsworth may have idealised the 'perfect Republic of Shepherds', the *Guide* marked a decisive shift of emphasis away from pictorial and towards environmental approaches to thinking about the Lakes. This shift can be detected in the guidebook-writing later in the century and into the next, from Harriet Martineau's *Complete guide to the English Lakes* (1856), to the much republished handbooks of Henry Irwin Jenkinson, M. J. B. Baddeley and W. G. Collingwood – all of which were concerned

[52] Wordsworth, *Description of the scenery of the lakes*, pp. 65ff. (pp. 65, 71, 76–7).
[53] Bate, *Romantic ecology*, pp. 50–1.

not only with the visual appearance and tourist amenities of the landscape, but also with the interrelationship between that landscape and its human inhabitants.[54] This environmental perspective was present even in the writing of those – like Martineau – who were scathing about the traditional society of the dales so valued by Wordsworth and others; it had become the norm.

More specifically, Wordsworth's environmentalism laid the groundwork for future preservation campaigns; it provided the basis of much of the argument that would be mobilised by the late Victorian and Edwardian defenders of the Lakes from all sides of the political spectrum. Wordsworth was routinely invoked in statements attesting to the wide extent of popular affection for the Lake District landscape. And while some preservationists were careful to distance themselves from his particular complaint against the Windermere railway, they were enthusiastic in adopting the general principle on which his objections had rested: that there should be preserved some 'nook of English ground secure from rash assault'. If his specific objection to the Windermere line had been misplaced, Wordsworth's more general objection to the despoliation of Lakeland where it was not necessary – where it would amount to 'rash assault' – proved more serviceable; indeed, it provided one cornerstone of the preservationist case. Another was provided by his insistence on the Lake District being 'a sort of national property'. In a sense it was irrelevant which sorts of people, exactly, Wordsworth thought had a claim on this property; what really mattered, once again, was the general principle. As we shall see, political democratisation and new ideas about the limits of landed property combined with the growth of popular engagement with the Lakes – of which tourism was an important manifestation – to effect a radical widening of the definition of 'those who had an eye to perceive and a heart to enjoy'. In this context, the Lake District came to be seen as the 'national property' not of a cultured few, but of the public as a whole;

---

[54] Jenkinson, *Jenkinson's practical guide* (1872), 8th edn (1885); H. I. Jenkinson, *Jenkinson's eighteenpenny guide to the English Lake District* (London, 1873); H. I. Jenkinson, *Tourists' guide to the English Lake District*, 1st edn (London, 1879), 7th edn (1892); M. J. B. Baddeley, *The thorough guide to the English Lake District*, 1st edn (London, 1880); M. J. B. Baddeley, *Black's shilling guide to the English Lakes*, 21st edn (London, 1897); H. Martineau, *A complete guide to the English Lakes*, 1st edn (Windermere, [1854]), 5th edn (Windermere and London, 1876); W. G. Collingwood, *The Lake Counties*, 1st edn (London, 1902).

indeed, it was 'national' in large part *because* it was understood to be in some sense the common possession of ordinary English men and women. Hence Wordsworth came to be deployed by those aiming both to preserve the Lakeland landscape unspoilt for future generations, and to improve public access to it: seeking to raise funds for the National Trust's acquisition of the Brandelhow estate on Derwentwater in 1901, for example, H. D. Rawnsley declared that the purchase 'will be blessing far-off generations and adding to the "joy in widest commonalty spread", which Wordsworth ... taught and wrought for'.[55]

The full implications of the ideological change initiated by Wordsworth were not immediately apparent, however. This was perhaps because, as James Winter showed some time ago, the impact of the age of steam on the Victorian environment was less severe than often thought.[56] Yet by the 1870s it seemed that technology, for all its limitations, was threatening the Lake District in new ways. A particular source of controversy was Manchester Corporation's proposal to convert Thirlmere, seventh largest of the Lakes, into a reservoir to supply that city's burgeoning demand for clean water.[57] In the end, Manchester won out, parliament approved the scheme in 1879, and it was finally brought to completion in 1894. But the emergent preservationist lobby put up a good fight, their resistance limiting the environmental impact of the development.[58] In her stimulating study, Ritvo has suggested that the origins of modern-day landscape preservationism were to be found in the debates over Thirlmere, the arguments then used by Lake District defenders being heard repeatedly in subsequent years.[59] Yet, while the fight over Thirlmere in the 1870s was certainly important, the preservationist debate of the following decade had at least as much significance. This debate was generated by new proposals to run railway

[55] H. D. Rawnsley, 'The Brandelhow estate, Derwentwater', *Northern Counties Magazine*, 2 (1901), 336–7.

[56] As Winter commented, 'the environmental effects on the homeland of the Victorian transport revolution' were 'relatively benign': *Secure from rash assault: Sustaining the Victorian environment* (Berkeley, 1999), p. 104, and *passim*.

[57] *Ibid.*, pp. 175ff.

[58] Although the battle to prevent the turning of Thirlmere into a reservoir was lost with the passage of the Manchester Water Act of 1879, a clause was inserted insisting that 'all reasonable regard' be shown by the developers for the preservation of the beauty of the scenery: *ibid.*, p. 183.

[59] Ritvo, *Dawn of green.*

lines in the Lake District, but it came to involve questions of public access – questions that were largely absent from the Thirlmere controversy. Moreover, it attracted unprecedented public attention. For the first time, the cause of preservation had powerful backers in parliament, the Liberal MP James Bryce being an especially valuable voice. The movement was also increasingly well organised (the first permanent Lake District-based preservationist organisation was established in 1883),[60] and its campaigning drew much press coverage, with most major national newspapers offering their support. Perhaps most tellingly, however, the battles of the 1880s were significant because, unlike that for Thirlmere, they ended in victories for preservation.

The first of these battles took place in 1883, when a proposal was made to run a railway from Braithwaite station to the Buttermere side of Honister Pass and the slate quarries there; it met opposition in and out of parliament, and was withdrawn in April.[61] The second was a scheme for a line down one side of Ennerdale to the head of the lake, with a view to exploiting mineral resources in the area; meeting opposition in the House of Commons, it was thrown out at committee stage in July.[62] Early in 1884, another Ennerdale Bill was introduced, and while this acknowledged preservationist concerns by proposing a cutting further from the lakeshore, the concession did not prevent its failure, once again at committee stage.[63] These three bills did much to galvanise the forces of preservation. H. D. Rawnsley and others established the Lake District Defence Society (LDDS) in direct response to the railway schemes, and local defence committees mushroomed in northern towns such as Leeds, Manchester and Sheffield, as well as in London. Perhaps most significantly, the Commons Preservation Society (CPS) and its associates – including powerful campaigners such as Octavia Hill and James Bryce – became increasingly concerned with the Lake District.[64] Hitherto focused on open spaces in and around

---

[60] The Lake District Defence Society (LDDS), of which more below.

[61] *The Times*, 10 April 1883, p. 11; *Spectator*, 14 April 1883, p. 471.

[62] *Hansard*, 3rd series, 281 (5 July 1883), 444–6 (6 July 1883), 596; *Spectator*, 21 July 1883, pp. 928–9.

[63] *Hansard*, 3rd series, 284 (21 February 1884), 1545–57 (25 February 1884), 1823–33. Having taken evidence, the committee threw the bill out 'after two or three minutes' conversation': *Manchester Guardian*, 17 May 1884, p. 8.

[64] O. Hill, *Octavia Hill's letters to fellow workers, 1872–1911*, ed. R. Whelan (London, 2005), pp. 525–7 (letter, 1904); Readman, 'Octavia Hill', pp. 164, 177–8; P. Readman,

London, the CPS contributed an activist drive, as well as much-needed legal and parliamentary support.[65] The strength of these newly gathered forces was made apparent in 1887, which saw them combine to lobby press, public and parliament, and by so doing defeat two new threats.[66] The first was another Railway Bill, this time proposing a line from Windermere to Ambleside. The scheme had more support than the previous proposals, and its promoters made strenuous efforts to demonstrate that their plans were designed so as to limit the environmental impact – the line would be in part concealed by a covered way, woods and the natural contours of the landscape.[67] Yet despite this, its fate was the same as the earlier Bills. The second threat was of a different order. Reports of people having being forcibly turned off a footpath up Latrigg, a hill near Keswick, sparked concerns about the restriction, by wealthy landowners, of public access to the landscape. Latrigg became a test case, and a site of protest: marches were organised up the disputed path and the ensuing court hearing resulted in formal acknowledgement of a public right of way. The cause of Lakeland footpath preservation was romantic ecology in action. Those involved were largely the same people who opposed the railway schemes; theirs was an agenda that asserted the existence of a popular – indeed national – stake in the landscape, one flouted by railway speculator and enclosing landlord alike.

This argument that Lakeland was 'national property' was central to the preservationist case against the railway schemes of the 1880s. The proposals, particularly the Ambleside Bill, attracted significant local support: resolutions were passed at public meetings, petitions were sent to parliament, and approving notices appeared in newspapers

'Walking and environmentalism in the career of James Bryce: Mountaineer, scholar, statesman, 1838–1922', in Bryant, Burns and Readman, *Walking Histories*, pp. 287–318.

[65] Bryce was in close touch with LDDS campaigners throughout, as evidenced by his letter to Rawnsley of 8 December 1886 urging the latter to 'Organize: organize: organize': Cumbria Record Office, DSO/24/20/2.

[66] For joint LDDS–CPS lobbying of the press, see the leaflet sent to newspaper editors explaining reasons for opposing the Ambleside Bill: Cumbria Record Office, DSO/24/20/2. The LDDS even produced special postcards, sent to people calling on them to write to their MP to urge him to vote against the second reading of the Bill.

[67] 'Reasons in support of the second reading of the Bill': Cumbria Record Office, DSO/24/20/2.

such as the *Ambleside Herald* and the *Cumberland Pacquet*. Railway
advocates buttressed their claims by noting that many of their opponents
were outsiders, a point certainly borne out by the composition of the
LDDS, not more than 10 per cent of whose members were Cumbrian
residents.[68] Historians, too, have made much of this, some seeing it as evidence of the exclusionary tendencies of a metropolitan-elite-dominated
preservation lobby.[69] Yet, such objections are (and were) misplaced. The
preservationist case was deliberately framed in national rather than local
terms; this, indeed, was the source of its strength. Lake District defenders repeatedly invoked the claim they saw the nation as having on its
landscape: 'The question of whether this or that Lakeland valley was or
was not to be destroyed rested neither with the inhabitants nor inheritors of the dale – "for the dales in their beauty were the heritage of every
Englishman".'[70] This was the principle the parliamentary opponents of
the Railway Bills of the 1880s strove to have recognised by the House
of Commons. Resistance to the proposals coalesced around the prospect that the public – that is, the nation at large – would have no *locus
standi* before the select committee appointed to consider them. Indeed,
the CPS solicitors advised opponents of the 1883 Ennerdale Bill that if
they wanted to fight it in committee, their case would need to rest on the
interests of Lake District residents whose property would be injured by
the railway, not on the wider claims of the national community.[71] Faced
by this, the parliamentary opposition to the railways departed from
orthodox practice with regard to private members' legislation by moving a wrecking amendment to the second reading of the Bill.[72] When this
manoeuvre failed, Bryce and his fellow Liberal E. S. Howard succeeded
in forcing through an Instruction that the select committee 'inquire and
report whether the proposed railway will interfere with the enjoyment of

---

[68] By contrast, 25 per cent came from Lancashire, and another 25 per cent from London
and the home counties: J. D. Marshall and J. K. Walton, *The Lake counties from
1830 to the mid-twentieth century: A study in regional change* (Manchester, 1981),
p. 214.
[69] '[T]here seems to have been a consensus that the full appreciation of the Lakes was
only for the educated mind ... The self-educated artisan was welcome, but he would
have to have the thrift and strength to beat his own path beyond the railroads': *ibid.*,
p. 215.
[70] H. D. Rawnsley, 'The proposed permanent Lake District Defence Society',
Transactions of the Wordsworth Society, 5 [1883], p. 48.
[71] Horne and Birkett to Rawnsley, 16 February 1883: Cumbria Record Office, DSO/24/
20/1.
[72] *Hansard*, 3rd series, 281 (5 July 1883), 444–6.

the public, who annually visit the Lake District, by injuriously affecting the scenery in that neighbourhood, or otherwise'.[73]

Although its significance was not fully appreciated at the time (even by sympathetic organs of opinion such as the *Pall Mall Gazette*), the Instruction was an important achievement, marking a formal recognition of some sort of wider public – as opposed to narrowly local – claim on the Lakeland landscape.[74] The stratagem was repeated when the Ennerdale Bill was re-introduced the following year, and again met with success.[75] It was also employed with regard to the Ambleside scheme of 1887, by which time Bryce found even wider acceptance for his view that, because 'the Lake District belongs to the whole of England', the preferences of local inhabitants were not of primary concern.[76] Politicians of highly contrasting ideological backgrounds agreed, ranging from the Conservative Henry H. Howorth, MP for South Salford, to the maverick socialist Robert Cunninghame Graham. All were clear that the interests of the nation had to come first, Cunninghame Graham combining utilitarian with patriotic considerations in declaring that 'every Englishman who loves his country' should prefer, as he himself did, 'the interests of the greater number of the inhabitants of this country to those of the lesser'.[77] Fleet Street agreed. Right at the outset of the Ambleside controversy, the Conservative-leaning *Daily Telegraph* had opined that 'questions of preserving the beauty of the most beautiful spots in England are not merely local, and can never be treated rightly from an exclusively local standpoint. It may be said with truth that the whole country has rights in Ambleside – rights which would be outraged if its natural charms were spoiled.'[78] In a pungent leader article in the aftermath of the debate in parliament, the Liberal *Manchester Guardian* declared that

> The citizens of Ambleside … have no right to be the sole judges of a matter interesting to every Englishman … And if the Ambleside people ask, '… may not we do what we like with our own?' after the fashion of the American slave-driver who asked if he might

[73] *Ibid.*, 281 (6 July 1883), 596.
[74] *Pall Mall Gazette*, 7 July 1883, p. 3.
[75] *Hansard*, 3rd series, 284 (25 February 1884), 1823–5.
[76] James Bryce, in *ibid.*, 310 (17 February 1887), 1734.
[77] *Ibid.*, 310 (17 February 1887), 1736–7 (Howorth); 1744–6 (col. 1744) (Cunninghame Graham).
[78] *Daily Telegraph*, 13 November 1886, p. 5.

not 'wallop his own nigger', the answer is that it is not their own. The Lake District belongs to all England. It is an utter delusion to suppose that there is anything 'aesthetic' or 'aristocratic' about the general feeling on this subject. The love of Nature is an instinct with almost all healthy minded, clean-living Englishmen who have the capacity of loving anything ... It is half-educated men of the middle class, bringing everything to the standard of £ s. d., who support such schemes, not working men, who cannot get away to Switzerland or Norway, and who have a paramount interest in keeping such bits of unspoilt Nature in their own country free from the inroads of the navvy and the jerry-builder, for the refreshment of tired mind and tired body.[79]

As the *Guardian* made clear, the Ambleside scheme offended the nation's stake in the Lakes by elevating the material interests of individuals above the priceless claims of the public. But the selfishness of locals who felt railways would give an economic boost to their businesses was only part of the problem. Another element of the preservationist critique was that the Railway Bills were speculative ventures. While they might benefit individual investors or landlords (who would receive monetary compensation for the lines crossing their property), they were of dubious value to the community more generally. In this sense they represented a 'rash assault' by sectional interests on a known national good. They were thus offensive to the patriotism that the mid-Victorian political hegemony of the Liberal Party had entrenched in mainstream discourse, and that – despite growing challenges from the left and the right – retained much of its cultural agency.[80] This patriotism was animated by an agenda of class reconciliation, standing for the interests of the people as a whole rather than those of sections of the community – the 'masses' rather than the 'classes', in Gladstone's famous formulation.[81] And it was a patriotism outraged by proposals

[79] *Manchester Guardian*, 26 February 1887, p. 7.
[80] For a discussion of the cultural purchase of Liberalism after *c.* 1880, and the (ultimately transformative) challenges it faced, see R. Colls, 'Englishness and the political culture', in Colls and Dodd, *Englishness*, pp. 53–84. As Colls writes, 'A capacious Liberalism remained the dominant force within the political culture between 1880 and 1920' (p. 54).
[81] For this theme, see J. Parry, *The rise and fall of Liberal government in Victorian Britain* (New Haven and London, 1993); also J. Parry, *The politics of patriotism: English Liberalism, national identity and Europe, 1830–1886* (Cambridge, 2006).

such as the Ambleside Bill – a scheme that, its detractors fulminated, was supported only by 'a handful of persons eager for dividend' or other material benefit, and that amounted to 'a shameless piece of pro-jected vandalism, prompted solely by greed'.[82] The 'destruction of beau-ties which are national property' by a 'small clique of persons' would amount to 'a national calamity' equivalent in awfulness to the ruination of St Paul's Cathedral for the sake of private gain. As the *Spectator* com-mented regarding the Braithwaite and Buttermere Railway Bill:

> The proprietors of the Honister Slate Quarries are now in the position of a dweller in St. Paul's Churchyard who should ask leave to run a street through the Cathedral, in order to pass from one side to the other more quickly. They propose to spoil the finest Pass in the English Lakes, in order to save themselves eight miles of carriage by road. The loss is altogether out of proportion to the gain, and what is more, the loss is sustained by the whole nation, while the gain is appropriated by a few quarry-owners.[83]

Like St Paul's, the Lake District was a national treasure on its own merits, but its status as such a treasure was greatly enhanced by the idea that it was considered to belong to all the people. This reflected a democratic conception of nationhood: scenery was 'really national in character' if it was something in which the public had a stake, if it was something 'which the nation is interested in preserving'. Being merely 'a contractor's speculation', a scheme such as the Braithwaite and Buttermere Bill could not be so regarded.[84]

This more democratic conception of 'the national' illustrated the widespread conviction that England was now a nation whose iden-tity was popularly defined. After the Third Reform Act of 1884–5, few doubted that this identity was reflected by the country's reformed

---

[82] Letter of Fred W. Jackson to the *Manchester Guardian*, reprinted in LDDS Sheet no. 7, 'The Ambleside Railway Bill', Cumbria Record Office, DSO/24/15/2; also *Manchester City News*, 29 January 1887 (DSO/24/15/2). Radical commentators were not slow to note that the Lowther and Cavendish Bentinck families, both large local landowners, were 'suspiciously eager in supporting the scheme': *Echo*, 23 February 1887, p. 2.

[83] Letter of Herbert Moser to *Kendal Mercury and Times*, February/March[?] 1883 (cutting, Cumbria Record Office, DSO/24/7); *Spectator*, 3 March 1883, 285.

[84] R. Hunter, *The preservation of places of interest or beauty* (Manchester, 1907), p. 29.

political system. Elected on a franchise understood (however errone-
ously) to be democratic, parliament was seen to represent the whole
people: the interests for which it was responsible were not those of the
rich and the powerful, but those of the great mass of the population.[85]
No longer could parliament privilege the interests of individuals over
those of the nation. 'The time has gone by', declared one MP in 1887,
'when by the permission of the House … commons [could be] stolen
from that great goose – the British public'.[86] Such explains why, just
before the second reading of the Ambleside Bill, the *Pall Mall Gazette*
saw fit to warn the Commons that it 'will fail shamefully in its duty as a
popular assembly unless it proclaims emphatically … that the days are
passed when the greed of private speculators can prevail over the right
of the people to have some spots … of their native land preserved'.[87]
Landscape like that of the Lakes was 'a great national reservoir … of
health, of beauty, and of recreation'. Over it the entire nation had a
claim: as such it 'must not be sacrificed either to the greed of contrac-
tors on the one hand or the convenience of a few local residents on the
other'.[88]

The protection of the Lake District landscape had thus become
'a public national cause', one in the 'national interest' precisely because
'all classes resort to this locality for health, rest, and recreation, and its
preservation is the concern of all'.[89] It was a cause, moreover, that had
real substance to its claims. Proponents of railways may have suggested
that their adversaries were 'professors of sentimentalism' who had no
real interest in the welfare of ordinary people,[90] but this charge carried
decreasing conviction in the face of mounting evidence of widespread
support for preservation. To start with, local backing for the railways
was by no means as strong as their champions claimed. Public meetings in support of the schemes could fall flat: one organised by the

---

[85] For some comments on this, see Readman, *Land and nation*, pp. 112–13.
[86] *Hansard*, 3rd series, 310 (17 February 1887), 1745. This was a reference to an anonymous doggerel verse of the eighteenth century: 'The law doth punish man or woman /
That steals the goose from off the common, / But lets the greater felon loose, /
That steals the common from the goose.'
[87] *Pall Mall Gazette*, 9 February 1887, p. 4.
[88] *Ibid.*, 14 February 1887, p. 3.
[89] Letter by leaders of LDDS (W. H. Hills, H. D. Rawnsley and others) to *Standard*, 26
February 1887, p. 3; LDDS Manifesto, Cumbria Record Office, DSO/24/15/1.
[90] *Hansard*, 3rd series, 284 (21 February 1884), 1548–51.

promoters of the Ambleside Bill in October 1886 was only attended by about sixty people, by no means an impressive turnout.[91] And for all that the LDDS membership was dominated by outsiders, its leading activists – men such as Rawnsley and W. H. Hills – were local residents, and they certainly received many letters of support from local people.[92] The local press, too, was by no means unanimously in favour of the schemes: by the time of the Ambleside Bill, one important organ that had previously supported railway extension – the *Westmorland Gazette* – was now opposed to it, judging that 'nearly the whole of the influential opinion of the district seems hostile to the project'.[93] Indeed, in 1886 the editor of the *Gazette* told the LDDS that, on the basis of conversations he had had with locals, the Ambleside railway 'would be anything but welcome to the bulk of the people'.[94] He was not misled in this opinion: a petition against the bill received the signatures of 800 men and women resident in or near the town, which at the time had a total population of around 2,000.

More important still was the support the preservationist case received from all round the country, and from people of all political and social backgrounds. By the time of the Ambleside Bill, this support was palpable. To be sure, protest petitions were sent to parliament from the ancient universities, and from metropolitan artists, men of letters and other intellectuals; but they also came from the great centres of population outside London, the manufacturing towns and cities of northern England especially.[95] The *Manchester Guardian* thought that 'The encouraging thing about the whole movement of opinion on this question is that it is a really popular and democratic movement, and that the masses are obviously determined that the "fair green garden of northern Europe", which England once was, shall not be converted into one vast Black Country.'[96] Working- as well as middle-class opinion swung behind the preservationist cause. A letter published in the *Bradford Observer*, for example, noted how a 'casual allusion' made

91 Cumbria Record Office, DSO/24/1: 'Copy of the evidence before the select committee on Ambleside Railway Bill, 1887', pp. 15, 21.
92 Letters to Rawnsley and Hills, Cumbria Record Office, DSO/24/20/2.
93 *Westmorland Gazette*, 20 November 1886, p. 5.
94 Letter to W. H. Hills, 22 November 1886, Cumbria Record Office, DSO/24/20/2.
95 Petitions in Cumbria Record Office, DSO/24/8/1; DSO/24/2–3; DSO/24/5.
96 *Manchester Guardian*, 26 February 1887, p. 7; also *Manchester Guardian*, 27 January 1887, p. 5.

against the railway by a speaker at a meeting of the Mechanics Institute 'elicited from a packed and appreciative audience almost unanimous applause'.[97]

Still more compelling, perhaps, is the evidence provided by the reception accorded the Ambleside Bill in parliament, where MPs from both sides lined up to denounce it as a measure antithetical to the interests of the 'general public'.[98] In opposing the Bill the Liberal MP for North Manchester, C. E. Schwann, declared his views to be aligned with those of his constituents, the workers of northern England being 'decisively and unanimously against' the scheme.[99] Indeed, both in and out of parliament, it was noted that representatives of working-class constituencies, such as Schwann, were in general hostile to the railway.[100] It was with considerable satisfaction that preservationists and their sympathisers noted how, in the vote on the Bill, 'the working-men representatives were against the railway in a body'.[101] This observation was correct. MPs for solidly working-class seats were among the most firmly and visibly opposed to the railway: the Manchester Committee for the Defence and Preservation of the Lake District included MPs for seats in Bolton, Salford, Liverpool, Stockport and Stalybridge, among others who voted against the bill.[102] Even the representatives of working-class constituencies in faraway London were in general opposed. Of the fourteen such MPs who voted, only four (all Conservatives) were in favour, while five Liberals, one Liberal Unionist and four Tories were against.[103]

Socialist opinion was especially hostile. Writing to complain of the Ambleside Bill in a letter to the *Pall Mall Gazette*, William Morris declared that

---

[97] Letter of H. Speight and J. H. Heighton to *Bradford Observer*, 16 March 1887, Cumbria Record Office, DSO/24/20/2.

[98] *Hansard*, 3rd series, 310 (17 February 1887), 1728–36 (James Bryce); 1736–7 (H. H. Howorth); and 311 (24 February 1887), 448–51 (G. J. Shaw Lefevre).

[99] *Ibid.*, 311 (24 February 1887), 447.

[100] See the comments to this effect of the Conservative MP for Wigan in *ibid.*, 311 (21 February 1887), 150.

[101] MPs such as W. Crawford, W. R. Cremer, C. Fenwick, George Howell, Charles Bradlaugh and J. Rowlands had all done their duty, in the opinion of the *Bradford Observer*, 19 February 1887; also *Pall Mall Gazette*, 18 February 1887, p. 8.

[102] *Manchester City News*, 5 February 1887 (Cumbria Record Office, DSO/24/20/2).

[103] *Echo*, 18 February 1887, p. 2. The definition of seats as 'working class' follows H. Pelling, *Social geography of British elections 1885–1910* (London, 1967), p. 43.

The external beauty of the country is a part of its wealth, and every citizen has a right to the enjoyment of it to the full extent of his capacity. No private person or group of persons has any right to deprive the rest of the citizens of this enjoyment, this wealth, on any pretext whatever; the whole community only has a right to determine what occasion may be pressing enough to make the sacrifice of some portion of this wealth necessary.[104]

Morris's position was informed by his hostility to landed property *tout court*: as he told Rawnsley in 1886, 'We shall be quite helpless against the landowners as long as there is any private ownership of land.'[105] While few preservationists took so extreme a position, there was more than a tincture of anti-landlordism in the case made by preservationists, as both their sympathisers and detractors acknowledged. In a letter to W. H. Hills in 1885, Gordon Wordsworth – grandson of the poet – noted that 'nearly all our active members are radicals'; while the following year, the fiercely Conservative *Observer* newspaper described hostility to the Railway Bills as expressive of 'the spite against capitalists and landowners which is almost daily developing itself in the various forms of communism'.[106] At any rate, central to the preservationist argument was the principle that considerations of public and national good ought to limit the claims of private ownership: a man should not be able, at least not in all circumstances, to do exactly what he liked with his own.

This strand of thinking came into sharp focus in the footpath dispute of 1887. The closure of the path up Latrigg involved much the same people who opposed the Railway Bills: Bryce, Rawnsley, Hills and others associated with the LDDS and CPS. The LDDS understood its role to be the protection of the public stake in Lakeland, and this included the protection of footpaths. It supported the work of the CPS in lobbying parliament to preserve commons and rights of way, and its propaganda asserted that 'the time has come for definite action with a view to their National defence'.[107] For Hills, the LDDS, CPS

104 *Pall Mall Gazette*, 22 February 1887, p. 2. See also the letter of Walter Crane, in *ibid.*, 9 February 1887, p. 3.
105 Morris to Rawnsley, 10 February 1886, National Trust Archives, Acc. 6/4.
106 Gordon Wordsworth to W. H. Hills, 8 November 1885, Cumbria Record Office, DSO 24/20/2; *Observer*, 27 February 1887, p. 4.
107 Leaflet, LDDS, Cumbria Record Office, DSO/24/7/3.

"OWNER UP" IN THE LAKE DISTRICT.

"Here y'are, Sir! Finest Waterfall in England! Sixpence a head, if *you* please! Owner don't allow nobody to look at his Waterfall for nothing!"

"Looking at that there Mounting was you, Sir? Then you're a-trespassing! I've orders from the Owner to stop anyone from looking at his Mounting."

"Hi! you Sir! Come off that grass, will you! I'm the Owner of this property, and I'll trouble you to walk in the middle of the road!"

"Here, I say, none of that! Owner's orders is no one's to disturb his Flies. You just leave 'em alone, will ye?"

15 '"Owner up" in the Lake District', *Punch*, 4 September 1886. Reproduced by kind permission of the Syndics of Cambridge University Library: L992.b.177.

and their supporters were 'the defenders of the rights of working men, of small farmers, of poor people everywhere, who are unable to maintain those rights which they have in the land, which have been enjoyed from time immemorial, but which are for ever being encroached upon by various kinds of people for selfish ends' – and he was quick to point to their defence of Lakeland footpaths. One of these was a path leading to Stock Ghyll waterfall, which a few years earlier had been closed by Colonel Godfrey Rhodes, local landowner and prominent promoter of the Ambleside railway scheme.[108] The other was that at Latrigg.

Trouble with Lake District footpaths had been brewing for some time, the Stock Ghyll affair being just one manifestation of a wider problem, the essence of which was nicely caught by a *Punch* cartoon published in September 1886 (see fig. 15). Around the time this cartoon

[108] W. H. Hills, letter to *Ambleside Herald*, 31 December 1886, p. 5.

appeared, the *Pall Mall Gazette* noted that over eighteen years to 1886, 'at least twenty ancient footpaths have been closed in the neighbourhood of Windermere Lake' alone.[109] But Latrigg was the tipping point. The paths on the hill were well used, not least because they provided one route to the summit of Skiddaw, still probably the most popular mountain in the Lakes – both as a climb (it was easy, after all), and on account of its majestic appearance, Wordsworth's comparison of it to Mount Parnassus being much quoted in guidebooks.[110] Reports that people – 'even some old ladies' – had been 'turned back and not very civilly' from three paths on the Greta Bank estate inflamed opinion,[111] and the recently established Keswick and District Footpaths Protection Association (KDFPA) got going in earnest. Attracting the support of Rawnsley and other prominent preservationists, its leading figure was Henry Irwin Jenkinson, writer of popular guidebooks to the Lakes and great admirer of the mountains around Keswick (his *Practical guide* had described Skiddaw as 'perhaps … the grandest mountain in Great Britain').[112] Advised by the CPS, on 30 August 1887 a group of KDFPA members marched up one of the disputed paths, which by this time had been blocked at several points by timber barriers, metal railings, an old iron plough, barbed wire, tar-covered thorn branches and other obstacles. This demonstration, however, did not prevent the re-erection of the obstructions, and further protests followed, including a mass rally on 1 October. Immediately after this meeting, the protesters – numbering at least 2,000 – confronted the landowners' agents (who threatened legal action), before breaking the chain on the gate barring the way, and walking to the top of Latrigg.[113]

---

[109] *Pall Mall Gazette*, 11 September 1886, pp. 4–5.

[110] M. J. B. Baddeley, *Black's shilling guide to the English Lakes*, 22nd edn (London, 1900), p. 116; *Jenkinson's practical guide* (1872), pp. 125, 185.

[111] *The preservation of ancient footpaths: The Latrigg case. Statement of the facts* (1888), Cumbria Record Office, WDX/422/214, pp. 2–3.

[112] Jenkinson, *Jenkinson's practical guide*, 1st edn, p. 125. Rawnsley was responsible for some of the Association's propaganda, including a leaflet calling for people to become members. The proximate cause of the formation of the KDFPA, in March 1886, had been a landowner's closure of a path on the Catbells side of Derwentwater: *Preservation of ancient footpaths*. The records of the KDFPA can be found in Cumbria Record Office, WDX/422/2/4, WDso 1/1/1–62.

[113] *English Lakes Visitor and Keswick Guardian*, 3 September 1887, p. 4; 8 October 1887, p. 5. *The Times*, 31 August 1887, p. 5; 29 September 1887, p. 4; 3 October 1887, p. 7. *Pall Mall Gazette*, 3 October 1887, pp. 1–2.

At the 1 October meeting, which was extensively reported by newspapers all around Britain, the leaders of the protest made their case clear. In part, they were standing up for the rights of locals, for whom the paths up Latrigg offered popular means of recreation. But at root theirs was an agenda founded on the claims of a national public: the question, as Jenkinson had put it, 'was one of national importance'.[114] In his speech on 1 October, he told the crowd that

> To-day you are showing to the world a spirit which will kindle such a fire as will light up the British Isles. (Cheers.) 'Latrigg' must be the watchword, and the question of access to our mountain tops having been disputed we must not rest satisfied until the ancient rights have been conceded, or the question is discussed and settled on the broadest principles. (Cheers.) If we have no right of access to the summit of Latrigg, then we have no right to ascend other similar mountains in Great Britain.[115]

These sentiments were reiterated by the veteran Radical politician Samuel Plimsoll, who was the principal speaker at the meeting. Invited up from London, the famous MP justified his presence at Keswick by denying 'that the rights, which you have met to-day in such great numbers and in such orderly array to vindicate, are the rights of the people of Keswick alone. I maintain they are the rights not only of the people of Keswick but of the people of England – (Hear, hear) – and as one of those I am here.'[116]

Helped by the CPS and sympathetic newspaper coverage, Latrigg attracted nationwide attention. In publicising it, and indeed the cause of footpath protection more generally, preservationists used patriotic rhetoric that appealed to national rather than local feeling. Writing in the *Contemporary Review* in 1886 with developments in the Lakes uppermost in his mind, Rawnsley declared that it was 'the duty of Englishmen and English sentiment and the English legislature ... to make every reasonable effort to preserve ancient rights of way'.[117] Resisting the impostures of those who had no qualms about

---

[114] *English Lakes Visitor and Keswick Guardian*, 3 September 1887, p. 4.

[115] *Ibid.*, 8 October 1887, p. 5.

[116] *Ibid.*

[117] H. D. Rawnsley, 'Footpath preservation: A national need', *Contemporary Review*, 50 (September 1886), 373–86 (p. 373).

'challenging all England'[118] often necessitated the physical removal of fences and other barriers, but true patriots, so the argument went, should not flinch from taking direct action. Reflecting on the lessons of the dispute in May 1888, the *English Labourers' Chronicle* advised its readers in an editorial that if a known public path be blocked, 'a band of indignant Britons may march to the spot, armed with the requisite implements, and forthwith level the obstruction, thereby laying the path open again'.[119] This, indeed, was precisely what had happened at Latrigg the previous autumn. Their demonstration described by the *Pall Mall Gazette* as 'at once polite and patriotic', the Keswick protesters of 1887 carefully removed the barriers and then marched up the hill singing 'Rule Britannia' and chanting 'Britons never shall be slaves', before giving a rendition of the first stanza of 'God save the Queen' once at the summit.[120]

After the march to the summit on 1 October, Jenkinson and others were served with writs charging them with damage to the landowner's property. Rawnsley helped raise funds for the defence, which was supported by the legal expertise of the CPS. The settlement that was eventually reached confirmed two of the three routes on the Greta Bank estate to be rights of way, with the KDFPA consenting to the closure of the third – which ran close by the landowner's residence.[121] Although the landowner would later hem in one of the opened paths with unpleasant barbed-wire fencing, this was a significant victory for the campaigners. Welcoming it as 'the first time in English history when the right of climbing a hill has been recognized in a court of law', the *Saturday Review* felt the case illustrated 'the curious change of opinion in the matter of open spaces which the public mind has undergone during the last three-quarters of a century'.[122]

This was a perceptive comment. Public opinion had indeed changed, and the basis of this change was the now democratised idea of Wordsworth's 'sort of national property' in the Lake District. It was

[118] Plimsoll's characterisation of the stance taken by the 'terrible little man' who, acting as the agent of the landowner, had dared to close the path up Latrigg: *English Lakes Visitor and Keswick Guardian*, 8 October 1887, p. 5.

[119] *English Labourers' Chronicle*, 12 May 1888, p. 1.

[120] *Pall Mall Gazette*, 1 October 1887, p. 6; 3 October 1887, p. 2. *The Times*, 3 October 1887, p. 7. *English Lakes Visitor and Keswick Guardian*, 8 October 1887, p. 5.

[121] *Manchester Guardian*, 9 July 1888, p. 7.

[122] *Saturday Review*, 14 July 1888, p. 37.

an idea, moreover, that was buttressed by the jurisprudential precept that in England absolute ownership of land by private individuals was impossible: what was termed 'private property' was simply an estate in the land – an entitlement to its exclusive or near-exclusive use. As land was different from other forms of property, being necessary for the very existence of the English people, this entitlement (at least in theory) was granted to individuals on the understanding that their 'ownership' of the soil would be of public benefit. Private property in land – originally a means by which its production could be maximised – was therefore limited by considerations of public or national interest: in principle this interest was in all cases prior.[123] This precept provided much of the ideological impetus behind proposals for land reform, the argument being that the public interest justified legislative attacks on the enervating system of 'landlordism'.[124] But more important for our purposes here, it underpinned the case made by the preservation movement: that the national benefit derived from landscape such as that of the Lake District justified action both to prevent its spoliation, and also to protect public access to this landscape. Plimsoll made this explicit in his Keswick speech:

> Property in land never was, is not now, and never can be, so absolute as it is in property [that is] the work of men's hands. You might put your money in a bag, row on to the lake and sink it there. You injure nobody but yourself; but the landlord can say whether he will grow crop or not [sic]. This is the *reductio ad absurdum* of their argument. If the whole of the landlords were to say, 'We will grow no food', you would soon bring them to their senses and show them it was never their land except as trustees for the nation, and for the good of the people. (Applause.)[125]

[123] See, e.g., J. S. Mill, *Principles of political economy*, 7th edn (London, 1877), pp. 226–7, 230–2; H. Sidgwick, *The elements of politics*, 2nd edn (London, 1897), pp. 67, 73–5, 147; T. E. Scrutton, *Commons and common fields* (Cambridge, 1887), pp. 174–5; J. M. Maidlow, 'The law of commons and open spaces, and the rights of the public therein', in J. M. Maidlow, H. W. Peek et al. (eds.), *Six essays on commons preservation* (London, 1867), p. 73; H. H. Hocking, 'The preservation of commons: Legal and historical aspects of the question', in Maidlow et al., *Six essays*, p. 293; R. Hunter, 'The preservation of commons in the neighbourhood of the metropole', in Maidlow et al., *Six essays*, pp. 357–8; H. Greenwood, *Our land laws as they are*, 2nd edn (London [1897]), pp. 7–8.

[124] See Readman, *Land and nation*.

[125] *English Lakes Visitor and Keswick Guardian*, 8 October 1887, p. 5.

Latrigg, then, did much to orient the preservation movement towards the assertion of this underlying national stake in the land. From the late 1880s, preservationists were as much concerned with the defence of the public access to valued landscape that this stake implied as they were with the prevention of scenic spoliation. Under the umbrella of the National Footpaths Preservation Society (NFPS), a body that had been founded in 1884, footpath preservation societies mushroomed throughout the country,[126] and the CPS made a formal commitment to campaign for the defence of rights of way, as well as the preservation of commons. This extension of the CPS's objects (which foreshadowed the eventual merger of the society with the NFPS in 1899) was prompted by Octavia Hill. In a speech at a CPS meeting in June 1888, Hill argued that the Latrigg case indicated that it was now

> incumbent on us all to do what in us lies to preserve for our countrymen and women and their children one of the great common inheritances to which they as English citizens are born – the footpaths of their native country ... I think that these little winding ways, that lead us on by the hedgerows and over brooks, through scented meadows and up grassy hill, away from dirty road, and into the silent green of wood and field, are a common possession we ought to try to hand down undiminished in number and in beauty for those who are to follow.[127]

Around the same time as Hill's Latrigg-inspired suggestion, CPS-supporting parliamentarians led by Bryce and G. J. Shaw Lefevre introduced bills aimed at improving legal safeguards against the improper closure of public footpaths.[128] In the early 1890s, the Liberals officially took up the cause, measures for the better protection and establishment of pedestrian rights of way being built into their party's proposals for

[126] Examples included the South West of England Footpaths Preservation Society (*c.* 1887); Wirral Footpaths Preservation Society (*c.* 1887); Leicestershire Footpaths Association (*c.* 1887); Northern Heights [Hampstead] Footpath Association (1888); Peak District and Northern Counties Footpath Preservation Society (1894); Blackburn and District Ancient Footpaths Association (1894).

[127] 'Miss Octavia Hill on the duty of supporting footpath preservation societies [1888]', Cumbria Record Office, WDX/422/2/4; also O. Hill, 'Open spaces of the future', *Nineteenth Century*, 46 (1899), 26–35 (p. 32).

[128] Bills were introduced in 1888 and 1892; for an example of press commentary, see *Manchester Guardian*, 25 May 1888, p. 5.

rural local government reform.[129] These proposals found their way onto the statute book via the 1894 Local Government Act, which gave the new Parish and District Councils powers to protect, regulate and create public rights of way – powers that Charles Roundell, one prominent parliamentary supporter of the measure, described as being 'of special value'.[130]

The growing centrality of questions of access found its culminating pre-1914 expression in the National Trust. It is not always appreciated that the primary focus of the Trust in its early years was not buildings, but open spaces: approximately two-thirds of its acquisitions before the Great War were open spaces, with about one-fifth being buildings and the rest monuments.[131] More specifically, the National Trust aimed to preserve not only valued natural landscape as unspoiled, but to facilitate free public access to this landscape. The Lakes soon emerged as the main locus of its activity outside south and southeast England. Before 1914 the Trust made no acquisitions in Durham, Lancashire, Lincolnshire, Nottinghamshire, Cheshire, Staffordshire or Northumberland, and only three in Yorkshire and Derbyshire together; but it made nine in the Lake District.[132] Among these were important properties in some of the most prized of all Lakeland landscape, notably Brandelhow Park on Derwentwater, and 750 acres of land at Gowbarrow Fell, by Ullswater, including the celebrated waterfall of Aira Force.

Despite the National Trust's emphasis on open space in the Lakes and elsewhere, some scholars have suggested that the organisation was animated by a reactionary and illiberal ideology. For John Walton, the Trust from its foundation 'celebrated a deeply conservative vision of England, with which Canon Rawnsley (for example) was completely at home'. Its 'dominant affinities', Walton says, were with an 'authoritarian paternalism' that aimed to sustain the 'preserved enclaves' of a Tory version of Englishness, one that over time came to involve celebration of 'a nationalistic and … militaristic patriotism'.[133]

[129] For instance, Sir E. Grey, *Rural land* (London, 1892), Oxford, Bodleian Library, John Johnson Collection, JJ/JCC 15.4.86, box 9.

[130] C. S. Roundell, *Parish councils: 'The village for the villagers'. An address before the Bradford Junior Liberal Club, on November 12, 1894* (London, [1894]), pp. 15–16.

[131] This estimate is mine; it is derived from the list of acquisitions given in National Trust, *Annual Reports*, Swindon, National Trust Archives.

[132] *Ibid.*, passim.

[133] J. K. Walton, 'The National Trust centenary: Official and unofficial histories', *Local Historian*, 26 (1996), 86; Walton, 'The National Trust: preservation or provision?'.

Certainly the agenda of the Trust was charged with patriotic purpose. In 1896, Rawnsley described it as 'the youngest-born of our patriotic societies that aim at preserving beautiful and historic Great Britain to future generations'.[134] But patriotic sentiment, even in the age of high imperialism, did not always correlate with Conservatism, and while the early National Trust drew some support from Tories, its leading lights were on the opposite side of the political spectrum (in this context, it is worth recalling Raphael Samuel's observation that 'Historically, preservationism is a cause which owes as least as much to the Left as to the Right').[135] Furthermore, Liberal and socialist languages of patriotism retained much vigour in these years,[136] and it was these languages that had most affinity with the Trust and its work before 1914. In a context of political democratisation, the Trust presented itself, to quote Rawnsley again, as 'a kind of Patriotic league for the public good'.[137] This was a patriotism allied with the interests of the whole people, rich and poor. It drew strength from Christian Socialism, a mode of thought that animated the open-spaces activism of Octavia Hill in particular,[138] and it looked to the hills and fields of England as fit objects of patriotic pride for all English men and women. Its monarchism made it mainstream – Princess Louise was its first patron – but, *pace* Walton, it disdained militarism. (During the Boer War, Rawnsley took to the pages of *The Times* to argue against a suggestion that St George's Day be celebrated as a 'Soldiers' Day', writing that 'We have enough and to spare of the love of battle in our blood and breed; we do not want to set apart solemnly a day for the nation to warm its heart at the fires of war.'[139]) As the Trust's second annual report explained, 'It is on the

---

For similar perspectives, see Gould, *Early green politics*, pp. 88ff.; N. P. Thornton, 'The taming of London's commons', Ph.D. dissertation (Adelaide University, 1988).

[134] H. D. Rawnsley, 'The National Trust: Its work and needs', *Nature Notes*, 7 (September 1896), 190–1.

[135] Samuel, *Theatres of memory*, Vol. 1, p. 288.

[136] Parry, *Politics of patriotism*; P. Ward, *Red flag and Union Jack: Englishness, patriotism and the British Left, 1881–1924* (London, 1998); Readman, *Land and nation*; P. Readman, 'The Liberal Party and patriotism in early twentieth century Britain', *Twentieth Century British History*, 12 (2001), 269–302.

[137] H. D. Rawnsley, 'The National Trust: Its aim and its work', *Saint George: The Journal of the Ruskin Society of Birmingham*, 2 (July 1899), 115.

[138] E. Baigent, '"God's earth will be sacred": Religion, theology, and the open space movement in Victorian England', *Rural History*, 22 (2011), 31–58.

[139] *The Times*, 10 April 1900, p. 11.

ground of patriotism and the poetry of great ideas that help a nation ... that we call upon the lovers of Britain to rally round the cause ... Men are beginning to learn ... that it is good to have a country to live for as well as a fatherland to die for.'[140]

This patriotism was much in evidence in the National Trust's fundraising campaigns to purchase land in the Lakes. The appeal for funds to buy Brandelhow Park was, as Rawnsley put it, 'the first attempt to nationalize ... any portion of the Lake District'. This terminology of 'nationalization' was echoed by other leading lights of the Trust, not least Sir Robert Hunter, and they understood it to mean an attempt to reify that originally Wordsworthian sense of 'national property' in landscape, in the interests of all.[141] Not least because the property bordered an unenclosed common, which would give visitors access to the nearby mountain summits, its purchase would add 'to the "joy in widest commonalty spread", which Wordsworth ... taught and wrought for'.[142] This was also very much the perspective of Octavia Hill, who in her own efforts to whip up donations told *The Times* that 'Such a national possession as the Brandelhow estate would be a great joy to thousands of English men and women; especially to those who have neither parks of their own nor friends to visit who possess country houses with woods and fields'; she hoped to see 'nearly a mile of sloping woodland ... part of the heritage of every English citizen'.[143] Such arguments reappeared in the Trust's other fundraising drives in the Lakes, notably in the Gowbarrow appeal of 1904–5. Once again, Rawnsley, Hill and Hunter presented the issue as being one not only of the preservation of beautiful landscape, but of the preservation of 'freedom of foot' over this landscape

---

[140] Cited in P. Horn, *Pleasures and pastimes in Victorian Britain* (Stroud, 1999), p. 1.

[141] See report of National Trust annual meeting (*The Times*, 11 July 1903, p. 10), at which the Brandelhow purchase was described by Hunter as 'but a beginning of the nationalization of many beautiful natural sites'. One National Trust leaflet published at the time of the Gowbarrow appeal contained the suggestion: 'Why not nationalise the English Lake District? ... If men had been wise enough to realise the worth of such a haunt of ancient peace the thing might have been done. Now every year the land is more locked up in private ownership': B. L. Thompson, *The Lake District and the National Trust* (Kendal, 1946), p. 43.

[142] Rawnsley, 'The Brandelhow estate, Derwentwater', 336–7.

[143] *The Times*, 10 June 1901, p. 7.

for 'man, woman and child for all ages'.[144] Either this freedom would be protected through purchase by the Trust, or it would be, in Hill's words, 'appropriated to one or two families, and fenced off with barbed wire; shut off from naturalist, hard-worked professional man, smoke-grimed city dweller, workman and child'.[145]

In making this case, the National Trust emphasised the increasing recreational popularity of the Lakeland landscape. Rawnsley pointed to the 'love of Nature' now apparent among 'the lowliest and the humblest', and appealed for funds in their name – for 'the sake of the future Nature-loving working men of England'.[146] Speaking at the formal opening of Gowbarrow, Hunter declared that the purchase had been made for the benefit of 'the large and ever-increasing numbers, who, escaping from the crowd and turmoil of town, seek quiet and a rest from the obtrusive presence of man's work'.[147] Such claims gained force, moreover, from the evidence of popular support for the Trust's appeals. Donations for the Gowbarrow and Brandelhow purchases came from all social groups. Hill and Rawnsley reported that the £6,500 raised to buy Brandelhow derived from more than 1,300 donors, the gifts ranging from single shillings to £300 and coming 'from all kinds of people – the octogenarian with all his memories, the young boys with all their hopes, from the factory worker and the London teacher'.[148] It was a similar story with Gowbarrow, the £12,000 required for its acquisition being raised from about 16,000 subscribers, many of whom were resident in the industrial areas of Lancashire and Yorkshire; the working-class membership of the Manchester-based Co-operative Holiday Association sent out thousands of appeals for funds.[149] Reflecting on the success of the Gowbarrow appeal, the Trust's annual report for 1905–6 noted that 'Perhaps the most satisfactory

[144] *Manchester Guardian*, 24 June 1905, p. 6 (Rawnsley); and 10 August 1906, p. 7 (Hunter).
[145] Hill, *Letters to fellow workers*, p. 526.
[146] *Manchester Guardian*, 14 June 1905, p. 6.
[147] *Ibid.*, 10 August 1906, p. 7.
[148] O. Hill, 'Natural beauty as a national asset', *Nineteenth Century*, 58 (December 1905), 940; H. D. Rawnsley, letter on Derwentwater appeal, in *Climbers' Club Journal*, 4 (1901), 45.
[149] *Manchester Guardian*, 10 August 1906, p. 6; Octavia Hill to Miss Schuster, 8 March 1905, Westminster City Archives, D Misc 84/1/6.

aspect' was 'the extensive support given ... by the small donor, and particularly the donor of the working class'.[150]

As illustrated by the controversies over railways and footpaths in the 1880s, and the National Trust's campaigns of the 1900s, the growing popularity of the Lake District was seen not as a threat to the landscape, but as justifying its protection for the benefit of the nation as a whole. As newspapers opposing the Ambleside Bill had it, Lakeland 'exists for the benefit of the public at large'; it was 'a national tourist field' that 'belongs to all England'.[151] By the late nineteenth and early twentieth centuries, then, tourism, preservation and ideas about public access were working hand-in-hand to help create a new cultural understanding of the Lake District, one rooted in a democratic reading of Wordsworth's idea of 'national property'. More and more, it was seen as a national landscape – part, indeed, of the nation's heritage – precisely because it was a place cherished by the whole people, and over which all had a claim.

This was not the only cause of its growing significance as national heritage, however. Another very significant factor was the new associational value that came to be attached to the Lake District. This was not just to do with the Lake Poets, though their influence remained important (as demonstrated not least by the Rawnsley-initiated fundraising campaign to buy Dove Cottage, opened to the public in 1891).[152] It was, rather, to do with history more generally. Once again, the activities of the National Trust are suggestive: among the Trust's pre-1914 Lake District acquisitions were the Roman fort at Borrans Field, near Ambleside, and a 9-acre field on Castlerigg containing a long-famous megalithic circle. Both sites were presented by the Trust and their supporters as valuable on account of their being 'storehouse[s] of history', *The Times* feeling that once purchased and excavated, Borrans Field would provide 'a striking object-lesson' in 'the history of our island'.[153] The historical associations of other Trust

[150] National Trust, *Annual Report* (1905–6), pp. 3–4.
[151] *Liverpool Daily Post*, 10 February 1887, p. 4; *Manchester Guardian*, 26 February 1887, p. 7.
[152] Gill, *Wordsworth and the Victorians*, pp. 244–6.
[153] *The Times*, 5 October 1912, p. 8; *Lakes Herald*, 7 June 1912, [p. 5]. See also H. D. Rawnsley, *Chapters at the English Lakes* (Glasgow, 1913), pp. 225–6; and

purchases also drew comment. In his speech at the 1913 opening of Queen Adelaide's Hill, Windermere, for example, Robert Hunter noted not only that the place had been visited by Queen Adelaide herself (on 26 July 1840), but that it had been known by the anti-slavery campaigner William Wilberforce.[154]

These remarks reflected a wider late Victorian and Edwardian historicisation of the Lake District. This was a new development. To a degree, it was associated with the Lake Poets, now firmly part of the nation's literary heritage. The ninth edition of Jenkinson's *Practical guide* (1893) made much of how 'in almost all parts' of the Lakes

> the traveller finds some worthy literary association, some ennobling memory, either of the habitation or the work of a man's mind, to lend the scene a human interest. Any one with a knowledge of English literature will find the hills and vales and houses of our English lakeland perpetually recalling some historic or literary figure, or monumental saying of the great dead in prose or poetry.[155]

The former homes and haunts of the Lake Poets had become popular tourist attractions. Something similar happened to Shakespeare around the same time; Stratford-upon-Avon was developed as a popular tourist destination, with the idea of 'Shakespeare's England' that it presented reaching its pre-war culmination in a large-scale exhibition of the same name at Earl's Court, London, in 1913.[156] But this growth in Lakeland heritage-consciousness was not confined to associations with past literary lives. It encompassed all of society, and all of human history, and its cultural purchase is perhaps best illustrated with reference to the writings of two men, both residents of the Lake District: Hardwicke Drummond Rawnsley and William Gershom Collingwood.

W. G. Collingwood, 'The Roman camp at Ambleside', National Trust pamphlet (Ambleside, 1912).

[154] *The Times*, 12 September 1913, p. 4.

[155] Jenkinson, *Jenkinson's practical guide*, 9th edn (1893), p. 8.

[156] Readman, 'Place of the past', pp. 166–8. The rapidly growing popularity of Stratford-upon-Avon at this time is evident from comparison of successive editions of Baedeker's handbook to Great Britain. See K. Baedeker, *Great Britain* (Leizig and London, 1887), p. 246 (3rd edn (1894), pp. 244–5; 4th edn (1897), p. 248).

Rawnsley was vicar of Crosthwaite, near Keswick, where he and his wife set up a school of industrial art. Collingwood was a water-colour artist, antiquary and writer, author of guidebooks, historical studies and novels; he was also one of the first biographers of John Ruskin, for whom he worked as a kind of secretary in the 1880s and 1890s. Both men were keenly appreciative of the Lake District land-scape and actively involved in footpath and landscape preservation activities; Rawnsley, whose activities in this area we have already dis-cussed, was one of the founder members of the LDDS and the National Trust. Both, too, were men of letters whose writing drew heavily on the Lake District. Rawnsley wrote a series of books, aimed at a middle-class market, with titles such as *Round the Lake country*, *A coach-drive at the Lakes* and *Life and nature at the English Lakes*. The sheer number of these volumes, which were quite similar in their content, was testi-mony to the public appetite for writing of this kind: they sold well, with a number going into multiple editions.[157] As for Collingwood, aside from a plethora of essays on Lake District antiquities, he published a successful guidebook, *The Lake counties* (1902), as well as two novels set in medieval Lakeland.[158]

For both men, the historical associations of the Lake District landscape were vital to its cultural value. Collingwood made this clear at the beginning of his guidebook, when he cited an experience Ruskin had had in a pine forest in the Jura, where the great man 'tried to imagine that this was in some new continent, uninhabited and with-out history, without any romantic associations' – and when he did the place lost all its appeal, 'a sudden blankness and chill' being cast over it. Ruskin's reaction, Collingwood explained, showed that 'story alone and scenery alone may interest specialists, but the thing that … charms us, and carries us out of ourselves, is the union of story and scenery'.

[157] H. D. Rawnsley, *Round the Lake country* (Glasgow, 1909); *Lake country sketches* (Glasgow, 1903); *Literary associations of the English Lakes*, 3rd edn, 2 vols. (Glasgow, 1906); *By fell and dale at the English Lakes* (Glasgow, 1911); *Chapters at the English Lakes* (Glasgow, 1913); *Life and nature at the English Lakes*, 2nd edn (Glasgow, 1902); *A coach-drive at the Lakes*, 3rd edn (Keswick, 1902); *Ruskin and the English Lakes*, 2nd edn (Glasgow, 1901); *Months at the Lakes* (Glasgow, 1906); *A rambler's note-book at the English Lakes* (Glasgow, 1902); *Past and present at the English Lakes* (Glasgow, 1916).
[158] Collingwood, *The lake counties*; W. G. Collingwood, *Thorstein of the mere: A saga of the northmen in Lakeland*, 2nd edn (London, 1909 [1895]); W. G. Collingwood, *The bondwoman: A story of the northmen in Lakeland* (London, 1896).

And in this, he thought, the Lake District was 'wonderfully rich'.[159] Indeed, it explained the popular appeal of the place, the scenery of which was 'all very tiny' and might otherwise appear unimpressive compared to that of the much grander European Alps. Yet,

> on the cloud-swept moor the cairn-dwellers come out, clad in skins of wolf and bear; or by the lake shore at twilight the ashes of the ancient furnace flame up, and the men from the hall ride past with hawk and hound. The scene is so peopled, what does it matter how large the canvas is – so rich in detail and variety, why trouble about the smallness of the picture-frame?[160]

Throughout the text that followed these preliminary observations, Collingwood drew attention to the historical associations of the Lake District landscape, inviting tourists to re-create the past through active, imaginative engagement with what they saw before their eyes. Thus, writing of the Roman camp at Ambleside, he advised the visitor to 'Ask for the football field, and you can trace the square ramparts plainly in the grass, and people it once again with the legionaries and their white-limbed British wives.'[161] It was a similar story for Rawnsley, whose writing repeatedly harped not simply on the visual qualities of landscape, but also on the history it embodied. This was as much a history of common people as it was of notables. It was also an ancient history, stretching back to the Neolithic 'Brigantes' who Rawnsley imagined had lived in his own vale of Keswick 5,000 years ago.[162] His views on the Gowbarrow estate are instructive here. For Rawnsley as for others, Gowbarrow was valued for its associations with Wordsworth, and specifically the daffodils the poet had seen while strolling along the shore of Ullswater with his sister Dorothy in 1802, an experience that had inspired perhaps his most celebrated poem.[163]

[159] Collingwood, *The lake counties*, pp. 3–4.
[160] *Ibid.*, p. 5.
[161] *Ibid.*, p. 35. See also Collingwood's speech launching the National Trust's successful fundraising campaign to purchase the site, the visiting of which brought 'us into touch with real people – so unlike ourselves and yet so like', who 'knew the look of the sunshine on Windermere and the rocks on Loughrigg just as we do. They were at home here, like us': *Lakes Herald*, 7 June 1912, [p. 5].
[162] Rawnsley, *By fell and dale*, pp. 1–5.
[163] Rawnsley, *Literary associations*, Vol. II, pp. 58–61; National Trust, *Scheme for the purchase of Gowbarrow Fell and Aira Force on Ullswater … some press comments* [1904], National Trust Archives.

But as Rawnsley noted a few years after the Trust had acquired the estate, it had a still more general historical appeal. For all that it was unmarked by the extant works of man (Lyulph's Tower excepted), the place was deeply evocative of the past. In his *Round the Lake country* (1909), Rawnsley described the view from Gowbarrow Fell as 'not only entrancingly beautiful, but ... full of history' spanning many centuries:

> Ullswater, the water of Ulph the Viking, was long before Viking days much beloved of Neolithic man; and on Barton Fell the traces of the encampments and hut-circles of the 'round-headed' race, who knew the use of bronze, and who succeeded the little, 'long-headed' race, who only knew the use of stone, are still in evidence ... Nor is the scene without some associations with Arthurian legend. Arthur's Pike or Peak rises up against the sky-line on Swarth Fell, while the Tristermont below, in Barton Park, nearer the Lake, is said to have taken its name from Sir Tristram, one of the knights of King Arthur's Table Round.[164]

Moreover, Rawnsley went on, the scene also brought to mind the Romans, who had built a road up on High Street, the mountain prominent to the east; and Christian history was evoked by the site of the thirteenth-century settlement of Benedictine Monks near Pooley Bridge. Even the animals that could be seen in the landscape were suggestive of earlier times: 'Above us the red deer stand in outline against the sky; below us, as we gaze, the fallow deer glance through the fern, and we are reminded how this vale was once part of the great Inglewood Forest, where Robin Hood and his merry men found hiding and wild-wood sport.'[165]

For Collingwood and for Rawnsley, the past immanent in the Lake District did not simply offer a collection of various historical associations; it was storied – in its features a coherent, continuous, narrative could be read. Writing of the view from Muncaster Fell in the western Lakes, Rawnsley described how

> a man may dream of all the historic pageant of the past that has gone to make our Cumberland. The Britons holding their 'strengths' of earth upon the shoulders of the inland fells; the Roman marching

[164] Rawnsley, *Round the Lake country*, pp. 101–5 (pp. 101–2, 105).
[165] *Ibid.*

along the sea-coast northward, or building their camp at Hardknot; the Christian missionaries landing with St. Bega at Tomlin Head; the Vikings filling the waterpool below with their beaked ships, or gathering for worship in the far hamlet of Gosforth; the monks of Calder building their Abbey in the woodland further north, the baron of mediæval time rearing his fortress hard by round the ancient tower which the Romans may have founded; the fishermen of Queen Elizabeth's time following the bends of the Irt and Mite and Esk and fishing the shallows for pearl-bearing oysters; the stranding of some Armada wreckage on the shore … – all these are pictures that may rise to the mind's eye, as one gazes.[166]

In this perspective, the Lake District landscape provided evidence of the interrelationship of Cumbrian and English history, the local, regional and national past overlapping and combining. Indeed, it showed how Cumbria had participated in the great events of the national past over centuries, from the Roman invasion to the defeat of the Spanish Armada and beyond. This helped bolster local patriotism, but it also presented the wider public with an additional reason to value the Lakeland land-scape as national heritage, and thus as 'national property'.

That said, some elements of this storied past were given more attention than others. Much was made of the contribution of the Vikings in particular. This focus on the Vikings was novel, and can be connected to a wider fascination with all things Norse in the later Victorian period.[167] Earlier in the nineteenth century, Thomas De Quincey, Robert Southey and Samuel Taylor Coleridge had taken some interest in the Norse influence on the Lake District. De Quincey claimed in 1819–20 that he had made the 'discovery' that 'the dia-lect spoken in Westmorland and Cumberland … is borrowed wholly from the Danish'.[168] But little notice was taken of these early pioneers (Wordsworth brusquely rejected De Quincey's offer of an essay on the subject to form part of the 1820 edition of his *Guide*),[169] and it was only in 1856 that the major breakthrough was made, with the

---

[166] Rawnsley, *Months at the Lakes*, p. 200.
[167] For this, see A. Wawn, *The Vikings and the Victorians: Inventing the old north in nineteenth-century Britain* (Cambridge, 2002).
[168] B. Symonds (ed.), *The works of Thomas De Quincey*, Vol. 1: *Writings, 1799–1820* (London, 2000), p. 294.
[169] *Ibid.*, p. 293.

publication of Robert Ferguson's *The northmen in Cumberland and Westmoreland*. Ferguson's book was extensively reviewed, and made a real impact – so much so, indeed, that as early as 1860 some protested that theories respecting Scandinavian influence had been 'carried very much too far'.[170] Drawing on Danish scholarship, Ferguson argued that it was Vikings from Norway, not Denmark, who had arrived in the Lake District, and presented much philological evidence in support of this contention – not least in relation to local place- and family names, many of which were of Norwegian origin.[171] And while later research exposed many shortcomings in the detail of Ferguson's work, his overall contribution had a lasting influence.

A distinctive feature of Ferguson's argument was his claim that the Viking invasions had had a *beneficial* impact, not only on Lakeland, but also on the nation as a whole. This challenged the hitherto dominant negative interpretation of the Vikings as destructive marauders. As Ferguson explained it, while the Vikings certainly raided and plundered, their eventual settlement in places such as Cumberland did much to strengthen England by infusing a vigorous spirit into its people, and the national character was the gainer:

> The fiery enterprise, the stern independence of those wild sea-rovers, were a necessary element in the greatness of England. Twice the languid Anglo-Saxon energy was stirred by the cross of Northern Blood; and, if the later [Norman] conquest was more imposing, it was not more important, than the slow and hard-fought footing gained by the more purely Scandinavian tribes … the dauntless seamanship of Britain … may be due, in no small measure, to the daring spirit of the old sea-rovers … our greatest admiral bears a Scandinavian surname … And the names, too, of Blake and Rodney are to be found in the Blaka and Hrodney of the Scandinavian vikings.[172]

This idea that the greatness of England owed much to the Vikings who came to the Lakes was seized upon in reviews of Ferguson's book, chiming with contemporaneous challenges to the Victorian cult

---

[170] W. Whellan, *The history and topography of the counties of Cumberland and Westmoreland* (Pontefract, 1860), p. 9.

[171] R. Ferguson, *The northmen in Cumberland and Westmoreland* (London, 1856).

[172] *Ibid.*, pp. 2–3; also pp. 144ff.

of racial Anglo-Saxonism.[173] These challenges grew stronger towards century's end, with new readings of history integrating not only the Normans, but also their Viking predecessors, into the *telos* of English progress towards present-day pre-eminence. One muscular expression of this was Frederick Metcalfe's *The Englishman and the Scandinavian* (1884), a compendious study of old English and Norse literature. In it Metcalfe presented ninth- and tenth-century England as in thrall to enervating Roman Catholicism, its people – having had 'all the spirit of manliness and of free intellectual play priest-ridden out of them' – being unable to cope with the vigorous Vikings, who 'transfus[ed] new blood into the body social and political, administering a tonic to a frame massive and strong, but lethargic and deficient in vital energy, thus leavening the torpid elements of the Saxon nature, and making a mark on the land never to be effaced'.[174]

Following Ferguson's cue, much commentary emphasised the martial and adventurous spirit of the Vikings, and how this spirit had laid the foundations of future naval greatness in particular. Metcalfe claimed that it was from the Norsemen, who 'were all agog for foreign travel', that 'our Frobishers and Drakes, our Percys and Franklins, and Rajah Brookes, are lineally descended'.[175] Around the turn of the twentieth century, however, arguments about the Norse impact took a new direction. The Viking invasions were still felt to have had lasting national benefits, but these benefits were now less associated with maritime derring-do or stern warlike virtues, and more with qualities peaceable and pastoral in nature. The catalyst for this shift in opinion was the deepening interest in the Norse heritage of the Lake District landscape. Ferguson's research was followed up by more detailed antiquarian and archaeological work on the ground, not least by members of the Cumberland and Westmorland Antiquarian and Archaeological Society. This work was supported by – and its conclusions reflected in – topographical volumes, tourist guidebooks, and articles in newspapers and periodicals. Even the rock climbers increasingly drawn to the Lake District showed interest in the Vikings. The publications of their societies carried essays on Norse antiquities and place-names, the interest

[173] See, e.g., 'The northmen in the Lake District', *New Monthly Magazine*, 108 (October 1856), 165.
[174] F. Metcalfe, *The Englishman and the Scandinavian; or, A comparison of Anglo-Saxon and Old Norse literature* (London, 1884), pp. 189–90, 193.
[175] *Ibid.*, p. 193.

of which, the prominent Lakeland mountaineer W. P. Haskett-Smith told readers of the *Climbers' Club Journal* in 1903, was something that 'appeal[ed] with special force' to those that ascended the heights.[176] This appeal was sufficient, indeed, for the same journal to publish two articles by Haskett-Smith in 1905–6 that were very largely devoted to the etymology of the word 'thwaite'.[177]

As Haskett-Smith noted in the second of these articles, 'Most of the commonest Scandinavian names' in the Lake District 'are to be found as prefixes to our word', which was originally used to mean a clearing for agricultural purposes.[178] This was a telling observation, reflecting a shift away from an understanding of the Vikings as warriors and adventurers, and towards an emphasis on their influence on the landscape of the Lakes, once they had settled there, as farmers. In this perspective they became the precursors of the modern-day dalesmen, their 'Viking' attributes of independence and hardiness being put to the purposes of agriculture, not rapine, and so creating a sturdily self-sufficient class of smallholders.

The wide currency of this new view of the Vikings owed a great deal to W. G. Collingwood. Collingwood was a leading member of the Norwegian Club and the Viking Club, serving as president of the latter; he contributed papers on Norse heritage to the journals of these societies, as well as other periodicals – not least the *Transactions of the Cumberland and Westmorland Antiquarian and Archaeological Society*, which he edited between 1900 and 1920. His careful empirical research led him to conclude that the Norse settlers in the Lakes should be seen not so much as raiders, but as agriculturalists whose lasting legacy was the peaceable society of the dales. Collingwood argued that Lakeland place-names provided convincing evidence of the past existence of Viking saeters, or summer farms: 'Summerhills, satters and

---

[176] W. P. Haskett-Smith, 'Wastdale Head 600 years ago', *Climbers' Club Journal*, 5 (1903), 3–15 (p. 3).

[177] W. P. Haskett-Smith, 'Lake Country place names', *Climbers' Club Journal*, 8 (1905), 18–20; 8 (1906), 78–88. Some climbers deliberately alluded to the Viking past of the Lake District in giving names to the routes they pioneered. Having made the first ascent of a gully on Haystacks, for example, the Manchester climber L. J. Oppenheimer remembered how, in discussion with his partners on the ascent, he had decided to 'recall the old Norse name – "High Stacken, the high cliffs" and so lighted on "Stack Gill" as the name': L. J. Oppenheimer, *The heart of Lakeland* (London, 1908), p. 58.

[178] Haskett-Smith, 'Lake Country place names', p. 80.

16 Frontispiece to W. G. Collingwood, *Thorstein of the Mere* (London, 1895). Reproduced by kind permission of the Syndics of Cambridge University Library: Misc.5.89.49.

seats, sels and sails, are common in the district, and show how pastoral was the life of the Vikings when once they had settled the dales of the lake Counties.'[179] And this was confirmed by archaeological research, which had uncovered remains that, as Collingwood pointed out, 'are not military, but pastoral – old farmsteads and saeters; and all we can gather of the Viking settlement points to this form of habitation, rather than defensible camps and castles, as the usual dwelling place'.[180]

Collingwood's scholarship fed into his other writings. His novel *Thorstein of the Mere* (1895), which developed out of his meticulous mapping of Norse settlements in Lakeland,[181] recounted how the

[179] *Saga-Book of the Viking Club*, 3 (1901), 143; also W. G. Collingwood, 'The Vikings in Lakeland: Their place-names, remains and history', *Saga-Book of the Viking Club*, 1 (1892–6), 182–96.

[180] *Saga-Book of the Viking Club*, 3 (1901), 18.

[181] D. H. Johnson, 'W.G. Collingwood and the beginnings of the *Idea of History*', *Collingwood Studies*, 1 (1994), 2–6.

eponymous hero's family had come to Cumberland from the Isle of Man not so much as warriors, but as farmers and traders.[182]

In both this book, and his less successful novel *The Bondwoman*, the day-to-day rural life of the Viking settlers is described in detail. In the same vein, Collingwood's tourist guide of 1902 presented the Norsemen as 'farming colonists', who cleared the woods, set sheep to graze on the hillsides and established sturdily self-sufficient communities whose virtues lived on in contemporary Lake District society.[183] And in 1908, Collingwood made this claim an integral part of his contribution to *Scandinavian Britain*, a major historical work he co-authored with the late Regius Professor of History at Oxford, Frederick York Powell. 'The Norse settlers did not come as conquerors', he wrote, 'but as immigrants seeking a livelihood'.[184]

The case made by Collingwood was further disseminated by others. Rawnsley's Lake District writings were suffused with regard for the Viking past, which he saw as being indelibly inscribed in the landscape – its 'ghylls and hawes and thwaites and dodds and kelds and forces' – and closely associated with a pastoral way of life.[185] For Rawnsley as for Collingwood, the Norse influence in the Lakes persisted over centuries down to the present, the dalesmen retaining Viking traits of independence and hardiness despite Saxon and Norman invasions, feudalism and other vicissitudes: 'the Vikings who settled here remained as the shepherds and farmers of the country all through these centuries of trouble and disturbance, and they are with us at this day'.[186] Even the Herdwick sheep that were such a feature of the Lake District landscape were of Norse origin, Rawnsley claimed. Co-founder of the Herdwick Sheep Association (1899), Rawnsley encouraged Beatrix Potter, among others, to farm the animals, and did much to popularise the idea that the breed – 'as hardy as the hardy Norseman himself' – had come over to England on the Viking

---

[182] Collingwood, *Thorstein*.

[183] Collingwood, *The lake counties*, esp. pp. 150–6.

[184] W. G. Collingwood and F. York Powell, *Scandinavian Britain* (London, 1908), p. 211. Collingwood was responsible for writing all but the first 35 pages of this 272-page book.

[185] Rawnsley, *By fell and dale*, pp. 9–11; also, for example, Rawnsley, *Round the Lake country*, *passim*.

[186] Rawnsley, *Chapters at the English Lakes*, p. 137; also Rawnsley, *A rambler's notebook*, pp. 205ff.

ships.[187] Their continuing presence in the Lakes was yet more evidence of the pastoral character of the Norse legacy in the landscape.

This reading of the Lakeland landscape made much of the character traits of the Viking settlers, but it was not founded on any crude biological assumptions about race, racial purity or racial superiority. As D. A. Lorimer has observed, 'the Victorians themselves were often uncertain about what meaning they assigned to "Race"'; their claims about the concept were 'fluid and contradictory', race often being conflated with culture.[188] Thus, to the Victorians, in the words of Peter Mandler, 'a "race" could be a physical stock, it could be something like a "tribe" or a "clan", or it could be both at once'.[189] Sometimes, and especially in imperial contexts, the term was used in a (pseudo-)scientific sense, associated with allegedly inherent physical characteristics; at other times it was deployed as a synonym for nations, ethnicities and peoples. It was in this latter sense that late-nineteenth- and early-twentieth-century Norse enthusiasts used the term. Collingwood and Rawnsley identified the persistence of a Norse ethnic heritage in the Lake District, but biological theories of racial contrasts and hierarchies were largely absent from their thought – for all that they believed in the superiority of British 'civilisation'.[190] For them, the point was not that the Norsemen were inherently superior to the native British; it was rather that their settlement in the Lake District (and elsewhere) had strengthened the

[187] Rawnsley, *By fell and dale*, pp. 10–11; 'A crack about Herdwick sheep', in *ibid.*, pp. 47–72; L. Lear, *Beatrix Potter* (London, 2007), p. 141. It did not escape notice that even the words used in connection with Lakeland sheep farming were of Norse origin: '*Gimmer* or *gymmer lamb* means the very same thing in this country and in Norway, and the *outrakes*, or sheep drives, to be found in almost every valley amongst our Lakeland mountains, have their counterpart in Scandinavia, and are from a well-known Norse word signifying to drive; while *Rake*, formerly a very common name for a sheep dog, is, as derived from that verb, literally, "The Driver"' (T. Ellwood, 'The mountain sheep', *North Counties Magazine*, 2 (1901), 256–7).

[188] D. A. Lorimer, 'Race, science and culture: Historical continuities and discontinuities, 1850–1914', in S. West (ed.), *The Victorians and race* (Aldershot, 1996), pp. 14, 16, 19.

[189] P. Mandler, *The English national character: The history of an idea from Edmund Burke to Tony Blair* (New Haven and London, 2006), p. 73.

[190] M. Townend, *The Vikings and Victorian Lakeland: The Norse medievalism of W. G. Collingwood and his contemporaries* ([Kendal], 2009); C. Parker, 'W. G. Collingwood's Lake District', *Northern History*, 38 (2001), 295–313. For the prevalence of non-biological 'civilisational' views of national differentiation in Victorian Britain, see Mandler, *English national character*, pp. 72–86.

national character by facilitating ethnic intermixing. Collingwood was especially clear that ethnic heterogeneity was a source of strength, both at a collective and at an individual level. Indeed, in accordance with this view that 'the exponent of a national ideal is rarely pure-bred', his biography of Ruskin went so far as to present his subject's greatness as being a consequence of mixed ancestry ('Celtic fire was fed with some west-country piety and tempered with an infusion of coolness from a sailor of the North Sea').[191] As for the Vikings, their arrival in the Lake District had resulted in a felicitous 'commixture of races', Celts, Norsemen, Welsh, Saxons and Angles blending together to local and national benefit.[192] *Thorstein of the Mere* gave powerful expression to this perspective in telling the story of the love and eventual union of Thorstein the Viking and Raineach, a young Celtic woman.[193] But Collingwood also celebrated ethnic hybridity through his more formal Lakeland researches. His philological studies suggested that there was 'a strong Gaelic infusion in the Lakeland Vikings', the linguistic compounds evident in many place-names indicating that the settlers were, in fact, of 'Irish-Norse' ancestry.[194] Moreover, not only were the Norse immigrants of mixed ethnicity, their arrival had not led to the displacement of native peoples. 'Cymric survivals' in the names of landscape features, such as 'Blen', 'Caer' and 'Pen', proved to Collingwood, as he put it in *Scandinavian Britain*, that 'the Welsh of Cumberland, as well as the Angles already settled there, lived side by side with the Norse immigrants'.[195] Still further evidence of this ethnic heterogeneity was provided by the impressive 14-foot-high stone cross in the graveyard of St Mary's Church in the village of Gosforth, on the western edge of the Lakes. Of tenth-century origin, the cross was especially important to Collingwood and his fellow Viking enthusiasts. For alongside depictions of the Crucifixion, and other Christian symbols, the cross bore carvings of scenes from the Poetic Edda of Norse mythology. This syncretism demonstrated the welcome ethnic commingling that followed the Vikings' arrival: the art on the cross was no confused melange of

[191] W. G. Collingwood, *The life and work of John Ruskin* (London, 1893), pp. 3–7.
[192] Townend, *The Vikings*, p. 196.
[193] Collingwood, *Thorstein*.
[194] Collingwood, 'Vikings in Lakeland', 182–96 (pp. 185, 195–6).
[195] Collingwood and York Powell, *Scandinavian Britain*, p. 216.

ideas; rather it, and the Edda it depicted, reflected 'the thought of the mixed race in its nascent energy'.[196]

Thus was the Norse heritage evident in place-names, archaeology and artefacts put to the use of a discourse that celebrated ethnic intermixture as a source of strength. At one level, this supported a sense of regional identity, the particular historical experience of the Lake District augmenting its distinctive specialness. Such pride in place is certainly evident in the writings of Collingwood and Rawnsley, with both men feeling a deep sense of attachment to their native fells and dales.[197] But it also fed into a wider discourse of Englishness, one that – as in the case of Northumberland – emphasised the importance of northern cultural landscapes to constructions of national identity. The historic greatness of England had its roots not only in the sleepy fields and villages of the home counties, or for that matter the bustling metropolis of London and the industrial powerhouse of Manchester (for all that both places were important in this respect, as we shall see); it was also to be found in the mountains of the Lake District, whose settlement by energetic Vikings had made a signal contribution to the English character. Furthermore, the history inscribed in the landscape of the Lakes, and particularly that associated with the Norsemen, demonstrated the centrality of ethnic heterogeneity to English greatness. It provided an object lesson in the virtues of racial intermixing for a culture that – at least insofar as this intermixing applied to an insular British context – was less wedded to biological ideas of racial purity than might be assumed.

The late nineteenth and early twentieth centuries saw the Lake District develop into a cultural landscape of special power and significance. Now seen as storied as well as beautiful, and a place in which all English people

---

[196] W. G. Collingwood, 'The Gosforth Cross', *Northern Counties Magazine*, 2 (1901), 313–21. See also W. S. Calverley, *Notes on the early sculptured crosses, shrines and monuments in the present diocese of Carlisle*, ed. W. G. Collingwood (Kendal, 1899), pp. 139–67.

[197] After Collingwood's death, his son, R. G. Collingwood, told the author of one of his father's obituaries that 'He never felt at home when away from them [the hills of the Lake District] … it was really literally true that, during the later part of his life, he could never be happy out of sight of mountains. Their absence was a kind of starvation to him, so that there could never be any question of his living anywhere except where he could see them daily': 'In memoriam: William Gershom Collingwood', *Alpine Journal*, 45 (1933), 150.

had a stake, it was the key locus of activity of the emerging preservation-ist movement, and it was valued as national heritage as never before. In one line of interpretation, these developments are evidence of a wider cul-tural conservatism, of a reaction against the modern spirit: English men and women turned to places such as the Lakes in revulsion from the con-tinually advancing pace of urbanisation and industrialisation. Thus the new value placed on Lakeland – and in particular the desire to preserve it from despoliation – can be seen as a function of a more general and distinctively British rejection of modernity.[198]

Conservative and reactionary sentiments were not absent from late Victorian and Edwardian commentary on the Lake District, or from the language of its defenders. Ruskin's interventions in the rail-way controversies of the 1870s and 1880s are often cited as providing a case in point. In a letter to the *Pall Mall Gazette* around the time of the Ambleside Railway Bill, for example, Ruskin inveighed against railways as 'to me the loathsomest form of devilry now extant, ani-mated and deliberate earthquakes, destructive of all wise social habit or possible natural beauty, carriages of damned souls on the ridges of their own graves'.[199] But these intemperate outbursts of a man whose mental health was disastrously poor by this time should not be taken as representative: the views Ruskin was expressing by the later 1870s and 1880s – in *Fors clavigera* for instance – were widely regarded as heterodox and extreme.[200] His earlier work, and indeed arguably his thought in general, should not be seen as espousing blanket resistance to modernity. As Collingwood's son, the noted historian and philos-opher R.G. Collingwood, was later to point out, while Ruskin saw much to admire in the civilisation of past societies, and particularly those of medieval times, 'He never for a moment wished to reinstate the Middle Ages, or to copy their characteristic features'; his point, rather, was that the present could learn much from the past, and take inspiration from its best elements.[201] It is in this vein that Ruskin's

[198] Wiener, *English Culture.*
[199] J. Ruskin, 'Arrows of the Chace', in *Library edition of the works of John Ruskin*, ed. E. T. Cook and A. Wedderburn, 39 vols. (London, 1903–12), Vol. XXXIV, p. 604.
[200] J. Batchelor, *John Ruskin: No wealth but life* (London, 2000), pp. 257, 260–2. Ruskin suffered the first of a series of debilitating mental breakdowns in 1878, and the remaining twenty-two years of his life were blighted by long periods of insanity.
[201] R. G. Collingwood, 'Ruskin's philosophy [1919]', in R. G. Collingwood, *Essays in the philosophy of art* (Bloomington, IA, 1966), pp. 3–41 (pp. 20–1). Cf.

work had had a profound impact on the views and work of many, not least Rawnsley and the elder Collingwood – both of whom had participated in Ruskin's Hinksey Road scheme while undergraduates at Oxford. H. D. and Edith Rawnsley's Keswick School of Industrial Arts owed much to Ruskin's ideas about the value of individual craftsmanship, as set out in his famous essay on the 'Nature of Gothic' (1853), for example.[202] And insofar as Ruskin's writings, published before his descent into madness, had influenced attitudes to landscape, they had more been in the direction of promoting the idea that the preservation of 'wild' nature – such as that of the Lakes – as a lived-in, inherited environment, was of vital social value, not least because exposure to this nature was of educative benefit to all in the here-and-now.[203] This, at any rate, was certainly the moral drawn by Rawnsley and his fellow supporters of preservation.

Indeed, the language and activities of Lakeland preservationists cannot accurately be described as running counter to the currents of modernity; in fact, speaking generally, they ran in the same direction. There was no automatic hostility to all schemes of development; what was objected to – as Wordsworth had put it – was 'rash' or unnecessary assault. As the writer of guidebooks that gave notably supportive attention to Lake District preservation, M. J. B. Baddeley defined the problem not as industrial or commercial activities per se, but their '*inconsiderate* extension'.[204] As we have seen, such a perspective informed opposition to railway schemes seemingly destined to benefit sectional interests, whether those of local businessmen or

J. Ruskin, *The two paths: Being lectures on art, and its application to decoration and manufacture, delivered in 1858–9* (London, 1859), lecture III, esp. pp. 125–7 ('We don't want either the life or the decorations of the thirteenth century back again' (p. 127)); and *ibid.*, lecture II, p. 56 ('If you glance over the map of Europe, you will find that where the manufactures are strongest, there art also is strongest').

[202] J. Brunton, *The arts and crafts movement in the Lake District* (Lancaster, 2001), esp. pp. 2–5, 89–90, 94–5.

[203] For Ruskin's view that the past and its landscape ought to be preserved, not as relics or 'curated artefacts' but as aids to the present and future, see G. Chitty, '"A great entail": The historic environment', in Wheeler, *Ruskin and the environment*, pp. 102–22, esp. pp. 119–21.

[204] Even quarries were acceptable in some circumstances, Baddeley felt, having 'an advantage over mines in so far that they only blur and blotch the surface of the ground to the extent of their own area, and when they are exhausted, time quickly repairs the harm done by them': Baddeley, *Thorough guide*, pp. xvii–xviii.

speculative investors, rather than the national good.[205] It also explains why many supporters of preservation could accept even major interventions in the landscape, where such interventions were seen as essential for the public good. Thirlmere was a case in point. Rawnsley for one accepted that Manchester needed a better supply of pure water, and having fought hard to limit the environmental impact of the reservoir, he officiated with a prayer at its opening.[206] Others were more positive about the appearance of the remodelled lake. In his *Highways and byways in the Lake District* (1901), the antiquarian A. G. Bradley did not think the locale had suffered much at the hands of the Manchester Corporation, venturing to suggest that the raising of the lake by means of the dam was 'perhaps … an improvement'.[207] Writing four years later, W. T. Palmer – a writer strongly supportive of National Trust activities in the Lakes – felt Thirlmere was still 'a place of beauty'. The stands of larch that the Corporation had planted around the reservoir offered 'romantic irregularity'; the new road along the lakeshore was 'cunningly' disguised from view, offering those who travelled it 'a beautifully engineered way through the mountains, giving entrancing glimpses up narrow ghylls'.[208] Baddeley was similarly enthusiastic. Although an LDDS member, he had never opposed the Thirlmere scheme, and the various editions of his popular guidebooks praised the final result. He agreed with Palmer about the new road, thinking it 'affords one of the most beautiful drives or walks in the District', and felt Thirlmere as a whole remained 'a noble sheet of water, but little impaired in appearance by its conversion' into a reservoir – something for which Manchester deserved to be 'heartily congratulated'. Even the straining well of the waterworks came in for admiration as 'a grand piece of engineering work'.[209]

Not all Lake District defenders went as far as Baddeley, but similar attitudes can be discerned even in the strongest of them. In their

[205] Baddeley was among the active opponents of such schemes: see, e.g., his letter to the *Standard*, February 1883, Cumbria Record Office, DSO/24/7.
[206] Ritvo, *Dawn of green*, pp. 138–41.
[207] A. G. Bradley, *Highways and byways in the Lake District* (London, 1919 [1901]), p. 244.
[208] W. T. Palmer, *The English Lakes* (London, 1905), p. 166. For Palmer's support of the Trust, see pp. 185ff.
[209] Baddeley, *Thorough guide*, 7th edn (London, 1895), p. 57; and 11th edn (London, 1909), pp. 58, 61, 62.

guidebooks, Collingwood and Jenkinson, to take two examples, were by no means disparaging of industrial modernity per se. Jenkinson's *Practical guides* recommended visits to lead mines near Borrowdale and Ullswater, as well as the pencil factory and museum at Keswick.[210] Collingwood's *Lake counties* looked forward to the time when 'the lake district water-power should be exploited' for electricity-generating purposes, so that the now down-at-heel towns of the Cumberland coast – places such as Whitehaven, which had been important as sites of engineering innovation – 'might have another chance' to achieve some better degree of prosperity.[211] And if as an LDDS executive committee member he certainly opposed the proposal to run a railway up to the slate quarries on Honister Crag, on account of the damage that would be done to the landscape through which the line would have passed, he did not deplore the quarries themselves. Given that the works produced 'the best of all roofing in England', their environmental impact on the fell was sufficiently slight to be acceptable; 1,000 feet up, they 'hardly detract[ed] from its impression as a mountain'. Moreover, Collingwood recommended the quarries as a tourist attraction productive of something like romantic wonder in the mind of the visitor, who from the vantage point on Honister Pass could see 'men – such little creatures they look … attack so stern a giant's castle and win its treasures, and slide down the beanstalk and away'.[212]

Such views were symptomatic of an accommodative attitude to industrial modernity, one typical of the preservation movement generally. Its leading lights at a national level – such as Bryce, Hill and Hunter – were no overly sentimental exponents of a pre-industrial 'simple life'; they accepted the progressive orientation of the British economy towards manufacture and commerce, and away from agriculture.[213] Landscape, as Hunter put it, 'might well be preserved without prejudice to the utilitarian concerns of to-day'.[214] This implied a posture of compromise and pragmatism, not doctrinaire resistance, and it was much in evidence in preservationist discourse on the Lakes, just

---

[210] Jenkinson, *Jenkinson's practical guide*, 9th edn (1893), p. 61.

[211] Collingwood, *The lake counties*, pp. 104–5.

[212] *Ibid.*, p. 112.

[213] Readman, 'Preserving'; Readman, 'Octavia Hill'; R. Hunter, 'The re-flow from town to country', *Nineteenth Century*, 56 (December 1904), 1023–32.

[214] Hunter, *Preservation*, p. 10.

as it was elsewhere. Thus, in mounting strenuous opposition to the Ambleside railway, the *Manchester Guardian* emphasised the unnecessary disfigurement the line would cause: as the railway was not really required, it was a case of 'rash assault' and therefore inadmissible. But the paper was also clear that where a significant public benefit could be demonstrated, 'the picturesque had to go to the wall' – as had been the case with other railway schemes.[215] It was in this spirit that the LDDS offered no opposition to plans for a branch railway from a village south of Penrith to the north end of Ullswater: such a line, the society felt, would improve public access to the northern Lakes without doing unacceptable scenic damage.[216] Similarly, in 1912 the National Trust was willing to admit the need for road widening in the Lake District, even on lands bordering its own property, and even involving the use of land it owned: it was not so much a question of blocking such developments as limiting any negative effects they might have.[217]

In making their pragmatic case, preservationists occasionally deployed commercial arguments. Opponents of the Braithwaite and Buttermere and Ennerdale railway schemes of 1883–4 emphasised that as 'beauty has a market value' the proposals were objectionable 'simply from the utilitarian and money point of view'.[218] Because, they claimed, the tourist trade could suffer as a result, and also – perhaps more plausibly – because the railways were speculative ventures of doubtful economic value (geologists and mineral experts thought them financially unviable), the proposals were as much 'commercial blunder' as aesthetic outrage.[219] Similar points were found in tourist guides, which cautioned against the wholesale sacrifice of Lakeland to 'enterprises which at the best only promise temporary gain': damaging the scenery that drew people to Lakeland in the first place would only kill 'the

---

[215] *Manchester Guardian*, 16 March 1887, p. 5.
[216] Letters of M. J. B. Baddeley and W. Little to W. H. Hills, 10 February 1884 and 1 June 1885, Cumbria Record Office, DSO/24/5/6. In the event, the line did not materialise.
[217] In this case the National Trust proposed that decisions as to the removal of any trees from a group of celebrated birches on Trust land should be made by an independent arbitrator: *Lakes Herald*, 24 May 1912, [p. 5].
[218] *Newcastle Daily Journal*, 13 March 1883, cutting, Cumbria Record Office, DSO/24/7/1.
[219] *Standard*, February 1883, Cumbria Record Office, DSO/24/7; Bryce: *Hansard*, 3rd series, 284 (21 February 1884), 1552; pamphlet [by Gordon Wordsworth] on the LDDS (1884), pp. 5–6, Cumbria Record Office, DSO/24/9/1.

goose that lays the golden egg for the hotel-keeper, the lodging-house keeper, and the farmer who has the food products to sell'.[220]

However, while such points showed sensitivity to bread-and-butter concerns, helping to counter accusations of head-in-the-clouds 'sentimentality', the utilitarian element of the preservationist argument had a still more important dimension. In objecting not so much to the 'industrial spirit', but to the 'purely industrial spirit' – that which threatened reckless and unnecessary damage to the remaining 'beauty-spots of our land' – preservationists were also affirming that such places were of practical value in the here-and-now.[221] The Lake District became a key site for the articulation of a new idea of amenity, predicated on the conviction that – as one newspaper put it vis-à-vis the Ambleside Bill – 'Man does not live by bread alone, and the utmost development of our manufactures would fail to protect our English life from impoverishment and failure, if there were no reservoirs of natural beauty and freshness remaining intact.'[222] In this perspective, the Lake District was a national resource, offering English men and women a vital means of reinvigorating themselves – and by extension the nation – through periodic contact with landscape rich in beauty and associational value. Such an amenity, moreover, was more necessary now than ever before, precisely because most people lived in towns and cities; as the *Manchester City News* put it, while there was once 'a time when it was right to cry speed to our infant industries when, spreading their arms over valley after valley … they might feed the unborn millions heralded by prosperity', those days were gone. The prerogatives of the present demanded that places such as the Lake District be preserved as a source not only of 'individual pleasure', but of 'elevating and humanizing ideas', and also of that 'natural vigour which goes so much to inspire and help inventive progress'.[223] Thus even Manchester opinion affirmed that the retention of the Lakes as a place of respite from what the LDDS termed 'the noise and bustle and dirt' of urban life was a matter of pressing 'national importance'.[224]

[220] Baddeley, *Thorough guide* (1880), pp. xvii–xviii; Jenkinson, *Jenkinson's practical guide*, 9th edn (1893), p. 16.

[221] 'LDDS sheet no. 7: The Ambleside Railway Bill', Cumbria Record Office, DSO/24/15/2; Rawnsley, 'The National Trust: Its work and needs', 190.

[222] *Newcastle Daily Leader*, 10 February 1887, p. 4.

[223] *Manchester City News*, 29 January 1887 (Cumbria Record Office, DSO/24/15/2).

[224] LDDS leaflet on Ennerdale Railway Bill 1884, Cumbria Record Office, DSO/24/15/3.

This implied not conservative revulsion from modernity, so much as a realistic appreciation of the needs of the modern-day English nation. That these needs included access to amenities such as the Lake District was in line with mainstream trends of thought. The 1889 edition of Baddeley's *Thorough guide* put this point across well:

> The desirability of reserving spaces for hygienic and recreative purposes is more and more recognized every year. In the Lake District the North of England has a ready-made park, of which Nature has been the architect, and which she has endowed with her choicest treasures. The 'practical' utilitarians who pooh-pooh the idea of mining and other speculations being objected to in the district and call the authors of these objections 'sentimentalists', should, if they have any regard for consistency, grow Jerusalem artichokes on their flower-beds at home and plough up their tennis-lawns for mangold-wurzels.[225]

This utilitarian understanding of the rationale for Lake District preservation was evident in the National Trust campaigns before 1914. It fused with the emphasis on access – the claim that Lakeland was 'national property' – to form a powerful and patriotic argument that addressed the felt needs of the present, of modernity itself. In making the case for the purchase of Gowbarrow Fell, for example, the Trust stressed its amenity value – the benefits it would give, in Hill's words, to the 'hard-worked professional man, smoke-grimed city dweller, workman and child' as well as, of course, the 'artist' and 'naturalist'.[226] The preservation of Gowbarrow, so the argument went, was a patriotic imperative on two related grounds: it would acknowledge the nation's stake in such places, and further, it would be of national benefit by providing the English people with what George Harwood, Liberal MP for Bolton, called 'that best of tonics, communion with the unspoiled beauties of nature'.[227] Speaking at a fundraising meeting in November 1905, Nigel Bond, Secretary of the Trust, gave a good summary of the case. There was 'only one Aira Glen and Aira Force and Gowbarrow Fell and Ullswater in the world', he told his audience, 'and if one

---

[225] Baddeley, *Thorough Guide*, 5th edn (1889), p. xvii.
[226] Hill, *Letters to fellow workers*, p. 526 (letter, 1904).
[227] *Manchester Guardian*, 24 June 1905, p. 6.

believed in the future need for the hard-worked townsmen of the north or south to spend a holiday on their own land and their own lake, and obtain the joy and inspiration for rest and future work that such a holiday could give, they could not as patriots make a much better investment for all time than in obtaining the possession of this 740 acres'.[228]

By the early twentieth century, the Lake District had indeed become 'a sort of national property'. But it was national not just in the sense of being valued for its beauty, distinctiveness or associations. It was also national because it was a place over which the whole people – not only the cultivated elite – were now understood to have a claim, and for which there now existed a strong groundswell of popular and patriotic affection. Collingwood caught this nicely in the introduction to his *Lake counties*, writing of how

> Just as Australians talk of England as home, so thousands of town-dwellers are Lake-folk at heart. They have every right to call the Lakes theirs, if affection and adoption count for anything. It needs no Act of Parliament or Land Nationalisation to make the district into a People's Park. That is what it is already – the garden of the towns. You will find, wherever you go in it, how little of the whole is forbidden ground; how rarely private ownership interferes. There have been footpath squabbles, and now and then a new landlord has tried to be selfish; but the tradition of the place is against exclusiveness … And in return for this welcome the public, far and wide, loves the Lake country as its own. When there is any fear that a corner of it is likely to be spoiled, high and low cry out. People of influence protest: they have spent happy summer there. Working men and women send their shillings: they have had glorious days on the heather and among the ferns.[229]

This understanding of the Lake District as national property would remain dominant throughout much of the twentieth century, informing future preservationist interventions. In 1951, of course, the Lake District did ultimately become a state-regulated National Park, but the rationale for this was not only the preservation of the landscape,

---

[228] *The Times*, 24 November 1905, p. 9.
[229] Collingwood, *The lake counties*, pp. 2–3.

but the preservation, also, of the nation's now well-established quasi-proprietorial interest in that landscape. The Lake District did not become a national landscape by becoming a National Park; it became a National Park because it was a national landscape. And its status as such a landscape lay in the largely nineteenth- and early-twentieth-century story told in this chapter, with the preservationist controversies of the 1880s being of special importance. Early enthusiasts – Gilpin, West, Gray and the like – established the cultural significance of the landscape, yet they presented its appeal in narrowly aesthetic terms: scenic appearance was paramount. In the course of the Victorian period, largely thanks to Wordsworth, there developed more environmental understandings of the Lake District, ones attentive to the past and present character of human interactions with its landscape. In connection with this, Lakeland came to be valued for its history and associations, those relating to the Vikings being especially notable. And this sensitivity to human interaction, over time, with the landscape, informed and gave strength to the developing preservation movement. Working in tandem with tourist discourse, this movement sought not to preserve Lakeland in aspic, as a last vestige of an unmodernised England. Rather, drawing strength from the increasingly democratic context of the times and also from new, patriotically inflected ideas about the public good, amenity and right living, it sought to preserve the distinctiveness of the Lake District as a cultural landscape offering particular, and tangible, benefits to the national community of the present day. By the Edwardian period, the case it presented had largely been won. Even very conservative organs of opinion were sympathetic. As the ultra-Tory *Quarterly Review* observed in a 1911 article on 'public amenities', there had been a sea-change in public feeling over the past few decades: stories on preservationist themes 'are among the most familiar topics in all intelligent newspapers'.[230]

Landscape preservation, in short, had entered the mainstream of English opinion. Its aims were directed at the felt needs of modernity, notwithstanding – indeed, in a sense, precisely because of – the value it placed upon environments as yet lightly affected by 'rash assault', and the traces of the past inscribed in them. That this was so was due largely to the Lake District – the ideas it catalysed and the issues it

---

[230] 'The National Trust and public amenities', *Quarterly Review*, 214 (January 1911), 159.

presented – over the course of the long nineteenth century. Yet the Lake District was not the only locus of preservationist concern. At the other end of the country, the New Forest of Hampshire also provides illuminating insights into this shift in opinion. More so perhaps even than the Lake District, the New Forest was a contested landscape. It was one that formed the focus for complex debates involving commoners, campaigners and crown officials over the meaning and implications of being a 'national' landscape. It is to this landscape, and to these debates, that we now turn.

4 THE NEW FOREST

Even by the standards of the time, Gerald Lascelles was inordinately fond of blood sports. His position as Deputy Surveyor of the New Forest between 1880 and 1915, which came with the enjoyment of a commodious manor house near Lyndhurst, afforded him ample opportunity to indulge his passion for the hunting, hawking and shooting of foxes, deer, badgers, otters, pheasants, rabbits, woodcock, teal, hares and much else besides.[1] Reviewing his memoirs on their publication in 1915, the *English Review* judged that 'what Mr. Lascelles did not know on this subject was plainly not worth knowing'.[2] Despite appearances to the contrary, however, Lascelles was not paid to hunt. As a senior official of the Office of Woods and Forests, his job was to look after the crown's interest in the New Forest, which dated from the reign of William the Conqueror; to see to the cultivation and preservation of its timber stocks; and to generate revenue for state coffers thereby. The diversions of the chase notwithstanding, his business was to manage the efficient planting, growing and felling of trees – a business he saw as a public service. For Lascelles, the New Forest was simultaneously a place of private sporting pleasure and a repository of timber for the nation.

But as the work of Doreen Massey reminds us, place is plural: Lascelles's New Forest was not the only New Forest.[3] For some, it

[1] G. Lascelles, *Thirty-five years in the New Forest* (London, 1915), esp. pp. 177ff.
[2] *English Review*, December 1915, p. 544.
[3] For Massey's stimulating theoretical reflections on the plurality of place, see in particular D. Massey, *Space, place and gender* (Cambridge, 1994); and D. Massey, *For space* (London, 2005).

was a timber and game preserve; for others, it was primarily a working agricultural economy. Much of the New Forest landscape was common land, and had been for centuries. And over this land many hundreds of landholders retained and continued to exercise inherited rights, such as turbary (the cutting of turf for fuel) and pannage (the turning out of swine to forage for beech mast and acorns). Regulated by an elected Court of Verderers dating back to medieval times, the most important of these rights were those which allowed pigs, cattle and other livestock to be depastured on the open forest. This was a boon to small farmers in particular, who were thus able to keep far more animals than the extent of their own holdings would have otherwise permitted. In 1875, the seventy-seven-year-old William Parnell kept five head of cattle, despite only having the tenancy of a 3½-acre smallholding. As he testified to the parliamentary Select Committee on the New Forest, which sat that year, this was because of his common rights: 'The turning out belonging to the small places was as valuable as the places themselves pretty near.'[4] Such rights did much to improve the quality of life of poor foresters, allowing some of them to maintain a self-sufficient livelihood free from reliance on wage earnings. One study published in 1907 found that the average size of a cottage holding in the forest was only 6 acres, with 12 acres being enough for complete independence.[5]

Other New Forests existed too, being conceptualised in different ways by different people. One important reading was provided by the 'tourist gaze', to which the forest was subjected – with ever-increasing intensity – from the mid eighteenth century on.[6] For the producer and consumer of guidebook, artistic and travelogue literature, as well as the holiday visitor, the New Forest was a place of sylvan beauty, primaeval wilderness, personal freedom and pleasure, a landscape freighted by associations with the past. Supposedly standing near the spot where the unpopular King William Rufus fell in 1100, killed by a stray arrow that glanced off an oak tree, the Rufus Stone operated as a synecdoche of this sensibility. Erected in 1745 in a glade in the heart of the forest, the Rufus Stone was a site of pilgrimage much beloved of

---

[4] Evidence of William Parnell, *Select Committee on the New Forest*, 13 (1875), p. 227.
[5] L. Jebb, *The small holdings of England: A survey of various existing systems* (London, 1907), pp. 293–303.
[6] For the concept of the 'tourist gaze', see J. Urry, *The tourist gaze* (London, 1990).

17 *New Forest: A country scene*. Photograph by J. G. Short of Lyndhurst, late nineteenth century. Courtesy of the New Forest Ninth Centenary Trust, Christopher Tower New Forest Reference Library, Hampshire Record Office: 20M92/2/Z34.

picnic parties, the acquisitive heritage-mindedness of souvenir-hunting visitors being such that so many pieces of the stone had been chipped away by 1841 that its mutilated form was encased in iron. As early as 1838, William Howitt reported how 'great numbers' of people came to sit under the trees nearby ('a pleasanter place for a day's excursion cannot be well imagined'); and by the 1870s and 1880s, 'vanload[s] of excursionists' – as well as more genteel visitors such as the Lury family (see fig. 18) – came daily from Salisbury, Southampton and elsewhere.[7]

As with other landscapes, then, the New Forest was a shared space, having multiple identities: Lascelles's New Forest was quite different from the commoner's New Forest, which was in turn different from that of the tourist. These differences gave rise to conflicts over the meaning and function of the place, as various interests and ideologies

[7] W. Howitt, *The rural life of England*, 2 vols. (London, 1838), Vol. II, pp. 91–2; M. G. Fawcett, 'The New Forest', *Magazine of Art*, 8 (1885), 6.

18 *The Lury family at Rufus Stone*. Photograph by Adams and Stillard, 1879. Hampshire Record Office: 105M93/3/15.

collided and struggled for dominance of the power geometry of the forest environment.[8] One very important intervention in these debates was made by the developing preservationist movement, which came to attach considerable importance to the New Forest as a national landscape valuable on account of its historical associations in particular. As we shall see, this intervention did much to promote public discussion of the interrelationship of nation and forest. The ensuing debate centred on competing conceptions of the national good and reveals much about the ways in which the patriotic discourse associated with valued landscapes could shape understandings of national identity.

The New Forest was part of the crown estate. Covering an area of comparatively poor soil, it had been heavily wooded since prehistoric times, but was constituted as a forest by William the Conqueror in or around 1079. Its original purpose was to provide the king with

---

[8] I borrow the term 'power geometry' from the work of Doreen Massey.

sport, specifically the hunting of deer, which were protected by the infamously harsh Forest Laws. Yet while medieval monarchs liked to hunt in the New Forest, many of their successors in later years found their pleasure in other pursuits, leading to the neglect of the forest and its governance. Things began to change in the later seventeenth century, with the development of anxieties about the nation's supply of naval timber – anxieties that found their most resonant and influential expression in the publication of John Evelyn's Royal Society-commissioned *Sylva* in 1664.[9] Evelyn urged timber cultivation as a national imperative and his call was heeded by many landowners, for whom tree planting, and the planting of oaks in particular, became a patriotic act – as well as one that, in a felicitous convergence of public and private interest, often added scenic and material value to their families' estates. Calls were also made for the better cultivation of wood in the crown estates, including the New Forest, which had become the second most important source of oak for the Navy behind the Forest of Dean in Gloucestershire.[10] In 1698, an Act of parliament was even passed providing for the enclosure of up to 6,000 acres of land in the New Forest for the better cultivation of naval timber.[11]

In the event, only about 3,300 acres were enclosed under the legislation of 1698, however, and the neglect of the forest continued.[12] Its officials enjoyed a well-deserved reputation for venality, being more concerned to preserve game for their own enjoyment and benefit than attend to the cultivation of timber. In 1789, the fifth report of the Commissioners of Woods and Forests found that three of the largest recent enclosures made – just twelve years previously – under the 1698 Act were now 'so over-run with Rabbits, that there are now no young Trees whatever in Two of them, and only a very

---

[9] J. Evelyn, *Sylva; or, A discourse of forest-trees, and the propagation of timber in His Majesties dominions* (London, 1664).

[10] R. Greenhalgh Albion, *Forests and sea power: The timber problem of the Royal Navy, 1652–1862* (Cambridge, MA, 1926), p. 108.

[11] 'An Act for the increase and preservation of Timber in the New Forest, in the County of Southampton', 9 & 10 Will. III (1698), 33.

[12] A total of 1,022 acres were enclosed in 1700; there were no further enclosures until 1751, when 300 acres were taken in. Two further enclosures, each of around 1,000 acres, followed in 1775: *Fifth report of the Commissioners appointed to enquire into the state and condition of the woods, forests, and land revenues of the Crown*, British Parliamentary Papers (hereafter PP), LXXVII (1789), pp. 24–6.

few in a Third'.[13] In this way, the unscrupulous keepers had made a rabbit warren out of 836 acres that were supposed to be reserved for timber cultivation.[14] And while the forest keepers were supposed to look after the deer, their overstocking of the woods with rabbits and other game further contributed to the depletion of timber supplies, as did the commoners' pasturage of livestock, the problem being that the animals – whether rabbits, deer, pigs or cows – destroyed the young trees. By 1783, the number of New Forest trees fit for the Navy was estimated at just 12,447, about one-tenth that which had been available in 1608.[15] This drew the ire of many contemporaries of an 'improving' cast of mind, John Byng's judgement on visiting the forest in August 1782 being that the place was 'neglected and wasted', with unenclosed clumps of trees existing in 'a wilderness of waste'.[16] In the context of the desperate wars with France after 1789, and further revelations of official corruption unearthed by the 1793 Report of the Royal Commission on Crown Lands, the situation generated considerable patriotic alarm, being seen by many as of 'infinite importance to the nation'.[17]

For these critics of the status quo the solution was the removal of the deer and the rights of the commoners, and the general enclosure of the forest. This would eliminate incentives for official corruption (and the demoralising practice of poaching) together with the allegedly

[13] *Ibid.*, p. 26.

[14] Of one of these enclosures (Wilverley Walk), the report noted that 'there is not any Appearance of it answering the Purpose for which it was intended, as not One Sapling is to be seen: the Pales are broken down, the Gates are continually open, Horses, Deer and Hogs have the same Liberty of agisting as in any other Part of the Forest, and it is stocked with great Numbers of Rabbits': *ibid.*, p. 109.

[15] P. Lewis, *Historical inquiries, concerning forests and forest laws, with topographical remarks, upon the ancient and modern state of the New Forest, in the county of Southampton* (London, 1811), pp. 120–33 (p. 121).

[16] C. B. Andrews (ed.), *The Torrington diaries: Containing the tours through England and Wales of the Hon. John Byng (later fifth viscount Torrington) between the Years 1781 and 1794*, 4 vols. (London, 1934–8), Vol. I, p. 82.

[17] Lewis, *Historical inquiries*, p. 122. See also, for example, A. Driver and W. Driver, *General view of the agriculture of the county of Hants, with observations on the means of its improvement* (London, 1794), pp. 37–41; T. Nichols, *Observations on the propagation and management of oak trees in general; but more immediately applying to His Majesty's New-Forest, in Hampshire* (Southampton, 1791); C. Vancouver, *General view of the agriculture of Hampshire, including the Isle of Wight: Drawn up for the Board of Agriculture and internal improvement* (London, 1810), pp. 474–6.

inefficient smallholding economy, and maximise the land's productive potential by allowing the systematic cultivation of timber plantations, the better to serve the needs of the Royal Navy. A number of schemes were proposed, many of these being characterised by a self-consciously rationalist Enlightenment vision of scientific progress. Perhaps the most striking was the plan sketched out in 1793 by Philip Le Brocq, domestic chaplain to the duke of Gloucester, which proposed that a circular enclosure of 50,000 acres be placed around Lyndhurst, the circumference of this huge timber plantation being marked out by a ditch and fenced off.[18]

Although a further act was passed in 1808 empowering the Office of Woods to enclose additional land in the New Forest for tree cultivation, more drastic action was not forthcoming. While not solving the timber problems of the Navy, the ending of the Napoleonic Wars in 1815 relieved the sense of acute crisis, and forest management continued very much along established lines. This was a source of exasperation for some reformers. For William Cobbett, who combined enthusiasm for the efficient use of land with a particular passion for tree growing,[19] the New Forest was a national disgrace, vividly emblematising the maladministration and wastefulness of *ancien régime* Old Corruption. Cobbett, who visited the forest in the course of his *Rural rides*, saw it as the rightful property of the public, held by the crown for the benefit of the nation as a whole. Yet the nation's interest in 'the *people's* forest'[20] was abused by the conduct of the Office of Woods, whose officials persisted in the enthusiastic preservation of game for their own pleasure, despite the public nuisance caused to the nation's timber supplies by tree-chewing deer. For Cobbett, the New Forest as presently administered was The Thing in action, a parasite on the body of the nation:

> And, again I say, *who* is all this venison and game *for*? There is more game *even in Kew Gardens* than the Royal Family can want! ... Here is another deep bite into us by the long and sharp-fingered Aristocracy, who so love Old Sarum! ... This New

---

[18] P. Le Brocq, *Outlines of a plan for making the tract of land, called the New Forest, a real forest: And for various other purposes of the first national importance* (London, [1793]; 2nd edn, London, 1794).

[19] W. Cobbett, *The woodlands* (London, 1825); Cobbett, *Rural rides*, pp. 253–7.

[20] Cobbett, *Rural rides*, p. 417.

Forest is a piece of property, as much belonging to *the public* as the Custom-House at London is. There is no man, however poor, who has not a right in it. Every man is owner of a part of the deer, the game, and of the money that goes to the keepers; and yet, any man may be *transported*, if he go out by night to catch any part of this game! We are compelled to pay keepers for preserving game to eat up the trees that we are compelled to pay people to plant![21]

Cobbett's indignant perspective on the New Forest was an expression of radical patriotism; it was predicated on a popular conception of the nation as the people of Britain as a whole, whose interests were being disregarded by a selfish elite bent on personal profit and aggrandisement.[22] But more mainstream discourses of improvement were also applied to the forest, pre-eminently those associated with the enclosure movement, and these, too, were infused with the language of patriotism. The man who in Jonathan Swift's memorable phrasing made 'two ears of corn grow where only one grew before'[23] was seen as a patriot performing a public good by increasing the nation's supply of agricultural produce – a vital consideration in the light of the experience of the Napoleonic Wars, which had seen sufficiently serious food shortages to spark popular protests, most notably in 1795–6 and 1800–1.[24] This perspective informed parliamentary support for enclosure. It was held to be in the national interest to enclose wasteland and maximise its productive capacity; any concern at the sufferings inflicted upon the rural poor through the extinction of their common rights was overpowered by invoking the wider claims of the nation. And while the New Forest lay on soil generally ill suited to large-scale arable agriculture (the stimulation of which enclosure was so often aimed at), it was nevertheless seen as a 'waste', and a singularly extensive and unproductive one at that. If its purpose was the supply of wood for the Navy – itself a national object, quite apart from the

[21] *Ibid.*, p. 418.
[22] For discussion of this radical patriotism, see the seminal article by H. Cunningham, 'The language of patriotism, 1750–1914', *History Workshop Journal*, 12 (1981), 8–33, esp. pp. 8–18.
[23] J. Swift, *Travels into several remote nations of the world … By Lemuel Gulliver* [*Gulliver's Travels*] (Dublin, 1726), p. 116.
[24] See R. Wells, *Wretched faces: Famine in wartime England, 1793–1801* (Gloucester, 1988).

patriotic imperative to improve the productivity of land qua land – the forest was spectacularly failing in this respect: between 1833 and 1848, its yield of timber was nil.[25]

Indeed, by the 1830s and 1840s, the New Forest was widely seen as an anachronism, its uncultivated lands supporting a population of squatters and poor commoners 'of very questionable character', who bore more resemblance to Pacific islanders than to civilised Englishmen. Replete with temptations such as poaching, timber-stealing and smuggling (given its proximity to the Channel coastline), the environment was seen as a brutalising one: 'It seems a general law of human nature, that if man either remains in the wild forest, or returns to it, there is no alternative to his being or becoming a ferocious savage.'[26] For exponents of classical political economy in particular, enclosure appeared a patriotic necessity, a means of extirpating a wasteful and demoralising relic of Norman brutality, the continued existence of which was a challenge to Britain's *soi-disant* status as the commercial-industrial powerhouse of the world. As house journal of the dismal science, the *Economist* ran a series of articles in 1847–8 criticising the persistence of what it called a 'criminal' state of affairs, sentiments that were widely shared at the time – even in the local newspaper press.[27] Providing a neat summary of the case for enclosure in June 1847, the *Hampshire Telegraph* felt it 'inexplicable' that 'the great evil of the extensive waste of the New Forest' should be allowed to go uncorrected.[28]

In the end, the enclosers did not quite get their way, but their agitation did help bring about new legislation designed to increase the productivity of the forest, and timber production in particular. With the ideology of 'improvement' in the ascendancy, the Office of Woods was more favourably disposed towards silviculture than had previously been the case, and the decision was taken to rid the New Forest of its deer. Under the terms of the 1851 Deer Removal Act, the ancient royal

---

[25] Albion, *Forests and sea power*, pp. 110–11.

[26] R. Mudie, *Hampshire: Its past and present condition and future prospects*, 3 vols. (Winchester, [1883]), Vol. II, pp. 218, 305.

[27] 'Reclamation of wastes – the New Forest', *Economist*, 10 July 1847, 5–6; *Economist*, 25 March 1848, p. 6.

[28] 'It supports a few public officers, it is maintained at a loss to the country, it affords no timber for public purposes, 54 gentlemen have a right to shoot over it, and some 3,000 or 4,000 deer range over 58,000 acres of unenclosed land': *Hampshire Telegraph and Sussex Chronicle*, 26 June 1847.

right to keep deer in the open forest was surrendered, the crown being granted as compensation the power to enclose an additional 10,000 acres for tree plantations, with the proviso that no more than 16,000 acres be enclosed at any one time.[29] One additional hoped-for benefit of the measure was that the elimination of the deer would reduce criminal activity, by removing a temptation to poaching.

The Office of Woods was quick to utilise the provisions of the 1851 Act. Large areas of open forest were enclosed for timber plantations, many of which comprised fast-growing conifers well suited to the local soil. This soon led to conflict with the commoners, who complained that the crown was deliberately seeking to injure their interests by taking prime pasturage for tree-growing purposes. These complaints were well justified: in a notorious letter of 1854, later made public in the course of a parliamentary select committee of 1875, the Deputy Surveyor of the forest had recommended to the Chief Commissioner of Woods that 'the Crown should, as soon as possible, exercise its right of enclosing the 16,000 acres because … by so doing all the best pasture would be taken from the commoners, and the value of their rights of pasture would then be materially diminished, which would be of importance to the Crown in the event of any such rights being commuted'.[30] In addition to this, furthermore, the forest officials revived old restrictions on pasturage in the open forest, despite the fact that these restrictions – the Fence Month and Winter Heyning – had been designed to protect the now-departed deer population.[31]

Predictably enough, the post-1851 policy of the Office of Woods drew strong opposition from the commoners, whose New Forest Association offered organised resistance from 1866. But as time passed, it also generated criticism in other quarters, having become something of a national scandal. Fears mounted that the crown would assert the rights of 'rolling enclosure' apparently implicit in the 1851 Act, throwing open plantations once matured then enclosing new

[29] New Forest Deer Removal Act, 14 & 15 Vict. (1851).

[30] Evidence of James Kenneth Howard, *Select Committee on the New Forest*, 13 (1875), p. 54.

[31] Fence Month (20 June–20 July) was the time around which the deer typically gave birth; during this period, the commoners were supposed to remove their livestock to allow the deer to calve undisturbed. Winter Heyning (22 November–4 May) was another period during which depasturage was restricted, in this case in order to protect forage for the deer.

areas, and repeating seriatim until the whole forest was converted into a dense, impenetrable wood, of no use to the commoners and their livestock. By the 1870s, much of the national press would have agreed with the *Saturday Review*, which in April 1871 reckoned crown policy amounted to 'a new code of forest law, framed in the straitest spirit of Scotch economy, and about as oppressive in other ways upon the commoners as that which was once supposed to have drawn down the vengeance of heaven upon the Red King [i.e. William II, commonly known as William Rufus]'.[32] Many parliamentarians agreed, and a few years later, following considerable debate and the report of a select committee, legislation was passed with the object of undoing the damage seen to have been done by the measure of 1851. Under the terms of the 1877 New Forest Act, the crown's power of enclosure was restricted to those lands that had been enclosed since 1698, the rest of the forest to remain open in perpetuity.

The reasons for this shift in opinion shed much light on the changing meaning and value of the New Forest. The 1877 Act was celebrated as a triumph for the commoners over the crown, but it was more than this. It was, as the Liberal intellectual Millicent Garrett Fawcett reflected in 1885, 'a victory that has been worth a good deal more to England than many of her victories of gunpowder and glory';[33] it was, in short, a victory for the nation as a whole. Fawcett's language is revealing. There had been a struggle; one side had won; the power geometry had changed. The patriotic discourses of timber cultivation and 'improvement' had been challenged and ultimately done down by alternative patriotic discourses, which saw the New Forest in a very different light, indeed as a different place entirely.

One key context for this change was technological: with the coming of the ironclad warship, 'the wooden walls of old England' passed into history, and the national imperative of sustaining a strategic reserve of naval timber disappeared with them too. Another was ideological. Classical political economy had enjoined the enclosure of unproductive wastes for the good of the nation, and certainly this argument died hard when it came to the New Forest. Indeed, in the 1860s and early 1870s some agriculturalists suggested that it should

[32] 'The New Forest', *Saturday Review*, 29 April 1871, 530.
[33] M. G. Fawcett, 'The New Forest – II: Historical', *Magazine of Art*, 8 (1885), 51.

be cut up into small freeholds precisely because its timber was no longer required by the Navy, Sir James Caird's opinion being that 'This country was too small to admit of the continuance of so large a tract of wild land within two hours of the metropolis.'[34] Increasingly, however, this point of view was coming under challenge. In fact, the suggestion that the forest be divided up into smallholdings reflected some shifts in economic thought. Peasant proprietors were rehabilitated by the writings of W. T. Thornton and John Stuart Mill, and – later on – by politicians and reformers who identified the smallholder as the ideal Englishman, sturdy of health, upright of character, and a source of national revival in the context of agricultural depression and rural depopulation.[35] With this new perspective, which resulted in organised campaigns for various land reforms from the 1860s on, came a concomitant rehabilitation of the people of the New Forest, many of whom were themselves small farmers and cottagers. If in the 1860s they could still be seen as exotic and uncivilised, 'a strange race of beings' leading a 'wild and reckless existence' at odds with the rest of the nation and its mores,[36] things were different a few years later. In part this was a function of a change in mainstream attitudes to the forest landscape, its wild character seen as imbuing its inhabitants with virtuous independence rather than uncultivated lawlessness, but the reappraisal of the economy of *petite culture* was equally important. From the 1870s on, the periodical press was full of articles extolling the practicality of small-scale cultivation for many items of agricultural produce, with numerous writers singing the praises of the New Forest smallholders as especially meritorious. As one commentator noted in 1885, the foresters were 'a hardy, robust, independent

---

34 Debate on Civil Service estimates, *Hansard*, 3rd series, 180 (19 June 1865), 478–84 (col. 480). Five years later, Clare Sewell Read, another noted agriculturalist MP, expressed similar views: the forest, he told the Commons, was of 'no use as a Royal domain, and last year it only provided a paltry net rent of £1,768, for growing timber that was not required for the Navy. It certainly employed a goodly number of officials, and it allowed the commoners to starve a few cattle and ponies, and it also encouraged a predatory population': *Hansard*, 3rd series, 199 (25 February 1870), 819–20.

35 W. T. Thornton, *A plea for peasant proprietors* (London, 1848); Mill, *Principles of political economy*, Book II, Chapters 6–7; C. J. Dewey, 'The rehabilitation of the peasant proprietor in nineteenth-century economic thought', *History of Political Economy*, 6 (1974), 17–47; Readman, *Land and nation*, pp. 43–85, and *passim*.

36 J. G. W., 'The children of the New Forest', *London Society*, 1 (1862), 365–7.

race, extremely poor, and yet sufficiently content'. They were hard-working, healthy, and 'untouched by the misery and discontent of the poor in the towns'.[37] The authors of agricultural tracts agreed, with Louise Jebb's important 1907 study finding that even very small holdings were viable in the forest, a conclusion corroborated by later research.[38]

In explaining the foresters' relative success, many pointed to the benefits conferred by their possession of common rights. This reflected a reappraisal of the value of commons more generally, which – so their defenders asserted – were no longer wastes that ought in all cases to be improved out of existence. At one level, the argument was economic: small farmers derived considerable material benefits from access to commons, benefits that if lost would drive them off the land into the towns, thereby contributing to the 'rural exodus' that so alarmed contemporaries.[39] But commons also exerted a more powerful and wide-ranging appeal. In the context of political democratisation, commons came to be seen as the people's heritage in the land of the country – a heritage, to be sure, that had been partially squandered by the self-serving actions of landlord-dominated parliaments, but whose remnants still survived in the form of the lands still unenclosed and open to all. In the 1860s, a powerful commons preservation lobby was got going by a group of prominent politicians and other public figures, its views finding expression in the shape of the CPS, which as we have already seen would become involved in the campaign to preserve the Lake District landscape – and access to it – from the 1880s on. Founded in 1865, the CPS had as its initial focus the prevention of further encroachments on the remaining tracts of common land. Drawing on considerable public sympathy, not least through the offices of sympathetic newspapers such as *The Times* and the *Pall Mall Gazette*, the CPS and its largely Liberal supporters achieved a number of notable early successes – including the saving of Hampstead Heath and

[37] M. Collins, 'In the New Forest: Part I', *English Illustrated Magazine*, June 1885, 587–8.
[38] Jebb, *Small holdings*, pp. 293–303; C. R. Tubbs, 'The development of the smallholding and cottage stock-keeping economy of the New Forest', *Agricultural History Review*, 13 (1965), 23–39.
[39] For an example of contemporary concern about rural depopulation, see P. A. Graham, *The rural exodus* (London, 1892). For more discussion, see Readman, *Land and nation*; and M. Freeman, *Social investigation and rural England, 1870–1914* (Woodbridge, 2003).

Epping Forest.[40] The rationale behind the campaign for commons preservation fused patriotic sentiment with more practical considerations. Commons were seen as vestiges of an older England, providing the inhabitants of an increasingly urban-industrial modernity with identity-bolstering connections to a popular past, while also affording them access to nature and the mental and physical benefits this bestowed.[41]

On this reading, then, commons were public amenities, and if their enclosure had in the past been justified as tending to the public good – by improving the productivity of the soil, from which the whole nation would gain – so now their preservation was enjoined on similar grounds. When it came to land use, the definition of public good had widened to encompass consideration of amenity, and while the New Forest had relatively little productive potential, it (along with other commons) was increasingly seen as conferring important – if necessarily unquantifiable – social and intellectual benefits. By the mid 1870s, even the *Economist* had changed its tune, opposing the Office of Woods's plantation policy as injurious to the attractions of the open forest landscape, which it judged senseless '[t]o surrender … for some paltry yearly gain of revenue, or even for a large increase in our supply of timber for the navy'. Such an action, it felt, would be 'something like cutting up the pictures in the National Gallery to mend the sails of her Majesty's ships'.[42] The *Economist*'s line reflected changes in political economic thinking. In the fourth edition of his famous book on the forest, which did much to disseminate the landscape's attractions to a wider audience, J. R. Wise identified an increase in 'love for natural scenery', a phenomenon he thought was due 'especially … to our new school of political economists, who … have preached the too-often forgotten truth, that man cannot live by bread alone'.[43] Among

---

[40] See G. Shaw Lefevre [Lord Eversley], *English commons and forests: The story of the battle during the last thirty years for public rights over the commons and forests of England and Wales* (London, 1894), published in a second edition as *Commons, forests and footpaths: The story of the battle during the last forty-five years for public rights over the commons, forests and footpaths of England and Wales* (London, 1910). For the political context, see Roberts, 'Gladstonian Liberalism and environment protection'.

[41] Readman, *Land and nation*, pp. 113–17. On the wider ideological context of the CPS's activities, see Readman, 'Preserving'.

[42] 'The New Forest', *Economist*, 24 July 1875, 7.

[43] J. R. Wise, *The New Forest: Its history and its scenery*, 4th edn (London, 1883 [1863]), preface, pp. ix–x.

the political economists of whom Wise may have been thinking was John Stuart Mill, whose humanistic utilitarianism came to encompass support for the CPS, as well as radical land reform to encourage small-holders.[44] Another thinker Wise may have had in mind was Henry Fawcett – professor of political economy at Cambridge, leading Liberal politician, CPS member, and an energetic defender of the New Forest and its commoners. Fawcett and his wife, Millicent Garrett Fawcett (whom we have already quoted), were influential figures, and their interest in the New Forest reflected a wider intellectual-reformist concern for the landscape, and indeed for common landscapes generally.[45]

The emphasis that Wise, the Fawcetts and others placed on the need to preserve New Forest commons in order to 'nourish not so much the body as the mind of man' came at a time when increasing numbers of people were resorting to the New Forest for recreational purposes – and indeed this idea was much repeated in the guidebook literature aimed at these visitors.[46] The forest had been a site of considerable antiquarian interest since the eighteenth century, with the ruins of Beaulieu Abbey (see fig. 19) exerting a particular attraction among gentlemanly enthusiasts for the medieval past.[47]

---

[44] Shaw Lefevre, *English commons*, p. 40; D. Martin, *John Stuart Mill and the land question* (Hull, 1981); Roberts, 'Gladstonian Liberalism and environment protection', 307.

[45] L. Stephen, *Life of Henry Fawcett* (London, 1885), esp. pp. 293ff. One author Wise certainly drew on was William Howitt, whose impassioned protests against enclosure, first aired in a rather unreceptive context in 1838, now found new resonance. Howitt had argued that '[o]ur mountains, forests and moorlands are the lungs of the whole country', and that 'true utilitarians' ought 'to keep them open, as we mean to keep alive the fine arts, poetry, the love of antiquity, and the love of nature amongst us; as we would retain and invigorate in us that higher life by which we have climbed to our present national altitude; by which our sages and poets have been nourished … by which we are made to feel our animal life even with a double zest; and yet, I trust, destined to make the name of England the greatest in the history of the world': Howitt, *Rural life of England*, Vol. II, pp. 117–18.

[46] As the fifth edition of W. H. Rogers's *Guide to the New Forest* enjoined in 1894, while 'man's first duty' might be the proper cultivation of the land, 'yet it must not be forgotten that the mind as well as the body requires food, and that the free and open country is able to afford this in the most lavish manner': W. H. Rogers, *Guide to the New Forest*, 5th edn (Southampton, [1894]), p. 2.

[47] See, for example, F. Grose, *The antiquities of England and Wales*, 8 vols. (London, [1772]–6), Vol. II, pp. 161–5; R. Warner, *A companion in a tour round Lymington* (Southampton, 1789), pp. 85–98; R. Warner, *Topographical remarks, relating to the south-western part of Hampshire*, 2 vols. (London, 1793), Vol. I, pp. 259ff.; J. Buller, *A companion in a tour round Southampton* (London, 1799), pp. 94–8.

19 *Beaulieu: Chapter House arches, Beaulieu Abbey.* Photograph by William Barfoot of Totton, late nineteenth century. Courtesy of the Beaulieu Estate Archive. Hampshire Record Office: HPP33/034.

Furthermore, largely thanks to the writings of Gilpin, its scenery had become closely associated with contemporary notions of the picturesque, drawing other elite visitors for this reason.[48] But until the later nineteenth century, popular interest in the New Forest was largely confined to those living within easy reach of the place by road, and even then focused overwhelmingly on the Rufus Stone. Later years saw the numbers of visitors grow exponentially, with one Stoney Cross innkeeper estimating in 1875 that as many as 1,000 people could visit in a single day.[49] Such, indeed, was the attraction of the Rufus Stone that some late Victorian and Edwardian commentators were apt to complain that the surrounding area had been 'vulgarised' as a consequence of its appeal.[50] An 1895 book aimed at the self-consciously discerning

[48] W. Gilpin, *Remarks on forest scenery, and other woodland views (relative chiefly to picturesque beauty) illustrated by the scenes of New-Forest in Hampshire*, 3 vols. (London, 1791).

[49] Evidence of G. E. B. Eyre, *Select Committee on the New Forest*, 13 (1875), p. 244.

[50] H. G. Hutchinson, *The New Forest* (London, 1904), p. 153.

20 *King and queen oaks, Bolderwood*. Photograph *c.* 1895 by James Coventry of Burgate Manor and deposited in Hampshire Record Office by the late Philip Allison. Hampshire Record Office: 33M84/16/1.

visitor warned that the '*al fresco* establishment of Messrs. Peckham Brothers, where cocoa-nuts are knocked down (or not knocked down, as the case may be) at "a penny a shy"' had been set up next to the Rufus Stone: 'All the summer and autumn this favoured spot is a heaven – or a pandemonium – of trippers.'[51] By this time, however, 'trippers' did not just come to see the Stone; they came to see other things too, for instance the grand beeches and oaks of Mark Ash Wood and Bolderwood, as well as celebrated individual trees such as the ancient Knightwood Oak (see figs 20 and 21).

[51] R. H. De Crespigny and H. Hutchinson, *The New Forest: Its traditions, inhabitants and customs* (London, 1895), p. 180.

With the extension of paid and bank holidays, more and more people were also taking vacations in the forest, staying for days on end: the New Forest was increasingly a tourist destination, and a popular one at that. At an 1892 public inquiry into the suitability of establishing a rifle range in the New Forest, one steamboat operator testified that around 130,000 people travelled from Southampton to Hythe each year. Another witness reckoned that the charabanc traffic on the roads of the forest each summer was such that 'you might imagine that all the middle classes in South Hampshire had married on the same day, and were all going out for a lark together'.[52] In the judgement of one guidebook, published around the same time, 'it seems impossible to imagine a district of the same area appealing to the tastes and predilections of so many classes and offering to all such rare enjoyment'.[53]

To an extent, the explanation for this growth in tourist interest is technological. Improved and cheaper means of transport made the New Forest – in common with other 'wild' places such as the Lake District – much more accessible to working- and middle-class people. The construction of the Southampton and Dorchester Railway in 1847 was important here,[54] but charabancs, bicycles (widely affordable from the 1890s on) and Solent steamboats also played their part. In addition to such technological factors, social developments had an impact too, in particular the expansion of leisure opportunities resulting from the increase in holiday provision and the growth of large suburban middle-class populations, for whom a vacation in the New Forest was a convenient, wholesome and fitting means of recreation. Yet important as these factors are, they do not take us to the heart of the matter; they were more facilitative than instrumental in their action. The New Forest was more accessible than it had been previously, but this on its own is insufficient to explain its growing popularity. Central to the increase in tourist interest in the New Forest was the widening appeal

---

[52] *Minutes of evidence taken before the Hon. T. H. W. Pelham in the inquiry as to the suitability & safety of the rifle range which it is proposed to establish in the New Forest* (15 March–23 April 1892), pp. 75, 102–4: Hampshire Record Office, 7M75/75.

[53] C. Mate, *Illustrated pocket guide to Bournemouth, the New Forest and district* (Bournemouth, 1904), p. 158.

[54] For details of the Southampton and Dorchester Railway, which ran from Southampton through Dorchester, Brockenhurst and Ringwood, and was linked to Bournemouth by an extension in 1863, see H. P. White, *A regional history of the railways of Great Britain*, Vol. II: *Southern England*, 4th edn (Newton Abbot, 1982), pp. 154, 161.

of its landscape, which meant more, to a broader cross-section of society, than it had done before.

In part, the change in attitude was a function of urbanisation and industrialisation. The dramatic demographic shift that saw Britain transformed from being a country where half the population lived in rural areas, in 1851, to one where less than a quarter did, in 1901,[55] had profound cultural consequences. One of these was the promotion of greater popular interest in the natural world, as the everyday lives of ordinary people became more uniformly urban. As the rural writer Francis Heath recalled in his 1878 book on *Our woodland trees*, which had much to say about the New Forest, it was only when he moved to live in London – after spending his youth in the countryside – 'that the latent love of Nature was developed with full force, and became a passion. The absence of woods and green fields gave rise to a painful longing to renew acquaintance with them on every possible occasion, and no recreation was so much prized as communion with Nature in her wildest haunts.' This, Heath felt, was a typical experience for the Englishman, whose great love of forests was a function of how much woodland had been destroyed in past years.[56]

The language with which this love was expressed drew heavily on that which had been developed by picturesque commentators of the late eighteenth and early nineteenth centuries. Writers such as Gilpin, Uvedale Price and Richard Payne Knight did much to establish what would become conventional understandings of picturesque forest scenery, emphasising the aesthetic superiority of open, deciduous woodland – what Knight called the 'uncorrupted … forest' – over systematic conifer plantations and the artificial landscaping of fashionable 'improvers' such as Capability Brown.[57] The 'stiff lines' of close-packed firs came in for particular criticism, their uniformity of form and colour being seen as the antithesis of the picturesque roughness and variation provided by places such as the New Forest, with

---

[55] J. Saville, *Rural depopulation in England and Wales 1851–1951* (London, 1957), p. 61.

[56] F. G. Heath, *Our woodland trees* (London, 1878), preface, pp. viii–ix; also F. G. Heath, *Tree gossip* (London, 1885), pp. 70–1.

[57] R. P. Knight, *The landscape, a didactic poem … Addressed to Uvedale Price, Esq.*, 2nd edn (London, 1793), pp. 31–3, 72. See also Gilpin, *Forest scenery*; Price, *Essay on the picturesque*.

its rugged old oaks, verdant glades, tangled undergrowth and furzy heath.[58] For Price, indeed, '[o]f all dismal scenes', the dreary interior of a conifer plantation

> seems to me the most likely for a man to hang himself in; he would, however, find some difficulty in the execution, for amidst the endless multitude of stems there is rarely a single side branch to which a rope could be fastened. The whole wood is a collection of tall naked poles, with a few ragged boughs near the top ... even its gloom is without solemnity; it is only dull and dismal; and what light there is, like that of hell, 'Serves only to discover scenes of woe, / Regions of sorrow, doleful shades'.[59]

Published in 1791, Gilpin's *Remarks on forest scenery* was especially important in establishing the New Forest's picturesque credentials, emphasising the varied quality of the landscape and pointing to the irregular forms taken by many of its beech and oak trees (an effect that was a function of the poor soil of the region). In common with other writers at the time, Gilpin's careful appreciation of the scenery of the New Forest co-existed with contempt for the character of its inhabitants, 'inferior people' who led unproductive and 'indolent' lives that were 'poor and wretched in the extreme'.[60] This was consistent with mainstream contemporary attitudes, which could praise the 'continually-varying harmony' of the New Forest, while at the same time urge its improvement on the grounds of economical, moral and national necessity.[61] Indeed, the picturesque sensibility and considerations of national need converged neatly over the issue of naval timber, the twisted boughs of New Forest oaks being both scenically appealing and peculiarly suited to the requirements of the shipwright. As Edward Wedlake Brayley and John Britton pointed out in their book on *The beauties of Britain*, published in the year of Trafalgar, the forest's trees 'seldom rise into lofty stems ... as oaks usually do in richer soils; but

---

[58] Knight, *Landscape*, p. 72.
[59] Price, *Essay on the picturesque*, pp. 210–24 (pp. 223–4). The verse quoted here is from Milton's *Paradise lost*.
[60] Gilpin, *Forest scenery*, Vol. III, pp. 39–42, and see also pp. 180–2.
[61] Mudie, *Hampshire*, Vol. II, pp. 311–15, and pp. 331–2 for his view that 'there cannot be a better national use of the [New Forest] than keeping it as a forest, and paying more constant and more scientific attention to the growth of timber than has hitherto been done'.

their branches, which are more adapted to what the ship-builders call knees and elbows, are commonly twisted into the most picturesque forms'.[62] Of course, the use of such oaks for the Navy destroyed them, but this was not unduly troubling, even for stronger partisans of the picturesque, for new trees would rise in due course to take their place. That the oaks felled might be large or venerable specimens was of little account: in contrast to earlier Enlightenment preoccupations with the age and size of trees, the picturesque privileged their appearance and forms, subjective judgments of taste supplanting objective scientific measurement.[63]

The picturesque's lack of concern with environment (as opposed to landscape, viewed in strictly aesthetic terms) and history (the age of trees being of little account) helps explain why increasing appreciation of the scenic value of woodlands such as the New Forest did not translate into demands for preservationist action in the late eighteenth and early nineteenth centuries. But in the later nineteenth century, the language of picturesque appreciation began to fuse with a conceptualisation of the New Forest as an historical – and hence valuable – environment, as part of the nation's heritage. This reading of the New Forest was that adopted by the increasingly democratic tourist gaze, and in the context of an altered political-economic climate newly cognisant of amenity as a national good, it came to exert significant and ultimately policy-shaping influence.

Of course, it took various forms. In one incarnation, it simply involved an appreciation of the New Forest as primeval nature, anciently wild and very largely untouched by the hand of man. One article in the *Cornhill Magazine*, published in 1893, described how in visiting the forest one 'finds oneself in company with Dame Nature in her best and most unspoiled aspect; all is still so little changed if, indeed, changed at all, since the times when the wolf and the wild boar ranged here'.[64] In this perspective, which was similar to that taken by contemporary admirers of the North American wilderness, the New

[62] E. W. Brayley and J. Britton, *The beauties of England and Wales* (London, 1805), Vol. vi, p. 175.
[63] C. Watkins, '"A solemn and gloomy umbrage": Changing interpretations of the ancient oaks of Sherwood Forest', in C. Watkins (ed.), *European woods and forests: Studies in cultural history* (Wallingford, 1998), pp. 105–8; Price, *Essay on the picturesque*, pp. 80–3.
[64] 'In the New Forest', *Cornhill Magazine*, n.s. 20 (January–June 1893), 591.

Forest offered a means of time travel back to prehistory.[65] That said, however, its landscape was relatively rarely consumed in this way. If a wilderness at all, the New Forest was a tame one, and in any case was not generally primeval, having been profoundly shaped by human activity over many centuries. Most people knew this, and indeed the forest's very connections with the human past do much to explain why its landscape was so widely and highly prized. With its charcoal-burners, commoners, old churches, abbey ruins, gypsies and ancient trees, the New Forest was imagined as 'a charming relic of the past life of a now shopkeeping nation'.[66] As Wise explained in his much-quoted book, it was understood to afford uniquely precious access to the national past, being

> [a]s good an example as could be wished of what has been said of English scenery, and its connection with our history. It remains after some eight hundred years still the New Forest ... the main features are the same as on the day when first afforested by the Conqueror. The names of its wood and streams and plains are the same. It is almost the last, too, of the old forests with which England was formerly so densely clothed. Charnwood is now without its trees: Wychwood is enclosed: the great forest of Arden – Shakespeare's Arden – is no more, and only a fragment of Sherwood has been saved. But the New Forest still stands full of old associations with, and memories of, the past.[67]

As with other valued landscapes, the New Forest provided an important sense of continuity with the English past, so acting as an antidote to the identity-sapping anomie of urban-industrial modernity.[68] Living things spanning numerous human generations, its trees were particularly important in this respect, being seen as witnesses to history: as John Ruskin understood, 'A very old forest tree ... is always

---

[65] R. Nash, *Wilderness and the American mind*, 5th edn (New Haven and London, 2014 [1967]); D. Lowenthal, 'The place of the past in the American landscape', in D. Lowenthal and M. J. Bowden (eds.), *Geographies of the mind* (New York, 1976), pp. 89–117.

[66] De Crespigny and Hutchinson, *New Forest*, pp. 2–3.

[67] Wise, *New Forest*, p. 3; also J. King, 'The New Forest and the War Office', *Westminster Review*, 137 (March 1892), 261.

[68] See Readman, 'Preserving'; and, for the importance of continuity, Readman, 'Place of the past'.

21 The Knightwood Oak. Photo courtesy of Hulton Archive/Getty Images.

telling us about the past.'[69] One such tree was the Knightwood Oak, near Lyndhurst, which by the turn of the twentieth century was several hundred years old. Lauded in guidebook- and belletrist writing since Gilpin, the much-visited tree attained the distinction of appearing on early Ordnance Survey maps of the forest.[70]

More particularly, the New Forest's associations with Norman England remained strong throughout. Pre-eminent among these associations was the story of the Conqueror's son, William II, whose dramatic and mysterious death near the spot marked by the Rufus Stone was a staple feature of discussion in the guidebook literature, and the

[69] Ruskin, *Works*, Vol. 1, p. 68.
[70] For example, Ordnance Survey Office, *New Forest* (Southampton, 1900): British Library Cartographic Items, Maps 2565(2).

root cause of its popularity as a tourist destination.[71] Despite the unpre-possessing nature of the memorial itself – a ruined old stone encased in cast-iron cladding – its historical resonance was considerable, one first-time visitor recording in 1881 'How vividly passed before one that scene that took place nearly a thousand years ago, when a king lost his life at the hands of a subject.'[72] There was a radical subtext to this: the king in question had the reputation of having been a capricious tyrant, zealous in his application of the bloody forest laws (which sent men to their deaths for killing royal deer), and there was a sense in which the Rufus Stone memorialised Anglo-Saxon resistance to the harsh rule of the country's new Norman regime. Although whether the Red King's death was murder or not was disputed, it certainly suited some com-mentators to see the stone as marking the site of an ambush 'to revenge by one swift act the injuries of an oppressed people'.[73] In any case, it was significant that the stone did not mark, so it was supposed, the actual spot where Rufus fell, but that where an oak which deflected the fatal arrow had once stood: this, then, was death as natural justice, and if a deliberate killing, it was one in which the forest was an accessory to the act of retribution.

This understanding of the meaning of the Rufus Stone was compatible with a broader Victorian–Edwardian conceptualisation of the New Forest as a landscape of popular liberty, one that had been passed down to the present as a survival from earlier times. Wild, open and unenclosed, the 'good greenwood' was seen as having offered ref-uge and succour to the common people over centuries.[74] It was a place where 'the bold yeoman' had 'sought shelter from Norman tyranny', the common rights he and his descendants enjoyed being 'a relic of Saxon liberties'.[75] Bolstered by more general ideas of quondam forest liberty, of which the myth of Robin Hood was most significant,[76] this conception of the New Forest as a historical site of native freedoms was strongly coloured by anti-authoritarian sentiment. Indeed, in some arguments it could even shade into a radical libertarianism, the leitmotif of which was deep suspicion of government and its works. For the philosopher

---

[71] Rogers, *Guide to the New Forest*, pp. 60ff.

[72] C. W. Wood, 'In the New Forest', *Argosy*, 31 (January 1881), 53.

[73] F. G. Heath, *Our English woodlands* (London, 1878), p. 148.

[74] Art[icle] V., *British Quarterly Review*, 38 (July 1863), 81.

[75] *Ibid.*; Fawcett, 'The New Forest – II: Historical', 50.

[76] Barczewski, *Myth and national identity*, esp. pp. 208–9.

and politician Auberon Herbert, 'the England of the greenwood time', as represented by the New Forest, was imperilled by the bloated bureaucracy of the Office of Woods, which aimed at replacing an open, varied, hardwood landscape – one that ought to be 'left absolutely to nature' – with the alien monotony of impenetrable conifer plantations.[77] Articulated in the 1880s and 1890s, Herbert's arguments were consistent with his own anti-statist ideology,[78] but they were nevertheless similar to many of those advanced by spokesmen for the commoners' interest from the late nineteenth century onwards. They presented the commoners as central to the survival of the New Forest as a quintessential landscape of liberty. By exercising and defending their ancient rights, preserving the forest as open and unenclosed in the teeth of state hostility, the commoners were helping to preserve the continuity of English popular freedoms.

These freedoms were represented by the time-honoured rights of common enjoyed by the smallholders, but more generally they were embodied in the unenclosed nature of much of the landscape, the fact that it was accessible to all. As Wise put it, 'the traveller can here go where he pleases, without any of those lets and hindrances which take away so much pleasure'.[79] The spacious grandeur of the open woodlands, intermixed with heath and pasture, added significantly to the status of the New Forest as a landscape of 'wild liberty' (see fig. 22).[80] This was particularly true from the perspective of the tourist, who was assured in one handbook, published in 1880, that he might 'at his own sweet will wander without let or hindrance, and breathe the air of life and freedom'.[81] As a leading figure in the New Forest Association, G. E. Briscoe Eyre alluded to these benefits in giving evidence to the 1913 Select Committee on Commons – benefits he felt were being eroded by the self-seeding of firs on the open forest, a development that if allowed

---

[77] Evidence of Auberon Herbert, *Select Committee on woods and forests and land revenues of the Crown*, 18 (1890), pp. 43ff. (p. 46); letters in *The Times*, 20 April 1889, p. 7, and 24 April 1889, p. 13. See also A. Herbert, 'The last bit of natural woodland', *Nineteenth Century*, 30 (September 1891), 346–60; A. Herbert, 'The slow destruction of the New Forest', *Fortnightly Review*, 49 (March 1891), 444–65.

[78] For which see S. H. Harris, *Auberon Herbert: Crusader for liberty* (London, 1943).

[79] Wise, *New Forest*, p. 8.

[80] P. Walker, 'In the New Forest', *Fraser's Magazine*, 77 (February 1868), 218; W. Allingham, *Varieties in prose*, ed. H. Allingham, 3 vols. (London, 1893), Vol. I, p. 6.

[81] C. J. Phillips, *The New Forest handbook: Historical and descriptive* (Lyndhurst, 1880 [1875]), pp. 9–12 (pp. 11–12).

22 *New Forest: Forest scene.* Photograph possibly by J. G. Short of Lyndhurst, late nineteenth century. Courtesy of Hampshire Cultural Trust. Hampshire Record Office: HPP39/011.

to continue would create masses of impenetrable coniferous woods and so extinguish that 'freedom which has got so much to do with the charm of the New Forest'. As Eyre went on the explain, 'Its freedom is its charm – the fact that you can come and go where you like, walk where you like and ride where you like, or you ought to be able to.'[82]

The idea of the New Forest as a freely accessible historical landscape of liberty was central to the claims of those who opposed the policy of the Office of Woods, who asserted the existence of a popular 'sense of possession' over the landscape, one that 'true patriotism elevates out of the sphere of selfishness'.[83] In line with arguments made by the CPS in other contexts, the case here was that unenclosed common land was the people's land – indeed, all the more so in this instance as the lord of the manor was not a private individual, but the state. Patriotism thus enjoined its preservation for the nation as a whole to enjoy.

Needless to say, this perspective did not go unchallenged. Fired by enthusiasm for replacing old and unremunerative ornamental trees with fast-growing conifers, forest officials sought to exploit the

[82] *Select Committee on Commons (Inclosure and Regulation)*, 6 (1913), p. 75.
[83] Heath, *Our English woodlands*, pp. 129–30.

provisions of the 1851 Deer Removal Act. Their tree-felling and planting activities drew criticism in parliament as early as 1854, with public
concern mounting thereafter.[84] Indeed, the Office of Woods even went
so far as to cut down several hundred ancient yews at Sloden – much
to the horror of Alfred, Lord Tennyson, for whom they had acted as
poetic inspiration.[85] Their timber apparently being sold for £30 to a
Southampton upholsterer, the yews were replaced with what one commentator called 'a sea of monotonous Scotch fir'.[86] When the controversy aroused by this and similar official attacks on 'ornamental' woods
led in 1868 and 1875 to two select-committee inquiries into the operation of the 1851 Act, the Office of Woods advocated disafforestation,
which would have amounted to the partition of the forest between
the crown and the commoners – much to the disadvantage of the latter.[87] By this stage faced with stiff opposition, the forest officers, led by
Commissioner of Woods J. K. Howard, defended their policy as conducive to the national interest. While the naval timber argument was
now obsolete, they still maintained that as the forest was crown land,
the revenue from which the monarchy had sacrificed under George III
in return for the civil list, it behoved them as public servants to maximise its income-generating potential. Failure to do so would be unfair
on the taxpayer – even 'unconstitutional'.[88] Following on from this,
Howard and his legal counsel suggested that it was grossly misleading
for the New Forest Association and its allies to portray themselves as
representing the public, when in fact the interests they served were necessarily local and sectional in nature: the rights claimed by the Office of
Woods, by contrast, were those of the crown and *ipso facto* 'exercised
for the benefit of the nation at large'.[89]

---

[84] *Hansard*, 3rd series, 135 (13 July 1854), 133–6.
[85] W. Allingham, *William Allingham: A diary*, ed. H. Allingham and D. Radford
(London, 1907), pp. 136–7.
[86] M. Collins, 'In the New Forest: Part I', *English Illustrated Magazine*, June 1885, 579;
also Fawcett, 'The New Forest – II: Historical', pp. 50–1.
[87] For the position of the Office of Woods at these select committees, see, e.g., evidence
of J. K. Howard, *Select Committee on the New Forest*, 13 (1875), pp. 49–50.
[88] *Report June 1871, to Treasury, by J. K. Howard, Com. of Woods, on New Forest and
position of Crown, and principles of management under Acts of Parliament*, PP, XXI
(1875), pp. 11–12.
[89] Evidence of Horace Watson, Solicitor to the Office of Woods, *Select Committee on
the New Forest*, 13 (1875), pp. 3–4 (p. 3); also evidence of Howard, *ibid.*, pp. 46ff.

The recourse to the 'national' here is significant, as what conduced to the national good was at the centre of the debate. It was a debate, however, that Howard and his officers were losing. Their opponents did not dispute the idea that the New Forest was state land, held for the benefit of the nation at large, but they insisted that this end was better served by attention to considerations of amenity, heritage and preservation than the efficient production of timber. Author of an influential preservationist pamphlet, Henry J. T. Jenkinson told the 1875 select committee that 'the public have a claim on the forest *quâ* forest, and as a national forest', and while in the past the national interest in the forest might have implied its silvicultural exploitation for naval or other purposes, those days were now gone. Instead, he suggested, the New Forest ought to be valued 'as much as we do the pictures in the National Gallery'.[90]

This comparison with the National Gallery was frequently aired, and it was no accident. The artistic value of the New Forest was now well established, the place being a popular subject for painters.[91] Members of the Royal Academy and the Society of Water Colour Painters presented preservationist petitions to parliament, and in May 1875, G. E. Briscoe Eyre's New Forest Association organised an exhibition of New Forest landscape art, evidently judging this an appropriate means of demonstrating the credentials of their cause.[92] But the analogy had a further significance, acting as a convenient way of emphasising the forest's aesthetic value, while at the same time suggesting that it was 'National Property', part of the national heritage, freely accessible for the edification and enjoyment of all – as indeed were the pictures of the National Gallery.[93] This was a point made with some force by Henry Fawcett and others in their parliamentary interventions on the subject. Like the works of art held in the great national collections, the ornamental woods of the New Forest, if destroyed, could never be restored; they constituted 'a creation of the past' that was absolutely

---

[90] *Ibid.*, pp. 120–1.

[91] By the 1880s, the New Forest was the subject of about one-third of all paintings of Hampshire scenes exhibited at Royal Academy Summer Exhibitions: Howard, 'Changing taste in landscape art', pp. 257–9.

[92] Evidence of Henry Fawcett, *Select Committee on the New Forest*, 13 (1875), p. 236; evidence of Eyre, *ibid.*, p. 243. The exhibition featured nearly 250 paintings of New Forest scenes, with visitors to the show being invited to sign a preservationist petition.

[93] J. Conlin, *The nation's mantelpiece: A history of the National Gallery* (London, 2006).

unique.[94] As such, it followed that they ought to be preserved, just as other elements of the national heritage were preserved by the agency of the state. In an 1871 speech supporting Fawcett's successful resolution prohibiting new enclosures or the felling of ornamental timber pending further enquiry into the operation of the Deer Removal Act, William Cowper-Temple reminded the House of Commons that no MPs had 'ever alleged that the public money was wasted when it was expended in purchasing the productions of great landscape painters for the National Gallery', yet the Commissioner of Woods

> could not believe that the public approved of the expenditure of money for the purpose of preserving the finest natural landscape existing in England. He wondered whether the Commissioner, if he had the charge of the National Gallery, would sell the pictures for what the canvas and paint would fetch; or whether, if he had the management of the British Museum, he would sell the Elgin Marbles for the value of the marble of which they were composed.[95]

The argument that the New Forest should be treated as part of the national heritage was considerably enhanced by the fact that it was widely perceived to be a distinctively English landscape, one agreeable to the sensibilities of patriots. Not only was its open landscape of self-sown woodland and heath inextricably linked to the long continuities of national history and thus worthy of preservation as 'some sort of remembrance of what England once was',[96] it was also seen – however misguidedly – as a monument to the variety and individuality of a particularly English natural environment. This made it very different from the 'German' sort of forest the Office of Woods allegedly wanted to create through its schemes of enclosure and conifer plantation – a sort of forest freeborn Englishmen would find uncongenial. As Eyre told the 1875 select committee, it would be a forest that

> differs only from a cropped field, in that it has cropped trees instead of cropped smaller vegetables; it consists simply of patches of this tree, that tree, or the other tree, one series following another in regular rotation, like rotation crops in agriculture: the effect is

[94] Fawcett, *Select Committee on the New Forest*, 13 (1875), pp. 236–9 (p. 238).
[95] *Hansard*, 3rd series, 207 (20 June 1871), 328–44 (cols. 339–40).
[96] W. C. D. Esdaile, *Select committee on the New Forest*, 13 (1875), p. 179.

simply that the wood is monotonous, it is close; there is no chance for any tree to assume any individuality, and therefore there is no picturesqueness … Your feeling is that you are in a vast timber-farm, everything is artificial and monotonous and to regulation pattern.[97]

The national-patriotic case made by the defenders of the New Forest overcame the alternative national argument made by the Office of Woods, which was that opposition to crown policy was to the advantage of the sectional interests of the commoners alone and thus contrary to the public interest rightly understood. The commoners certainly played a leading part in the controversy, their particular claims on the forest looming large throughout. Yet as Gerald Lascelles shrewdly observed in his memoirs, heritage-amenity arguments were now neatly 'dovetailed' with the local concerns of the commoners.[98] This amounted to more than sleight of hand, however. For a start, enclosure and the plantation of conifers were anathema to preservationists and commoners alike. The restriction of common rights and the destruction of pasturage meant the disappearance of the easily accessible landscape of ornamental old woods, wild liberty and historical associations – a landscape now dear not only to the hearts of foresters, but also to the public at large. Perceptive contemporaries recognised this. As the *Saturday Review* remarked in the context of the 1871 debate on disafforestation, 'The cause of popular enjoyment calls for open glades, acceptable to riders, walkers, and picnic parties, rather than tangled copse-woods; and the profit of the commoners who enjoy rights of pasturage and pannage lies in the same direction.'[99] At a deeper level than this convergence of interest, moreover, lay an important ideological factor. At a time of growing public concern with landscape preservation, common land came to be freighted with special cultural significance. In an increasingly democratic political context, commons were seen to stand for the people's rightful inheritance in the soil of their country. Thus commoners were the guardians of this inheritance, the rights they claimed over the landscape ensuring that it remained open for the enjoyment of the nation at large; fitting it was,

---

[97] Eyre, *ibid.*, pp. 242–3.
[98] Lascelles, *Thirty-five years*, p. 19.
[99] 'The New Forest', *Saturday Review*, 29 April 1871, 531.

too, that the image of the smallholding commoner now conformed to the ideal of the Englishman, frugal, manly and free.[100]

This perspective inspired land reformers desirous of righting the wrongs of enclosure. It also inspired the early preservationist movement, the increasingly influential CPS and its parliamentary supporters arguing that common land was not to be enclosed unless it could be shown that doing so would benefit the public (the assumption being that in most cases, the public would be best served through commons preservation). When it came to judgments about the proper use of commons, the public interest was increasingly seen as taking priority, and this interest was increasingly understood to consist in their heritage-amenity value above all else.[101] It was in the context of this shift in mentality that the 1877 New Forest Bill was passed. This legislation was essentially a measure for the preservation of common land and rights. Under its provisions, further enclosure was prohibited, the old woods so characteristic of the open forest were to be preserved (no ornamental timber could be felled), and the ancient Verderers' Court was reconstituted as a body more representative of the commoners whose rights it administered.[102] The New Forest Act was landmark legislation, indicating and acknowledging a shift of public opinion away from the idea of the public interest in the natural environment being primarily economic in character, and towards its conceptualisation as a social-cultural asset of considerable national importance. As a prominent member of the CPS and co-founder of the National Trust, Sir Robert Hunter remarked in 1895 on how the wider significance of the New Forest Act was that it was a measure that 'distinctly recognised the paramount right of the nation to forbid the destruction of a beautiful and unique district'.[103]

Hunter's was an acute observation, but 1877 was not the end of the story. Emboldened by their effective control of the Verderers' Court,

---

[100] For this stereotype, see Readman, *Land and nation*, esp. 62–71.
[101] See Readman, 'Preserving'; and Readman, 'Octavia Hill'.
[102] The new Court would be composed of five verderers elected by the commoners, and one appointed by the crown. This was bitterly resented by the Office of Woods, Lascelles regarding the new body as 'a committee of commoners' pure and simple: Lascelles, *Thirty-five years*, p. 37.
[103] R. Hunter, 'Places of interest and things of beauty', *Nineteenth Century*, 43 (April 1898), 570–89 (p. 570).

commoners and preservationists mounted further campaigns against the Office of Woods, which they charged with violating the terms of the 1877 settlement, conspiring to obtain more extensive powers of enclosure, and generally neglecting its duty of care for the open forest. The subjects of these complaints included the cutting of ornamental timber for the satisfaction of fuel rights; the failure to prevent the self-seeding of conifers beyond the bounds of plantations; and the intro-duction of what Auberon Herbert called 'new and fanciful specimens of non-indigenous trees' such as scarlet oaks, coloured maples and cedars into what was, after all, a quintessentially English landscape.[104] In vain did the Office of Woods and its supporters repeat the argument that the public's real interest in the forest – as a source of revenue – had been subverted by a self-serving group of commoners who were 'really the enemies of the nation or public generally'.[105] The wind of opinion was now blowing in a different direction. Even *The Times* was happy to present the commissioners as bureaucratic philistines, content to destroy a national heritage for their own dubious ends. In April 1890, a leader article suggested that were officialdom to get its way and more statutory enclosures be granted, 'deeds of darkness will be done':

> Without sufficient reverence for the genius of the place even to abstain from whistling, or to keep his hands out of his pockets and his head respectfully erect, a triumphant functionary, with a pot of red paint in attendance, will go marking patriarchal trees for destruction at his caprice. He will rejoice to make gaps, and will fill them with gaudy foreign interlopers, scarlet oaks, coloured maples, and, worst of all, with cedars. Then will the surface be scraped bare of trees, as if it were a French Cathedral, with its carved capitals, in course of deep restoration.[106]

Such was the nature of public sentiment, indeed, that threats or poten-tial threats to the integrity of the 1877 settlement met with protest, from whatever quarter those threats came, Office of Woods or elsewhere. In the early 1890s, controversy arose over the passage of the 1891 Ranges Act. Smuggled through parliament at the tail end of the session, it allowed the War Office to acquire common land for rifle ranges, one of

---

[104] A. Herbert, 'Scraping, spending, and spoiling', *The Times*, 18 April 1890, p. 13.
[105] Letter of J. Campbell Water, *The Times*, 30 April 1889, p. 9.
[106] *The Times*, 18 April 1890, p. 9.

which the government proposed to establish on 800 acres of the New Forest, at Blackdown near the Lyndhurst–Beaulieu road. News of this proposal led to New Forest Association-organised protest meetings in the forest, CPS-led agitation at a national level, and much coverage in the newspaper and periodical press. Alarm was expressed across the ideological spectrum, from respectable Conservative Party-supporting dailies such as the *Morning Post* and *Pall Mall Gazette*, through to *Land and Labour*, organ of the Land Nationalisation Society.[107] Drawing on all the now-standard patriotic arguments, the consensus was that the 'mischievous and insidious' Ranges Act was 'a tool to cut at the roots of the rights of Englishmen', the application of which to 'the people's' New Forest constituted an assault on a 'national inheritance' that was 'a bit of old England'.[108] Faced with this barrage of public criticism, which also included petitions from scientific bodies, naturalists' societies, working-class botanists, presidents of mechanics institutes and much else besides, the government caved in and agreed to a public inquiry. Chaired by T. H. W. Pelham, a leading barrister, the inquiry heard much evidence attesting to the public stake in the New Forest and the preservation of its common land being of national as well as local concern. As a consequence its report duly advised against establishing a rifle range, advice that the government heeded in June 1892.[109] Further concessions followed in the Military Lands Consolidation Bill, introduced to supersede the problematic Ranges Act. As passed into law, this measure explicitly excluded the New Forest from its operation, as well as prohibiting the appropriation of common land anywhere for rifle ranges without parliamentary consent.[110]

The principle of treating the New Forest as deserving of protective attention was carried over into the detail of other legislation. A clause in the 1897 Military Manoeuvres Act required the army to consult the Verderers before using any part of the forest for its

---

[107] See, e.g., *Morning Post*, leader, 19 February 1892, pp. 4–5; *Saturday Review*, 20 February 1892, p. 203; *The Times*, 15 February 1892, pp. 4, 9, and 19 February 1892, p. 9; 'The New Forest and the War Office', *Land and Labour*, May 1892.

[108] 'The New Forest in danger', *Nature Notes*, 3 March 1892, p. 41, and 3 April 1892, pp. 61–4; King, 'The New Forest and the War Office', 261–7.

[109] *Report of T. H. W. Pelham on suitability and safety of rifle-ranges proposed in New Forest*, PP, LXIV (1892); *Hansard*, 4th series, 5 (13 June 1892), 915.

[110] Military Lands Act 1892 (55 & 56 Vict., 43); Shaw Lefevre, *Commons, forests, and footpaths*, p. 168.

seasonal manoeuvres, with no activity to take place in the same district more than once every five years.[111] Similarly, an offending clause was removed from the 1894 Crown Lands Act that, if retained, would have allowed new enclosures to be made;[112] and commoners' rights were given due consideration by the terms of the New Forest (Sale of Land for Public Purposes) Act of 1902, which gave the crown power to sell or let limited portions of land to meet local sanitary needs.[113] This practice would continue in the interwar years, with special protection being granted in Addison's 1919 Housing and Town Planning Act, which restricted to just 30 acres the amount of forest land that could be taken for housing under its provisions, and the 1922 Allotments Act, which placed strict limits on the use of forest land for allotment purposes.[114]

The post-1877 solicitude for the New Forest was based on the assumption that adherence to the terms of the New Forest Act would ensure the preservation of the region's heritage-amenity value as an important national landscape. In doing so, a second assumption was made: that the unenclosed forest was capable of 'natural' regeneration, the only substantive human intervention being made indirectly, through the commoners' exercise of their rights of pasturage, pannage and so on. It was, in fact, a bogus assumption. The ancient hardwoods of the open forest had not grown up spontaneously, but were in their present form in significant part the consequence of earlier forest management. Many of the most highly regarded old oaks and beeches – those of Ridley Wood, for example, and indeed even the mighty Knightwood Oak itself – had in the past been pollarded, a procedure that had done much to contribute to the picturesque forms they now assumed.[115] Encoppicement and enclosure had also ensured the survival of many

---

[111] Military Manoeuvres Act 1897 (60 & 61 Vict., 43). For the government's acceptance that the New Forest was a special case, see *Hansard*, 4th series, 39 (21 April 1896), pp. 1394–5.

[112] Crown Lands Act 1894 (57 & 58 Vict., 43); *Hansard*, 4th series, 15 (19 July 1893), pp. 53–4; 28 (3 August 1894), pp. 113–14.

[113] New Forest (Sale of Lands for Public Purposes) Act, 1902 (2 Edw. VII, 198).

[114] Housing and Town Planning Act 1919 (9 & 10 Geo. V, 35). *Hansard*, 5th series, Lords, 35 (17 July 1919), 699–795; 50 (24 May 1922), 711. Under the terms of the 1922 Act, no more than 60 acres of New Forest land could be taken for local-authority-provided allotments, in addition to land already being used for that purpose: Allotments Act 1922 (12 & 13 Geo. V, 51).

[115] Lascelles, *Thirty-five years*, pp. 150–6.

admired hardwood giants when they were but saplings. Lascelles, who had examined historical evidence from the reigns of Edward IV, Henry VI and Henry VIII, knew this well. 'Without the fostering fence and care', he wrote in 1915, great old woods such as Mark Ash 'never could have come into existence, or survived the ravages of the King's deer and commoners' cattle and ponies'.[116] Although challenged by his opponents, Lascelles was right: the removal of the deer may have prevented their munching the young trees, but the commoners' numerous livestock were, after 1877, free to roam year-long throughout the open forest, eating whatever they found toothsome. With the Office of Woods unable to throw up protective enclosures around saplings, even of a temporary kind, the old forest was falling into decay. Chancellor of the Exchequer and New Forest resident Sir William Harcourt was asked in a House of Commons question of June 1894 if he had noted that 'the young trees are being utterly destroyed by cattle, and that the provision of any protection is prevented by a well-meant but ill-drawn Act of Parliament; that the glory of the greatest of our national estates is being slowly destroyed; that the woods are gradually disappearing; and that the forest will ere long become entirely denuded of trees'.[117] Revealingly, while Harcourt in his reply did not agree that the 1877 Act was a failure – predictably enough, as he had been party to its drafting – he did acknowledge, on the basis of his personal knowledge of the place, that more could be done 'to prevent the denudation of the forest'.[118]

From a purely silvicultural perspective, 'the denudation of the forest' meant the squandering of a potential source of revenue: land that might have yielded a good crop of timber was being underutilised, the Office of Woods being unable to develop the productive potential of the increasingly senescent open forest. It was a point of view that found favour in the proceedings of Sir John Lubbock's 1885–7 Select Committee on Forestry, which received damning evidence from experts such as M. Boppe, the Inspector of French Forests, whose verdict was that the unenclosed lands were 'hurrying to destruction in a manner deplorable to behold, and before very long there will be a worthless barren heath'.[119] A noted scientific writer, Lubbock was clearly swayed

[116] *Ibid.*, pp. 138–46.
[117] *Hansard*, 4th series, 25 (14 June 1894), 1096.
[118] *Ibid.*, 25 (14 June 1894), 1096–7.
[119] *Select Committee on Forestry*, 8 (1884–85), appendix, p. 49.

by such testimony, as was his committee generally, the report of which concluded that much of the New Forest was in a state of degradation, and that the operation of the 1877 Act was serving to speed the process of decay.[120]

This was not a conclusion that found much public favour, the claims of science and technical expertise being trumped by the prevailing view that the New Forest was a unique national landscape that ought not to be sacrificed 'for profit and for Scotch firs' in imitation of continental practice.[121] Lubbock's committee did, however, make clear that a non-interventionist approach to the much-prized old ornamental woods was hastening their destruction – and in later years, this point was made more forcibly, forestry experts recasting their arguments in ways that addressed heritage-amenity concerns more sympathetically. Thus, instead of focusing on undercultivation and the loss of revenue this implied, they suggested that the 1877 Act meant the decay of the New Forest qua New Forest. While it might suit the commoners to see the open forest turn into rough pasture as the old trees died out – and indeed one of their spokesmen told the 1913 Select Committee on Commons that the forest ought to be seen as 'a huge grazing farm'[122] – the now well-established public interest in the preservation of ancient woodland conflicted with this. Set up in 1912, the forestry branches of the Board of Agriculture lost little time in making this point, their first annual report lamenting the irony that while the New Forest Act had broken new ground in emphasising the cultural as opposed to the financial worth of the forest to the nation, it prevented crown officials from acting to preserve the 'aesthetic value' of the open woods. As enclosure was impermissible, it was 'impossible to protect and regenerate them', and thus it was 'certain that ultimately these woods, which form one of the chief beauties of the forest, must disappear'.[123] Thus it was that by the outbreak of the First World War, silvicultural opinion had come to accept the legitimacy of

---

[120] *Ibid.*, 9 (1887), report, pp. iv–v. Lubbock, indeed, was personally responsible for inserting a paragraph in the report drawing attention to 'the present unsatisfactory condition of the New Forest' from a silvicultural point of view (pp. xi–xii).

[121] Editorial, *The Times*, 19 September 1885, p. 9.

[122] Evidence of Arthur Cecil, Chairman of New Forest Commoners' Defence Association, *Select Committee on Commons (Inclosure and Regulation)*, 6 (1913), p. 61.

[123] *Joint Annual Report of the Forestry Branches [of the Board of Agriculture], for 1912–13*, PP, XII (1914), p. 29.

the contention that the national value of the New Forest was not solely concentrated on its timber-producing potential.

The implications of these new perspectives for actual forest management became clearer after 1918. In the context of an ever-growing body of empirical evidence that the ancient woods were indeed decaying, opinion slowly moved towards the view that further intervention was required to supplement the 1877 Act. In the interwar period, the Forestry Commission (established in 1919 as the successor to the Office of Woods) made a determined and ultimately success-ful case for the enclosure, plantation and selective thinning of stands of mature hardwood – not to raise revenue, but in order to effect the regeneration of the forest, and preserve its amenity value.[124] This con-firmed the acceptance of the heritage-amenity case by forest officials, and paved the way for further recognition of the nation's claim on the forest, which would finally come in the aftermath of the Second World War. Drawing on the conclusions of the 1946 New Forest Committee, the 1949 New Forest Act confirmed the forest's status as what the then Minister of Agriculture called 'a great national park',[125] the place being now recognised as definitively the possession of 'the 47,000,000 peo-ple of the country whose heritage it is'.[126] This understanding would underpin future policy in relation to the forest, culminating in the for-mal establishment of a state National Park in 2005; as has been demon-strated here, however, the origin of such thinking – and its expression in policy – can be traced back to the late Victorian and Edwardian periods.

This chapter has plotted a paradigm shift in attitudes to the landscape of the New Forest. Over the course of the nineteenth century, the

[124] In 1927, the commission's chairman Lord Clinton told the House of Lords that his organisation's duties ought to be seen as 'three in number ... to cut, to maintain the picturesque character of the woods, and to replenish those woods. It is clear, and I admit, that the case of the picturesque overrides all those, but the work of replen-ishment must be done to preserve the picturesqueness.' In enclosed areas of the forest, Clinton explained, conifers were only planted where oaks would not thrive, and much of the felling of hardwood timber in the plantations was done to stimulate growth, broadleaved trees requiring access to light in order to grow properly. Lord Clinton, *Hansard*, 5th series, Lords, 204 (7 April 1927), 910–11.
[125] Thomas Williams (Minister for Agriculture): *Hansard*, 5th series, Commons, 469 (1 November 1949), 221.
[126] Lord Lucas of Chilworth: *Hansard*, 5th series, Lords, 154 (25 February 1948), 105.

power geometries of place had been transformed. By 1914, Lascelles's New Forest, a place that was primarily a (public) source of crown revenue and secondarily a (private) source of gentlemanly recreation, was in eclipse. In the context of political democracy, urbanisation, mass tourism and the development of a popular heritage consciousness, an alternative New Forest had come to prominence. This was the New Forest as a national landscape, as the people's property, and its cultural valence owed much to the associations attaching to common land. Here as elsewhere in England, the movement for commons preservation played a key role in establishing the idea of an ancient and rightfully inalienable popular stake in the soil – one that had been ridden over roughshod in less enlightened times, but that demanded recognition now that parliament was understood as representative of the whole people. In a perspective much coloured by a demotic patriotism that hymned the virtues of freeborn Englishmen, sturdy yeomen and self-sufficient smallholders, local rights of common came to be seen as standing proxy for the wider claims of the nation. In this way, the New Forest became a national landscape, part of the national heritage, long before it finally, formally, became a National Park early in the twenty-first century. Yet, as we shall see in the next chapter, it was not just rural landscapes that came to be perceived as national possessions over the course of the long nineteenth century.

PART III

Beyond the South Country

5 MANCHESTER: SHOCK LANDSCAPE?

Elizabeth Gaskell's novel *North and south* (1854–5) begins in the New Forest. Its heroine, Margaret Hale, is the daughter of the vicar of Helstone, a secluded village amid the woods, and a place Margaret loves. For her, like many of its other Victorian admirers discussed in the previous chapter, the New Forest with its accessible commons is a landscape of personal liberty. It affords opportunities for direct and unfettered engagement with wild nature, and also with the ordinary people of the countryside – the commoners – to whom Margaret feels closely attached:

> It was the latter part of July when Margaret returned home. The forest trees were all one dark, full, dusky green; the fern below them caught all the slanting sunbeams; the weather was sultry and broodingly still. Margaret used to tramp along by her father's side, crushing down the fern with a cruel glee, as she felt it yield under her light foot, and send up the fragrance peculiar to it, – out on the broad commons into the warm scented light, seeing multitudes of wild, free, living creatures, revelling in the sunshine, and the herbs and flowers it called forth. This life – at least these walks – realized all Margaret's anticipations. She took a pride in her forest. Its people were her people … she was continually tempted to go off and see some individual friend – man, woman, or child – in some cottage in the green shade of the forest. Her out-of-doors life was perfect.[1]

[1] E. Gaskell, *North and south* (Harmondsworth, 1970 [1854–5]), p. 48.

The perfection of Margaret's free and easy outdoor life is not to last, however. Beset by religious doubts, her father proves unable to continue his Anglican ministry, and resigns, telling his family that they must move away from the forest to the industrial town of Milton in the north of England. Margaret is distraught; she is appalled at the prospect of leaving the forest and the freedoms and pleasures it confers. But her father is implacable; his only real prospects are in Milton, and there they must go. Her first impressions of the town, a lightly fictionalised Manchester, are not encouraging:

> For several miles before they reached Milton, they saw a deep lead-coloured cloud hanging over the horizon in the direction in which it lay … Nearer to the town, the air had a faint taste and smell of smoke; perhaps, after all, more a loss of the fragrance of grass and herbage than any positive taste or smell. Quick they were whirled over long, straight, hopeless streets of regularly-built houses, all small and of brick. Here and there a great oblong many-windowed factory stood up, like a hen among her chickens, puffing out black 'unparliamentary' smoke, and sufficiently accounting for the cloud which Margaret had taken to foretell rain.[2]

And once settled in Milton, Margaret is soon homesick for Helstone. She tells Bessy, a sickly factory operative girl she befriends, about its beautiful, peaceful landscape, with its great trees 'making a deep shade of rest even at noonday', its 'turf … as soft and fine as velvet', its 'tinkling brooks', its 'billowy ferns'.[3] It is a landscape that contrasts very sharply with that of the urban environment of Milton, where the people appear hemmed in amongst dense agglomerations of small houses and towering factories, and are generally oppressed by the noise and dirt of industry. Their cramped and restricted lives do not permit free roaming in the woods, and on what Margaret calls the 'wide commons, high up as if above the very tops of the trees' – places that Bessy finds especially appealing when they were described to her:

---

[2] Ibid., p. 96.
[3] Ibid., pp. 144–5.

'I've always wanted to get high up and see far away, and take a deep breath o' fulness in that air … Now on these commons, I reckon, there is but little noise?'

'No', said Margaret; 'nothing but here and there a lark high in the air'.[4]

Margaret's early impression of Milton/Manchester, then, is of a place antonymous to Helstone and the New Forest. The forest, with its unenclosed commons, offers nature, tranquillity, beauty and liberty; Milton is a dystopia, a place of man-made squalor, ugliness, clamour and confinement. It seems to represent the antithesis of right living, a wrong turn in the course of civilisation, a shaming of England. Gaskell has other things to say about Milton further on in the novel (of which more later), but her presentation of the place in the early parts of the book can be taken as reflecting a well-established – indeed stereotypical – view of Manchester and its landscape. Generations of commentators have passed unfavourable judgement on the place: even in the 1950s, A. J. P. Taylor thought the city 'irredeemably ugly'.[5] For many, it represented the dark side of industrialisation: pollution, dirt, disease, capitalist class oppression. Its built landscape was often seen as either hateful or – being squarely and designedly utilitarian – not worthy of much in the way of approbatory comment.

The impress of this stereotype is evident in scholarly writing as well as cultural discourse more generally. Historians, art historians and historical geographers have not generally associated industrial environments with valued landscapes: the accent has often been on the negative, even when the cultural, economic and intellectual vitality of the urban environment is acknowledged. That said, there have been exceptions to this perspective. Some time ago, Andrew Lees made a strong case for the persistence of positive views of the city in Britain and elsewhere across the nineteenth century, though his focus was not so much on urban landscape specifically as on broader intellectual responses to rapidly changing urban culture and society.[6] Lees's book

---

[4] *Ibid.*

[5] A. J. P. Taylor, 'Manchester' [*Encounter*, 1957], in A. J. P. Taylor, *Essays in English history* (London, 1976), p. 309.

[6] A. Lees, *Cities perceived: Urban society in European and American thought, 1820–1940* (Manchester, 1985); and see also A. Lees and L. H. Lees, *Cities and the making of modern Europe, 1750–1914* (Cambridge, 2007).

has not been noticed as much as it might have been, but recent years have seen the publication of more work emphasising the significance not only of favourable views of the city in general, but of the urban environment in particular. Richard Dennis, for example, has stressed the progressive modernity embodied in Victorian cityscapes, while Tristram Hunt has delineated the various ways in which industrialists sought to improve the civic life of the places from which they drew their wealth.[7] More recently still, Katy Layton-Jones has pointed to the diversity of visual representations of the nineteenth-century city: even at the height of the Industrial Revolution, the rapidly transforming provincial landscape was not seen as necessarily inimical to aesthetic ideals.[8]

Valuable and suggestive as these and other such correctives are, however, the landscape of the city has not generally been associated with constructions of national identity – or at any rate the assumption remains fairly well entrenched that the countryside plays a vastly more important role in this respect. It is here worth repeating Krishan Kumar's remark, made in his landmark study of English national identity, that by the later nineteenth century the 'essential England was rural'.[9] In this interpretation, the progress of urban-industrial modernity provoked a valorisation of its imagined antithesis, a peaceful, pastoral, village England, and a concomitant deprecation of those places – such as Manchester – where it found its most vigorous expression. Modern British culture, so the argument goes, shied away from the environment of 'dark satanic mills', and by extension what Martin Wiener called 'the industrial spirit' more generally, constructing an alternative, ruralised sense of national identity, one that was socially – if not necessarily politically – conservative, opposed to the tenor of the times.[10] The landscape of Englishness was not to be found on the streets of Manchester but in the fields and lanes of the south country.

The present chapter challenges this still-persisting view. Building on some of the work mentioned above, what follows will

---

[7] R. Dennis, *Cities in modernity: Representations and productions of metropolitan space, 1840–1930* (Cambridge, 2008); T. Hunt, *Building Jerusalem: The rise and fall of the Victorian city* (London, 2004).

[8] K. Layton-Jones, *Beyond the metropolis: The changing image of urban Britain, 1780–1880* (Manchester, 2016).

[9] Kumar, *Making of English national identity*, p. 211.

[10] Wiener, *English culture*.

argue that from the Industrial Revolution of the late eighteenth and early nineteenth centuries, and on through the Victorian and Edwardian periods, Manchester and its landscape were seen in a far more positive light than is often suggested. But it was not just that the elite of the town sought to project an image of commercial and civic vitality through public works and public architecture, as Tristram Hunt has shown.[11] For all that the social conditions of the city attracted concern, especially but not exclusively in the years of the 'Hungry Forties', the landscape of the place more generally was a potent source of patriotic pride throughout the period, local opinion asserting the national importance of the city, and national cultural discourse acknowledging this importance. In this way, Manchester became an integral part of the patriotic landscape imaginary, its urban environment supporting rather than contradicting mainstream constructions of national identity. As will become clear, Manchester was valued as an important national landscape: the essence of England was not only located in the countryside.

Manchester was the first industrial city. Situated on level ground with a good water supply and a moist climate favourable to cotton spinning, it was well placed to exploit the technological advances in textile manufacturing of the later eighteenth century. Large mills were built in the town along the Rivers Irwell, Irk and Medlock, one notable landmark being Richard Arkwright's construction, in 1782, of Britain's first unified cotton mill, a large, five-storey manufactory driven by a huge waterwheel.[12] Steam-powered factories followed soon afterwards, the use of steam being facilitated by the duke of Bridgewater's canal, which had reached Manchester by the early 1760s and which greatly reduced the carriage costs of coal.[13] A Watt engine was installed in Piccadilly Mill in 1789, and its success prompted the widespread adoption of steam technology in Manchester cotton factories from the 1790s.[14] Industrial development was accompanied by an explosive growth in the town's population. In 1758, around 17,000 people lived

[11] Hunt, *Building Jerusalem*.

[12] H. L. Platt, *Shock cities: The environmental transformation and reform of Manchester and Chicago* (Chicago, 2005), p. 38.

[13] W. H. Chaloner, 'Manchester in the latter half of the eighteenth century', *Bulletin of the John Rylands Library*, 42 (1959–60), 40–60 (pp. 46ff.); Platt, *Shock cities*, p. 28.

[14] Platt, *Shock cities*, p. 39.

in Manchester; by 1788 the number had reached nearly 43,000, and by the turn of the century it exceeded 70,000.[15] At the time of the Great Reform Act of 1832, Manchester – with a population of 142,000 – had become 'Cottonopolis' and what Asa Briggs has memorably called 'the shock city of the age'.[16]

Industrialisation had a transformative impact on the landscape of Manchester. Great blocky mills mushroomed; thousands of houses, shops, offices and other buildings were thrown up; and the town expanded rapidly. Some commentators did not like what they saw. Significant atmospheric pollution was apparent as early as 1789, one visitor in that year describing as 'abominable' the 'smoke and dirt on approach to Manchester' and finding the town itself correspondingly 'dull, smoky, dirty'.[17] Others were more withering still. John Byng, later Viscount Torrington, visited Manchester twice in the 1790s, finding it 'a great, nasty, manufacturing town' with nothing whatever to recommend it. The market and bookshops were disappointing, the singing in the collegiate church was execrable, the food at his inn was inedible (and the port undrinkable); he wandered about the streets for a whole day 'without seeing anything that I should wish to see again'. The place was, he felt, 'a dog hole' marooned in 'gloom and dirt'. It had nothing to offer the sensitive man of taste: 'who but a merchant could live in such a hole', he wondered.[18]

Byng was a country gentleman, and in his remarks we see the shudder of aristocratic disdain for 'trade', whose rank growth in Manchester had come, so he felt, at the expense of the traditional landed interest. Dramatic changes such as those seen in late-eighteenth-century Manchester are never universally welcomed, however, and criticism such as Byng's is best understood not as reflective of mainstream opinion, but as constitutive of protest against prevailing trends. Manchester was at the head of these trends, and many other commentators were positively enthusiastic about the part the town was playing in the progress of the nation, the transformation through industry of its landscape being an

[15] Chaloner, 'Manchester in the latter half of the eighteenth century', pp. 41–2; A. Briggs, *Victorian cities*, 2nd edn (Harmondsworth, 1968 [1963]), pp. 88–9.

[16] Briggs, *Victorian cities*, pp. 88ff. (p. 96).

[17] A. Walker, cited in C. Bowler and P. Brimblecombe, 'Air pollution in Manchester prior to the Public Health Act, 1875', *Environment and History*, 6 (2000), 71–98 (p. 76).

[18] Andrews, *Torrington diaries*, Vol. II, pp. 116–17, 206–9.

object of keen patriotic pride.[19] In 1771, the London-based Scottish writer Robert Sanders reckoned that '[t]he trade and manufactories, particularly in all sorts of cotton, carried on in this opulent town, may be considered as one of the brightest jewels in the diadem of Great Britain'.[20] William Thomson, another London Scottish man of letters and author of a treatise on the principles of beauty in nature and art, was similarly impressed when he visited Manchester in 1785. Like Sanders, he took the opportunity to conscript the town into the service of Britishness, declaring that 'the industry in the manufactures carried on here and in the neighbourhood, cannot fail to excite the most agreeable emotions in the minds of all Britons'.[21]

For the late-eighteenth- and early-nineteenth-century man of taste, the wealth generated by Manchester was a source of pride and wonder, more particularly so because it was seen to be aesthetically beneficial. As we will see in the case of the Thames Valley, the proceeds of trade and manufacturing were held to have a visually as well as materially enriching effect on the landscape. Approaching Manchester from the north around the turn of the nineteenth century, the well-travelled west-country antiquarian Richard Warner reached the top of a hill about two miles outside the town, which afforded him a view over 'a prodigious champaign of country … watered by the river Irwell, filled with works of art; mansions, villages, manufactories, and that gigantic parent of the whole, the widely-spreading town of Manchester'.[22] Far from being a welt on the landscape, Manchester was seen to enhance it – not least by providing the means of its improvement and ornamentation. This perspective was still more clearly expressed in Kinder Wood's popular poem of 1813, *A prospect of Manchester and its neighbourhood*, which hymned the attractions of the 'noble … rich, populous, beautiful, and variegated … plain … in which Manchester is placed'.[23] The poem described a view of this plain, here figured as 'the

[19] See, e.g., M. W. Thompson (cd.), *The journeys of Sir Richard Colt Hoare through Wales and England 1793–1810* (Gloucester, 1983), p. 155.
[20] N. Spencer [Robert Sanders], *The complete English traveller; or, A new survey and description of England and Wales* (London, 1771), p. 535.
[21] T. Newte [William Thomson], *A tour in England and Scotland in 1785: By an English gentleman* (London, 1788), p. 39.
[22] Warner, *A tour*, Vol. II, p. 140.
[23] [K. Wood], *A prospect of Manchester and its neighbourhood, from Chamber, upon the rising grounds adjacent to the Great Northern Road: A poem* (Manchester, 1813), p. vi.

wide extended scene, / Where spreading Commerce, Britain's favorite child, / Supplants the shepherd's reed, and Doric measure wild'. This was a place where 'joys from commerce spring', a place whose manufactures had spread across the world, so much so that 'thy bright name extends from pole to pole'. Far from degrading the landscape, then, Manchester nurtured its surrounding 'vassal country', whose settlements were as 'tender ivy' strengthened and sheltered by the 'broad oak' of the burgeoning metropolis of cotton.[24]

Such a sensibility could even be shared by visitors to northwest England intent on admiring the picturesque, of which there were increasingly large numbers by the later eighteenth century, in large part owing to the pull exerted by the Lake District. One traveller included a stop at Manchester in a tour, taken in 1791, from London to the Lakes. But far from unfavourably contrasting the man-made town with the celebrated scenery of Cumberland and Westmorland, he made a point of admiring both. While Manchester offered relatively little in the way of picturesque attractions (though he did mention the collegiate church and Chetham's College as two examples), it was a place whose wealth was progressively improving and civilising the local landscape:

> To see barren hills and vallies laugh and sing under the influence of an auspicious trade, must give the benevolent heart the most agreeable sensations … [to see] a great part of the old pulled down to make room for spacious and ornamental mansions – these are thy blessings, O Commerce! – These are thy rewards, O Industry![25]

Appreciation of the picturesque in nature co-existed with appreciation of modern, expanding townscapes.[26] This was consistent with the contemporary view that polite and social virtues – indeed, civilisation generally – could only really find full expression in an urban context.[27] It was a view that found strong expression in the

---

[24] *Ibid.*, pp. 15, 17–18.
[25] A Gentleman [Adam Walker], *A Tour from London to the Lakes: Containing natural, œconomical, and literary observations, made in the summer of 1791* (London, 1792), pp. 30–3.
[26] Layton-Jones, *Beyond the metropolis*, esp. pp. 42–6.
[27] R. Sweet, *The English town, 1680–1840: Government, society and culture* (Harlow, 1999), pp. 220–2.

urban histories and guidebooks published in increasingly large numbers from the later eighteenth century onwards.[28] Such publications
were produced not only for fashionable society destinations such as
Bath, but also for places such as Manchester. The first guidebook to
the town, intended as 'a kind of Vade-mecum for strangers', was James
Ogden's *Description of Manchester*, which appeared in 1783;[29] similar
volumes followed in the early and middle years of the nineteenth century.[30] These books, and the local histories that were also brought out,
made much of Manchester's growing national importance; expressions
of civic pride, they were designed to impress the British public at large
with a sense of this importance, indeed with the idea – as one put it – of
the place as being 'the second town in the kingdom'.[31] Their contents
emphasised not only the industry and wealth of Manchester, but also
the improving usages to which wealth was put: cotton manufacture was
presented as supporting rather than undermining decorous improvements to the landscape. Much was made of the laying out of elegant
new streets and the widening of narrow old ones, their buildings being
torn down to make way to create what one visitor in 1802 described
as 'spacious and healthy' thoroughfares, with 'large, handsome, and
uniform' houses.[32] Much also was said in praise of the architecture
of modern public buildings such as the Infirmary (1755) and – later
on – Thomas Harrison's John Soane-inspired Portico Library (1802–
6) and stately Exchange building (1806–9). By 1815, one Manchester
guidebook saw fit to declare that 'the many great improvements' made
in recent years to the civic architecture and street layout of the town
'surpass[ed] belief'.[33] Industry-derived wealth had entered into a felicitous alliance with refined taste:

> The numerous and splendid public structures for devotion, charity,
> pleasure, and business; the immense ranges of newly-erected

[28] R. Sweet, *The writing of urban histories in eighteenth-century England* (Oxford, 1997), esp. pp. 100ff.
[29] J. Ogden, *A description of Manchester* (Manchester, 1783), pp. 3–4.
[30] See, in particular, J. Aston, *The Manchester guide: A brief historical description of the towns of Manchester and Salford, the public buildings, and the charitable and literary institutions* (Manchester, 1804); and *The new Manchester guide* (Manchester, 1815).
[31] Aston, *Manchester guide*, p. 1.
[32] Ogden, *Description of Manchester*, pp. 63–71; Aston, *Manchester guide*, pp. 42–3; Warner, *A tour*, Vol. II, p. 142.
[33] *New Manchester guide*, pp. 45–7.

dwelling-houses, distributed into streets and squares, in the most eligible situations, and in a style of superior elegance … exhibits at one view the effects of industry directed by genius, and supported by public spirited and benevolent characters.[34]

The development and approbation of a polite Manchester townscape was not done in the face of any significantly increasing unease about the visual effects of the industry that had made such civic improvements possible. At least until the 1820s, negative commentary on the appearance of Manchester cotton factories was thin on the ground. This might seem odd, given the utilitarian design of Industrial Revolution-era mill buildings; the early cotton masters of northwest England did not intend for their works to beautify the landscape. Yet at the same time, the buildings they threw up had an undeniably powerful visual impact on perceptions of that landscape; indeed, they became important features of it in their own right. The Manchester manufactories, huge and novel as they were, did not escape the notice of contemporaries, for many of whom they were less an eyesore than an object of curious and even touristic attraction. Genteel visitors consumed mills as 'sights' in a manner not too dissimilar to how they might have consumed favoured views in the Lake District or the Wye Valley. Finding himself in Manchester in July 1800, the antiquary Sir Richard Colt Hoare made sure to call in to the library of Chetham's College, with its fine collection of medieval texts, but he also explored the nearby textile manufactories.[35] Similarly, Richard Warner, another antiquary visiting Manchester around the turn of the century, also made a point of visiting the mills of the town, discovering 'machines of the most beautiful contrivance' in the cotton works of Messrs Atkinson.[36] Indeed, so common was this kind of activity that the *Manchester Guide* of 1804 felt 'it is become a fashion for strangers to visit spinning factories'.[37]

This fashion was part of a wider phenomenon. As Francis Klingender and Esther Moir showed some time ago, for all the influence of the picturesque in these years, the landscape of the Industrial

[34] *Ibid.*, pp. 45–6.
[35] Thompson, *Journeys of Sir Richard Colt Hoare*, pp. 155–6.
[36] Warner, *A tour*, Vol. II, p. 145.
[37] Aston, *Manchester guide*, p. 279.

Revolution exerted considerable aesthetic appeal. Along with the cotton mills of Lancashire, the tin and copper mines of Cornwall, the salt mines of Cheshire and the ironworks of Shropshire all attracted tourist interest.[38] Arkwright's Cromford Mill (1771) near Matlock in Derbyshire, the first water-powered cotton spinning facility in the world, caused a sensation not just on account of its technological modernity but also because of its appearance – especially at night, with its fires and gas lights flaring. Sights such as this received approving comment from influential arbiters of taste such as Humphry Repton;[39] they were even seen as fit subjects for artists, inspiring the work of painters such as Joseph Wright of Derby.[40]

In some cases, and particularly before the turn of the century, manufactories and mines could be accommodated within a picturesque aesthetic. The rural location of many of the more notable sites was one reason for this, innovative technologies of production being sited amid attractive natural landscape and providing a visually striking contrast with it. Over time, however, such readings of the industrial landscape became problematic. Urbanisation and the increasing economies of scale associated with steam power made the picturesque much less compatible with industry. Factories became larger and were more typically found in built-up areas. But yet they retained some visual appeal. In particular, they could be seen as sublime objects. As Edmund Burke had put it in his hugely influential *Philosophical enquiry*, the qualities needed to produce a sublime effect included obscurity, power, privation, vastness, infinity, succession, uniformity and 'a quick transition from light to darkness'.[41] The huge, rectilinear

---

[38] F. D. Klingender, *Art and the Industrial Revolution*, 2nd edn (Chatham, 1968 [1947]); E. Moir, 'The Industrial Revolution: A romantic view', *History Today*, 9 (September 1959), 589–97; E. Moir, *The discovery of Britain: The English tourists 1540–1840* (London, 1964), pp. 91ff. See also B. Trinder, *The making of the industrial landscape* (London, 1982), pp. 54–5, 96. As Moir wrote, 'Tourists who travelled down the Wye in search of the picturesque, under the inspiration of the Rev. William Gilpin saw Tintern Abbey in alls its splendid detail, but then turned to the nearby iron-works to gain an almost equal pleasure': Moir, 'Industrial Revolution', 593.

[39] For whom the massive Bean Ing Mill (1792) in Leeds, then the largest woollen mill in the world, could 'never fail to be an interesting object by daylight, and at night presents a most splendid illumination of gas light': E. Jones, *Industrial architecture in Britain 1750–1939* (London, 1985), p. 27.

[40] Klingender, *Art and the Industrial Revolution*.

[41] Burke, *Philosophical enquiry*, pp. 54–74 (p. 73).

forms of mills and warehouses, with their regular lines, serried rows of identical windows and flaring nocturnal light effects, had these qualities in spades. By the early nineteenth century, the cotton factories of Manchester, though in no way picturesque, were visually interesting elements of the landscape because of their sublimity. Exuding blocky, massive power, Sedgwick Mill and McConnel's Mill, at Ancoats, were two prominent examples.

Into the nineteenth century, then, the industrial landscape of Manchester excited more wonder and awe than it did disapprobation. The factories themselves were impressive touristic 'sights', and the wealth they generated was seen to have had a civilising effect on the townscape while also doing much, as one antiquary declared, to make 'the British nation the most powerful in Europe … enabl[ing] us to dispute the sovereignty of the world, with an host of surrounding and envying kingdoms'.[42] Industry was doing patriotic work, and – especially in view of the wars with Revolutionary and Napoleonic France – its landscape was a fit object of patriotic valorisation. For many historians, however, this did not last. As industrialisation progressed, so the argument goes, more and more critical voices were heard lamenting its ill effects: it disfigured the countryside, polluted the environment and brutalised the people. In the context of the 'condition of England' question that climaxed with the publication of Edwin Chadwick's *Report on the sanitary condition of the labouring classes* in 1842, it seemed to many far less a national benison than a national evil. For the landscape historian Barrie Trinder, 'The popular image of mining and manufacturing became one of smoke and squalor, of overcrowding, muddy streets, drunkenness and disorder … [B]etween 1815 and 1850 … and particularly [in] the years around 1840 … the English industrial landscape … became a source of shame.'[43] Whatever aesthetic appeal factories and workshops had exerted had disappeared by this time, or so it is claimed. The 'romanticism of industry had completely evaporated', writes Esther Moir. Tourists now looked exclusively elsewhere for their pleasures, as 'Mills built of uglier materials, using cheap brick and slate, outgrowing their rural settings, sprawling

[42] J. Butterworth, *The antiquities of the town, and a complete history of the trade of Manchester* (Manchester, 1822), p. 46.
[43] Trinder, *Making of the industrial landscape*, pp. 198–201.

with trails of shoddy houses across miles of the Northern countryside, retained little that was pleasing to the eye.'[44]

There is something to be said for this interpretation. No doubt there were more voices raised against living conditions in industrial areas in the 1830s and 1840s than previously, Friedrich Engels's *Condition of the working class in England* only being the most famous example (though as Tristram Hunt has pointed out, the book's historical significance in the British context is often overstated: it was not until the 1880s and 1890s that English-language editions appeared, first in the United States in 1886, then six years later in Britain).[45] But examination of this critical commentary suggests that many of those who contributed to it did not see the social problems they identified as inevitable or systemic effects of industrialisation, or of the environment that industry created. For sure, the squalid living conditions of the labouring poor in Manchester could not be denied: as one observer wrote of the Ancoats district of the town in the year of Chadwick's report, 'Many of the houses are equal in wretchedness to the worst part of St. Giles' [a notorious London slum]; some are in a state of dilapidation, scarcely tenantable, the garrets and cellars literally crowded with inhabitants, whilst half-fed creatures are seen hanging about the doors like hungry wolves.'[46] But the city and the factory system were not typically identified as the causes of this squalor, the urban-industrial world being seen as inescapable, but also as a good thing per se.[47] Some took the line that 'the vices of the poor labouring man are the principal source of his alleged sufferings'.[48] Others, such as J. P. Kay in his influential enquiry into *The moral and physical condition of the working classes employed in the cotton manufacture in Manchester*, or William Cooke Taylor in his *Notes of a tour in the manufacturing districts of Lancashire*, argued

---

[44] Moir, 'Industrial Revolution', 597.

[45] F. Engels, *The Condition of the working class in England* (London, 2009 [1845]). For the publication history see *ibid.*, pp. 24–5; and Hunt, *Building Jerusalem*, p. 33. The book, Hunt writes, 'made almost no political impact in nineteenth-century Britain'.

[46] H. Heartwell, 'Characteristics of Manchester', *North of England Magazine*, 1 (1842), 166.

[47] Lees, *Cities perceived*, pp. 39ff.

[48] J. Wheeler, *Manchester: Its political, social and commercial history* (London, 1836), p. 201.

that 'foreign and accidental causes' were to blame.[49] Prominent among
these causes, Kay, Taylor and others suggested, were the Corn Laws,
which increased the price of bread, and Irish immigration, which – so
they claimed – brought with it a host of problems.[50] Like Liverpool,
Manchester attracted large numbers of migrants from Ireland in the
early-to-mid nineteenth century, the desperately poor conditions of life
on the west coast of that country driving people from their homes.
By 1841, over 30,000 inhabitants of Manchester were Irish-born (up
from around 5,000 in 1787); ten years later, the number had reached
45,136, equivalent to 15.2 per cent of the town's total population.[51]
These people lived in dire poverty. The area southwest of Oxford Road
known as 'Little Ireland' was especially notorious, the cotton manufacturer and political radical Richard Cobden condemning it as exhibit-
ing 'all the filth, depravity, and barbarism that disgrace its patronymic
land'.[52] For commentators such as Cobden, the problem was nothing
less than 'a moral cancer'; accustomed to living more barbarously than
the native English of Manchester, perhaps on account of their racial
difference, the immigrants from Ireland drove down the cost of labour
and so depressed living standards generally, as well as encouraging the
adoption of depraved 'Irish habits' of behaviour.[53] Indeed, even the
minority of observers who accepted that environmental factors made
'moral and virtuous' living 'almost physically impossible' for many of

[49] J. P. Kay, *The moral and physical condition of the working classes employed in the cotton manufacture in Manchester,* 2nd edn (London, 1832), p. 78; also W. C. Taylor, *Notes of a tour in the manufacturing districts of Lancashire,* 2nd edn (London, 1842), pp. 14–15, 288.

[50] Kay, *Moral and physical condition,* pp. 80ff; M. Poovey, 'Curing the "social body" in 1832: James Phillips Kay and the Irish in Manchester', *Gender and History,* 5 (1993), 196–211; Lees, *Cities perceived,* pp. 42–3.

[51] M. Busteed, 'Little islands of Erin: Irish settlement and identity in mid-nineteenth-century Manchester', in D. M. MacRaild (ed.), *The Great Famine and beyond: Irish migrants in Britain in the nineteenth and twentieth centuries* (Dublin, 2000), pp. 95–127 (p. 99).

[52] [R. Cobden], *England, Ireland, and America,* 6th edn (Edinburgh, 1836), p. 18. Engels visited Little Ireland in the 1840s, finding the cottages there 'old, dirty, and of the smallest sort, the streets uneven, fallen into ruts and in part without drains or pavements; masses of refuse, offal and sickening filth lie among standing pools in all directions; the atmosphere is poisoned by the effluvia from these, and laden and darkened by the smoke of a dozen tall factory chimneys. A horde of ragged women and children swarm about here, as filthy as the swine that thrive upon the garbage heaps and in the puddles': Engels, *Condition of the working class,* p. 98.

[53] [Cobden], *England, Ireland, and America,* p. 18.

the Manchester poor tended to note the debasing effects of 'the lower order of Irish, who, familiar with dirt and discomfort at home, were content with any sort of habitations that would receive them'.[54]

Suggesting that the problems experienced in Manchester were of foreign rather than English origin was one response to the 'condition of England' question as it affected the town, one means of protecting the image of the place from (autochthonous) taint. Another, more substantive, response was accomplished through the shaping of the Manchester landscape itself. From the 1820s on, the project of civic improvement begun in the later eighteenth century intensified markedly. Attempts were made to mitigate the effects of the air pollution caused by industrialisation, and these were far more systematic and less ineffective than often supposed, being limited by inadequate technology rather than any failure of will.[55] More important than this, however, was the ongoing architectural transformation of the town. Inspired by a keen sense of local pride, the increasingly confident Manchester middle class (which controlled the levers of power in the absence of any significant aristocratic presence) was the motive force behind this transformation.[56] New streets were laid out, and old ones were widened and improved. In the 1820s and 1830s narrow roads such as Toad Lane (previously 'one of the filthiest suburbs of the town'), King Street and Market Street were developed into stately thoroughfares more in keeping with the town's civic identity as the world metropolis of cotton.[57] In the 1840s, Manchester (and Salford) acquired three public parks, their provision being presented as evidence of local manufacturers' benevolent concern for the welfare of the common people.[58] Further middle-class involvement in philanthropy and good works

---

[54] G. R. Catt, *The pictorial history of Manchester* (London [?1845]), p. 36.

[55] Bowler and Brimblecombe, 'Air pollution in Manchester'.

[56] For the assertive civic culture and activities of the Victorian middle class in Manchester and other northern industrial cities, see in particular Hunt, *Building Jerusalem*; and S. Gunn, *The public culture of the Victorian middle class: Ritual and authority and the English industrial city, 1840–1914* (Manchester, 2000).

[57] The improvement of Market Street was particularly important. As one local writer noted in 1836, 'Market-street was previously a mere "lane"; along which two carriages could scarcely move in line: the houses were of antique structure, for the most part in a dilapidated state, and the flag-way was in many places hardly a yard wide': Wheeler, *Manchester*, p. 258.

[58] E.g. H. G. Duffield, *The stranger's guide to Manchester* (Swinton, 1984 [Manchester, 1850]), p. 37.

found expression in a proliferation of civic institutions and societies, many of which were housed in impressive buildings.[59] The most notable of these was the Manchester Athenaeum Club for the Advancement and Diffusion of Knowledge (1835), which offered its membership courses of lectures in various subjects, foreign language instruction, and the use of a library and newspaper room. The Athenaeum had premises from 1837 in a Charles Barry-designed palazzo-style building on Princess Street, greatly praised by contemporary commentators ('exceedingly beautiful', according to one guidebook).[60] Also important was the earlier-established Manchester Royal Institution (1823), which played a leading role in promoting the fine arts in the town, and occupied a much admired Greek Revival building also designed by Barry ('very handsome', and 'a splendid example of modern architecture' were typical judgments).[61] Public buildings connected with the town's administration were also erected. Although Manchester was not incorporated as a borough until 1838 and did not achieve city status until 1853, the erection of a new town hall in 1822 supplied a tangible, visible representation of local civic authority, providing a prestigious architectural mask for what was in reality – at least before granting of borough status in 1838 – a confused array of local government institutions.[62] Designed by Francis Goodwin at a cost of more than £40,000, an enormous sum at the time, the Manchester Town Hall was modelled on the Erechtheum temple of the Acropolis in Athens and had an interior decorated with specially commissioned frescoes.[63] For all that its practical shortcomings would be exposed by the 1860s (necessitating a new town hall), early Victorian opinion concurred in praising the structure and its features, finding them 'fine', 'beautiful', even 'magnificent', and appropriately emblematic of

[59] M. E. Rose, 'Culture, philanthropy and the Manchester middle classes', in A. J. Kidd and K. W. Roberts (eds.), *City, class and culture: Studies of social policy and cultural production in Victorian Manchester* (Manchester, 1985), pp. 103–17.

[60] G. Bradshaw, *Bradshaw's hand-book to the manufacturing districts of Great Britain* (London, [1854]), pp. 74, 75–6.

[61] *Osborne's guide to the Grand Junction, or Birmingham, Liverpool, and Manchester Railway*, 2nd edn (Birmingham, 1838), p. 333; T. Roscoe, *The book of the Grand Junction Railway* (London, 1839), p. 131.

[62] For this confusion, see the summary in A. J. Kidd, *Manchester: A history* (Lancaster, 2006), pp. 58–63.

[63] For descriptions, see *Manchester as it is* (Manchester, 1839), pp. 145–6.

Manchester's claims that the determined pursuit of money-getting was not inimical to cultivated taste.[64]

Neoclassical buildings such as the Royal Institution and town hall can be seen as reflecting the persistence of a polite eighteenth-century urban aesthetic. Indeed, it might even be suggested that the creation and maintenance of a 'civilised' townscape – town halls based on Greek temples, and so forth – was thought all the more necessary precisely *because* of Manchester's status as a centre of bur-geoning industry: the business of manufacturing needed offsetting, camouflaging even, by expressions of elevated culture. Yet, while ele-ments of a 'polite' visual vocabulary can certainly be detected in the discourse, it was not a predominant presence. This is evident from the pictorial representations of the Manchester landscape popular at the time. Working-class people, ordinary passers-by, and even loiterers and beggars were notably present in many of these. The engravings in George R. Catt's cheap *Pictorial history of Manchester* (*c.* 1845) provide a case in point, showing scenes suffused with what the text described as 'an air of bustle and business-like activ-ity becoming to the metropolis of the north of England'.[65] Other examples can readily be found. One of George Measom's engravings in his official guide to the North-Western Railway depicted poor street vendors plying their wares outside the town hall, while the 1857 edition of *Cornish's guide* had illustrations of Market Street, the collegiate church and other locations showing pavements featur-ing people of all classes (see fig. 23).[66]

By the middle decades of the nineteenth century, then, visual representations of the Manchester landscape were typically figured in the here-and-now, not in accordance with the conventions of an older aesthetic of politeness, for all that vestiges of this aesthetic still existed (not least because older images could readily be reproduced). Something of the character of this visual vocabulary, or at any rate the

---

[64] *Cornish's stranger's guide to Liverpool and Manchester* (London, 1838), p. 96; Roscoe, *Book of the Grand Junction Railway*, p. 132; *Osborne's guide*, p. 333.

[65] Catt, *Pictorial history*, pp. 8–9.

[66] G. Measom, *The official illustrated guide to the North-Western Railway … Including descriptions of the most important manufactories in the large towns on the line* (London, 1859), p. 439; *Cornish's stranger's guide through Manchester and Salford*, 2nd edn (Manchester, 1857), pp. 3, 37.

View of Market Street, from a Photograph by Mr Pyne.

23 *View of Market Street.* Engraving, from *Cornish's stranger's guide to Manchester and Salford* (Manchester, 1857). British Library, London, UK/ Bridgeman Images.

boisterous and popular spirit of civic pride with which it was associated, is nicely captured in the language of the ballad 'Manchester's improving daily', various versions of which were in circulation between 1820 and 1850:

> Oh! Manchester's a famous town,
> The great metropolis of trade, sirs,
> And still is rising in renown
> By the great improvements daily made, sirs.
> All strangers view it with surprise,
> And townsfolk scarce believe their eyes,
> And, looking round, cry out quite gaily,
> Manchester's improving daily.
> Where Blackfriar's Bridge was made of wood,
> 'Twas dangerous for folk to pass, sirs;
> But now it is built of stone so good,

> And nightly lighted up with gas, sirs.
> Then Market-street, it was so narrow,
> There scarce was room to wheel a barrow;
> But see it now, it's made so wide,
> Six coaches can run side-by-side.[67]

As well as being consistent with such demotic expressions of local landscape-patriotism, this new visual vocabulary did not eschew pictorial representation of explicitly industrial scenes. Indeed, in the context of the undeniably strengthening associations between industrialisation, pollution and social problems, what is striking is the extent to which industry and its appurtenances were *not* marginalised in visual renderings of Manchester. To take an early example, the section on Manchester in W. H. Pyne's *Lancashire illustrated* (1829–31) gave much attention to new and elegant civic landmarks such as the Royal

---

[67] Copied from MS Song book, *c.* 1842, in Vol. X of twelve scrapbooks compiled by Luke, James and Sam Garside, New Mills History Society, D983/10. A variant ran:

> This Manchester's a rare fine place, / For trade and other such like movements; / What town can keep up such a race, / As ours has done for prime improvements /
>
> ...
>
> Our fine town hall, that cost such cash, / Is to all buildings quite a sample; / And they say, sir, that, to make a dash, / 'Twas copied from Grecan temple /
>
> ...
>
> Once Market-Street was called a lane, / Old Toad-Lane too, a pretty pair, sir; / While Dangerous-Corner did remain, / There was hardly room for a sedan chair, sir; / But now they both are open'd wide, sir, / And dashing shops plac'd on each side, sir
>
> ...
>
> With bumping stones our streets wur paved, / From earth like large peck-loaves up rising: / All jolts and shakings now are saved / The town they're now McAdamizing: / And so smooth and soft is Cannon-Street, sir, / It suits the corns on tender feet, sir ...
>
> (anon., 'Manchester's improving daily', in A. Clayre (ed.), *Nature and industrialization: An anthology* (Oxford, 1977), pp. 119–20)

See also T. Swindells, *Manchester streets and Manchester men*, 2nd series (Manchester, 1907), pp. 97–8; and R. W. Procter, *Memorials of Manchester streets* (Edinburgh and London, 1874), p. 40. Ballads celebratory of Manchester life and landscape remained popular into the late nineteenth century. See P. Joyce, *Visions of the people: Industrial England and the question of class, 1840–1914* (Cambridge, 1991), pp. 230ff., esp. pp. 241–2.

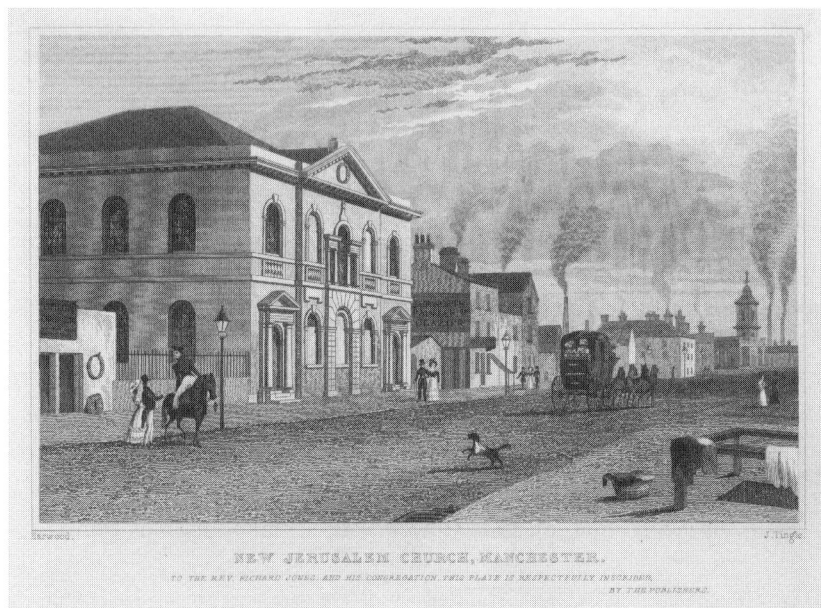

24 James Harwood, *New Jerusalem Church*, engraved by R. Wallis, from
W. H. Pyne, *Lancashire illustrated, in a series of views* (London, 1829–31).
Reproduced by kind permission of the Syndics of Cambridge University
Library: Eb.9.28.

Institution, but the physical evidence of manufacturing was far
from absent from its pictorial treatment of the place. Some engravings caught the sublime visual effect of massive cotton mills such as
Messrs Murray and Sons. Others made clear the inescapable presence
of industry in the landscape generally. One engraving showed the New
Jerusalem Church against a backdrop of smoke-belching chimneys
(fig. 24); another, of the medieval Chetham's College, was similarly
inclusive of obvious signs of industrial modernity.[68]

A later illustrated guide to Lancashire, published at the height
of the 'condition of England' debate, was similarly content to portray
the quotidian reality of industry cheek-by-jowl with civil and religious
life. One particularly striking view, which was reproduced elsewhere,[69]
showed the recently constructed Victoria Bridge (1839) over the Irwell
in the foreground, with the collegiate church flanked by a large factory

[68] W. H. Pyne, *Lancashire illustrated, in a series of views* (London, 1829–31).
[69] E.g. Catt, *Pictorial history*, p. 22; Measom, *Official illustrated guide*, p. 438.

chimney in the middle distance (see fig. 25). Yet, rather than presenting this as a visually incongruous curiosity, let alone an obscenity, the accompanying text felt it a sight in which any visitor ought to find pleasure:

> The view of and from the Victoria Bridge offers many objects of interest to the spectator. On the Manchester side we catch a glimpse of the old Collegiate Church and Cheetham [*sic*] College … while in the direction of Salford we see the best constructed and tallest chimneys of factories that are to be found in the district. Indeed some of them have a good architectural effect, and were they built of stone instead of brick, when they cease to vomit forth smoke they might pass for triumphal columns.[70]

One of the leading suppliers of engraved views of factories was George Measom, who made a considerable fortune from his popular, affordable and much republished 'official' railway guides, which began to appear in the early 1850s.[71] These volumes were intended not only to provide practical information about railway travel, but also advice to the tourist as to what was worth seeing. As might be expected, they contained extensive coverage of established attractions: the Lake District, picturesque old market towns and medieval castles got a good deal of attention. Yet, at the same time, the guides also had much to say about objects of tourist interest in industrial England. This was reflected in the textual commentary, but perhaps even more tellingly in the accompanying engravings, which were executed by Measom himself. So, while W. H. Smith's 1859 edition of Measom's *Guide to the North-Western Railway* included eighteen views of Oxford, fifteen of Chester and ten of Warwick Castle, it also featured thirty of Manchester.[72] Among these were more views of the collegiate church amid a landscape of railway bridges, chimneys and factories, as well as pictures of factories themselves.[73]

[70] [C. Redding], *An illustrated itinerary of the county of Lancaster* (London, 1842), p. 33.

[71] G. H. Martin, 'Sir George Samuel Measom (1818–1901), and his railway guides', in A. K. B. Evans and J. V. Gough (eds.), *The impact of the railway on society in Britain: Essays in honour of Jack Simmons* (Aldershot, 2003), pp. 225–40.

[72] Measom, *Official illustrated guide*.

[73] *Ibid.*, pp. 428, 438, 456, 471.

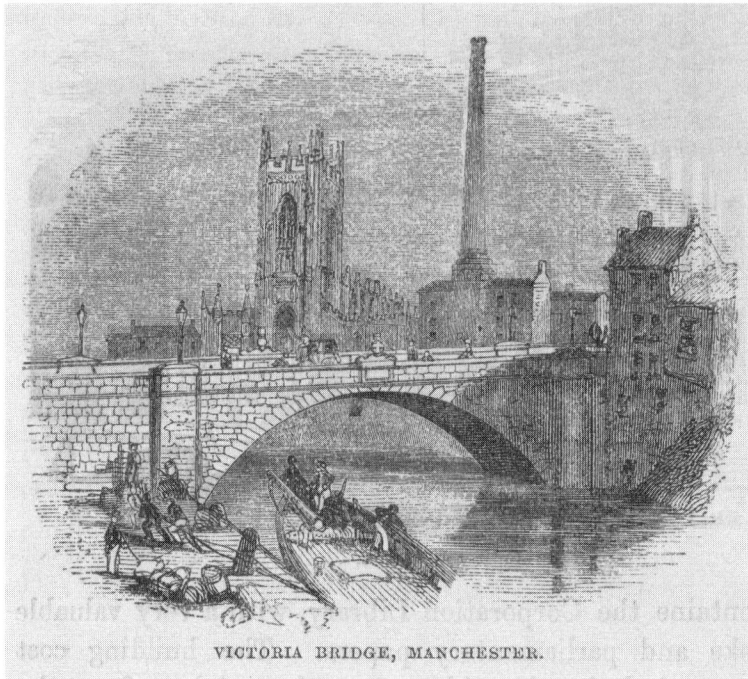

VICTORIA BRIDGE, MANCHESTER.

25 *Victoria Bridge, Manchester*. Engraving, from George Measom, *The official illustrated guide to the North-Western Railway* (London, 1859). Reproduced by kind permission of the Syndics of Cambridge University Library: 1859.7.324.

Measom was probably aware of the advantages of currying favour with Manchester entrepreneurs, whose works and productions received approving notice in his guidebooks, but his presentation of Cottonopolis as a site of tourist interest was far from fanciful. Indeed, industrial England retained considerable tourist appeal throughout the nineteenth century. Herself a Manchester resident, Elizabeth Gaskell was fond of taking her visitors to see the impressive Bridgwater Foundry at Patricroft, which her friend James Nasmyth, inventor of the steam hammer and model for John Thornton (Margaret's love-interest in *North and south*), had established on the outskirts of the town.[74] Indeed, Gaskell often furnished Manchester visitors with introductions to facilitate their being shown round some of the more notable factories.

[74] E. H. Chadwick, *Mrs Gaskell: Haunts, homes, and stories* (London, 1910), p. 216.

Writing to one man in March 1864, she was careful to 'enclose some of my cards', adding that

> they will enable you to see the things best worth [sic] in Manchester; viz '*Murray's* FINE spinning-mills', in *Union* St (I think) just off Ancoats Lane … You would there see the whole process of preparing & spinning cotton …
>
> '*Hoyle's*' print-works, Buxton St (Ardwick) off the London Road … You would there see the process of printing cotton goods, – very well explained too by the person who takes you about.
>
> '*Whitworth's*' Machine[ry] Works … these works are very interesting, if you do not get a stupid *fine* young man to show you over – try rather for one of the *working* men.[75]

Into the late Victorian period, middle-class travellers found it relatively easy to visit Manchester factories. Such visits were encouraged in the tourist literature. *Bradshaw's* famous railway handbook suggested that a visit to a factory 'is one of the chief sights of Manchester', and provided a list of some of the more interesting of them.[76] Firms recommended in this way expected to be visited by tourists, and many actively welcomed them – with or without letters of introduction. Nasmyth's Patricroft works was one example.[77] The huge Atlas Locomotive works at Ancoats was another, the volume of visitors there causing its management to put up notices advising tourists to make donations to the employee sick fund rather than tendering direct payments to the workmen detailed to show them round.[78] Established in southwest Manchester in the 1820s, Macintosh's India rubber factory even opened a model room at their plant to satisfy the curiosity of interested visitors.[79]

[75] Letter to an unknown man, 9 March 1864, in J. A. V. Chapple and A. Pollard (eds.), *The letters of Mrs Gaskell* (Manchester, 1997 [1966]), pp. 729–30.

[76] *Bradshaw's descriptive railway hand-book of Great Britain and Ireland* (Oxford, 2012 [1863]), Section III, p. 38

[77] James Nasmyth, *James Nasmyth: Engineer: An autobiography*, ed. S. Smiles, new edn (London, 1885), pp. 295–6; *The pictorial history of the county of Lancaster* (London, 1844), p. 8.

[78] *Cornish's stranger's guide through Manchester and Salford*, p. 142; Duffield, *Stranger's guide*, pp. 45–6.

[79] Duffield, *Stranger's guide*, pp. 41–2; Measom, *Official illustrated guide*, pp. 455–61.

Curiosity, of course, was a good part of the draw. As implicit in Gaskell's letter, many visitors were intrigued by the processes of industrial manufacture. In particular, and encouraged in this direction by guide-books, they were fascinated by the power of modern machinery and the magnitude of the operations carried on in the mills. At the Atlas works tourists experienced a pleasurable frisson of awe on encountering the iron guillotine of the punching and clipping machine: 'its descending knife deals as complacently with the thickest iron bars, as a lady's scissors with a piece of cambric'.[80] Their action memorably described in 1836 by Sir George Head in his much quoted *Home tour through the manufacturing districts of England*, the hydraulic presses used to compact finished fab-rics also drew much comment, and so too did the mighty steam hammers pioneered by Nasmyth.[81] As one guidebook remarked of the machinery used to compress clothes for transportation, 'He who sees this, will soon see how easily the Alps might be crushed to powder, by a few thousand gallons of water, plenty of fuel, and machinery of requisite magnitude.'[82]

With its emphasis on the pleasurably terrible power and scale of machinery, such commentary reflected the persistence of a close con-nection between industry and the sublime. The aesthetics of the sub-lime, indeed, retained some hold on the British cultural imagination, as evident, for example, in the motivations of Victorian mountaineers,[83] and – more relevant to our purposes here – the apocalyptic paintings of John Martin. But it was not just the fiery inner workings of facto-ries that addressed the sublime dispensation; their external appearance continued to do so as well. Something of this almost infernal aesthetic was caught by Benjamin Disraeli's description of Coningsby's late-night arrival at Manchester in his eponymous novel of 1844: 'He had passed over the plains where iron and coal superseded turf and corn, dingy as the entrance of Hades, and flaming with furnaces; and now he was among illumined factories with more windows than Italian pal-aces, and smoking chimneys taller than Egyptian obelisks.'[84]

---

[80] T. A. Bullock, *Bradshaw's illustrated guide to Manchester and surrounding districts* (Manchester, 1857), p. 15.

[81] G. Head, *A home tour through the manufacturing districts of England in the summer of 1835* (London, 1836), pp. 73–7.

[82] Bullock, *Bradshaw's illustrated guide*, p. 19.

[83] See P. Readman, 'William Cecil Slingsby, Norway, and British mountaineering, 1872–1914', *English Historical Review*, 129 (2014), 1098–1128.

[84] B. Disraeli, *Coningsby*, 3 vols. (London, 1844), Vol. II, p. 5.

To be sure, this was no conventional landscape of pleasure, but it was nonetheless one that fascinated many. It was interesting; it was also thrilling, transfixing. For this reason tourists did not just explore the interior of Manchester mills. They also sought views of the exterior aspect of industrial buildings – the 'brilliant appearance' their gas-light-illuminated windows presented at night exerted a particular appeal[85] – and wandered the streetscapes in which they were situated. Guidebooks enjoined the visitor to 'notice Birley's, at Chorlton, and Dewhurst's, in the Adelphi, Salford, with its tall stone chimney, 243 feet high, on a base 21 feet square and 45 feet high'; to see 'The bleach and dye works … placed up and down the Irwell and its tributaries'; to 'direct his steps to an interesting cluster situated in Chorlton-cum-Medlock, leading out of Oxford Street, on the right hand, on the banks of the river, including the large pile, known as the Oxford Road Twist Company's Mill, in that street'; and so on.[86] Such instructions ministered to the appeal of modern industrial buildings as things stupendous, awesome; as landscape features they retained the capacity to evoke the sublime that had first become apparent in the late eighteenth century. As one piece of advice to Manchester visitors had it, 'To get his mind thoroughly impressed with the magnitude of the manufactures of Manchester, the visitor should take a walk among the mills; and whatever his notions may be respecting their smoke and steam, and dust, he will be compelled to indulge in feelings of wonder at their stupendous appearance.'[87] Such language recalled that used by contemporaries to describe the sublime in nature. For many, the landscape of Cottonopolis offered experiences quite as awesome – if of course very different in form – as those to be found in the high mountains of Switzerland, or even the remote wildernesses of the New World. In a revealing comparison, Thomas Carlyle described Manchester as 'sublime as a Niagara, or more so'.[88] Others agreed. In the course of recommending that the visitor make more than one excursion to a Manchester cotton mill, one author of an itinerary of Lancashire borrowed directly from

[85] Catt, *Pictorial history*, p. 10.
[86] *Bradshaw's descriptive railway hand-book*, p. 38; *The visitor's guide to Manchester and hand-book to the attractions of the city and suburbs* (London, 1857), p. 67.
[87] *Manchester as it is*, p. 201.
[88] Thomas Carlyle, 'Chartism', in *Sartor resartus / Lectures on heroes / Chartism / Past and present* (London, 1894 [1839]), p. 51.

Carlyle in reckoning that 'The din of machinery' pervading the town 'beats the Falls of Niagara all to nothing'.[89]

Early-to-mid Victorian Manchester was thus less a polite landscape than one of drama, sublimity and business-like bustle. The street improvements and public buildings for which the town's increasingly assertive middle class was responsible did not run counter to this image, but complemented it. The wealth so dramatically created was perceived as having been put to architecturally wholesome civic uses, which in turn helped undermine suggestions that the factory system was having a degrading effect on the town's character and population. By mid-century, even in the decade of the Hungry Forties, positive appraisals of the overall built environment of Manchester were routine. In 1845, the *Builder* described the town as presenting 'a striking example of good taste' in its architecture, and three years later the same journal went so far as to claim that 'There is less bad *building* in Manchester than in London.'[90]

Approving readings of the Manchester landscape became still more prevalent as the century progressed. This was in part a function of the town's economic development. Manchester was becoming increasingly important in commercial as well as manufacturing terms. Cotton textile production remained crucial to the town's economy – and was in fact the prime motive force behind the commercial expansion.[91] But, as R. J. Morris has remarked, by the mid nineteenth century 'Manchester was as much a place of warehouses, banks and shops as it was of factories',[92] many more of the latter now being found in satellite towns such as Oldham that clustered in its hinterland. Manchester was now not only the hub of the entire textile industry of northwest England, it had established itself as a major centre of trade and finance more generally. As Measom put it in one of his railway guides, the

---

[89] Redding, *Illustrated itinerary*, p. 10.

[90] *Builder*, 3 (15 November 1845), p. 546; *Builder*, 6 (2 December 1848), p. 577 (emphasis in original).

[91] R. Lloyd-Jones and N. J. Lewis, *Manchester and the age of the factory: The business structure of Cottonopolis in the Industrial Revolution* (London, 1988).

[92] R. J. Morris, 'Structure, culture and society in British towns', in M. Daunton (ed.), *The Cambridge urban history of Britain*, Vol. III: *1840–1950* (Cambridge, 2000), p. 401.

'wonderful city' was now an 'emporium of commerce'; it was, indeed, 'the great emporium of England's manufactures'.[93] This economic transformation had a crucial effect on the physical appearance of the town. In its central streets, old houses and other buildings were swept away to make room for enormous and much admired warehouses. The successively rebuilt, increasingly large and elaborate Manchester Exchange came to stand as a monument to the commercial vigour of the place, quite apart from its practical function as a venue for trade transactions. With its huge central hall, the grand neoclassical building was celebrated as the largest trading exchange in Europe by the late 1830s,[94] being a popular tourist attraction as well as an object of civic pride. A visit to see the 'Parliament of cotton' assembled to broker hugely valuable deals 'with a mere word or a nod' at 'High 'Change' on Tuesdays was recommended in the guidebooks.[95] One suggested that it was 'the first great object of curiosity to a visitor of Manchester', another that the interior of the 'handsome and commodious edifice' offered 'one of the most attractive sights Manchester can present to the stranger'.[96]

But in fact it was the warehouses, of which according to one estimate there were 1,724 by 1857,[97] that commanded the most attention. They became emblematic of Manchester and its landscape, to the extent that *Heywood's* 1857 guide could declare that 'Warehouses form ... the staple of Manchester; to describe *them* is to describe *it*.'[98] To a limited extent, these often massive structures could be accommodated within the same aesthetic sensibility that valued the forms of cotton mills. At night, particularly when illuminated, they could produce attractively sublime or mysterious effects – helped in this respect by their sheer size. One popular recommendation made to visitors was to take time in the early evening to admire the blazing lights of the warehouse windows high in the sky, and perhaps to

[93] Measom, *Official illustrated guide*, pp. 428, 450.

[94] Briggs, *Victorian cities*, p. 107.

[95] Redding, *Illustrated itinerary*, p. 9; *Manchester as it is*, p. 200; Bullock, *Bradshaw's illustrated guide*, pp. 28–9.

[96] Redding, *Illustrated itinerary*, p. 9; J. Perrin, *The Manchester handbook: An authentic account of the place and its people* (Manchester, 1857), pp. 121–2, 123.

[97] Bullock, *Bradshaw's illustrated guide*, p. 6.

[98] A. Heywood, *Heywood's pictorial guide to Manchester and companion to the Art Treasures Exhibition* (Manchester, 1857), pp. 35–6 (emphasis in original).

linger a while to see them disappear, a row at a time, as the working day came to an end.[99]

During most of that working day, however, warehouses presented less a sublime than a magnificent or even a beautiful appearance. Following the model that had been pioneered by Barry in his Palazzo-style Athenaeum, local architects such as Edward Walters (1801–72) and John Edgar Gregan (1813–55) turned to Italy for inspiration in their warehouse designs.[100] It was a sound choice. Purely utilitarian brick boxes would no longer do for Manchester's increasingly self-confident class of merchant princes, who wanted their firms to project a distinctive and attractive face to the world, and more specifically to their clients, who visited the warehouses in person to make purchases and strike deals. Classical styles based on capitals and columns, while suitably grand, imposed restrictions on scale, building materials, and the dimensions and placement of windows and doors; they were thus deemed impracticable for warehouses.[101] By contrast, a style based on the mansions of the Italian Renaissance offered much more flexibility, enabling buildings to be designed to any size and constructed of brick, stone or a combination of materials, and allowing for the numerous windows that warehouses required.

In addition to these practical considerations, however, Italianate designs – such as Walters's for James Brown and Sons on Portland Street (1851–2) – projected an image perfectly in step with Manchester's developing civic identity as a great trading capital. Without sacrificing function to form, architects such as Walters and Gregan – and by extension their clients – intended the massive, boldly ornamented warehouses they erected to evoke the splendour and wealth of the city states of Renaissance Italy. In this they were triumphantly successful. By November 1847, the *Builder* could declare that Manchester demonstrated that 'we need not now point exclusively to the commercial cities of Italy' for 'the proof that warehouses may be designed of a character in accordance with their purpose, and yet without any absence

[99] *Cornish's stranger's guide through Manchester and Salford*, pp. 142–4; Duffield, *Stranger's guide*, p. 40; Heywood, *Heywood's pictorial guide*, pp. 35–6.
[100] C. Stewart, *The stones of Manchester* (London, 1956), pp. 34–8; R. Dixon and S. Muthesius, *Victorian architecture* (London, 1978), pp. 127–8.
[101] J. H. G. Archer, 'Introduction', in J. H. G. Archer (ed.), *Art and architecture in Victorian Manchester* (Manchester, 1985), pp. 14–16.

of the graces of art'.[102] Six years later, another observer told readers of *Fraser's Magazine* that the warehouses of central Manchester 'rival in architecture the palaces of Venice'.[103] Guidebooks declared that the warehouses of Mosley Street, Portland Street and elsewhere had become 'a very striking object of attention to the stranger', and indeed 'one of the most attractive features of the streets of Manchester'; they felt sure that 'No one would think of a visit to this city' without seeing them.[104] Certainly it seems many visitors to Manchester followed such advice; directions to tourists as to which warehouses to see, and how best to inspect their interiors (this presented 'no difficulty' according to *Black's guide*) continued to be issued right up until the First World War.[105]

Aside from warehouses, other buildings contributed to Manchester's presentation of itself as, in the words of local architect Thomas Worthington, 'the Florence … of the nineteenth century'.[106] Pre-eminent among these was Walters's Free Trade Hall (1853–6; fig. 26). Built on the site of the Peterloo Massacre of 1819, which had seen soldiers bloodily disperse a mass meeting assembled to demand parliamentary reform, the hall was a powerful monument to the city's political liberalism and commercial identity, both of which were closely associated with support for free trade – not least on account of Manchester's having played a leading role in the anti-Corn Law agitations of the 1840s.

The building was (and is) an architectural masterpiece. Writing in 1969, Nikolaus Pevsner judged it to be 'perhaps the noblest monument in the Cinquecento style in England',[107] and indeed it was very deliberately designed to evoke – as with Walters's warehouses – the spirit of the Renaissance. This was well understood at the time. *Heywood's* 1857 guide described the building as 'Italian, or Lombardo-Venetian, a style which, taken in connexion with many of the new buildings of Manchester, not inappropriately recalls the glories of the Italian

[102] *Builder*, 5 (6 November 1847), p. 526.
[103] 'Manchester, by a Manchester man', *Fraser's Magazine*, 47 (June 1853), 615.
[104] *Cornish's stranger's guide through Manchester and Salford*, p. 142; H. G. Duffield, *The pocket companion; or, Stranger's guide to Manchester* (Manchester, [c. 1852/3]), p. 23; Bullock, *Bradshaw's illustrated guide*, p. 17.
[105] *Black's guide to Manchester and Salford* (Edinburgh, 1868), p. 24; J. E. Morris, *Black's guide to Manchester and Salford,* 14th edn (Edinburgh, 1909), p. 32.
[106] Stewart, *Stones of Manchester*, p. 86, quoting Thomas Worthington.
[107] N. Pevsner, *Lancashire, I: The industrial and commercial south* (Harmondsworth, 1969), p. 270.

26 The Free Trade Hall, Manchester, from *Our own country* (London, 1898). Photo courtesy of Universal History Archive/Universal Images Group via Getty Images.

commercial cities in their best period'.[108] Similar assessments were offered by other commentators, the consensus being that the Italianate style of the Free Trade Hall – whatever the rights or wrongs of free trade as a policy – was a great ornament to Manchester, a fitting symbol of the city's commercial and national greatness.[109]

The dominance of the Palazzo style reached its apogee in the 1850s and 1860s. By this time, Italianate influences could even be detected in the design of factories, with double pilasters, stone mouldings and decorative windows being seen on some mill buildings.[110] Victoria Mills (1867) on the eastern side of Manchester provides one such example, its architect, George Woodhouse, being a prominent exponent of Italianate-inflected factory design. One of the most striking

---

[108] Heywood, *Heywood's pictorial guide*, p. 39.
[109] Bullock, *Bradshaws's illustrated guide*, pp. 25–7; *Varley and Robinson's guide for the stranger in Manchester* (Salford, 1857), p. 9; *Visitor's guide*, pp. 51–2.
[110] M. Williams with D. A. Farnie, *Cotton mills in Greater Manchester* (Preston, 1992), p. 79.

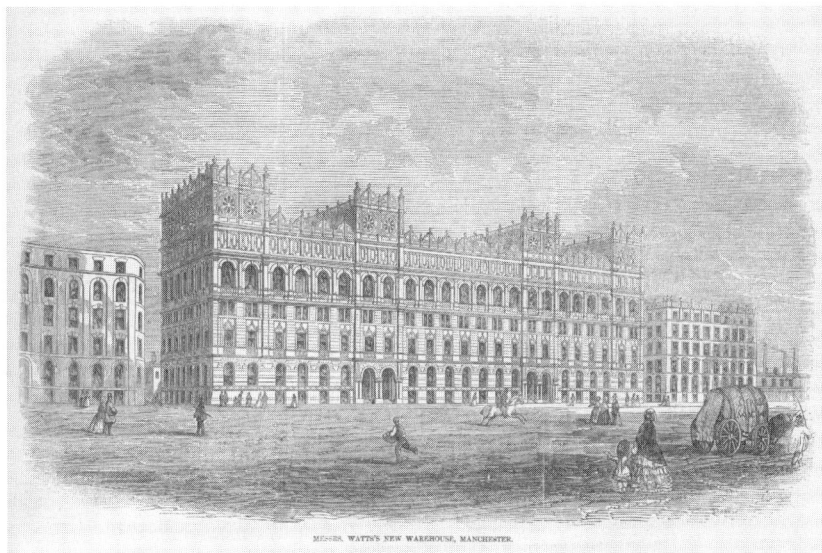

MESSRS. WATTS'S NEW WAREHOUSE, MANCHESTER.

27 *Messrs. Watts's new warehouse, Manchester*, Illustrated London News, 6 December 1856. Reproduced by kind permission of the Syndics of Cambridge University Library: NPR.C.313.

features of the Victoria Mills building was its ornate arcaded chimney, the shaft of which towered up from a massive seven-storey octagonal base.[111] Chimneys could provide opportunities for architectural expression, and indeed had been praised as 'elegant' from the early nineteenth century on.[112] Worthington – another architect influenced by the Italian Renaissance – even constructed a furnace chimney at Salford in the style of the tower of Siena.[113] But stylistic eclecticism was beginning to creep in. An early and notable example of this tendency was presented by S. and J. Watts's new warehouse complex on Portland Street (fig. 27), which was designed by the architects Henry Travis and William Mangall and completed in 1856. This 'majestic pile of buildings'[114] departed from the coherent and more restrained Italianate pioneered by Walters; lavishly and variously ornamented, each storey offered a different architectural style, from Renaissance to Elizabethan.

---

[111] I. Beesley and P. De Figueiredo, *Victorian Manchester and Salford* (Halifax, 1988), n.p., Plate 12.

[112] Layton-Jones, *Beyond the metropolis*, p. 96.

[113] Stewart, *Stones of Manchester*, pp. 80–1.

[114] Bullock, *Bradshaw's illustrated guide*, p. 18.

Yet for all its stylistic eclecticism, Watts's design was much acclaimed by contemporaries as a virtuoso essay in magnificence and grandeur, as a suitably palatial symbol of the power of Manchester commerce and of the city's significance in national life. Surveying the scene in Portland Street in 1857, *Bradshaw's* guide took a sly dig at the state of affairs on the European Continent in describing the Watts buildings as

> structures fit for kings … which many a monarch might envy. There are some eight or ten sovereign princes in Germany, whose entire revenues would not pay the cost of these warehouses. The industrial and scientific energy which has reared them is an honour to our country, and speaks well for the future of Manchester. The artistic display is all but equal to the noble enterprise which gave them being. They are, indeed, the most splendid adornment of this city.[115]

Routinely mentioned in the tourist literature as one of the sights of Manchester, Watts's 'princely structure' became a monument to the city's Victorian commercial identity and an object of patriotic pride.[116] Later warehouses, while not surpassing Watts's in the richness of their decoration, also featured bold, sumptuous and stylistically various ornamentation, an impression of palatial splendour being the visual effect typically intended.[117] A nice illustration of their connotation with luxury is given by the fact that, as early as 1880, one warehouse was converted into an upmarket hotel (such repurposing would become more prevalent in the twentieth and twenty-first centuries; at the time of writing, Watts's is owned by the Britannia hotel group).[118]

The increasing eclecticism seen in warehouse designs was in part a function of the Victorian 'battle of styles' in architecture, the inconclusiveness of which resulted in diversity of architectural form. As J. Mordaunt Crook has shown, the struggle over architectural style

---

[115] *Ibid.*, pp. 17–19.
[116] W. A. Shaw, *Manchester old and new*, 3 vols. (London, 1894), Vol. II, pp. 38, 39.
[117] S. Taylor, M. Cooper and P. S. Barnwell, *Manchester: The warehouse legacy* (London, 2002), pp. 28–33.
[118] Jones, *Industrial architecture*, p. 89.

was a function of the historicism of the age, of the Victorian habit of looking back to find inspiration for progress. What Crook calls this 'acute awareness of history', this very self-conscious knowledge of the past, presented a range of architectural styles from which to choose and gave rise to heated debate.[119] Arguments over the suitability of Gothic as a model for buildings in Britain were at the heart of this debate, and had a significant impact on Manchester. As was also the case elsewhere, in and around Manchester the Gothic had provided a staple template for the design of churches since the early decades of the nineteenth century, finding expression, for example, in Francis Goodwin's St George's, Hulme (1826–8) and Barry's St Matthew, Castlefield (1822–5).[120] Its popularity in this regard continued into the mid Victorian period, as seen in the erection of religious buildings such as G. S. Scott's Christ Church, Denton (1853), A. W. N. Pugin's St Francis, Gorton (1863), and G. E. Street's St Peter, Swinton (1868). Following the commissioning of the new Gothic Houses of Parliament in 1836, however, the popularity of the style as one suited to secular uses grew markedly. This was particularly the case in northern England, where Gothic was perceived by many to offer an ideal model for the new civic buildings now required by burgeoning and increasingly populous urban centres.

Manchester, of course, was one such centre, and Gothic made a lasting mark on its secular quite as much as its religious architecture. Supported by Ruskin's advocacy, a Venetian-Gothic aesthetic made the early running. Helpfully evocative of commercial greatness as well as refined taste, and so seeming especially apposite in a Manchester context, it found its most authoritative exponent in Alfred Waterhouse, who followed up works such as his Binyon and Fryer warehouse (1855–6) with the Manchester Assize Courts (1859–64). An astonishingly accomplished application of the style to a public building, the Assize Courts was much admired by contemporaries (including Ruskin, who regarded it as 'much beyond anything yet done in England on my principles').[121] Guidebooks declared it to be an 'architectural triumph'

[119] See J. M. Crook, *The dilemma of style: Architectural ideas from the picturesque to the post-modern* (Chicago, 1987), esp. pp. 98, 126–31 (p. 131).

[120] C. Hartwell, *Manchester* (New Haven and London, 2002), p. 20.

[121] Cited in G. Tyack, 'Architecture', in F. O'Gorman (ed.), *The Cambridge companion to John Ruskin* (Cambridge, 2015), p. 109.

and 'one of the finest Gothic buildings of modern days'.[122] Its Venetian-Gothic style provided an influential model for the work of other Manchester-based architects, including Worthington's Memorial Hall (1863–6) and Police Courts (1868), and Edward Salomon's Reform Club (1870).

Soon after the completion of the Assize Courts, Waterhouse was responsible for a perhaps still more impressive Gothic public building for Manchester: a new town hall (1867–77; fig. 28). Located on an awkward, triangular-shaped site off Albert Square in the city centre, the town hall was the brainchild of the middle-class Liberal businessmen who dominated mid Victorian Manchester's local government, in particular Joseph Thompson and Abel Heywood, the building being opened in Heywood's second term as mayor.[123] These individuals were motivated by a keen, historically informed sense of civic pride, by a patriotic desire – as Heywood put it afterwards – to present 'a worthy monument of the industrial greatness of Manchester and an outward and visible sign to the world that we are not wholly given up to Mammon and that the higher culture is not neglected among us'.[124] In this, they – and their architect Waterhouse – were triumphantly successful. In the years after its completion, the building was celebrated throughout Britain as 'the most magnificent Town Hall in England' and, by extension, 'the finest municipal building in the world'.[125] It soon became a tourist attraction, one of the established sights of the city. As cheap guidebooks to the town hall explained, tours of the main parts of the building, such as the state rooms and council chamber, were available every day (a three-person ticket cost 6d); and on Saturday mornings its corridors and large rooms were thrown open to the public for free.[126]

[122] *J. H.'s complete pocket guide to Manchester and Salford* (Manchester, [1869]), pp. 14–15; *Black's guide to Manchester and Salford*, p. 10; also E. P., *Hand-book to the Manchester Assize Courts* (Manchester, 1864).

[123] For detailed discussion of the town hall and its construction, see C. Dellheim, *The face of the past: The preservation of the medieval inheritance in Victorian England* (Cambridge, 1982), Chapter 4; for Heywood, see M. Beetham, 'Heywood, Abel (1810–1893)', in *Oxford dictionary of national biography*.

[124] Dellheim, *Face of the past*, pp. 144–5.

[125] *Official guide to the Midland Railway* (London, 1893), p. 247; *Manchester of to-day* (London, 1888), p. 50. See also, e.g., W. Tomlinson, *Gossiping guide to Manchester and Salford* (Manchester and London, 1887), p. 113.

[126] [W. E. A. Axon], *Guide to the new town hall* (Manchester, [1878]); *Guide to Manchester town hall* (Manchester, [1884]).

28 Manchester Town Hall, from *Sights and scenes in England and Wales* (London, [*c.* 1899]). Photo courtesy of The Print Collector/Getty Images.

Chosen as the winner of a city council-run competition that had drawn 137 entries, Waterhouse's design this time was not Venetian in its inspiration. Its precedents were instead the thirteenth-century forms of Gothic seen in the medieval civic buildings of northern France and Belgium. Redolent of the robust spirit of liberty and self-government thought to have animated the prosperous trading towns of medieval northern Europe, this language of Gothic seemed as appropriate a model as its Italian variant for a nineteenth-century city keen to memorialise its present-day industrial and commercial pre-eminence. (It certainly now seemed more appropriate than the elegant classicism of the old town hall, a building anyway too small to accommodate the great volume of local government business transacted.) As one commentator reflected in 1894,

> The hall is worthy of the city which has been the birthplace of Free Trade and nineteenth-century commerce ... If ever the candlestick be removed from her midst, and the commercial glory

of Manchester extinguished, let us hope that the City Hall will remain a memento as redolent of high association as those grand old City Halls of the Low Countries, which still live to speak of commercial greatness memorable, not for itself alone, but from its intimate connection with loftiest national endeavour.[127]

The commemorative force of the building was further underlined in the details of its decoration, much of which celebrated Manchester's connections with free trade, commerce and industry – and by extension its contribution to national identity, national greatness and the course of national history. Adorning the exterior were roundels depicting spinning and weaving, and the coats of arms of leading manufacturers, as well as figures of St George and Queens Victoria and Elizabeth. The interior was similarly redolent of local and national pride, benefiting from such features as three huge staircases, each one built of granite from a different part of the United Kingdom; a large statue of the great free trader John Bright; and – most strikingly of all – a series of murals by the pre-Raphaelite artist Ford Madox Brown. These paintings told a confident and optimistic story of Manchester's history from medieval times, paying notable attention to the city's economic development. Painted on the walls of the Great Hall, their subjects included 'the establishment of Flemish weavers at Manchester AD 1363', 'John Kay, inventor of the Fly Shuttle, AD 1753' and 'the opening of the Bridgewater Canal, AD 1761'.[128]

Throughout all its various iterations, Manchester's Victorian Gothic revival did not reflect any revulsion for the strident commercial-industrial modernity of Cottonopolis. In his work on the town hall, Waterhouse saw himself as designing a building fit for the present-day needs of local government. Function was not sacrificed to form, the design being as attentive to the building's practical operation as it was to its appearance and iconographic significance (considerations of utility were, in fact, important in the council's decision to choose

[127] Shaw, *Manchester old and new*, Vol. I, p. 96.
[128] On the artwork of the murals, see J. Treuherz, 'Ford Madox Brown and the Manchester murals', in Archer, *Art and architecture in Victorian Manchester*, pp. 162–207. On the murals as evidence of a desire, on the part of civic leaders, to draw on the past to craft a positive and forward-looking narrative, see Joyce, *Visions of the people*, pp. 182–3.

Waterhouse as winner of the competition).[129] As guidebooks to the building had it, 'The style of the Town Hall may be best described as thirteenth century Gothic', but – they were also careful to add – 'so far from being medieval in execution it is distinctly modern in its conception and adaptation to the multifarious requirements of the present age'.[130] Such adaptation included provision of a state-of-the-art heating system, among other modern conveniences that were integrated into Waterhouse's overall design.[131] This felicitous marriage of modernity and historicity was also pulled off in other Gothic buildings of the later Victorian period. One example from London was Tower Bridge, opened to the public in 1894: for all its kitsch, this mock-medieval construction was, as Richard Dennis has shown, an effective and popular embodiment of the 'integration of tradition and modernity' characteristic of the Victorian city.[132] In Manchester, in the years after the erection of the town hall, perhaps the most prominent example of such a building – and one more artistically satisfying than Tower Bridge – was Basil Champneys's Arts-and-Crafts-inflected late-century masterpiece, the John Rylands Library (1890–9). Built in the distinctively English style of Perpendicular Gothic and deliberately drawing on the architecture of Oxford and Winchester, the library was lauded by contemporaries as 'eminently an English building founded on English types'.[133] Yet, for all its imaginative flights of Gothic fancy, it remained emphatically modern in its functional design. Among other things, it was one of the first public buildings in Britain to benefit from internal electric lighting, and also boasted an ambitiously high-tech ventilation system designed to filter the polluted Manchester air before circulating it around the building.[134]

Yet, despite all this attention to present-day needs, the Gothic was nevertheless inescapably evocative of pre-industrial times. Surveying the efflorescence of Gothic architecture in mid-to-late

---

[129] Dellheim, *Face of the past*, p. 149.

[130] *Guide to Manchester town hall* (Manchester, n.d.), p. 10; *Guide to the new town hall*, 2nd edn (Manchester, n.d.), p. 6.

[131] Dellheim, *Face of the past*, pp. 136–9.

[132] Dennis, *Cities in modernity*, pp. 10–14 (p. 10).

[133] W. Whyte, 'Building the nation in the town: Architecture and identity in Britain', in W. Whyte and O. Zimmer (eds.), *Nationalism and the reshaping of urban communities in Europe, 1848–1914* (Basingstoke, 2011), p. 219.

[134] J. Hodgson, '"Carven stone and blazoned pane": The design and construction of the John Rylands Library', *Bulletin of the John Rylands Library*, 89 (2012), 60–4.

Victorian Manchester, Charles Dellheim has observed that 'All these buildings created a sense of the past in one of the major citadels of modernity.'[135] In a sense, this is a curious conjunction. With their connotations of commercial wealth and splendour, Renaissance Venice and the prosperous medieval trading cities of the Low Countries may have provided appropriate historical models for the architectural landscape of Manchester, but why reference these precedents at all? Why did the burghers and merchants of now brashly self-confident Cottonopolis need the past as much as they did?

Certainly, their need for the past was strongly felt, and perhaps unusually so. The Gothic revival took hold with greater force in Manchester than in many other British towns and cities. But its purchase was not the only – or perhaps even the most significant – index of the city's engagement with history. Interest not just in the past in general, but in Manchester's past in particular, grew steadily over the course of the nineteenth century. Early histories had followed the lead of John Whitaker's *History of Manchester* (1771–3) in making claims for the town's being of ancient origin.[136] While few went as far as Whitaker in asserting that the history of Manchester dated from pre-Roman times, that the place was the site of a Roman fort (Mancunium) established by Agricola in or around AD 79 was routinely mentioned. In these texts, a good deal of attention was also paid to the medieval and early modern history of the town, with authors showing a particular desire to date the origins and trace the development of its manufacturing industry.[137] The findings of local historians were drawn on by contemporaneous tourist guides, which presented their own historical narratives emphasising the great age of what might at first sight seem to the visitor to be the most modern of modern towns.[138] 'Manchester has high claims to antiquity' was the leitmotif of these often quite lengthy accounts.[139]

---

[135] Dellheim, *Face of the past*, p. 132.

[136] J. Whitaker, *The history of Manchester*, 2 vols. (London, 1771–3).

[137] See, e.g., Aston, *Manchester guide*; Wheeler, *Manchester*. One indication of contemporary interest in the early records of the town is the publication, in 1839, of a new edition of Hollingworth's 'Chronicles of Manchester': R. Hollingworth, *Mancuniensis; or, An history of the towne of Manchester and what is most memorable concerning it*, ed. W. Willis (Manchester, 1839 [c. 1656]).

[138] See, e.g., *Cornish's stranger's guide through Manchester and Salford*, pp. 8–16.

[139] *Manchester as it is*, p. 12; and for an example of extensive treatment, Perrin, *Manchester handbook*, pp. 11–40.

The engagement with Manchester history evident in these publications was both cause and consequence of the growth of organised
antiquarianism in the town. Along with botany, geology, art collect-
ing and other self-improving intellectual activities, antiquarianism and
local history had considerable appeal for the cotton-enriched members
of the Manchester middle class, and societies devoted to their pursuit
flourished as a consequence. The most important of these organisations
were the Chetham Society, established in 1843, and the Lancashire and
Cheshire Antiquarian Society (LCAS), which was set up in 1884.[140]
Both attracted healthy memberships; published papers and proceedings; and, by the mid Victorian period, had achieved a significant
place in the civic life of the town. Many of the individuals involved
in these societies became local figures of some prominence on account
of their historical activities. A founder member of LCAS and author
of *Annals of Manchester* (1886), an impressively comprehensive year-
by-year digest of local history 'from the earliest times', the journalist,
folklorist and librarian William E. A. Axon was one such example.[141]
Another representative figure was William Arthur Shaw, editor of several Chetham Society volumes and fellow of Owens College (precursor to the modern-day Manchester University, housed from 1873 in
handsome Waterhouse-designed Gothic premises on Oxford Road,
to the south of the city centre). Shaw, who became a noted economic
historian of seventeenth-century Britain, was also keenly interested in
the local history of Lancashire and Manchester, and along with other
works reflecting this interest published, in 1894, a lavishly illustrated
three-volume antiquarian topography, *Manchester old and new*.[142]

By the time this book appeared, public engagement with
the Manchester past was entrenched in local civic culture. This
reflected a general nationwide broadening and deepening of popular historical-consciousness in the late nineteenth century, the indices
of which were as apparent in Manchester as they were elsewhere.[143]

---

[140] For the histories of these societies, see A. G. Crosby, *A society with no equal: The
Chetham Society, 1843–1993* (Manchester, 1993); J. W. Jackson, 'The Lancashire
and Cheshire Antiquarian Society, 1883–1943', *Transactions of the Lancashire
and Cheshire Antiquarian Society*, 57 (1943–4), 1–17. See also B. Hollingworth,
'Lancashire writing and the antiquarians', *Journal of Regional and Local Studies*, 6
(1985), 27–35.

[141] W. E. A. Axon (ed.), *The annals of Manchester* (Manchester and London, 1886).

[142] Shaw, *Manchester old and new*.

[143] Readman, 'Place of the past'.

This historical-consciousness, moreover, was closely bound up with place: the fast-changing Manchester landscape was increasingly read as storied. Such was apparent from books like Shaw's, of which a number appeared in the 1870s, 1880s and 1890s. One example was James Croston's *Old Manchester* of 1875, which, in the words of its subtitle, presented 'a series of views of the more ancient buildings in Manchester and its vicinity, as they appeared fifty years ago'.[144] Perhaps more telling as evidence of the late-century interconnections between landscape and history was the magazine *Manchester Faces and Places*. Launched in October 1889, it contained articles on local personalities and sights of note, together with 'fine reproductions of portraits, public buildings, and the various places of interest and picturesque beauty contained in and around the city'.[145] Strikingly, in its coverage of 'places' the past loomed large. Historical landmarks such as the medieval Chetham's College were given much attention, as were the historical associations attaching even to apparently very modern streetscapes. The domestic architecture of Tudor and Elizabethan times was a particular preoccupation. In article after illustrated article, the small and often quaint black-and-white buildings that remained in the city centre were noted and discussed, as were the very much grander timber-framed manor houses of the same era, such as Wardley Hall, that were still to be found in its hinterland.

The value so placed on the vernacular architecture of the sixteenth century was of a piece with the contemporaneous, and nationwide, appeal of an ideal of an older, more picturesque and 'Merrie' England, of which the folk-song and dance revival and to a certain extent the emergent landscape preservation movement were also manifestations. As with this wider phenomenon, it is possible to read Manchester's variant of it as expressive of a reactionary impulse, a culturally conservative rejection of a now exponentially developing modernity. As also with this wider phenomenon, however, such a reading would be a mistake. Cultural engagement with the past had become more intense and pervasive as the nineteenth century progressed, and towns such as Manchester were no exception to this.[146] Indeed, the industrial-commercial landscape of such places may itself have been an

[144] J. Croston, *Old Manchester: A series of views of the more ancient buildings in Manchester and its vicinity, as they appeared fifty years ago* (Manchester, 1875).
[145] 'To our readers', *Manchester Faces and Places*, 1 (1890), 90.
[146] Joyce, *Visions of the people*, esp. Chapter 7, 'The sense of the past', pp. 172ff.

important additional stimulus to this engagement. After all, the expansion and development of Manchester had led to the disappearance of many sixteenth-century buildings in and around the city. As Patrick Joyce has commented, 'in the new industrial towns of the north of England … the rapidity of urban and industrial changes called into being both the awareness of a past believed slipping away, and a history in which town and industry figured as symbols of national and industrial progress … economic and social advance were emphasised all the more by being given a pedigree'.[147] Thus the increased interest shown by Mancunians in their history did not reflect revulsion for their present, but rather a desire to make sense of it, to preserve and celebrate a sense of continuity with the past, for the benefit of current and future generations. Something similar was happening in London at the same time, where – as Lynda Nead has shown – the appeal of the historical and the picturesque persisted amid the sweeping improvement works that were transforming the Metropolitan landscape.[148] In Manchester, as elsewhere, this holding on to the past was a means of preserving a coherent sense of civic identity, of better understanding the city's national significance and how it had come to attain this significance. It helped form the building blocks of very modern-day sentiments of local pride; as evident from the accounts in tourist guidebooks, the long and continuous history of Manchester was a subject about which many saw fit to boast. In the late Victorian and into the Edwardian period, the world did seem to be changing faster than it had done before,[149] but the concomitant rise of what might be termed heritage-consciousness worked in step with rather than against the pace of these changes. Awareness of and care for the past and its landscapes, which involved appreciation of the still-existing and identity-bolstering continuities with former ages, made the experience of change less dislocating – perhaps even more possible – than it might otherwise have been.

Attitudes to the late Victorian cultural landscape of Manchester provide a good illustration of this phenomenon in action, and all the more so because of the immutable modernity of the place, its status as one of the 'shock cities' of the nineteenth century. A particularly revealing case study in this regard is the 1887 Exhibition, an elaborate

---

[147] *Ibid.*, pp. 180, 181.
[148] Nead, *Victorian Babylon*.
[149] Kern, *Culture of time and space*.

civic event held in honour of Queen Victoria's Golden Jubilee. In contrast to the earlier 1857 Art-Treasures Exhibition, the city council this time resolved to celebrate manufacturing, science and handicrafts as well as high culture. To this end, the enormous exhibition building erected at Old Trafford was divided into sections, the intention being to emphasise the diversity of Manchester's contribution to national life. There were displays of musical instruments, paintings, sculpture and pottery, but also areas devoted to chemistry, manufactured goods and machinery. Indeed, the Great Hall of the exhibition building was entirely given over to machinery, presenting – or so the organisers claimed – the largest and highest-quality collection of its kind ever assembled.[150] The exhibition was a great success, achieving large attendance figures in comparison with comparable events held around the same time.[151] More than 4.7 million people visited over the course of 166 days between May and November, with nearly 75,000 coming on one day alone.[152]

Described in guidebooks as 'probably … the greatest treat of the whole show', and after the event as being of 'immense' popularity and 'a conspicuous success', the outdoor display of 'Old Manchester and Salford' was one of the real draws of the exhibition. Masterminded by local architect Alfred Darbyshire, this was a life-size exhibit of Manchester architecture from Roman to late Georgian times. Visitors entered via a carefully researched replica of the Porta Decumana of ancient Mancunium, guarded by Roman soldiers, and went through into a mock-up of Market-Sted Lane and other old Manchester streets. There they could wander among and into reproductions of old buildings, encountering as they did so exhibition employees dressed in historical costumes. The avowed intention of the organisers was to emphasise the richness of Manchester's architectural heritage, while at the same time demonstrating – as contemporaneous guidebooks and local histories also did – the long continuities of the city's history, stretching back to

[150] W. Tomlinson, *The pictorial record of the Royal Jubilee Exhibition, Manchester, 1887* (Manchester, 1887), p. 103.
[151] Total attendance was 4,765,137. The Liverpool Exhibition of 1886 drew 2,668,118 visitors over 156 days, with the figures for the Edinburgh International Exhibition of 1886 being 2,769,632 over 151 days. The footfall at the Jubilee Exhibition compared favourably even to that at the Art-Treasures Exhibition of 1857 (1,336,715 over 141 days). See *ibid.*, p. 142.
[152] *Ibid.*

Roman times. It was a memorial to the historic landscape of the place, and its popularity was a telling indication of the rising strength of heritage-consciousness. Above all, it reflected a concern – later shown in the pages of *Manchester Faces and Places* – with the vernacular architecture of the sixteenth century. In Old Manchester and Salford, half-timbered shops, inns and manor houses abounded, the now largely disappeared black-and-white buildings of the early modern town being resurrected for modern-day perusal and appreciation.[153]

This valorisation of a Tudor aesthetic bled over into the rest of the exhibition. Far from looking outwards to the empire for their visual cues, as might perhaps be expected at this time, the organisers turned inwards to the English past. In a telling demonstration of modernity's need, in Richard Dennis's words, for 'picturesque props',[154] the walls of the main exhibition hall, which housed the great display of machinery, featured Tudor-style timber-frame decorations, as did some of the doorways and entrances. As the official *Pictorial Record* described it, the sides of the nave of the exhibition building had 'quaintly picturesque decorations … consisting principally of reproductions of old English gabled and half timbered house fronts'.[155] Along with Old Manchester and Salford, such decorative touches expressed a desire to bring the past into the service of the present, to frame the great advances of modernity – all that sophisticated new machinery and so on – in an historical context. Of course, the 'Merrie England' Tudor aesthetic was no discovery of the late Victorian period, having animated the early-nineteenth-century popular 'Olden Time' cult, as Mandler has shown.[156] But it did gain renewed currency in these years, finding expression in musical tastes, art and design, and – by the Edwardian period – the fashion for historical pageantry.[157] Unlike the

---

[153] For details, see A. Darbyshire, *A booke of olde Manchester and Salford* (Manchester, 1887).

[154] Dennis, *Cities in modernity*, pp. 175–7.

[155] Tomlinson, *Pictorial record*, pp. 18, 20.

[156] P. Mandler, '"In the Olden Time": Romantic history and English national identity', in Brockliss and Eastwood, *Union of multiple identities*, pp. 78–92. See also P. Mandler, 'Revisiting the olden time: Popular Tudorism in the time of Victoria', in T. C. String and M. Bull (eds.), *Tudorism: Historical imagination and the appropriation of the sixteenth century* (Oxford, 2011), pp. 13–35.

[157] S. Banfield, 'Tudorism in English music, 1837–1953', in String and Bull, *Tudorism*, pp. 57–77, esp. p. 63; J. M. Woodham, 'Twentieth-century Tudor design in Britain: An ideological battleground', in String and Bull, *Tudorism*, pp. 129–53, esp. p. 134; Readman, 'Place of the past'. Queen Elizabeth was by some distance the

self-consciously 'civilised' architecture of the eighteenth century (much disparaged in the souvenir guide to Old Manchester and Salford),[158] Tudor buildings seemed picturesque, homely, and suggestive of communal pleasures and comforts. They were evocative of rude but wholesome pleasures – May Day celebrations and the like – and of lifestyles of plenty for the humble as well as the great. This helps explain the appeal of the Tudor past to radical reformers and socialists in these years,[159] but also accounts for its more general appeal in a country increasingly democratic both in social-cultural and political terms. Great towns and cities such as Manchester were great centres of this burgeoning democratic sensibility; it is thus perhaps unsurprising that civic celebrations such as the 1887 Exhibition should reflect so strong an engagement with this past and its landscape.

In Manchester as elsewhere, then, the relationship between heritage and modernity was supportive rather than conflictual; the two went together. A further indication of this was the way in which the Old Manchester and Salford exhibition combined heritage with consumerism. Visitors were encouraged to buy illustrated guidebooks and other souvenirs, some of which could be purchased from costumed vendors in the replica old buildings. In Harrop's Printing Office, for example, employees of the modern-day Manchester publisher John Heywood and Sons (one of them impersonating Joseph Caxton!) could be found operating old wooden presses to run off facsimile copies of the 28 November 1769 number of *Harrop's Mercury*, which were then offered for sale. Other Manchester firms ran displays in and around the houses of Old Manchester and Salford, showing the manufacture of jewellery, watches, confectionery and much else besides, examples of which could be bought by visitors. 'Withecomb's pipemakers … engaged in the manufacture of briar-root and meerschaum pipes, and the drilling and shaping and polishing of amber, attracted the men-folk greatly', while it might be supposed that children were more drawn to the scene 'in front of old Hulme Hall', where 'a bevy of maidens charmingly dressed in the style of Queen Anne's

most popular figure in the Edwardian craze for historical pageants: see A. Bartie, P. Caton, L. Fleming, M. Freeman, T. Hulme, A. Hutton and P. Readman, *The redress of the past*, www.historicalpageants.ac.uk/pageants/ (accessed 12 May 2017).
[158] Darbyshire, *Booke of olde Manchester*, pp. 53–4, 56, 67, 81.
[159] Ward, *Red flag and Union Jack*; also Readman, *Land and nation*, esp. pp. 187–8.

days, bore about ices, and creams, and chocolate, under the aegis of Messrs. Parker and Sons'.[160]

Although not so chaotically interblended, heritage and consumerism also sat cheek-by-jowl in *Manchester Faces and Places*, which combined appreciation of the surviving picturesque buildings of the sixteenth century with enthusiasm for the brash, up-to-the-minute commercialism of department stores such as Lewis's on Market Street ('a huge emporium of everything, garnished on the exterior with all the architectural embellishments of a handsome and highly ornate building … and brilliant at night with electric light and the reflections of thousands of lamps').[161] In its pages, articles breathlessly puffing the virtues of 'our business places' (principally shops) sat alongside others extolling the appeal of 'picturesque' relics of times gone by. This reflected a mindset that sought to preserve memories of the past while at the same time celebrating the bright benisons of modernity as manifested in the city's landscape. Sometimes, indeed, the old buildings to which these memories attached were objects of attention precisely because they acted as monuments to a worse past, of progress made since the days they were erected. Writing of the Rover's Return, a tiny 'quaint and picturesque' public house on Shude Hill, for example, *Manchester Faces and Places* averred that such buildings 'give us some idea of the appearance of the town in its earlier days when the streets were few, narrow, and tortuous, when Market street was an old alley, and its houses, of overhanging gables, were so close that, when a broad-wheeled wagon was dragging along, the pedestrian had to exercise both patience and ingenuity to avoid destruction' (see fig. 29).[162]

This was a perspective that acknowledged change and modernisation as inevitable and welcome. Thus it was that *Manchester Faces and Places* could be relatively sanguine about the ongoing destruction of many of the remaining old buildings in the city centre while at the same time carrying articles detailing their history and associations. (Something similar happened in other urban contexts: as Nead has shown in her work on London, from the 1860s the *Illustrated London*

---

[160] On the appeal of Old Manchester and Salford to children, see the illustrated paperback aimed at them: E. E. Haugh, *The adventures of little Man-Chester; or, Recollections of the Royal Jubilee Exhibition* (Manchester, 1887). Significantly, the sole focus of this book is Old Manchester and Salford, not the exhibition generally.

[161] *Manchester Faces and Places*, 1 (1890), p. 175.

[162] *Ibid.*, 4 (1893), p. 76.

29 Samuel L. Coulthurst, *Rover's Return*. Photograph, from *Manchester Faces and Places*, 1893. British Library, London, UK/Bridgeman Images.

News 'assumed the role of archivist of the city, carrying images and descriptions of old buildings demolished in the course of improvement works'.[163]) So, for all that it was important to remember buildings such as St Mary's Church, which was demolished in 1891, it was also important to recognise when they had 'outlived [their] necessity'.[164] Similarly, while the half-timbered Seven Stars and Sun Inn pubs in Long Millgate were powerfully evocative of past centuries and hallowed by local associations (the Sun Inn, as 'Poet's Corner', had been

---

[163] 'In regular columns with titles such as "Nooks and corners of old England" and "Archaeology of the month" it illustrated the disappearing inns and houses of Elizabethan London, creating in its pages a lexicon of the metropolitan picturesque': Nead, *Victorian Babylon*, pp. 30–1.

[164] *Manchester Faces and Places*, 1 (1890), pp. 163–5.

the meeting place of an early Victorian literary circle), they were now out of keeping with the character of the modern city:

> 'Poet's Corner' is probably about the most ancient bit of old-fashioned Manchester … The dilapidated front leans forward on its timber support in the last stage of tottering age, looking like a ghost of the past nestling up to the proud seat of modern culture, as though to catch from juvenile voices and laughter a refrain of the jocund spirit which from under its own roof has now for ever fled. This 'poet's corner' forms now an ugly angle in the street outline. Its presence spells obstruction, and even toleration for relics of the past cannot long defer its removal.[165]

In the event, Poet's Corner survived until 1923, but the attitude of *Manchester Faces and Places* to the continued existence of 'tottering remnant[s] of antiquity' in the heart of the modern city was a typical one by the late Victorian period. Antiquarian and topographical surveys pointed to the visual incongruity such survivals presented; they seemed out of place in the city-centre landscape and disruptive of the discourse of improvement it ought to embody. In his *Old Manchester* of 1875, James Croston thought the few remaining old buildings on Deansgate were 'in the midst of surroundings entirely out of character with their antiquated features', noting that 'until very recently Deansgate was only a narrow and inconveniently-crowded thoroughfare' but 'by the spirit of modern enterprise it has become transformed into one of the most spacious as well as one of the handsomest streets in the kingdom, rivalling even Regent-Street itself in the imposing character of its buildings'.[166] Twenty years later, the continued presence of at least some of these buildings on Deansgate drew a still blunter response in W. A. Shaw's *Manchester old and new*: 'It produces something like an effect of grotesqueness and incongruity when we think of these odd buildings with their old-time associations surviving with the modern city, in the midst of the cotton mills and busy warehouse life that are becoming its chief characteristics.'[167]

The problem here was not the buildings per se, but their survival in the modern landscape of central Manchester. This perspective

---

[165] *Ibid.*, 2 (1891), p. 103.
[166] Croston, *Old Manchester*, p. 20.
[167] Shaw, *Manchester old and new*, Vol. i, p. 26.

reflected cultural attitudes to the English landscape more generally. Despite the arguments of some historians, it is simply not the case that late Victorian and Edwardian opinion came to see the rural landscape of the past as very much more 'national', more essentially English, than the urban landscape of the present. This was a culture that accommodated both in its nationalist topography; it celebrated both – in their right place. For some commentators, indeed, the very sharpness of the contrast between town and country was perceived to be a good thing, as if the more thoroughly urbanised places such as Manchester became, the more complementary they were to the very different landscape of the English countryside. Arriving in Manchester by train, the journalist T. H. S. Escott found the scene around him 'profoundly impressive'. He observed 'the flaming beacon-lights of a never-ending labour' and the 'endless vista of watch-fires of industry'; his ears were assailed by 'the tremendous reverberation of forges mightier than those of the Cyclops'. The stark contrast between this industrial landscape and the fields and moors of rural England, from which he had come, was inescapable, yet at the same time he felt 'the continuity of national life and feeling is preserved unbroken … The new is ever being incorporated with the old, and the result of the process is a growing identity of interests and of feeling.'[168]

Such sentiments illustrate a patriotic confidence about change. The growing conception of landscape – or certain landscapes – as being valuable on account of their associations with the past, or for their natural beauty, was not incompatible with this confidence. The men and women of Victorian and Edwardian Manchester could welcome modernising urban improvements while simultaneously involving themselves in historical societies, nature study, and even preservationist campaigns. Many ordinary Mancunians were active in botanical clubs, rambling and footpath associations, and the like, making full use of the city's proximity to the Lake and Peak Districts.[169] Yet these activities

[168] T. H. S. Escott, *England: Its people, polity, and pursuits*, new edn (London, 1885), pp. 74–5.

[169] See, e.g., A. Secord, 'Elizabeth Gaskell and the artisan naturalists of Manchester', *Gaskell Society Journal*, 19 (2005), 34–51; J. Percy, 'Scientists in humble life: The artisan naturalists of south Lancashire', *Manchester Region History Review*, 5 (1991), 3–10. For a balanced account of the later-nineteenth-century development of recreational walking as an organised activity involving all social classes, see Taylor, *Claim on the countryside*.

did not imply distaste for the urban landscape in which people passed their everyday lives. One of their spokesmen was the adult education pioneer and botanist Leo Hartley Grindon, whose nature writings appeared regularly in the columns of local newspapers from the 1850s on, and also in book form.[170] For Grindon, the rapid growth of Manchester (a town 'bosomed in beauty') did not threaten wild nature, readily accessible as it was by means of the railway, which he thought a great boon to the botanist.[171] 'Let the bricks and mortar stride far as they will over the greensward', Grindon thought, 'there are always sanctuaries beyond – sweet spots where we may yet listen to the singing of the birds, and pluck the early primrose and anemone'.[172] Moreover, for all his love of nature and the great outdoors, Grindon – author of a history of Manchester – also had a positive regard for the urban environment. As he told readers of his *Manchester walks and wild-flowers*,

> The streets lead the way to as much pleasure as the field-paths. It is nothing but a thoughtless mistake which lauds the country at the expense of the town … Like the sexes, each is complementary to the other, and each offers pleasures which only itself can give; each is best in turn, and full of compensation for what we leave behind in the other.[173]

It is true that Grindon, like many others by the later decades of the nineteenth century, was increasingly aware of the negative environmental impact of great towns. For residents of Manchester it could hardly be otherwise. The smoke from houses and factories was all-pervasive. Continually hanging over the city, it blackened buildings and caused respiratory disease; such was the atmospheric pollution that the

---

[170] L. H. Grindon, *Manchester walks and wild-flowers* (London and Manchester, [1859]); *Summer rambles in Cheshire, Derbyshire, Lancashire, and Yorkshire* (Manchester and London, 1866); *Country rambles and Manchester walks and wild flowers: Being rural wanderings in Cheshire, Lancashire, Derbyshire and Yorkshire* (Manchester, 1882).

[171] 'Honoured for ever be the name of Stephenson! It is in facilitating men's intercourse with nature, and the purest and most ennobling recreations they can enjoy and are capable of, that the social blessings of railways have their highest realisation': Grindon, *Manchester walks and wild-flowers*, p. 7.

[172] *Ibid.*, p. 1.

[173] *Ibid.*, p. 82.

rain was often dirty with soot (the so-called 'blacks'). For years, the factories that lined the rivers in and around Manchester had pumped waste into their waters, leading foreign observers from mid-century on to describe the city-centre reaches of the Irwell, Medlock and Irk as 'black and fetid'.[174] But to most English eyes, such things were an inevitable consequence of Manchester's – and England's – greatness; their capacity to cause wider, nationwide damage to the environment was not yet fully appreciated (as Grindon said, a lot of nature still remained to be spoiled). There was good reason to think in this way. As James Winter has demonstrated, the environmentally deleterious potential – and impact – of Victorian technology was relatively limited: while it could have transformative effects, these were largely localised, steam power lacking the capacity to wreak the more widespread damage that the twentieth-century spread of the internal combustion engine would bring.[175] Perhaps in part because of this, contemporaries did not condemn the urban landscape of Manchester as hateful, begrimed though it was. The Irwell was celebrated as 'a noble work-a-day river, with smutty face, winning the children's bread' through 'labours only paralleled by those recorded in the fable of the mighty Hercules of old'.[176] Indeed, the very pollution of Manchester rivers could stand as evidence of their worth as valued landscapes. Grindon certainly thought so: while 'A limpid stream among the hills' may be 'lovely and poetical ... the most pleasing of all rivers are those of which the banks are occupied by an industrious and intelligent population'.[177] And, as he wrote on another occasion, if the once plentiful trout were now extinct in the Medlock and Irwell, 'Are we then to murmur? – to feel as is robbed? By no means. Nothing can be regretful that is inseparable from the conditions of the industry and the prosperity of a great nation. The holidays will be here by and by. A couple of hours' railway

[174] M. L. Faucher, *Manchester in 1844* (London, 1844), p. 17. For other examples, see L. D. Bradshaw (ed. and comp.), *Visitors to Manchester: A selection of British and foreign visitors' descriptions of Manchester from c. 1538 to 1865* (Manchester, 1987), pp. 34–5 (Alexis de Tocqueville; Victor Huber), 36 (Eugène Buret); also Engels, *Condition of the working class*.
[175] Winter, *Secure from rash assault*.
[176] T. Newbigging, *Lancashire characters and places* (Manchester, 1891), pp. 126–7.
[177] Grindon, *Manchester walks and wild-flowers*, p. 47.

journey enables one to listen to the "liquid lapse" of streams clear and bright as Cherith.'[178]

Some went further still in their appreciation of Manchester waterways. Artists and photographers began to find interest and even beauty in the scenes that they offered. In this they were influenced by contemporaneous trends in visual culture towards the aestheticisation of urban landscapes, two of the more significant indications of which were James Abbott McNeill Whistler's Thames nocturnes in the 1870s, and – later on – Claude Monet's London series of paintings (1900–3), which also had the Thames as a focus. In January 1903, *Manchester Faces and Places* featured an article about photography in and around the city. Entitled 'Picturesque Manchester', it noted that at a recent exhibition held by the Manchester Amateur Photographic Society, 'no photograph commanded more attention' than T. Longworth Cooper's misty, foggy view of the River Irwell from Blackfriar's Bridge, featuring barges, chimneys and other appurtenances of industry. Yet, the writer continued, the 'beautiful photograph' was evidence that '"Cottonopolis" may lay claim to the picturesque', even 'along the course of the inky and evil-smelling Irwell'.[179] Similar scenes were increasingly popular with artists, one especially notable example being Adolphe Valette, a French Impressionist painter who came to England in 1904 and settled in Manchester, where he taught at the Municipal School of art.[180] In works such as *India House, Manchester* (1912), and *Under Windsor Bridge on the Irwell* (1912), Valette conjured up images of striking beauty from the dank and murky rivers and canals of the city (see fig. 30). Valette's paintings of Manchester waterways were well received at the time. In its report on the inaugural exhibition of the Manchester Society of Modern Painters, of which Valette was a member, the *Manchester Guardian* commended one of his views 'of [a] canal or river crossed by a heavy iron bridge' for its 'extreme delicacy of atmospheric effect', judging it to be 'one of the best interpretations of our city landscape that we have seen at any time'.[181]

---

[178] L. H. Grindon, *Lancashire: Brief historical and descriptive notes* (London, 1892), pp. 101–2.

[179] *Manchester Faces and Places*, 14 (1903), pp. 50–3.

[180] For Valette, see Manchester Art Gallery, *Adolphe Valette: A French Impressionist in Manchester* (Manchester, 2007); S. Martin, *Adolphe Valette: A French influence in Manchester* (London, 2007); C. Lyon, *Adolphe Valette* (Chichester, 2006).

[181] *Manchester Guardian*, 19 September 1912, p. 5.

30 Adolphe Valette, *India House, Manchester*, 1912. Oil on jute. Manchester Art Gallery, UK/Bridgeman Images.

Manchester remained a valued national landscape into the twentieth century. Until the First World War, its architecture of enterprise was designedly splendid, and perceived as such by contemporary opinion. Its streets were bustling; its warehouses and department stores were palatial; its public buildings were suitably evocative of commercial greatness and civic virtue; even its polluted rivers could be seen as beautiful. As one observer noted in 1900, its status as 'the undoubted metropolis of the north' could be read in its landscape:

> Manchester is in many respects a microcosm of England and a replica of London. In its public spirit and enterprise we see the national characteristics which have created modern England. In

its main thoroughfares we are reminded of the City of London; Market Street is the counterpart of Cheapside; substitute tramcars for omnibuses, lorries for vans, and, amid the keen bustling throng of men and women, intent on commerce or shopping, you may fancy yourself within sight of the Mansion House; what difference exists is often in the line of greater intensity in the northern centre.[182]

Still recommended as worth visiting in the guidebook literature,[183] even Manchester's factories retained visual merit in the landscape, not least because of the further increased attention given to ornamentation in their design – as shown, for example, in the use of polychromatic bricks; terracotta decorations; and the adornment of stair towers with parapets, balustrades and even copper domes.[184]

To be sure, the negative elements of the Manchester urban environment were never ignored, but its connotations with industry, enterprise and modernity generally made it a great national landscape. Despite spikes of concern, most notably in the 1840s, it was a fit object of patriotic pride not only for residents of Cottonopolis but also for the country at large, and remained so throughout the nineteenth and into the twentieth century. And while the historical associations of this landscape were less strongly evident than in other of the landscapes discussed in this book, they were certainly valued: Manchester too was storied ground. These associations were integrated into a forward-looking narrative of civic progress that brought the past into the service of the present and future. In the interwar period, this use of the past would become further evident in the large-scale historical pageants and civic weeks held in the city, those of 1926 and 1938 being the most important examples. As Tom Hulme has shown, Manchester pageants – like many of their counterparts in North America – were great festivals of civic boosterism, which re-enacted the past as a means

---

[182] F. W. Newland, 'The city of Manchester: I', *The Sunday at Home*, 1 January 1900, 150.

[183] K. Baedeker, *Great Britain*, 3rd edn (Leipzig, 1894 [1887]), p. 334. 'No traveller should quit Manchester without having seen one at least of its great factories': K. Baedeker, *Great Britain*, 7th edn (Leipzig, 1910), p. 358.

[184] Williams with Farnie, *Cotton mills*, pp. 100–1. Constructed in Accrington brick with sandstone and terracotta embellishments, Paragon Mill and Royal Mill (1912) presents one example of such a structure (*ibid.*, pp. 166–7).

of stimulating pride in past achievements with a view to inspiring hope for the future.[185] In Manchester's case, this meant a patriotic celebration of the city's industrial and commercial heritage at the heart of the workshop of the world, and thus its contribution to the nation's economic greatness and sense of identity; it did not involve any nostalgic lamentations for a lost and supposedly more authentically English rural idyll.

The story told in the Manchester pageants reflected an acceptance of change, and specifically England's transformation from a largely rural- to a largely urban-dwelling nation. Yet it was a story that had long been embodied in the landscape of the city, and in readings of that landscape. This chapter began with Elizabeth Gaskell's *North and south*; its denouement is suggestive here, and presents an appropriate point on which to conclude. Once settled in Milton/ Manchester, Margaret comes to realise that she cannot return to the land of the south. This realisation bursts upon her in the course of a visit to her old home of Helstone, in the New Forest. The landscape still retains its scenic appeal – Helstone 'to her ... would always be the prettiest spot in the world' – but Margaret's exposure to the very different environment of Milton has transformed her attitude to change. Whereas in her youth she had revelled in the apparently timeless aspect of her sylvan home, now she sees 'change everywhere' (even in Helstone), and it is on the side of change that she wishes to be: 'If the world stood still, it would become retrograde and corrupt ... Looking out of myself, and my own painful sense of change, the progress all around me is right and necessary.' Thus it is that on returning north Margaret resolves to marry her lover, the mill owner John Thornton, and make her life amid the smokestacks and factories of Milton – for all that she retains strong affection for the commons, fields, flowers and trees of the New Forest.[186] Margaret's bifurcated sensibility stands proxy for that of wider cultural attitudes. For all that nineteenth- and early-twentieth-century English men and women

---

[185] T. Hulme, '"A nation of town criers": Civic publicity and historical pageantry in inter-war Britain', *Urban History*, 44 (2017), 270–92. For details of the Manchester pageants, see A. Bartie, L. Fleming, M. Freeman, T. Hulme, A. Hutton and P. Readman, 'The Manchester Historical Pageant [1926]', *Redress of the past*; and Bartie, Fleming, Freeman, Hulme, Hutton and Readman, 'The Manchester Pageant [1938]', *ibid.*

[186] Gaskell, *North and south*, pp. 481, 488, 489–90.

displayed an increasing sensitivity to the problems of poverty, dirt and disease that afflicted towns and cities, landscapes such as Manchester could still be associated with change, progress and national greatness, and valued as a consequence. Yet, at the same time, as we saw in the previous chapter, places such as the New Forest remained valued landscapes too, though for rather different reasons. The patriotic landscape imaginary of the long nineteenth century was a capacious one, encompassing both rural shires and city streets, and the extent of this capaciousness is further illustrated, as we are about to see, by the example of the River Thames.

6 THE THAMES

In his *General account of all the rivers of note in Great Britain*, published in 1801, Henry Skrine devoted most attention to the River Thames, which he declared to be 'The mighty king of all the British rivers, superior to most in beauty, and to all in importance'.[1] This emphasis was clear from the frontispiece, which, as Skrine described it, showed 'Thamesis, the River God of the Thames, attended by Tava, the nymph of the Tay in Scotland, and Vaga, the Nymph of the Wye in Wales, presenting a Chart of Great Britain, intersected by its Rivers, to Neptune' (see fig. 31).[2] It was, perhaps, an appropriate image of British unity in the context of the ongoing wars with France, the white cliffs and naval fleet in the background underlining the book's patriotic intent and evoking the sort of insular, sea-girt national identity that was discussed in Chapter 1. Like the cliffs of Dover, the Thames – as the greatest of all British rivers – could easily be brought to bear on mainstream ideas of Britishness.

As with the white cliffs, the importance of the Thames in the patriotic imaginary is long established. Since the eighteenth century it has routinely been described as 'the first of all British rivers',[3] drawing forth great torrents of admiration. Its cultural significance has

[1] H. Skrine, *A general account of all the rivers of note in Great Britain* (London, 1801), p. 319.
[2] *Ibid.*, frontispiece; also preface, p. ix.
[3] W. Westall and S. Owen, *Picturesque tour of the River Thames* (London, 1828), p. iii.

31 Frontispiece from H. Skrine, *A general account of all the rivers of note in Great Britain* (London, 1801). Reproduced by kind permission of the Syndics of Cambridge University Library: Ll.34.16.

also been discussed by historians. In sweeping book-length studies, Jonathan Schneer and Peter Ackroyd have surveyed the history of the river over centuries.[4] This chapter has a more modest aim, seeking to provide not a general but a detailed treatment, with a view to demonstrating precisely how and why the Thames, over the course of the long nineteenth century, became so important in the national imagination. In doing so it examines the different ways in which the landscape of the river supported constructions of national identity through its associations with commerce, culture and – most important of all – the course of history. The symbolic force of the Thames, it will be argued, owed most to its associations with the national past. From its source in rural Gloucestershire through London to the North Sea, the Thames was understood to describe the progress of the nation from obscurity to greatness, while at the same time standing for the still-existing – and

---

[4] J. Schneer, *The Thames* (New Haven and London, 2005); P. Ackroyd, *Thames: Sacred river* (London, 2007).

much valued – connections between past and present, countryside and capital, backwater and bustling port.

The national significance of the Thames is in part attributable to its association with London, the capital city. But valid as this observation is, it only gets us so far. Larger rivers, of course, have tended to attract more in the way of admiration than smaller ones, and the Thames is the third longest in the British Isles (behind the Shannon and the Severn). But at just 215 miles in length, it has never counted as one of the great world rivers in terms of size, a fact of which its British admirers were well aware from an early stage, and that indeed they frequently admitted as a prelude to assertions that it was a truly noble river nonetheless. One reason for such assertions is suggested by the frontispiece to Skrine's book, with its linking of the Thames to the sea – Thamesis and his entourage were paying homage to Neptune, after all. In part this was a reference to British naval power, and to the claimed Britishness of the sea, but it also suggested a more intimate relationship between the maritime and the riverine. Neptune was shown receiving a chart of the rivers of Britain because many of these rivers were tidal to a large degree, in contrast to the typically less tidal rivers of continental Europe. This was a function of Britain's island status, and was generally understood to be part of that blessing Providence had bestowed on the country in so configuring its geography. In this connection, the Thames stood out, being tidal for approximately 100 miles of its course, from Teddington Lock, west of London, to the mouth of its estuary. This made the river more readily navigable, especially in the days before steam, when sail-powered craft could use the action of the tides to go up- and downstream with relative ease. In this way, as one guidebook to London observed in the 1770s, 'every tide brings in a fresh number of ships from all parts; so that it may be said, the riches of the world are continually flowing into the river of Thames'.⁵ It was largely because of the tidal Thames that London was thought to have become a great port, indeed a great city, and as British commercial prosperity advanced in the eighteenth and into the nineteenth century, the river's connection with this prosperity grew stronger. In text after text, the Thames was presented as 'the principal source' of London's

---

⁵ *A companion to every place of curiosity and entertainment in and about London and Westminster*, 4th edn (London, 1774), p. 8.

burgeoning 'wealth and magnificence', its 'opulence and grandeur'.[6] Selected lines from John Denham's still enormously popular *Cooper's Hill* (1642) or Alexander Pope's *Windsor-Forest* (1713) were frequently quoted to underline how, as Pope had it,

> … from his Oozy Bed
> Old Father *Thames* advanced his rev'rend Head.
> His Tresses dropt with Dews, and o'er the Stream
> His shining Horns diffus'd a golden Gleam:
> Grav'd on his Urn appear'd the Moon, that guides
> His swelling Waters, and alternate Tydes;
> The figur'd Streams in Waves of Silver roll'd,
> And on their Banks *Augusta* rose in Gold.[7]

Closely linked to the tidal character of the Thames, this Augustan prosperity appeared a happily natural state of affairs, ordained as much by God (or the moon) as determined by man, the produce of the world flowing into the metropolis 'with a never-failing stream'.[8]

Given the close relationship between commercial and national greatness in the construction of Britain's self-image from the mid eighteenth century on,[9] the Thames soon emerged as a source of patriotic pride on account of its wealth-creating role. Guidebooks and topographical literature made much of the 'forest of masts' to be seen filling the Port of London, and extolled 'The commerce of this mighty river' as 'the boast of all Englishmen'.[10] But the river's service in facilitating money-getting was only part of the story. The wealth brought in by the flowing tide was perceived to support not only material prosperity, but taste, elegance and beauty; and it was of particular significance that these benisons were so much in evidence along the Thames Valley

---

[6] *The ambulator; or, The stranger's companion in a tour round London* (London, 1774), pp. 166–8; *A view of London; or, The stranger's guide through the British metropolis* (London, 1803–4), pp. 55, 92.

[7] A. Pope, *Windsor-Forest* (London, 1713), p. 14.

[8] *Pigot and Co.'s metropolitan guide and book of reference to every street court lane passage alley and public building in the cities of London and Westminster* (London, 1824), p. 5.

[9] P. Langford, *A polite and commercial people: England 1727–1783* (Oxford, 1989), esp. pp. 1–7.

[10] T. Nicholls, *The steam-boat companion* (London, 1823), p. 7; J. Britton, *The original picture of London*, 26th edn (London, 1828 [1802]), p. 386.

landscape itself. Pope gave early expression to this in *Windsor-Forest*; later in the eighteenth century, prose accounts amplified the idea. Thomas Pennant's *Account of London* (1791), for example, described the wealth brought in by the river as combining with natural agricultural fertility to produce a pastoral landscape of tranquil graciousness. 'The whole course of the river', he wrote,

> is through a country abounding with every idea of opulence, fertility, and rural elegance: meadows rich in hay, or covered with numerous herds; gentle risings, and hanging woods; embellished with palaces, magnificent seats, or beautiful villas, a few of the hereditary mansions of our antient gentry, but the greater part property transferred by the effects of vice and dissipation, to the owners of honest wealth, acquired by commerce, or industrious professions.[11]

This pastoral Thames-side scenery was much extolled in topographical literature and art, of which there was a proliferation from the later eighteenth century. Catering to the tastes of the traditional elite as well as those enriched by the great expansion of industry and commerce, and also the rising 'middling sort', lavishly illustrated books and prints popularised the aesthetic of the landscape beautiful, as represented by the fashion for paintings by Claude, Salvator Rosa and Gaspard Poussin. The result was, as John Brewer has commented, that 'By the end of the century, these landscape prints, whether sold individually, in series or as illustrations to travel books, had become ubiquitous.'[12] If the Lake District was an important focus of attention at this time, so too was the Thames, particularly its mansion- and park-studded course west of London. One key publication was Samuel Ireland's *Picturesque views on the river Thames* (1792), the plates from which were widely reprinted; and the book itself was followed by a slew of imitators over the next few decades, most immediately William Combe's *History of the principal rivers of Great* Britain (1794), which very largely focused on the Thames, through to William Westall and

[11] T. Pennant, *Some account of London*, 5th edn (London, 1813 [1791]), pp. 628–30.
[12] J. Brewer, *The pleasures of the imagination: English culture in the eighteenth century* (London, 1997), p. 458.

Samuel Owen's *Picturesque tour of the River Thames* (1828), a large-format volume illustrated with twenty-four coloured views.[13]

In these topographical works, the landscape esteemed was polite and gentrified. Much attention was paid to the fine houses, parks and country seats, many of them of recent construction, to be found along the river.[14] The natural environment was a beautiful one, to be sure, the 'windings' and 'graceful' curves of the river in its meandering describing the serpentine line of beauty.[15] But this nature was felt to have been 'embellished' and 'ornamented' by the riverside houses, parks and gardens of the cultivated wealthy, whose sensibilities were commended in often sycophantic terms.[16] The parkland of Nuneham Courtenay near Oxford, seat of the Earls Harcourt, was singled out for special praise in many accounts, one remarking of it that 'nature gave the outline, and taste has completed the picture'.[17] So too were the elaborately landscaped grounds of General Henry Seymour Conway's Park Place near Henley, with its 'rustick' bridge, menagerie, 'Druids' temple' and artificial ruin of a Roman amphitheatre, of which William Combe commented that 'Nature has done much, nor has taste done less: the genius of the place has every where been consulted, as it has been happily completed, by the present owner of it.'[18] The 'exquisite taste' of people such as Conway and the Harcourt family had combined with the natural charms of riverside scenery to create a landscape of gracious elegance, consistent with Claudian conceptions of beauty while at the same time reflective of that prosperity which the Thames had done so much to foster.[19]

[13] S. Ireland, *Picturesque views on the river Thames from its source in Glocestershire to the Nore,* 2 vols. (London, 1792); [W. Combe], *An history of the principal rivers of Great Britain,* 2 vols. (London, 1794). Later books included Skrine's *General account; The Thames; or, Graphic illustrations of seats, villas, public buildings, and picturesque scenery, on the banks of that noble river,* 2 vols. (London, 1811); and Westall and Owen, *Picturesque tour.*

[14] See, e.g., *Forer's new guide for foreigners, containing the most complete and accurate description of the cities of London and Westminster, and their environs, that has yet been offered to the public* (London, [1798]), pp. 50ff.; *A new display of the beauties of England; or, A description of the most elegant and magnificent public edifices, royal palaces, noblemen's and gentlemen's seats, and other curiosities, in different parts of the kingdom,* new edn, 2 vols. (London, 1787), Vol. II, pp. 47ff., 286ff.

[15] Skrine, *General account,* pp. 340, 385.

[16] *The ambulator,* p. 167; Skrine, *General account,* pp. 333–4.

[17] W. B. Cooke and G. Cooke, *Views on the Thames* (London, 1818), n.p.

[18] [Combe], *History of the principal rivers of Great Britain,* Vol. I, p. 250.

[19] Skrine, *General account,* pp. 333–4.

It was a matter of patriotic pride that inherited wealth, commerce, taste and nature should be in such harmony. And nowhere else was this felt to be more evident than on the Thames around Richmond, a town about eight miles southwest of central London whose attractions were felt to rival the lions of the continental grand tour: Samuel Ireland called it 'the Frescati of England'.[20] In particular, the view of the river and its surrounding countryside from the terrace on Richmond Hill had a uniquely strong appeal, encapsulating the ideal of nature and art in felicitous fusion. As Combe described it, 'Beneath the hill the Thames winds its silver stream through meads and gardens, where nature luxuriates, and which taste adorns; while the villas, seats, and villages that enrich its banks, with their blended beauty, heighten the enchanting scene.'[21] The view's increasing popularity as a subject for artists (including Sir Joshua Reynolds, who painted it in 1788, and later on J. M. W. Turner) both reflected and added lustre to its appeal.[22] So too did its literary associations. Two noted poets of the Thames, John Denham and Alexander Pope, had lived nearby; but most important of all was the association with James Thomson and *The seasons*, a series of poems first written between 1725 and 1730 but which remained enormously popular throughout the rest of the eighteenth and into the nineteenth century (the British Library catalogue records that it had been republished more than 130 times by 1820).[23] In *Summer*, the second instalment of the series, Thomson paid tribute to the 'calmly magnificent' view from the hill, suggestive of a 'Happy Britannia' of pastoral prosperity and plenty, in lines that came to be quoted countless times in topographical and guidebook literature.[24]

This literary and artistic valorisation of the view from Richmond Hill was instrumental in establishing it as a key site in the late-eighteenth- and early-nineteenth-century touristic and aesthetic imaginary. Along with many other Thames-side landscapes, it was

[20] Ireland, *Picturesque views*, Vol. II, p. 107. 'Frescati', i.e. Frascati: a historic town in central Italy, famous for the magnificent villas built there from the sixteenth century as country residences for the elite of Rome.
[21] [Combe], *History of the principal rivers of Great Britain*, Vol. II, p. 25.
[22] Sir J. Reynolds, *The Thames from Richmond Hill* (1788); Howard, 'Changing taste in landscape art', p. 297.
[23] Thomson revised the text of *The seasons* a number of times over the course of his life. The references to the view from Richmond Hill seem to have been added in the version first published in 1745: J. Thomson, *The seasons* (London, 1744).
[24] *Ibid.*, pp. 112–14.

commended as being 'particularly worthy of Notice' in the *Supplement to Thomas Gray's* hugely influential *Tour through Great Britain*.[25] In the context of the Revolutionary and Napoleonic Wars, appreciation of its charms was linked with patriotic feeling – as was the case with other British landscapes seen as beautiful or distinctive at the time, that of the Lake District being the most obvious example.[26] Many of the landscapes so valued were commended for their picturesque qualities, following the pattern set by Gilpin, Price and other popularisers of this new aesthetic sensibility.[27] With its softly verdant and elegantly prosperous riverine appeal, the view from Richmond Hill was perhaps more strictly a beautiful than a picturesque landscape. Yet it was certainly compatible with the hazily defined mainstream ideas of the picturesque as they developed from the 1780s and – in relation to the Thames in particular – as were represented by Ireland's *Picturesque views* and Westall and Owen's *Picturesque tour*, both of which had much to say in praise of Richmond and its environs.[28] From the early years of the nineteenth century, Turner provided his imprimatur by means of a number of works, not least *The Thames from Richmond Terrace* (1836; fig. 32), a watercolour executed for his series of *Picturesque views in England and Wales* (1825–38). In this painting, and in contrast to his earlier Claude-inspired renderings of the view,[29] Turner shows Richmond Hill as being a popular destination for real people in the here-and-now – indeed, for all social classes, the aristocracy, middle and working classes alike (the latter being shown on the right, strolling on the terrace in their best Sunday outfits).[30]

A good number of the people featured in Turner's paintings had probably come to Richmond by steamboat. Indeed, the early-nineteenth-century advent of steam-powered craft played a crucial

[25] T. Gray, *A supplement to the tour through Great-Britain, containing a catalogue of the antiquities, houses, parks, plantations, scenes, and situations, in England and Wales* (London, 1787).
[26] J. Buzard, 'The Grand Tour and after (1660–1840)', in P. Hulme and T. Youngs (eds.), *The Cambridge companion to travel writing* (Cambridge, 2002), pp. 37–52.
[27] W. Gilpin, *Observations on the river Wye* (London, 1782); Price, *Essay on the picturesque*.
[28] Ireland, *Picturesque views*, Vol. II; Westall and Owen, *Picturesque tour*.
[29] D. Hill, *Turner on the Thames: River journeys in the year 1805* (New Haven and London, 1993), pp. 53–62, 150–2.
[30] E. Shanes, *Turner's picturesque views in England and Wales 1825–1838* (London, 1979), p. 48.

32 J. M. W. Turner, *The Thames from Richmond Terrace*, 1836. Watercolour on paper, Walker Art Gallery, Liverpool.

role in popularising the Thames as a focus of recreational activity, not just around Richmond but also along its whole course. In fact, it was the lower and not the upper Thames that was most affected by this development, at least at first. Steam travel was introduced on the Thames from about 1820, with the focus being on downriver traffic to Gravesend and Margate, which themselves were developing as seaside resort towns in this period. As early as 1831, steamers could reach Gravesend from London in three hours; by 1839 the journey time had been reduced further, to around two hours, allowing half-day trips.[31] The companies operating the route offered a fast and reliable service, one that had the advantage of running to a timetable. The new steamboats represented a considerable improvement on the sail-powered hoys that had previously worked the route, which unlike steamers were vulnerable to the caprices of tides and weather (in 1797, one hoy had taken twenty-seven hours to go from London to Margate).[32] Travel was reasonably affordable, too, at least for the middle classes: day

---

[31] D. M. Williams and J. Armstrong, 'The Thames and recreation, 1815–1840', *London Journal*, 30 (2005), 25–39 (p. 27).

[32] J. Whyman, 'Water communication to Margate and Gravesend as coastal resorts before 1840', *Southern History*, 3 (1981), 111–38 (p. 116).

excursions to Gravesend and back could be had for 1s 6d in 1827, and 1s by 1834.[33] Thousands of people quickly took advantage. By the early 1830s the number of passengers leaving and disembarking at Gravesend had reached 300,000 per year; by the early 1840s, this number exceeded 1 million.[34]

A significant proportion of these passengers were commuters, the speed and certainty of the service helping to establish Gravesend as a dormitory town (at least in the summer months) for London white-collar workers as early as the 1830s. But a larger number were holidaymakers and excursionists. Day trips were popular, particularly on Sundays, and indeed special Sunday services were soon put on to meet the demand: by 1836, over 8,000 people were landed at Gravesend on one day alone.[35] For these travellers in particular, the appeal of the outing was less to do with the destination, whether Gravesend or Margate, and far more to do with the journey on the Thames. The glamour and novelty of steam was part of the draw, particularly in the early years, but this was soon overshadowed by the attraction of the river landscape itself. So much is clear from the great mass of literature produced to cater for these downriver tourists. This included annotated panoramic illustrations of the buildings and scenery to be seen on each bank, designed for use on board, and cheap paperback guides (available for 6d by 1835), as well as more substantial publications, often brought out under the aegis of the steamboat companies themselves.[36] Predictably enough, these publications drew attention to picturesque and beautiful sights where they could be found, the riparian scenery of Kent and Essex offering some idea of a rural, village England. (The scope for such excursuses was inevitably limited, however, the

---

[33] Ibid., p. 129.

[34] Ibid., pp. 123–6; Williams and Armstrong, 'The Thames and recreation', p. 32.

[35] Williams and Armstrong, 'The Thames and recreation', p. 28; Whyman, 'Water communication', p. 132.

[36] Examples included G. H. Davidson, *The Thames and Thanet guide, and Kentish tourist*, 6th edn (London, [?1840]); W. Camden, *The steam boat pocket book: A descriptive guide from London Bridge to Gravesend, Southend, the Nore, Herne Bay, Margate, and Ramsgate* (London, 1835); *A new picturesque companion, in an excursion of Greenhithe, Northfleet, Gravesend* (London, [1834]); *The steam-boat companion from London to Gravesend* (London, 1830); *Boyles's Thames guide* (London, [?1839/40]). The *fons et origo* of all this literature appears to have been Nicholls's comprehensive *Steam-boat companion*, from which other guides borrowed heavily.

flatlands of the estuarial Thames being unpromising candidates for inclusion in any nineteenth-century aesthetic pantheon.) More attention was paid to the associational value of the landscape, in particular its connection with the national past, and with the boats starting out near the Tower of London this value was high indeed. Aside from the Tower, the tourist gaze was directed to places such as Greenwich Hospital, home to retired sailors of the Royal Navy, with its agreeable links to British naval supremacy (and national gratitude to those who had maintained it); Swanscombe Wood, where the 'Men of Kent' had extracted gavel-kind from William the Conqueror; and Tilbury Fort, site of Queen Elizabeth's rousing speech to her army at the time of the Spanish Armada. Even in the popular and panoramic guides, historical associations loomed large. One of the latter, *Boyles's Thames guide*, found space for the recondite alongside the obvious in the annotations to its illustrations, remarking in its entry for West Tilbury church, for example, that 'West Tilbury appears to have been the episcopal seat of Cedda, or St. Chad (in the times of the West Saxons), one of the first propagators of the Doctrines of Christianity in this country.'[37]

But whether well-known or not, the historical associations that preoccupied these publications reflected a patriotic purpose as evident as that which had animated the accounts offered in earlier topographical literature. As had been the case with the cultivated aficionados of picturesque and beautiful scenery in the 1790s and 1800s, the more socially heterogeneous trippers down the Thames in the 1830s and 1840s were also urged to combine travel with 'patriotic pleasure'.[38] This is clear from Thomas Nicholls's *Steam-boat companion* of 1823, perhaps the earliest steamboat guide and one that provided the basis for many subsequent handbooks, its agenda being spelt out by the epigram on its title page: 'Leave all the Foreign Shores alone, / Till you have seen and known your own.'[39] The scenery of the downriver Thames, one of Nicholls's imitators declared, was 'abounding with reminiscences and associations, interesting not only to the poet, the painter, the merchant, the naturalist, and the antiquary, but to every man who has an eye for the beauties of nature, or who feels the slightest interest in the means and monuments of his country's power and glory'.[40]

37 *Boyles's Thames guide.*
38 Cf. Brewer, *Pleasures of the imagination*, p. 633.
39 Nicholls, *Steam-boat companion.*
40 Camden, *Steam boat pocket book*, p. iii.

In offering opportunities for such patriotic heritage-tourism, the steamboat companies naturally ministered to more material pleasures too. The steamers offered comfortable accommodation, food and drink, and sometimes music and other entertainments. One special excursion in summer 1833 from London to the Nore, for example, included a concert, an illusionist, a ball and a band in its ticket price. But as apparent from the advertisement put out by its promoters, such pleasures would be combined with appreciation of the river scenery and its historical-patriotic connotations. 'The vessel', the advert stated,

> will proceed along the Kent and Essex shores; and from the Deck will be visible the various works of art and nature that grace those romantic situations. The Thames Tunnel, that effort of national science and industry, which if completed would be the glory of the world; that splendid Palace for decayed Seamen GREENWICH HOSPITAL; WOOLWICH DOCKYARD; GRAVESEND PIER AND FISHERIES; and TILBURY FORT, from when Queen Elizabeth addressed her patriotic partisans, to the ultimate destruction of the Spanish Armada; and so onward to the Nore. The Company will also have the opportunity of witnessing the LAUNCH OF THE WATERLOO 120 GUNS.[41]

It is of course very difficult to recover the popular response to such sights: just how interested were Thames excursionists in the storied landscape with which they were presented? Following John Urry's influential argument, it could be argued that the 'tourist gaze' in this context, as in others, was largely about the search for novelty and pleasure, divorced from authenticity and the acquisition of knowledge.[42] Yet, as work on the history of tourism in Germany and elsewhere has suggested, 'the search for knowledge and an "authentic" identity beyond the marketplace characterizes even some of the most apparently mindless and commodified forms of touristic behaviour', with 'tourism's ability to promote national identity' being 'one example of that search for meaning beyond the marketplace'. Tourists, in this interpretation, are more than 'passive' consumers, seeking to develop their own knowledge and sense of identity

[41] F. Burtt, *Steamers of the Thames and Medway* (London, 1949), pp. 23–4.
[42] Urry, *Tourist gaze*.

through the experience of tourism.[43] The same was true in the British context. For the Thames trippers of the early-to-mid nineteenth century, the novelty of steam travel and the various on-board distractions accounted for some of the appeal, but patriotic engagement with the (mainly historical) associations of the landscape was also important. After all, the content of excursion guides and advertisements as much reflected popular tastes as stimulated them, given that steamboat companies and guidebook publishers were operating in a competitive market. Some sense of the popular response is given in Angus Bethune's *London on the Thames* (1848), a series of comic sketches about pleasure-seeking on the river, which *inter alia* testified to the popularity of downstream tripping for working- as well as middle-class families by mid-century.[44] In one of these sketches, Bethune described the scene on board a steamer once it has set off, loaded to the gunwales with 'Gravesenders':

> Now do people in pursuit of useful knowledge, and voyaging 'with a purpose', produce penny panoramas of the river, and find that the Long Room in the Custom House measures 470 feet; and that the Tower was founded by Julius Caesar; and that the Thames Tunnel was the work of Isambert [*sic*] Brunel. Now do affectionate parents point out to Billy and Tommy and Jane the water-gate by which traitors were conveyed to the Tower, and Greenwich Hospital which is 'a memorial to the gratitoode of bold Hengland to her brave defendiars'. Now do respectable gentlemen cluster above the engine, and after watching for some five minutes the regular rush of the ponderous iron beams, and the steady throbbing of the working mechanism, remark to each other, 'Wonderful thing steam, sir – and only in its infancy yet'. Now are large families of small children out for a holiday ordered to begin to enjoy themselves and be happy, under the penalty of corporal punishment in case of disobedience. Now does the band consisting of a fiddle, a trombone, and a

[43] R. Koshar, '"What ought to be seen": Tourists' guidebooks and national identities in Modern Germany and Europe', *Journal of Contemporary History*, 33 (1998), 323–40 (p. 325). See also, e.g., the essays in S. Baranowski and E. Furlough (eds.), *Being elsewhere: Tourism, consumer culture and identity in modern Europe and North America* (Ann Arbor, 2001).
[44] A. B. Reach [Angus Bethune], *London on the Thames*, 2 vols. (London, [1848]), Vol. I, esp. pp. 49–50, on the activities of benefit clubs and philanthropic societies.

cornet-a-piston, begin to regale the ears of all listeners with that novelty, *Jullien's Polka*.[45]

As Bethune observed, different pleasures were combined here, but it is clear that involved in these was popular engagement – however unsophisticated – with the heritage presented by the landscape of the river. Simpler pleasures were combined with rational recreation; tourism was a means of patriotic self-improvement.

The popularity of excursions down the river persisted into the mid Victorian period. It was dealt a blow, however, by the *Princess Alice* disaster of 3 September 1878, in which the eponymous Thames steamer, en route back to London from Sheerness with perhaps 900 people on board, collided with the *Bywell Castle*, off Tripcock Point near Woolwich. The *Princess Alice* was cut in half by the other, much heavier, vessel, and sank rapidly with more than 650 people killed. Numerous deaths were attributed to the heavily sewage-contaminated water in that part of the river, with many of the people who were rescued from drowning dying later as a result of ingesting it.[46] Sensational and grisly, the tragedy administered a major blow to the downriver excursion traffic, and one from which it never properly recovered.[47] In another sense, however, the disaster represented a shift in attitudes to the landscape of the Thames. The *Princess Alice* had met her doom at the hands of a screw-powered collier, a type of ship that after its introduction around 1850 proved instrumental in the spread of industry along the lower river, and that would account for more than half of all Thames craft by century's end. Screw colliers enabled the construction of huge river-fronting gasworks, as were built at Greenwich and Beckton, such facilities requiring the very large, regular and certain supply of coal that only vessels such as the *Bywell Castle* could supply.[48] In this context of increasing industrialisation downstream from London Bridge, the lower Thames became less accessible – both in reality and imaginatively – as a tourist landscape, for all that it continued to be valued according to other criteria (of which more later). The

45 *Ibid.*, Vol. 1, pp. 17–18.
46 For an account of the *Princess Alice* disaster, see *The Times*, 4 September 1878, p. 7.
47 Burtt, *Steamers*, pp. 52–3.
48 A. Pearsall, 'Greenwich and the river in the 19th century', *Transactions of the Greenwich and Lewisham Antiquarian Society*, 8 (1972–3), 20–6 (pp. 24–5).

Bywell Castle and its ilk saw off the likes of the *Princess Alice* in more ways than one.

   This was not to say, however, that the Thames ceased to serve as a landscape of pleasure. Against the later-nineteenth-century backdrop of advancing urban-industrial modernity, its upper reaches gained in popularity as a destination offering pastoral tranquillity and other rural charms for the inhabitants of an increasingly teeming metropolis. Steamers had gone upriver in the 1820s and 1830s, but numbers had remained relatively low compared to those involved in the more profitable downstream trade.[49] Traffic had increased in the 1840s, Bethune's sketches testifying to the growing appeal and accessibility of Richmond to middle- and working-class excursionists, with Sunday lunch at the Star and Garter Hotel on Richmond Terrace being a fashionable desideratum of those who could afford it.[50]

   Steam revolutionised travel on land as well as on water, of course, and railways made the upper Thames more accessible still. Brunel's Great Western Railway reached Maidenhead in 1838 and Oxford in 1844, with a branch line to Henley opened in 1857. In combination with the availability of increasingly affordable fares in the wake of the 1844 Railway Regulation Act, and later on the coming of bank holidays, this helped establish the upper Thames as a supremely popular landscape of leisure for Victorian and Edwardian Londoners of all social classes. By the 1880s, the South Western Railway was advertising a range of cheap special excursion tickets from Waterloo to Teddington, Kingston, Hampton Court and Windsor.[51] But perhaps the particular contribution of railways was their facilitating of boating holidays on the Thames, as, on alighting from their trains at riverside towns, vacationers could hire small craft for short-term private use. By the late Victorian period, firms such as Salter Bros of Oxford were doing a roaring trade in the rental of small boats, many of which were used for trips down the Thames from Oxford to London (Salters undertaking to ship the boat back on completion of the journey). By the 1890s Salters had a regular stock of 700 boats, employed 100 people, and had 12 boathouses in Oxford alone; according to John H. Salter,

[49] Of the thirty-four steamers active on the Thames before 1828, only three ran to Richmond: Burtt, *Steamers*, pp. 18–19.

[50] [Bethune], *London on the Thames*, Vol. II, pp. 16–17, 33–4.

[51] R. R. Bolland, *Victorians on the Thames* (Tunbridge Wells, 1974), p. 13.

eldest of the brothers, the company might hire out up to 900 boats in a single season, such was the level of demand.[52]

The late Victorian success of companies such as Salters was a function of an explosion in popularity of the landscape of the upper Thames. This explosion can be dated with some precision to the 1880s, a decade that saw seemingly ever-increasing numbers of people take to the river for their holiday and weekend recreation, especially in the summer months. In 1884, one Thames Conservator told a parliamentary select committee that 2,000 boats passed through Boulter's Lock near Maidenhead every summer Sunday.[53] That year, the Chief Constable of Berkshire reported to the same forum, the pretty Thames-side village of Pangbourne was so overrun by visitors that 'they were hiring sheets to make tents of, and they were sitting in chairs all night long in the street, because they could not get accommodation'.[54] Such observations were confirmed by official statistics. As the records of the Thames Conservators showed, the fees paid by pleasure boats for the use of the river saw a great increase in the 1880s, rising from £1,647 in 1879 to £3,805 by 1887 (over the same period, takings from barge traffic had declined from £1,779 to £1,174, a telling sign of the times).[55] By the end of the Edwardian period, the total number of registered pleasure vehicles on the Thames approached 15,000, a figure that has not since been exceeded, and did not of course include unregistered craft, of which there were probably significant numbers.[56] And in addition to the great increase of small-boat-based recreation, excursions by steamer remained popular, particularly with working-class people, who often lacked the time or money to take longer holidays. More steamboats were built to meet demand, and more services were put on by the operating companies. Indeed, the popularity of the Kingston-to-Oxford stretch of the river alone was sufficient for Salters to design and build four steamboats specifically to serve the needs of the 'Thames trips' they began offering in 1888.[57] Also in the 1880s, businesses

---

[52] Interview with John H. Salter: *Lock to Lock Times and River Life*, 5 August 1893, 1.
[53] Evidence of Sir Gilbert Clayton East, *Select Committee on the Thames River Preservation*, 16 (1884), pp. 206–7.
[54] Evidence of Adam Blandy, *ibid.*, p. 359.
[55] Bolland, *Victorians on the Thames*, p. 14.
[56] Conservators of the River Thames, *The Thames Conservancy 1857–1957* (London, 1957), p. 77.
[57] *Lock to Lock Times*, 5 August 1893, p. 1.

began to provide days out on the Thames as treats for their employees, renting steamers for the purpose; and steamboat excursions were also arranged by voluntary organisations and occupational groups – from music hall artistes, railway servants and cab-drivers to Early Closing Associations and Freemasons.[58]

This enormous increase in the popularity of the upper Thames can be observed in the parallel proliferation of guidebooks, maps and belletrist publications, which both stimulated and reflected the phenomenon. The Oxford photographer Henry Taunt's pioneering *New map of the river Thames*, which went through many editions after its first publication in 1872, was one of the earliest and most influential of these.[59] Other, later, examples included the revealingly titled *Thames guide book from Lechdale to Richmond for boating men, anglers, picnic parties and all pleasure seekers*, and *Pearson's gossipy guide to the Thames*, which for the price of 1s gave the busy *fin-de-siècle* Londoner a range of advice on how to go about having a peaceful riparian day – or few days – away from it all.[60] From June 1888 there was even a newspaper aimed specifically at the frequenters of the upper Thames. Priced at 2d, the *Lock to Lock Times* contained practical information for river-users and gave coverage of regattas and other sporting events; it also reported boating and local news and the doings of the Conservators, as well as carrying gossipy pieces on river personalities and articles about the various attractions of the Thames Valley landscape.

The content of these publications gives a good sense of what drew people to the Thames in such numbers. Part of the appeal can be put down to water sports of different kinds. Fishing was popular, not least because of the near impossibility of finding edible fish in the central London stretch of the river by the nineteenth century, pollution being the major reason for this.[61] According to an 1894 estimate, there were by that year nearly 200 angling clubs in London alone,

---

[58] P. Burstall, *The golden age of the Thames* (Newton Abbot, 1981), pp. 105–13.

[59] H. W. Taunt, *A new map (illustrated with eighty photographs) of the river Thames … taken during the summer of 1871* (Oxford, 1872).

[60] *Thames guide book from Lechdale to Richmond for boating men, anglers, picnic parties and all pleasure seekers*, 2nd edn (London, 1890 [1882]); *Pearson's gossipy guide to the Thames from source to sea* (London, [1902]).

[61] B. Luckin, *Pollution and control: A social history of the Thames in the nineteenth century* (Bristol, 1986), pp. 12–16.

and for their memberships the readily accessible reaches of the upper Thames offered a convenient field of activity.[62] Fishing was often combined with boat trips, and information for anglers routinely featured in Thames guidebooks and the *Lock to Lock Times*. The suitability of the upper river for competitive athletic activity was another draw, and was also evident from the content of contemporary publications. The popularity of the University Boat Race is well known, of course, but these years also saw the development of large-scale annual regattas at many riverside towns, featuring club, public-school and university contestants – that held at Henley being the largest and most prestigious. Aside from rowing, competitive punting was also popular, a Thames Championship being held once a year. Indeed, one of the most successful wielders of a punt pole was W. H. Grenfell of Taplow Court near Maidenhead, who earned the distinction of winning the championship three years in a row between 1888 and 1891 (having in his youth rowed twice for Oxford in the Boat Race).[63] Grenfell, later Baron Desborough, was in some ways a key figure in the world of the late Victorian and Edwardian Thames. His wife Ettie presided over a fashionable salon at Taplow, holding glittering house parties on the banks of the river, while he – alongside many other public commitments – served as longstanding chairman of the Thames Conservators.[64] His sporting exploits and glamorous connections made him a particularly effective exemplar of the masculine 'muscular athleticism' of the day (among his other achievements were stroking an eight across the English Channel, and climbing the Matterhorn by three different routes). The Thames proved well suited to the performance of this athleticism, which since the time of 'Tom Brown's Schooldays' was indelibly associated with public schools, Oxford and Cambridge, and their milieu.[65] After all, the relationship between competitive boating on the Thames, the public schools (not least Eton, sited on the river) and the ancient universities

[62] C. H. Cook, *Thames rights and Thames wrongs: A disclosure* (London, 1894), p. 140.

[63] I. F. W. Beckett, 'Grenfell, William Henry, Baron Desborough (1855–1945)', *Oxford dictionary of national biography*.

[64] For Ettie see R. Davenport-Hines, *Ettie: The intimate life and dauntless spirit of Lady Desborough* (London, 2008).

[65] For this context, see J. A. Mangan, *Athleticism in the Victorian and Edwardian public school: The emergence and consolidation of the educational ideology* (Cambridge, 1981).

33 Lucien Davis, *At Boulter's Lock, Maidenhead, on the way to Henley Regatta, Illustrated London News*, 3 July 1886. Photo courtesy of Hulton Archive/Getty Images.

was especially strong – and positively celebrated at events such as the Oxford and Cambridge Boat Race and the Henley Regatta.

These associations overlaid the upper Thames with a patina of glamour. Henley and the Boat Race became fixtures of the London Season. Fashionable society prospected for invitations to Taplow Court or Cliveden (the latter bought by American millionaire Waldorf Astor in 1893, and visited by the Prince of Wales in 1896). Boulter's Lock, near Maidenhead, became one of the places to see and be seen, thousands of boats filled with bedizened socialites, swells and cockneys passing through over the course of a typical summer weekend (see fig. 33).

Yet, alongside the stimulus provided by sport and fashion, the landscape itself still mattered. Indeed, the persisting aesthetic and associational appeal of the landscape of the Thames is central to any understanding of the late Victorian and Edwardian upriver craze. It was not all about striped blazers and straw hats, or Cockney 'Arries and 'Arriets enjoying the novelty of messing about in boats.

First of all, and continuing some of the emphases found in late-eighteenth- and early-nineteenth-century discourse, the upper Thames was consumed as a peaceful, tranquil, rural landscape, loosely definable as picturesque as well as beautiful. This is evident from trends in the visual arts, which were in constant dialogue with developments in tourism and recreation more generally. From about the 1870s, the upper Thames was popular with creative types, who descended in numbers upon old parish churches, rustic mills, quiet backwaters and sylvan riverbanks. Old-world villages such as Pangbourne and Mapledurham formed subjects for photographers and artists, among whom Henry Taunt, Vicat Cole and G. D. Leslie were the most prominent. Writing in 1888, Leslie remarked that the villages of Goring and Streatley were now infested with 'sketching tents and white umbrellas … perched on any coign of vantage', while 'in the sketching season the little coffee-room at the "Swan" has easels and artists' traps in every corner, and the village swarms with geniuses and their aesthetically dressed wives'.[66] Three years later, two American visitors judged 'Goring Church, with the deep red roof and gray Norman tower, so beautiful from the river', to be 'almost as familiar in modern English art as the solitary cavalier once was in English fiction'.[67] Secluded spots such as Bolney Reach, a quiet backwater near Henley, were also popular subjects with painters (indeed, the hidden-away Thames backwater evidently held a particular artistic attraction, the *Art Journal* running a whole series of articles on the subject in 1883).[68]

The work of these Thames artists and photographers was popular, reflecting a more general appeal. Photographers such as Taunt and J. S. Gatford produced bound volumes of their pictures of placid upriver scenery at affordable prices.[69] Some even gave lantern slide-shows of their work. Taunt's lecture on 'A trip down the Thames from its source to London', which he first gave to the Oxford Churchman's Union in January 1871, went on to run in revised form for 200 nights at the

---

[66] G. D. Leslie, *Our river* (London, 1888), p. 152.

[67] J. Pennell and E. R. Pennell, *The stream of pleasure: A month on the Thames* (London, 1891), pp. 62–3.

[68] W. Senior, 'The backwaters of the Thames', *Art Journal* (May, July, August, September, October, December 1883).

[69] J. S. Gatford, *Silvery Thames: Well known spots, Richmond to Oxford* (London [?1900]) was priced at 1s.

London Polytechnic.[70] What Edward Walford described in his encyclo-paedic *Greater London* (1894) as the 'calm and tranquil beauty' of the Thames was a major reason why the landscape exerted the attraction it did, over not just aesthetes, but also the public at large.[71] It informed their recreational engagement with the river. As one guidebook asked in 1899, who '[i]n these days of brain fag and nerve strain … does not turn lovingly to the broad bosom of good old Father Thames, there to rest and recreate at will?', its conclusion being that 'There is no restora-tive in pharmacopoeia like unto an up-river holiday.'[72]

This promise of tranquil repose amidst a beautiful variety of scenery was seen to be offered by other rivers, not least those of North America.[73] The rapid late-nineteenth-century economic develop-ment of the United States encouraged its urban-dwelling inhabitants to view rivers as recreational and restorative amenities, offering res-pite from some of the pressures of fast-paced modern life. Gilded-Age Chicagoans saw the Dells of the Wisconsin River in precisely these terms, making claims for the superior quality of the benefits offered by this restful environment.[74] So too, of course, did English people in relation to the Thames. The thirteenth edition of *Salter's guide* thought the tranquillity of the landscape of the upper Thames was a mark of distinctiveness – one way in which the river stood apart from the other great rivers of the world – while Taunt described the scenery around Goring and Streatley as being 'of that soft, flowing character which is essentially English'.[75]

But even now, the distinctive appeal of the Thames as 'essen-tially English' was only partly attributable to the beauty and tranquil-lity that its upper reaches offered to metropolitan pleasure-seekers. The

---

[70] B. Brown (ed.), *The England of Henry Taunt: Victorian photographer* (London, 1973), p. xiii; G. H. Martin and D. Francis, 'The camera's eye', in H. J. Dyos and M. Wolff (eds.), *The Victorian city: Images and realities*, 2 vols. (London, 1977 [1973]), Vol. II, pp. 240–1.

[71] E. Walford, *Greater London*, 2 vols. (London, 1894), Vol. I, p. 569.

[72] *Royal Thames guide* (London, 1899), p. ii.

[73] See, e.g., Cusack, *Riverscapes*, Chapter 2 (on the Hudson River).

[74] S. Hoelscher, 'Viewing the Gilded Age river: Photography and tourism along the Wisconsin Dells', in T. Zeller (ed.), *Rivers in history: Perspectives on waterways in Europe and North America* (Pittsburgh, 2008), pp. 149–71.

[75] J. H. Salter and J. A. Salter, *Salter's guide to the Thames*, 13th edn (Oxford, 1910), pp. 2–3; H. W. Taunt, *Taunt's map of the river Thames, from Lechdale to London* (Oxford, [1881]), p. 13.

Thames remained a national landscape because of its association with the past, which was an important element of its appeal even in the late Victorian and Edwardian periods. This is evident from tourist publications. The *Lock to Lock Times* carried a series of detailed articles on 'A new history of the Thames', while even cheap guidebooks gave much space to sites of historic interest, and took pains to present the Thames Valley as 'the real centre of English life and of English history'.[76] Texts such as *Salter's guide* pointed to how the river and its hinterland included ancient villages and countryside, famous institutions of learning (Eton and Oxford), royal palaces, and the great historical capital city itself. As a consequence, the landscape was 'a long historical Museum' presenting 'a wonderful series of ancient memories and monuments', with 'No century since the Conquest [having] passed without depositing both material relics and the tradition of great events' along the course of the river.[77] More literary treatments of the river also emphasised its connections with the past.[78] Like the Cotswolds, whose southeastern limits abutted the upper Thames Valley, the landscape was seen as richly storied; described by one writer as 'haunted with imperishable memories of pathetic beauty and of secret, unmolested, peace', its very tranquillity contributed to the impression it imparted of 'bygone English life'.[79] For some, the environment offered appealing opportunities for experiences akin to time travel, so little affected by modernity did much of the landscape seem. A volume in the 'Heart of England' series edited by Edward Thomas, Hilaire Belloc's *Historic Thames* (1907), gave forceful expression to this sentiment:

> There are dozens of reaches upon the upper Thames where little is in sight save the willows, the meadows, and a village church tower, which present exactly the same aspect to-day as they did when that church was first built. You might put a man of the fifteenth century on the water below St. John's Lock, and, until he came to Buscot Lock, he would hardly know that he had passed

[76] *Lock to Lock Times*, 22 September 1888, p. 1; *The Thames Valley, from Kew to Oxford*, 2nd edn (Bournemouth, 1904); Salter and Salter, *Salter's Guide*, p. 1.

[77] Salter and Salter, *Salter's guide*, p. 4.

[78] See, e.g., Sir W. Besant, *The Thames* (London, 1903).

[79] F. S. Thacker, *The stripling Thames: A book of the river above Oxford* (London, 1909), p. 448. For the growing contemporaneous popularity of the Cotswolds as an exemplar of 'Old England', see Brace, 'Looking back'.

into a time other than his own. The same steeple at Lechdale would stand as a permanent landmark beyond the fields, and, a long way off, the same church of Eaton Hastings, which he had known, would show above the trees.[80]

Such evocations of a timeless and unchanging England can easily be read as reactionary protest against modernising trends (Belloc, for one, thought the introduction of railways to the Thames Valley was sadly destructive of 'its historic tradition').[81] Yet at the same time, such sentiments also reflected a wider interest in a vernacular, popular past, in the social experience of ordinary people rather than great men, in the farmstead and not the stately home. And for all that some of the manifestations of this phenomenon were conservative in character, it was a distinctly modern development, and one closely connected to contemporary and democratising trends of thought. It found expression in the new, more social history of J. R. Green and others, the folk-song and dance revival, the enthusiasm for cottages and cottage gardens, and the appeal of the pre-Reformation village community (this last doing much to inspire radical schemes of land reform). Perhaps most relevant for our purposes here, however, is the rural aesthetic popularised by artists such as Myles Birket Foster (1825–99), originator of the 'cottage idyll' genre, and his followers – among the more notable of whom were Joseph Kirkpatrick (1872–1930) and, in particular, Helen Allingham (1848–1926).[82] In her late-nineteenth- and early-twentieth-century watercolour pictures of village scenes, which attracted high prices, Allingham presented a sentimentalised image of a rural England of old. Yet her business was not simple nostalgia. In part motivated by a preservationist desire to paint a record of picturesque old vernacular buildings before they disappeared from the landscape, her paintings were deliberately intended to function as records 'in line and colour [of] a most interesting, but unfortunately vanishing phase of English domestic architecture', one that embodied 'a piece of Old England' that, once lost, was irrecoverable by 'all the genius in the world and

[80] H. Belloc, *The historic Thames* (Exeter, 1988 [1907]), p. 29.
[81] *Ibid.*, p. 125.
[82] M. B. Huish, *Happy England as painted by Helen Allingham* (London, 1903); H. M. Cundall, *Birket Foster* (London, 1986 [1906]).

34 Helen Allingham, *On Ide Hill*, 1900. Watercolour on paper, from Helen Allingham and Marcus B. Huish, *Happy England* (London, 1904). Reproduced by kind permission of the Syndics of Cambridge University Library: 404.c.90.4.

the money in the bank'.[83] Moreover, for all its roseate wistfulness and apparent blindness to the hardships of the rural poor, Allingham's country aesthetic centred on the common people: aristocracy, gentry and rich farmers were very largely absent from its purview.

Evidently of the belief that the 'typical English home' could be found in the 'humble cottages' of the countryside, Allingham rarely featured larger houses in her paintings, and never the 'country gentleman's seat'.[84] Like that of Birket Foster, her landscape was almost totally dominated by representations of ordinary people.[85] The old England

---

[83] Huish, *Happy England*, p. 118; R. Treble, 'The Victorian picture of the country', in G. E. Mingay (ed.), *The rural idyll* (London, 1989), p. 54. Allingham and her husband, the Irish poet William Allingham, were themselves active in supporting landscape-preservationist activities near their Surrey home. In 1883, for example, William Allingham organised a petition to Lord Derby, requesting that he refrain from enclosing roadside wastes on his property near Hindhead: H. Allingham and D. Radford (eds.), *William Allingham's diary*, 2nd edn (Fontwell, 1967), p. 319.

[84] S. Dick, *The cottage homes of England: Drawn by Helen Allingham and described by Stewart Dick* (London, 1909), pp. 4–8 (p. 8); Huish, *Happy England*, pp. 143–4.

[85] For Birket Foster see Cundall, *Birket Foster*.

it memorialised, in paintings such as *On Ide Hill* (1900), suggested the England that was widely believed to have existed before the enclosure movement of the late eighteenth and early nineteenth centuries (see fig. 34). It was a place where 'the sturdy British yeoman', 'the real old John Bull', still possessed common rights – a place where the smallholder remained free to turn geese out on to the village green.[86]

This view of the rural had powerful cultural purchase from the late Victorian period on. As was the case with those of Birket Foster, Allingham's paintings were extensively reproduced as cheap prints; and her style had many imitators.[87] Moreover, the artistic aesthetic she promoted was one that chimed with the increasing popularity of old-world village England as a destination for tourists and weekend excursionists (many of whom, by the 1890s, would have ridden out into the countryside by bicycle).[88] Advised by publications such as Methuen's *Little guides* or Ward Lock and Bowden's *Pictorial and descriptive guides*, holidaymakers sought out the past in the cottages, churches and laneways of the English countryside, many using the increasingly inexpensive technology of photography – as Allingham used painting – to record the rustic picturesque for posterity.[89] The correlation with the artistic and the touristic was further made evident by the burgeoning trade in picture postcards, thousands of which were illustrated with reproductions of photographs and paintings of tranquil rural scenes.[90] The watercolours of Alfred Robert Quinton (1853–1934) provide a good example here, being used extensively by major postcard manufacturers such as J. Salmon Ltd.[91]

---

[86] Dick, *Cottage homes of England*, pp. 21, 183.

[87] Wood, *Paradise lost*, p. 131.

[88] Bicycles were widely affordable by the 1890s, and provided a means by which urban-dwellers – women as well as men – could get into the countryside under their own steam: D. Rubinstein, 'Cycling in the 1890s', *Victorian Studies*, 21 (1977), 51–2. To meet the needs of these cycling enthusiasts, specialist publications such as *Lady Cyclist*, the *Rambler* and the *Wheelman* carried features on the pleasures and curiosities of the rural landscape, one example being the *Rambler*'s series of articles on 'the prettiest village in England' (*Rambler* 5 February–26 March 1898).

[89] See Taylor, *Dream of England*.

[90] M. Willoughby, *A history of postcards: A pictorial record from the turn of the century to the present day* (London, 1992), pp. 62, 81.

[91] *Ibid.*, pp. 79–80; J. Salmon Ltd, *The England of A. R. Quinton: Rural scenes as recorded by a country artist* (Sevenoaks, 1978).

35 George Price Boyce, *The Mill on the Thames at Mapledurham, Oxfordshire*, 1860. Watercolour and bodycolour on paper, © The Fitzwilliam Museum, Cambridge.

Significantly, Quinton also supplied the illustrations for Belloc's *Historic Thames*, and the wider cultural enthusiasm for the rural vernacular that his pictures represented was also evident in later Victorian and Edwardian discourse on the Thames landscape generally. Just as Allingham eschewed the grand for the homely in her paintings of Surrey, Sussex and Kent, so too were painters of the upper Thames increasingly drawn to scenes demotic rather than magnificent in nature. Despite the large number of splendid mansions and parks in the Thames Valley, it was now the quaint old mills, rustic cottages and quiet backwaters that drew most attention. This move towards the picturesque vernacular was apparent from the 1860s, as is well illustrated by the paintings of the Pre-Raphaelite George Price Boyce (1826–97). Boyce spent most of his summers that decade in and around the villages of Pangbourne, Mapledurham, Whitchurch and Streatley, where he painted carefully observed pictures of cottages and mills, the atmosphere of these scenes being one of calm, reposeful domesticity (see fig. 35).[92]

As G. D. Leslie attested in 1888, such scenes became still more popular with other artists in later years.[93] The *locus classicus* was probably Iffley Mill, a picturesquely dilapidated building of

[92] C. Newall and J. Egerton, *George Price Boyce* (London, 1987).
[93] See above, p. 269.

eleventh-century origins, which stood beside the Thames near Oxford (it burnt down in 1908). So popular, indeed, was the scene with artists that *Dickens's dictionary of the Thames* (1893) suggested in its entry for Iffley that 'It is hardly necessary to visit Iffley to see the mill. It has been painted in every kind of medium, and photographed in every sort of camera, till it must be as familiar to most people as Windsor Castle itself. Rarely, indeed, is there an exhibition at the Academy, or the Dudley, or any of the water-colour societies, without at least one bit of Iffley.'[94]

As elsewhere, changing artistic preferences related to changing tourist tastes. One reflection of this was the tendency for late Victorian and Edwardian Thames guidebooks to praise the rustic vernacular. Even cheap 1d handbooks, such as those produced by the *Lock to Lock Times* in the 1890s, waxed lyrical over the attractions of 'very picturesque old villages' such as Goring, Streatley and Sonning, as well as recommending notable individual sites such as Shiplake Mill near Henley, and its 'much painted and photographed' counterpart at Iffley.[95] Throughout these texts, the bias was towards old-world domesticity and riverside tranquillity, with Elizabethan architectural features – for instance the gabling at Pangbourne and Mapledurham – being especially esteemed.[96] Such preferences were also evident in more highbrow contexts. Perhaps predictably, William Morris favoured the cottage architecture of Sonning to the aristocratic landscape around Cliveden ('a lacquey's paradise'), his upriver boat trip of August 1880 doing much to inspire the socialist utopia of *News from Nowhere*.[97] But similar perspectives could also be found in mainstream belletrist accounts. Two Edwardian examples were J. E. Vincent's *Story of the Thames* (1909) and Mortimer Menpes and G. E. Mitton's lavishly illustrated *The Thames* (1906),

[94] C. Dickens, *Dickens's dictionary of the Thames* (Oxford, 1972 [London, 1893]), p. 113.

[95] *'Lock to Lock Times' and 'River Life' pocket guide to the River Thames* (London, [1896]), pp. 10, 17, 21, 23.

[96] A. S. Krause, *A pictorial history of the Thames* (London, 1889), pp. 102–8 and *passim*.

[97] N. Kelvin (ed.), *The collected letters of William Morris*, Vol. 1: *1848–1880* (Princeton, 1984), pp. 581–2; J. M. Baïssus, 'The expedition of the Ark', *Journal of the William Morris Society*, 3 (1977), 2–11; William Morris, *News from Nowhere* (London, 1891).

both of which contained much admiring discussion of the cottages, villages and parish churches to be found along the upper course of the great river.[98]

This emphasis on the vernacular landscape – that of ordinary people, however idealised – contrasted sharply with earlier accounts, which had focused on the opulent mansions of the rich. By the late nineteenth century, in the context of widening divisions between landlords and people,[99] it was not only socialists such as Morris who disdained the latter. While others were by no means as critical as he, armchair accounts and tourist handbooks alike paid relatively scant attention to the country seats of the Thames Valley (some were even underwhelmed by Windsor Castle).[100] Revealingly, *Dickens's dictionary of the Thames* contained no entries for Cliveden or Park Place, or indeed many of the other piles that had hitherto been so lionised, while the third edition of *Up and down the Thames* (1897), a paperback guide issued on behalf of the Thames Steamboat Company, dismissed the once-lauded Syon House as 'not a very pleasant or beautiful … country mansion'.[101] And those country seats that retained some popularity did so mainly on account of their surrounding scenery, not because of their architecture or associations. Cliveden remained popular not for its house, but for its 'fine situation' and 'grand woods' – even if William Waldorf Astor, owner of the estate from 1893, did all he could to prevent river-going excursionists from appreciating its landscape by walling it off from view.[102] Few landowners went quite so far as 'Walled-off' Astor (as he became known): the Harcourts of Nuneham Courtenay, for example, continued to permit public access to their tree-lined stretch of riverbank, which enjoyed great popularity as a picnic spot into the

---

[98] J. E. Vincent, *The story of the Thames* (London, 1909); M. Menpes and G. E. Mitton [text: Mitton], *The Thames* (London, 1906).

[99] For the political expression of which, see Readman, *Land and nation*; for the broader cultural context, see P. Mandler, *The fall and rise of the stately home* (New Haven and London, 1997).

[100] *Pearson's gossipy guide*, pp. 68–70 (for Windsor).

[101] Dickens, *Dickens's dictionary*; *Up and down the Thames, from London Bridge to Hampton Court and Oxford and from London Bridge to the Sea*, 3rd edn (London, [1897]), p. 39. For earlier laudatory commentary, see, e.g., *A new display of the beauties of England*, Vol. II, pp. 64ff.

[102] Vincent, *Story of the Thames*, p. 235; Mandler, *Fall and rise of the stately home*, p. 206.

twentieth century, with anything up to 20,000 people visiting on the two days it was open each week. Yet even so, very little was now said in praise of Nuneham House (the best *Dickens's* could do was to remark that it was 'fortunately free' from 'over magnificence').[103] And for all that its park attracted the crowds, the pleasures offered there seemed anachronistic to some commentators, harking back to an aristocratic time now being eclipsed with the advance of democracy. As Walter Armstrong noted in his *Thames from its source to the sea* (1886), the 'half-artificial beauties' of the gardens at Nuneham were 'the relics of a state of society which is becoming more obsolete every day'.[104] For Armstrong, as for many others by this time, the real 'beauties of the Thames culminate[d] at Streatley', amongst the old-world cottages of ordinary people, not in the sylvan demesnes of the elite.[105]

These late-nineteenth- and early-twentieth-century preferences correlated with the great explosion in popularity of the upper Thames as a place of leisure and recreation. They were also associated with the democratising tenor of the times more generally; in the context of broadening parliamentary and local government electoral franchises, they chimed with new understandings of nationhood as defined in popular terms. Increasingly, English identity was seen as rooted in the common people, in their culture and ways of life (however fancifully imagined these sometimes were). This nationalist imaginary did much to inspire land reformers of a very wide range of political persuasions, from radical Conservatives to socialist land nationalisers. The idea here was that getting people back to the land would undermine or offset the system of 'landlordism', which had been a creation of past aristocratic parliaments, and give the ordinary people of modern England – who now determined the fate of governments – more of a stake in the soil of their native country.[106] But the political utility of this demotic-patriotic ruralism was a function of its cultural currency, and there was no better evidence of its currency than the new readings now being offered of the Thames Valley.

---

[103] Krause, *Pictorial history*, p. 66; evidence of Frederick Mair, *Select Committee on the Thames River Preservation*, 16 (1884), p. 391; Dickens, *Dickens's dictionary*, pp. 158–60 (p. 158).

[104] W. Armstrong, *The Thames from its source to the sea*, 2 vols. (London, [1886]), Vol. 1, p. 62.

[105] *Ibid.*, Vol. 1, p. 83.

[106] Readman, *Land and nation*.

Revealingly, many of the publications that emphasised the charms of this landscape often voiced complaints about local landlords denying the public adequate access to them.[107] By the 1880s, with the picturesque villages and quiet backwaters of the upper river increasingly popular among excursionists of all classes, tensions between riparian owners and pleasure-seeking members of the public were more and more apparent. Newspapers carried reports of proliferating 'private' notices, the blocking of backwaters, and even the enclosure of towpaths and strips of land along the river. The concern was such that a Thames Rights Association was established in 1882 to support those who were 'wrongfully assailed and threatened by riparian owners', and to campaign for the defence of public rights in the river. As the debate intensified, it drew the attention of *The Times*, which in a leading article of November 1883 went so far as to declare that the selfish action of landowners was such that 'the river, as a pleasure resort, is in danger'. *The Times*'s intervention prompted the CPS to undertake an investigation, the conclusions of which alarmed preservationist opinion, and later that year a Thames Preservation League, composed of representatives from the CPS and local footpaths and open spaces committees, had come into being.[108]

Central to the contention of the CPS and its allies was that the Thames was a national possession and that, as such, rights of access for all should be preserved. As the Thames Preservation League put it in its statement of aims and objects, 'The Thames has been for many years one of the most popular of the Nation's pleasure resorts … The interest of the Nation in the Thames was recognised as long ago as the reign of King John in the Magna Charta.'[109] This argument was analogous to that which was successfully being made with respect to common land in urban areas. In the case of these tracts of land – Hampstead Heath, for instance – the CPS had argued that while ancient common rights were no longer of any economic utility for ordinary people, the new public use-value of such places as sites of recreation made enclosure unjustifiable.[110] This perspective was further buttressed by the jurisprudential precept that in making judgments on the proper use of land,

---

[107] See, e.g., Leslie, *Our river*, pp. 69, 127; Menpes and Mitton, *The Thames*, pp. 65–6.

[108] Sir Robert Hunter papers, Surrey History Centre, 1621/13/1; 'Encroachments on the Thames', *The Times*, 12 November 1883, p. 8.

[109] 'The Thames Preservation League: Aims and objects', Hunter Papers, 1621/13/1.

[110] Readman, 'Preserving'.

public benefit ought to be the primary consideration. Hence private property could be justified on the grounds that security of possession encouraged the maximisation of agricultural or other forms of production, so conducing to the general good; hence, also, public access to commons could be justified on the grounds that such places were conducive to the general good by providing an increasingly urbanised people with opportunities for healthful open-air leisure and enjoyment of nature.[111] So far as the Thames was concerned, the argument was that public access to the river had previously been legitimated by economic considerations, the river being an important artery of trade, but that now the public use-value of the river was based on its importance – to quote *The Times* – as 'a national pleasure-ground'.[112] Thus, while the rationale for the nation's stake in the Thames had always been the maximisation of the public good, the means by which the Thames might contribute to that good had changed. It was widely felt that if the river had been 'a great national possession' in the past by virtue of its significance as a navigable waterway, it remained so in the present not on this account, but because of its new utility and popularity as a site of healthful recreation.[113] The response of riparian owners to this popularity was to assert their private proprietary rights, often overzealously, in some cases illegally, and this was seen as an attack on the nation's rightful stake in the landscape: 'Father Thames in Danger', cried an article in the 22 March 1884 number of *Punch*.[114]

Public opinion and CPS campaigning drew the attention of MPs, and in March 1884 a parliamentary select committee on Thames preservation was established under the chairmanship of the Liberal Unionist Nevil Story-Maskelyne, professor of mineralogy at Oxford University. The report of the committee affirmed the existence of a public right to move boats on Thames waters; it also urged the establishment of a free towpath along the whole length of the river, recommending that any such amenity should be usable as a footpath as well as for towing.[115] Doubtless such conclusions were cheering to the CPS and its allies. Perhaps less welcome was the recommendation that more by-laws be introduced for the regulation of behaviour on or near the

[111] Readman, *Land and nation*, pp. 113–18.
[112] 'Encroachments on the Thames'.
[113] *Ibid.*; cf. Menpes and Mitton, *The Thames*, Chapter 19: 'Our national possession'.
[114] *Punch*, 22 March 1884, p. 142.
[115] *Select Committee on the Thames River Preservation*, 16 (1884), Report.

river (the foul language and 'indecent' bathing of river trippers were notable concerns of a number of witnesses, including Sir Gilbert East, a prominent local landlord and chairman of a committee of riparian owners).[116] And certainly less welcome was the committee's view that it was 'impossible to recognise anything like a general right to take fish as now existing': while the water of the Thames might be public property, the animals in it were not.[117]

Story-Maskelyne's report led to the passage of an Act 'for the preservation of the River Thames above Teddington Lock for purposes of public recreation and for regulating the pleasure traffic thereon'. Following the select committee's recommendation, this measure – the 1885 Thames Preservation Act – laid down that there existed an inalienable public right to travel by boat on the waters of the upper river, but it was far from perfect from the access campaigners' point of view. For a start, a clause was inserted legalising obstructions to the navigation extant for twenty years previous to the passage of the Act, which had the effect of permanently ruling some backwaters out of bounds. This disappointed CPS leaders such as Robert Hunter; it also disappointed *The Times* and other organs of mainstream opinion.[118] Furthermore, the measure gave extensive powers to the Thames Conservators to make by-laws for the regulation of the river, and for all that the introduction of fines for 'indecent' bathing probably commanded significant

[116] In his evidence before the committee, East made much of alleged nuisances caused on the Thames by 'roughs', in particular 'the London "'Arry"' type ('a class of savages born on purpose'). Their sins were various. Not only did they 'dress in short trousers not reaching down so far as their knees, and a jersey without sleeves', but they used 'disgusting' language; 'trespass[ed] everywhere'; scattered papers and bottles; vandalised trees, hedges and buildings; picked flowers; shot wildlife and game indiscriminately (while trespassing, naturally); and let their dogs worry the cattle. Still worse, the young men bathed naked in plain sight of the riverside residences of people such as East, and – in even plainer sight – some went so far as to run about unburdened by clothes on private lawns beside the river, in order to dry themselves after their exertions. To cap it all, East and his friends felt, these 'river roughs' lacked all respect for ladies, using indecent language in their earshot. 'I have been in a sailing boat', East fulminated, 'and ... they have come round the sailing boat and said, "Oh, how nice it is to be alone with a woman!" and made remarks of that description, which is very unpleasant; and it made one long to kick them, only you cannot get at them.' *Select Committee on the Thames River Preservation*, 16 (1884), pp. 205, 274–83.

[117] *Ibid.*, p. xxiii.

[118] Robert Hunter: *The Times*, 1 August 1885, p. 7; 'The Thames as a pleasure resort', *The Times*, 3 September 1885, p. 5.

support,[119] there was a concern that the Conservators' powers would be exercised in the interests of riparian owners. And in any case, as it stood, the act made trespassing on the banks of the river a criminal offence, and prohibited houseboats from loitering within 200 yards of riverside residences – a clause that Henry Allnutt, founder of the National Footpaths Preservation Society, thought would make 'a person … rub his eyes and consider, in these times, whether he is still living in a free England'.[120]

Yet, for all the criticism of the Thames Preservation Act – criticism that persisted in some quarters into the 1890s and 1900s[121] – it was nonetheless a landmark piece of amenity legislation. As *The Times* recognised when it passed into law, while certainly flawed, the measure was 'valuable in its frank recognition of the fact that the Thames is now a pleasure river, and must be preserved and managed as such'.[122] In legitimising the new understanding of the landscape as a 'national possession', the act facilitated the making of complaints against private landowners thought to be blocking public access. Buttressed by the law in this way, such complaints grew more frequent, bold and vociferous from the later 1880s on. They were aired in editorials in the *Lock to Lock Times*; they surfaced in belletrist accounts; they even appeared in tourist handbooks.[123] The legislation also helped stimulate practical acts of defiance. G. D. Leslie's advice to readers of his *Our river* (1888) was to ignore 'the notice board about private waters, &c.'; while *Pearson's gossipy guide* (1902) went so far as to suggest that for the river holiday-maker 'a very good plan is to go down **all** backwaters … Don't you trouble as to infringement of rights; leave it to the putative owners to assert them.'[124] Such advice seems to have been followed by river users. In their 1891 account of a month spent boating on the Thames, an American couple observed that 'no one seems to heed' signs saying 'private water'; indeed, they reported having 'heard men read aloud "private water", and add at once, "Oh, that's all right. Come on!"'.[125] And while the 1885

[119] Burstall, *Golden age*, pp. 154–5.
[120] *First Annual Report of the National Footpath Preservation Society*, 1884–5, p. 27.
[121] See, e.g., Cook, *Thames rights and Thames wrongs*, esp. pp. 158–64.
[122] The Thames as a pleasure resort', *The Times*, 3 September 1885, p. 5.
[123] 'Rights of way on the Thames', *Lock to Lock Times*, 1 September 1888, pp. 1–2; Menpes and Mitton, *The Thames*, pp. 65–6.
[124] Leslie, *Our river*, p. 127; *Pearson's gossipy guide*, p. 51 (emphasis in original).
[125] Pennell and Pennell, *Stream of pleasure*, p. 80.

act criminalised trespassing on private riverbanks, this did little to deter excursionists from disembarking for Thames-side picnics. As one such excursionist told the *Lock to Lock Times* in September 1888:

> The other Sunday I camped for lunch on the favourite bit of ground under the willows by Kempton Park. As is getting so usual now, a man came round to know if everybody knew that this was private ground, etc. I saw many people give him a shilling – he must have made some half-a-sovereign in about ten minutes. When he came to me, I took no notice of him. He blustered a good deal, and I told him to go and fetch his master, and offered him my name and address. He went off very excited to fetch his master, who, he said, was only a few steps off, and he'd precious soon show me, etc., etc. We waited very comfortably for an hour, but neither he nor his master came. Who was he, and what did he do with the money, and what would you call the people who are simple enough to part [with it]?[126]

The stalwart picnicker was none other than Jerome K. Jerome, who would later fictionalise this lunchtime experience to good effect in *Three men in a boat*, his hugely popular and comic account of three clerks' holiday jaunt on the Thames.[127]

Perhaps the person who accosted Jerome that Sunday afternoon was a confidence trickster and not the agent of any landowner; but even if so, the reaction of the excursionists is telling, suggestive of a determination to assert a claim to the Thames landscape (if at financial cost in some cases).[128] This reflected the shift in public opinion marked by the passage of the Thames Preservation Act, however

---

[126] *Lock to Lock Times*, 1 September 1888, p. 10.

[127] See J. K. Jerome, *Three men in a boat* (London, 2004 [1889]), pp. 58–9. For Jerome's affection for the Thames, and boating activities on it, see J. K. Jerome, *My life and times* (London, 1926), pp. 103–7, 229.

[128] In *Three men in a boat* the clerks' picnic-time experience prompts a philippic, by the narrator, against the behaviour of riverside landowners: 'The selfishness of the riparian proprietor grows with every year. If these men had their way they would close the River Thames altogether. They actually do this along the minor tributary streams and in the backwaters. They drive posts into the bed of the stream, and draw chains from bank to bank, and nail huge notice-boards on every tree. The sight of those notice-boards rouses every evil instinct in my nature. I feel I want to tear each one down, and hammer it over the head of the man who put it up, until I have killed him, and then I would bury him, and put the board up over the grave as a tombstone' (Jerome, *Three men in a boat*, p. 59).

imperfect the details of that measure may have been. With the statutory affirmation of the idea that the Thames was 'a national possession' in terms of its amenity value for the populace as a whole, the river, increasingly, was contested ground, a place where competing interests collided.

As was the case with disputes over footpaths and commons, the conflict between Thames landowners and pleasure-seekers could be presented as one between selfish and public interests, between private greed and national good. Such was the argument of the CPS, and it was one that had considerable traction in an increasingly democratic public culture. The currency of this argument had led riparian landowners such as Gilbert East to portray Thames excursionists as rough, drunken and indecent rabble, whose behaviour was akin to that of 'Nubians' or 'complete savages' rather than civilised Englishmen (reports of naked bathing seem to have been especially suggestive here).[129] But this was a defensive response, and one that was itself testimony to the widespread popularity of the Thames to people of all classes; the landscape was now a place in which ordinary men and women felt a real stake, and its soaring recreational popularity with them had helped make it the 'national possession' that the legislation of 1885 acknowledged it to be. As the *Lock to Lock Times* put it in 1888, the river was now 'free to all'; in this sense, it belonged to the nation.[130]

This new conception of the Thames as a national possession created other tensions, as more and more people took to the river. Since the late 1860s, concerns had been raised about the impact of steam-launches in particular. To some, the velocity and noise of these vehicles seemed destructive of the tranquillity of the environment, their swell disturbing other users of the upper river, from artists, to bankside fishermen, to those seeking relaxation by pottering about in rowing boats (see fig. 36).[131] Some of the complaints were hyperbolic, but the issue was real enough and increasingly drew the attention of the Thames Conservators – and even, on occasion, the courts. In July 1876 charges were brought at Henley County Court against the

---

[129] 'Exploring the wilds', *Fun*, 19 July 1876, p. 27; Burstall, *Golden age*, pp. 154–5; *Select Committee on the Thames River Preservation*, 16 (1884), pp. 157, 205, 366.

[130] *Lock to Lock Times*, 9 June 1888, p. 1.

[131] 'The Thames Conservancy', *Saturday Review*, 26 June 1869, 833; *Punch*, 21 August 1869, p. 74; C. Black, *Frederick Walker* (London, [1902]), p. 178; 'Exploring the wilds', *Fun*, 19 July 1876, p. 26.

CAPTAIN JINKS (OF THE "SELFISH") AND HIS FRIENDS ENJOYING THEMSELVES ON THE RIVER.

36 *Captain Jinks (of the 'Selfish') and his friends enjoying themselves on the river*, *Punch*, 21 August 1869. Reproduced by kind permission of the Syndics of Cambridge University Library: L992.b.177.

unfortunately named Horatio Nelson Hall, who was accused of dangerously navigating his steam launch (the *Flying Dutchman*) at several points along the Thames. The court heard how on 25 May that year his boat had travelled at speeds of up to 15½ mph, creating 2½ feet of surf, which carried away about a tonne of earth and a willow tree near Wargrave, and also damaged boats moored at a riverside pub. Worse still, later that evening the swell from the *Flying Dutchman* had caused a boat to be swamped near Mapledurham, leading to a person being drowned.[132] This was an extreme example, perhaps, but concerns over steam launches did lead to their increased regulation. The 1883 Thames Act and the 1885 Thames Preservation Act required the registration of steam-powered craft, imposed stiffer penalties for misbehaviour such as Nelson Hall's, and empowered the Conservators to

---

[132] Nelson Hall was given the maximum penalty (fines totalling £30), with a civil action being taken against him for the fatality: *Illustrated Police News*, 15 July 1876.

make by-laws for the control of river traffic.[133] These measures did not end the complaints about steamboats, and the Conservators were still occasionally castigated for not doing enough to tackle the problems they posed;[134] nevertheless, the legislation had an impact. Certainly the *Lock to Lock Times* was wrong when it claimed, in July 1888, that the Conservators generally failed to bring proceedings against those in breach of by-laws relating to steamcraft.[135] In fact, between 29 June 1883 and 31 December 1887 a total of 102 prosecutions were brought against steam launches under the provisions of the 1883 Act alone – a high figure, given that there were no more than 250 such vessels on the river at this time.[136]

Among those concerned about the impact of steam on the Thames environment was the preservationist lobby. In a memorial presented to the mayor of London in 1883 the Thames Preservation League mentioned 'the reckless … mismanagement … of steamboats and other craft' as one of the 'impalpable wrongs' being done to the Thames.[137] It is possible to read such sentiments as expressing a more general hostility to the modern world and its (in this case steam-powered) appurtenances. But as with valued landscapes elsewhere in England, such as the New Forest and the Lake District, preservationist activity in relation to the Thames was motivated not by the abjuration of modernity, but by a conviction that the amenity benefits conferred by such landscapes were now more than ever important. This was a very modern impulse, one proceeding from an acceptance that the vast majority of British people would continue to live in towns and cities, and that because of this, the preservation of common access to places rich in wild nature or historical associations was a vital social good – that it was, indeed, a patriotic imperative. This was the position of the CPS and the National Trust. And more particularly related to the Thames context, it was also the position of those involved in the turn-of-the-century campaign for the preservation of the view of the

---

[133] E. H. Fishbourne, *The Thames Conservancy* (London, 1882).

[134] See, e.g., the polemical Cook, *Thames rights and Thames wrongs*, pp. 16ff.

[135] *Lock to Lock Times*, 14 July 1888, pp. 1–2.

[136] Krause, *Pictorial history*, p. 59; *Lock to Lock Times*, 28 July 1888, pp. 1–2. Moreover, that only 35 of these 102 proceedings resulted in convictions suggests that the conservators were, if anything, over-zealous in their application of the by-laws; any complaints of inaction were unjustified.

[137] 'Memorial to the Mayor of London', Hunter Papers, 1621/13/1.

Thames Valley from Richmond Hill, a campaign that culminated in 1901–2 with the local-authority-funded purchase of an estate of land adjoining the river, and the passage of legislation preventing building on other land near the hill.[138] Supported by leading organs of opinion, notably *The Times*, this preservationist activism had been sparked by fears that the land around the hill would be sold for building purposes, so alarming 'the consciences of men to whom the silvery flowing Thames is a sacred river'.[139] One prominent supporter of the campaign, the novelist George Meredith, described the view as 'one of our national treasures'; while *The Times* reckoned that there was no prospect 'more characteristic of English scenery at its best … Yet nowhere in this broad and beautiful England can the English eye look upon a landscape more purely and essentially English, most instinct with the very spirit of our land.[140] As we have seen, the view had formed the subject of paintings by artists such as Turner and Reynolds; it had also featured in the writings of Thomson, Scott and others. It was thus rich in associational value, widely understood to be part of the nation's heritage, or – as one local councillor involved in the campaign put it – 'a natural living picture which painters and poets have for ages extolled, handed down to us as a national heirloom'.[141]

The description of the view from Richmond Hill as a 'national heirloom' was one that many late Victorian and Edwardian English men and women would have thought applicable to the Thames landscape more generally. This was a national landscape in the sense that it was an inheritance in which all had a stake. It was also an inheritance on account of the connections it offered between England old and new. The world of the upper Thames was prized for its evocation of an ancient, rural England; while that of the lower Thames was valued for its associations with the nation's capital and contemporary commercial

---

[138] For an account of the campaign, see Anne Milton-Worssell, 'The need for a rural idyll: Preserving the view from Richmond Hill', *Richmond History*, 24 (May 2003), 68–81.

[139] *Westminster Review*, 13 March 1896. *The Times*, 28 December 1895, p. 9; and 15 July 1901, p. 9.

[140] Letter of George Meredith to *Richmond and Twickenham Times*, 15 June 1901, 6; *The Times*, 15 July 1901, p. 9.

[141] Councillor James Hilditch, quoted in *Richmond and Twickenham Times*, 8 June 1901, p. 6.

greatness.[142] Linking these two worlds, the river connected past, present and future, the flow of its water representing the onward flow of time; the Thames became a physical representation of the historical continuity that underpinned national identity. Thus, in combining the 'lovely and English' countryside of its upper course with the industry and commerce of London, the landscape of the Thames stood for the history of England.[143] This was a lived history; the river landscape suggested a past immanent in the everyday life of late Victorian and Edwardian modernity, not one preserved in aspic. *Salter's guide to the Thames* may have described the Thames as 'a long historical Museum', but almost in the same breath it offered the reflection that

> museum is perhaps hardly the right word. For the Thames has comparatively few mere relics and ruins – the dry bones of history. It is characteristic that Windsor Castle, founded by Norman kings, is still a royal residence; that the modern Oxford undergraduate still sleeps in fifteenth century bedrooms, and that regular services are still celebrated in the church of the Vicar of Bray. Destruction there has been, but not disuse. A long procession of noble Abbeys has perished – for the most part perished utterly. A longer series of churches, of castles, of ancient manor houses remain, not in ruins but in continuing usefulness. They do not merely record the past, like relics, but unite it to the present by still serving a useful purpose. It has always been the pride of England to turn the past to the uses of the present, and nowhere can this be better seen than in the Thames Valley.[144]

The point here was that time, like the waters of the Thames, did not stand still, and moreover that its progress was no cause for regret so long as a sense of historical continuity remained embedded in lived experience. Commentators presented Joseph Bazalgette's great sewage scheme, which involved the construction of huge artificial

---

[142] *Salter's guide* thought the 'peculiar glory of the Thames' was that 'within the small compass of about a hundred miles it shows just what is most characteristic in English scenery, history, and modern life. The monuments of the past, the placid and prosperous life of the present, the quiet pastoral beauty of meadow, woodland and silver stream, are all seen here, and all at their best': Salter and Salter, *Salter's guide*, p. 5.

[143] 'The conservancy of the Thames', *London Journal*, 5 October 1872, 212–13; 'The Thames: Its history and scenery', *London Journal*, 1 September 1870, 84–5.

[144] Salter and Salter, *Salter's guide*, p. 4.

embankments along the Thames in central London, as no jarring novelty but as 'a continuance, or rather a revival, of a policy first commenced by the Saxons, probably thirteen centuries ago, and carried on during every subsequent period on some part of the river'.[145] Indeed, as the example of Bazalgette's engineering illustrates, even quite drastic human interventions in the Thames landscape were not generally abjured. The visual qualities of many of the modern bridges that spanned the river had long been admired, in self-consciously 'aesthetic' commentary as well as tourist guidebooks and technical accounts. Not long after it was constructed, for example, Shillingford Bridge had been lauded in Ireland's *Picturesque views on the River Thames* (1792) as 'light and elegant' in appearance, and conferring a significant addition to 'the natural beauty of the landscape'.[146] Bridges continued to attract such compliments into the late nineteenth and early twentieth centuries.[147] The new iron bridge built between Pangbourne and Whitchurch in 1902 was praised in one belletristic text as having augmented the scenic appeal of the already much-valued locality, despite the fact that it had replaced a picturesque wooden structure.[148] And even solidly utilitarian iron or brick railway bridges, such as those at Maidenhead and Richmond, came in for commendation.[149]

[145] 'The Thames: Its history and scenery', p. 85; 'The conservancy of the Thames'; W. L. Wyllie and G. Allen, *The tidal Thames: Catalogue of the drawings of Mr W. L. Wyllie exhibited at the Fine Art Society 148 New Bond Street with introductory chapter by Mr Grant Allen* (London, 1892), p. 130. The reference here was to the embankments constructed by the Saxons on the Surrey and Kent shores of the Thames with a view to improving navigation and reclaiming otherwise flooded land for agriculture.

[146] Ireland, *Picturesque views*, Vol. 1, p. 144. Ireland was particularly taken by the bridges spanning the river; of the fifty-two prints in the two volumes of his *Picturesque views*, forty-three are of bridges, or feature them prominently.

[147] Nicholls, *Steam-boat companion*, p. 7; 'Bridges on the Thames', *London Journal*, 22 November 1873, 324; A. T. Walmisley, *The bridges over the Thames at London* (London, 1880), p. 8; J. H. Herring, *Thames bridges from London to Hampton Court* (London, 1884); J. Dredge, *Thames bridges, from the Tower to the source*, 2 vols. (London, 1897), Vol. 1, pp. 27, 50; *County of London sketches of bridges over the Thames* (London, 1903).

[148] 'At Pangbourne the old wooden bridge has given place to an iron one, but the deed has been carried out in a manner that reflects credit on the doer, for the new bridge runs in a graceful curve, and its sides of latticed ironwork are painted white': Menpes and Mitton, *The Thames*, p. 63. Menpes was an artist, and friend of J. A. M. Whistler's.

[149] Herring, *Thames bridges*, n.p.; Menpes and Mitton, *The Thames*, pp. 132–3; Armstrong, *The Thames*, Vol. 1, p. 85.

Aside from bridges, the weirs that studded the course of the river constituted another particularly noticeable man-made intervention in the landscape, but one that was not generally condemned. The weirs had originally been designed to facilitate commercial navigation, especially by barges; but after the decline of such traffic from the mid Victorian period their maintenance was urged on the grounds of amenity. Not only did pleasure craft also require a navigable river, but the weirs and their locks were felt to preserve the beauty of the landscape. In his July 1864 report on the state of the upper river between Oxford and Staines, S. W. Leach, engineer to the Thames Commissioners, had pointed out that 'those beautiful reaches for which this part of the Thames is noted owe not a little of their attractiveness to the fullness of their stream being maintained by the weirs, to which the locks are an essential adjunct. Newnham, Basildon, Cliefdon [Cliveden], and other spots would have their beauty sadly marred by the river being reduced, as it were, to a streamlet.'[150] Such arguments helped ensure that relatively few objections were directed at projects for the maintenance and improvement of weirs, and even the making of new ones. While voices were occasionally raised against the design of modern weirs and locks,[151] their necessity was generally accepted. Admiration of the Thames as 'redolent of the past of this our Britain' could go hand-in-hand with enthusiasm for modern river technology, such as that embodied in the iron and granite structure of Teddington Weir, built in 1871 at the cost of almost £8,000,[152] and a popular subject for picture postcards. Some quite ardent defenders of Thames nature and heritage even felt that more weirs should be constructed. The naturalist C. J. Cornish was a strong preservationist: he thought the Thames should be protected by making it into a national trust because it was 'our national river' and 'as important as the British Museum'. But as Cornish suggested in his book, *The naturalist on the Thames*, he also thought new locks should be placed further downstream, so as to make it easier for boats to come on the river at all times, thereby improving public access to nature.[153]

---

[150] *Bell's Life in London and Sporting Chronicle*, 25 March 1865, p. 10. *The Times* agreed, remarking in its commentary on Leach's report that 'There is perfect harmony, therefore, on this question between artistic taste and utility' (15 March 1865, p. 9).

[151] Cook, *Thames rights and Thames wrongs*, pp. 58–9.

[152] 'The conservancy of the Thames', p. 213.

[153] C. J. Cornish, *The naturalist on the Thames* (London, 1902), pp. 250–1, 254ff.

In his book, Cornish also complained about the quality and quantity of accommodation for tourists on the upper river, and suggested the building of more holiday cottages by landowners.[154] It was a comment that reflected a wider truth about the late Victorian and Edwardian touristic consumption of the Thames landscape: enthusiasm for natural beauty and the storied past – all those quiet backwaters and picturesque villages – went hand-in-hand with a desire for the enjoyment of modern conveniences. Here as elsewhere, the two impulses were not incompatible. In *Our river*, the artist G. D. Leslie recommended that the tourist make overnight stops at towns such as Reading rather than out-of-the-way villages; this was because in the larger places the accommodation would be superior, and newspapers and provisions more readily available. It was also because the hubbub of urban life provided a striking and agreeable sense of difference with nearby rural beauty:

> After a long day on the river in comparative solitude there is much pleasure in the contrast afforded by the bustle of the streets and shops in a town, and the appetite for the beauties of nature receives a fresh sharpening. On Saturday night the market place at Reading is a most amusing place in which to stroll about after dinner. Quack medicine vendors and Cheap Jacks are in great force, the country people flocking around them in picturesque crowds.[155]

In this way, the appreciation of rustic riverside quietude was complemented and enhanced by contact with urban modernity; experience of the one made more intense experience of the other.

Leslie was not the only artist whose interest in the rural landscape of the upper Thames co-existed with enjoyment of and interest in the more advanced appurtenances of modernity. George Vicat Cole (1833–93) presents another example. Personally interested in chemistry and electricity, and a member of the Royal Institution,[156] Cole was no nostalgic reactionary; many of his paintings, indeed, were made from his own steam launch, which he delighted in piloting (not

[154] *Ibid.*, pp. 182–7.
[155] Leslie, *Our river*, p. 230.
[156] R. Chignell, *The life and paintings of Vicat Cole, R.A.*, 3 vols. (London, 1898), Vol. III, p. 146.

inconsiderately, it was generally agreed) up and down the river. And while he was certainly drawn to rural and picturesque scenes, many of Cole's paintings depicted a working river: barges often featured in them, including those presenting otherwise rustic upriver scenes.[157] Furthermore, even the more pastoral of Cole's Thames-side works, such as *Oxford from Iffley* (1884), did not portray a ruralism insulated from the vicissitudes of time. It is not just that the picture is one of a lived-in and working countryside – the sheep in the foreground, the men at work in the fields – but that it describes a landscape both historical and susceptible of change. This is no static scene, but one filled with life and movement, looking to the future as well as the past. The key here is the painting's emphasis on the changefulness of the weather, clear in Cole's handling of the sky; and it was an emphasis readily apparent to contemporary commentators. As Robert Chignell noted in his 1898 biographical study of Cole, in the painting

> A glorious day of June throws its beams over the landscape; the foliage is in its summer prime; the sky tells of movement and change; the scene is peaceful, yet imbued with life. Beyond lies the city which the painter delights to honour. How many summer days have shone on its spires and towers? What generations of men have come forth from its walls to gaze on the stream, and watch the unfolding of life and the play of light over the landscape! Everything changes; but the city remains: it will see many such a glorious day, and be the chosen home of learning for many a year, Still, Nature renews herself, and outlives man and all his works. The stream reflects the sky as it has done for thousands of years, and will do for thousands to come. A double suggestion of mutability is thus conveyed; the daily changes of Nature are contrasted with the stability of man's work; and again, as a further thought, the inner permanence of Nature is compared with the brief life of even the most enduring structures reared by human hands.[158]

Other paintings Cole made of upriver scenes were similarly imbued by a sense of change and liveliness, whether it was the rush of water through sluices under the darkening sky of a windy day in *Iffley Mill*

[157] *Ibid.*, Vol. III, pp. 8–10.
[158] *Ibid.*, Vol. III, p. 26.

37 George Vicat Cole, *Iffley Mill*, 1884. Oil on canvas. Towneley Hall Art Gallery and Museum, Burnley, Lancashire/Bridgeman Images.

(1884; fig. 37), or the movement animating the sky and water in *The meeting of the Thames and Isis at Dorchester* (1890).[159]

Cole's interest in the Thames extended to its lower reaches, where he found subjects quite as 'English', though rather different from those he encountered in its upper course. His *View of the Thames at Greenwich* (1890; fig. 38) recalled Britain's long traditions of naval greatness (note the aged sailors, residents of Greenwich hospital, on the bench in the foreground) as well as other historical associations, particularly connected with those royal figures for whom Greenwich had been a site of both personal pleasure and philanthropic activity.[160] At the same time, however, it gave due attention to the great industrialised

---

[159] *Ibid.*, Vol. III, pp. 31, 40–1.

[160] As Chignell commented, the Spanish chestnut trees in the foreground of the picture 'are typical of the many grand old trees of their species to be found in the park, which have shaded generations of men for three centuries or more. They have seen Queen Bess when she "rose to chase the deer at five". James I may have passed under them in hunting ... Cavalier and Roundhead, with their wives and children, spent the day, each after his own manner, beneath their shade ... King William III and Queen Mary, perhaps, sat under the old trees while discussing plans for converting the palace ... into a hospital for sailors wounded in the sea-fight off Cape la Hogue. In truth, the whole scene is full of historic memories, not the least touching of which is connected with the hospital itself' (*ibid.*, pp. 133–5).

38 George Vicat Cole, *View of the Thames at Greenwich*, 1890. Oil on canvas, private collection. Photograph © Christie's Images/Bridgeman Images.

metropolis beyond, a tall chimney looming prominently on the northern side of the river.

But it was with two of his larger paintings, *Westminster* (1892) and *The pool of London* (1888) that Cole really demonstrated the persistence, into the late nineteenth century, of patriotic admiration for the lower Thames, and indeed the continuing variety of the river's nationalistic associations. *Westminster* combined national heritage and urgent modernity in a way that was both realistic and appealing; the mother of parliaments and the cathedral church of London stood cheek-by-jowl with docks and cranes, while steam-tugs and barges laden with goods floated on the waters of a turbid, workaday Thames. It was a picture, the *Art Journal* reflected, in which 'past and present are delightfully interblended': one that was 'an epitome of the life of the English nation – all the chief features of its greatness – England's faith, England's commerce, England's government'.[161] Chignell thought it 'intensely English', and quite as much so as Cole's equally English rural paintings of the upper Thames.[162] Depicting a dense crowd of

---

[161] G. R. Kingsley, 'Westminster', *Art Journal*, 55 (February 1893), 34.
[162] Chignell, *Life and paintings of Vicat Cole*, Vol. III, pp. 122–3.

39 George Vicat Cole, *The pool of London*, 1888. Oil on canvas. © Tate, London, 2017.

ships, their forest of masts framing a distant St Paul's, *The pool of London* (fig. 39) also drew much praise, being widely hailed as a masterpiece when exhibited in the Royal Academy Summer Exhibition of 1888. Gladstone felt a 'seizure' on seeing the painting, writing of his 'admiration for the genius of a man who had been able ... so to represent a scene of commercial activity as to impress upon it, as I thought, the idea and character of *grandeur*. The picture seemed to speak and to say, "You see here the summit of all the commerce of the world." '[163]

Of course, not all contemporaries would have viewed the commercial bustle of the Thames with such favour. The novelist and historian Walter Besant, for one, was disgusted by the same ships in the pool of London that had so delighted Cole, thinking them 'hideous things made of iron, black and dismal'.[164] But such views were in a minority. In part this was because of James Abbott McNeill Whistler, whose Thames paintings from the 1860s on had done much to elevate the urban-commercial river as a subject for art.[165] Yet while Whistler's nocturnes represented an avant-garde aestheticisation of the Thames,

[163] Letter of Gladstone to Chignell, 15 January 1894, reproduced in *ibid.*, pp. 126–7.
[164] Besant, *The Thames*, p. 105.
[165] J. P. Ribner, 'The Thames in the age of the great stink: Some artistic and literary response to a Victorian environmental crisis', *British Art Journal*, 1 (2000), 38–46.

40 William Lionel Wyllie, *Toil, glitter, grime and wealth on a flowing tide*, 1883. Oil on canvas. © Tate, London, 2017.

its dirt and grime being transformed into formal beauty, for other more mainstream artists, riparian realities had a romantic appeal. Cole was one such. Another was William Lionel Wyllie, who made his reputation in the 1880s and 1890s with a series of pictures of the lower Thames and Medway. Of these paintings, *Toil, glitter, grime and wealth on a flowing tide* (1883) was particularly important, influencing the work of other artists (not least that of Cole).

Centrepiece of his breakthrough one-man show at the Fine Art Society, 'The tidal Thames' (1884), the painting (fig. 40) had as its main subject the working of heavily laden barges by squat, steam-powered tugs. Along with his other pictures of the lower river, it was well received, suggestive of a contemporary appreciation of the pictorial and nationalistic appeal of such gritty, busy, commercial scenes. As one critic wrote in 1889,

> The Thames Mr Wyllie paints is the Thames as it is, with all its grime and much of its wonder, all its business and something of its pathos, and suggestions (always right and often vivid) of its contrasts of hurry and rest, its mingling of dignity and degradation, its material embodiment of British supremacy and

prosperity, and its enormous testimonies to the dark romance of these coal-and-iron times.[166]

Wyllie transformed the dirty, bustling, foggy Thames, with its forests of masts and funnels, into what the writer Grant Allen – who was also a keen admirer of the upper river – called a 'wonderful epitome of British civilisation'.[167] As Allen glossed it in his commentary on the 'Tidal Thames' collection of pictures, Wyllie's art showed this river landscape to be the 'most central and essential fact in our national existence', the 'prime highway of our commercial greatness' and the 'ultimate origin of our naval supremacy'.[168] Thus, just at the time the upper river was being valued for its associations with an older, rural England, so was its lower course being celebrated as an embodiment of national greatness in the here-and-now. This demonstrated the power of the Thames as a national landscape linking past and present, rural and urban. It was a power the river had retained throughout the period.

Wylie's evocative portrayal of the Thames as the source of British commercial-maritime strength might suggest a close association between the Thames and empire. Certainly, a number of scholars have suggested that, just as London was an 'imperial metropolis', the Thames was an imperial landscape: as John Broich has put it, 'The Thames, a *place* in Britain, was part of imperial *space*.'[169] In a sense, this is undeniably true – indeed, one might say it is necessarily true of all places in Britain across the long nineteenth century. It is certainly the case that the patriotic valorisation of the river was compatible with imperial sentiment throughout the period, and even more so with a generalised idea of the nation's power and influence on the global stage – as implicit, not least, in the paintings of Wyllie, among other things. It is also the case that the real economy of the river was closely linked to the empire: of the 121 ships that arrived in London Port on 17 September

[166] H. V. Barnett, 'By river and sea', *Magazine of Art*, 7 (1883–4), 312; R. Quarm and J. Wyllie, *W. L. Wyllie: Marine artist, 1851–1931* (London, 1981), pp. 26, 60–1.

[167] W. L. Wyllie and G. Allen, *The tidal Thames with twenty full-page photogravure plates* (London, 1892), p. 128.

[168] *Ibid.*, pp. 132–3; and see also Wyllie and Allen, *The tidal Thames: Catalogue.*

[169] J. Broich, 'Colonizing the Thames', *Journal of Colonialism and Colonial History*, 11.3 (2010), https://muse.jhu.edu/ (accessed 24 October 2017); also J. Schneer, *London 1900: The imperial metropolis* (New Haven, 2001).

1849, for example, 52 brought cargoes from the colonies.[170] Yet for all that, the Thames was less an imperial than it was a British – and especially an English – river. The empire was by no means the dominant element of the nationalist imaginaries discussed in this chapter. One reason for this, perhaps, was the persisting importance of the national past in the discourse on the Thames. The Thames was a national river of surpassing importance in large part because of the strength of its associations with the long story of the nation, and this story was still largely an insular one. Increasingly consumed as popular heritage, and understood to be an amenity in which all had a quasi-proprietorial stake (as we saw in relation to the debates over access to its upper course), the river was a cultural landscape that stood for the whole history of England, and the vicissitudinous but still progressive continuity of that island history. As Samuel and Anna Hall observed in their *Book of the Thames*, published in 1859, while the river lacked 'the grander features of landscape', this did not detract from its national significance. In common with the other landscapes discussed in this book, associational value was crucial. 'Its history', the Halls explained,

> is that of England: the Britons, the Romans, the Saxons, the Danes, and the Normans, in turn made it their 'seat of war', or, setting upon its banks, sought the repose of peace and the blessings of agriculture and commerce. In all the civil contests of centuries it obtained melancholy renown: the intrenched camp, the castle, the baronial hall, the mansion, the villa, occupied adjacent steeps, commanded fords, or adorned its sides, as harmony took the place of discord, and tranquillity succeeded strife.[171]

As we have seen in this chapter, similar statements were made by many others, and found in a variety of contexts. One of the most evocative of such utterances was made at the end of our period, by H. G. Wells, in his novel *Tono-Bungay* (1908), which ends with a description of a trip on a new type of destroyer from Hammersmith to the open sea. For all the melancholia and uncertainty about the future that suffuses the novel's plotline, Wells's language here pays testimony

[170] T. Howell, *A day's business in the Port of London* (London, 1850), p. 9.
[171] Mr and Mrs S. C. Hall [Samuel Carter Hall and Anna Maria Hall], *The book of the Thames* (London, 1859), pp. 1–2.

to the power of the Thames as a synecdoche of England, and of the course of England's history as a nation:

> To run down the Thames ... is to run one's hand over the pages in the book of England from end to end. One begins ... as if one were in the heart of old England. Behind us are Kew and Hampton Court with their memories of Kings and Cardinals, and one runs at first between Fulham's episcopal garden parties and Hurlingham's playground for the sporting instinct of our race. The whole effect is English. There is space, there are old trees and all the best qualities of the home-land in that upper reach ... And then for a stretch the newer developments slop over ... until you come out ... with Lambeth's old palace under your quarter and the houses of Parliament on your bow! ...
>
> For a stretch you have the essential London; you have Charing Cross railway station, heart of the world, and the Embankment on the north side with its new hotels overshadowing its Georgian and Victorian architecture, and mud and great warehouses and factories, chimneys, shot towers, advertisements on the south. The northward skyline grows more intricate and pleasing ... Somerset House is as picturesque as the civil war, one is reminded again of the original England, one feels in the fretted sky the quality of Restoration lace ...
>
> And then the traditional and ostensible England falls from you altogether ... Comes London Bridge, and the great warehouses tower up about you waving stupendous cranes, the gulls circle and scream in your ears, large ships lie among their lighters, and one is in the port of the world.[172]

Throughout the long nineteenth century, the Thames was a potent symbol of the nation's past and its continuities; it was the history of England in landscape. But the story it told ran forwards as well as back. Linking the rural and the urban, the past and the present, and increasingly seen as a recreational landscape for the whole people – the whole nation – the Thames was a crucial element in a capacious nationalist topography that encompassed the city as well as the country, and indeed celebrated their interconnectedness. Englishness, as figured by the Thames, was in step with modernity.

---

[172] H. G. Wells, *Tono-Bungay*, 2 vols. (London, 1908), Vol. II, pp. 486–8.

CONCLUSION

This book has explored the multifarious ways in which the English landscape contributed to constructions of English national identity between the late eighteenth and early twentieth centuries. This is not to deny the role of other influences on the shaping of Englishness, but it is to stress the special importance of landscape. In particular, the book has argued that the associations attaching to places valued for their nationalistic significance, especially historical associations, were a crucial determinant of this significance. Physical characteristics and visual distinctiveness, while not unimportant, counted for less than the sense of the past, the collective memories, and the people and events to which these places were linked. Such associations were the active ingredients of the glue that bound landscape to nation. The modern idea of English national identity, as it developed over the course of the long nineteenth century, was founded on a sense of the nation having a very lengthy and largely continuous history; at a time of great change – social, cultural, political, technological, demographic – this sense of continuity had great attraction and power. But the sources for this patriotic identity-bolstering narrative were not just written histories, the development of the historical profession, state-sponsored commemorative activity and other more familiar elements of historical culture. As has not been sufficiently appreciated by scholars – and certainly not scholars working on English national identity – they were also to be found in landscape.[1]

---

[1] Even Daniels's *Fields of vision*, for example, has little to say about the historical associations of landscape in its relationship to national identity.

The places discussed in this book show how landscape provided a sense of connection between the national past and the national present, thus helping to maintain a coherent idea of Englishness in the context of nineteenth- and early-twentieth-century modernity.

As discussed in the first two chapters, landscape helped define the boundaries of the nation, its geographical extent and its relationship with the world outside England, whether continental Europe in the case of the white cliffs of Dover, or the nation of Scotland in the case of the Northumbrian borderland. The white cliffs were valued for their association with the sea, acting as markers of England's – and Britain's – historic status as an island nation. Standing guard on the coast of the channel and surmounted by the ancient castle of Dover, they were a powerful symbol of defence and defiance over centuries, of a long history of resistance to foreign threats; their height often exaggerated, the cliffs were imagined as the walls or ramparts of the nation. At the same time, in a more peaceable vein, and on account of Dover port's longstanding status as the main route in and out of the country, they also functioned as a reassuringly unchanging marker of home and homecoming, as a stable idea of a familiar, historic homeland.

The associations attaching to border landscape were different in Northumberland, but here as on the Channel coast links with the past were important. Indeed, the landscape of the English border was especially heavily freighted with history. The history in this case was largely one of Anglo-Scots enmity, the long story of medieval and early modern strife between the two nations indelibly scoring the bleak uplands and remote valleys. This heritage made the landscape a powerful and distinctive locus of Englishness, one quite different from that founded on a sedately pastoral, south country ideal. A key feature of its difference from this ideal was the work it did in supporting a wider Britishness. The borderland was an important site for the articulation of 'unionist-nationalism', of both the Scottish and the English variety: aided by ballad culture, the legacy of conflict so visible in the landscape was re-imagined as a heritage of romance and valour, one that both nations – now happily united – could look back on with pride. The Northumbrian border was thus a space for the performance of a regional Englishness that acknowledged the differences between Scotland and England while simultaneously, through the historical associations of its cultural landscape, putting these differences to the service of a larger British identity.

As shown by the examples of the white cliffs and the Northumberland borderland, then, English landscapes subject to patriotic valorisation were compatible with, and indeed supported, a wider sense of Britishness (one that, interestingly enough, was largely independent of languages of empire and imperialism, for all that it was not antithetical to them). But the particular connection between the English landscape and discretely *English* discourses of national identity was more apparent elsewhere, being especially evident in the case of landscapes subject to preservationist concern. Two of these landscapes, the Lake District and the New Forest, were discussed in Part II of this book. In the case of the Lake District, its associations with national identity seem almost axiomatic: beyond question it was – and is – one of the most highly valued landscapes in the country, and approbation of its qualities was suffused with patriotic sentiment of one kind or another throughout the period. Some of this, particularly in the early years, was bound up with lyrical appreciations of the distinctive qualities of Lakeland scenery – its picturesqueness, beauty, sublimity and so forth. But as time went on the associational value of the landscape, and notably its connotations of the past, came to be asserted more strongly. Alongside this, and related to it, there developed an idea of the Lake District as part of the national heritage, with Wordsworth's conception of the place as 'national property' being broadened out, in the context of democratisation and the growth of popular tourism, to encompass all sections of society. This development was a key factor behind the emergence of the landscape preservation movement, a movement shot through with patriotic intent, and one for which the controversies over railways and footpaths in the 1880s acted as an important catalyst of activism. Thus it was that preservationism had its origins in the Lakes, and in the patriotic discourses with which its landscape was associated.

Patriotic discourses of preservation were also much in evidence in relation to the New Forest. Here, as in the Lakes, landscape was a focus for the articulation of new and more inclusive understandings of the public or national good. As the nineteenth century progressed, the forest was increasingly valued for its ancient beauty, and its connotations of a popular and distinctively English myth-heritage of liberty and freedom. Although part of the crown estate, much of the forest was subject to rights of common, and at a time of political democratisation – and new understandings of the limitations on the prerogatives of private property – these rights came to stand proxy for a wider, national stake in the landscape. To a large extent, this stake was based on the historical associations of the forest environment, from generalised ideas of the immemorial 'liberty of the greenwood', to more specific appreciation of the significance of particular sites, as well as an understanding of the antiquity of popular claims on the place as embodied in the rights of commoners. Allying a concern for the preservation of the old woods with desire to maintain free public access, defenders of the New Forest propounded a new idea of amenity, one infused with a patriotic conviction that places such as the forest needed to be protected for the sake of modern England and the welfare of its inhabitants. It was a point of view that collided with the conception of public utility articulated by the forest commissioners, but in the ensuing debate the new ideas won important ground: by the early twentieth century, the New Forest was a national landscape not on account of its value as a source of timber, and thus of crown revenue, but because it was understood to be a place over which the people – and therefore the nation – had a controlling moral claim. Crystallised into a point of principle by the debates over the New Forest and the Lake District, as well as other landscapes subject to preservationist concern (London commons, for example), this was an understanding that would underpin later developments – not least the establishment of state-supported National Parks.

Both the New Forest and the Lake District were largely rural environments, of course, and there is certainly no doubt that the English countryside played a vital part in mainstream constructions of English national identity. Aside from the cultural productions associated with many of the landscapes discussed in this book, one might recall the burgeoning late Victorian popularity of Constable as a painter of 'purely and thoroughly English' scenes, and the associated creation of 'Constable Country', in the Stour Valley, as a tourist hotspot.[2] At a rather less elevated artistic level, the cottage watercolours of Allingham, Birket Foster, Alfred Robert Quinton and others presented a roseate 'happy England' of old-world cottages and villages, many of which were often reproduced (or imitated) by the manufacturers of

---

[2] Fleming-Williams and Parris, *Discovery of Constable*; E. Helsinger, 'Constable: The making of a national painter', *Critical Inquiry*, 15 (1989), 253–79; Daniels, *Fields of vision*, pp. 210–13; R. and S. Redgrave, *A century of painters of the English school*, 2nd edn (London, 1890), p. 314.

late Victorian and Edwardian picture postcards.[3] Above all, rural land-scapes were powerfully suggestive of the past, of an older England, and the celebration – and preservation – of places such as the Lakes, the New Forest, or the upper Thames Valley was a means of maintaining a sense of the continuity of national life at a time of change: hence, to a significant degree, the felt value of these locales in nationalistic terms. As David Miller reminds us, one key 'feature of nationality is that it is an identity that embodies historical continuity'; hence the despoliation of or loss of connection to landscapes that were themselves held to be embodiments of this continuity perforce generated patriotic concern.[4]

But it is an important claim of this book that the countryside was not the predominant topographical repository of national iden-tity, for all that 'the ideology of England and Englishness' may appear 'to a remarkable degree rural'.[5] The 'essential England' was not only to be found in rural contexts; it could be found in diverse places and it took diverse forms, and this, indeed, was one of the key sources of its strength. While the south country ideal certainly made a mate-rial contribution to nationalistic discourse – as evident, for exam-ple, in responses to the rustic vernacular of Thames-side villages – it is wrong to say that, by the beginning of the twentieth century, 'the north was imagined as entirely overrun by industrialisation and con-sequently ceased to be available as a representative image at a time when England and therefore Englishness was popularly conceived as profoundly anti-industrial and anti-modern … The nation, redefined culturally and geographically, shrank to southern sites and to isolated, supposedly more authentic locations like Cornwall.'[6] As demonstrated by the exploration, in Chapter 5, of the industrial (and latterly com-mercial) landscape of Manchester, popular understandings of England and Englishness drew not only on the country, but also on the city – and the northern city at that. Despite its being the quintessence of the Victorian 'shock city', and a focus of concern about the negative effects of industrialisation, Manchester was a key part of the geog-raphy of Englishness. Not only could its architecture of enterprise

[3] Huish, *Happy England*; Cundall, *Birket Foster*. Salmon Ltd, *The England of A. R. Quinton*.
[4] Miller, *On nationality*, p. 23.
[5] Howkins, 'Discovery of rural England', p. 85.
[6] D. P. Corbett, Y. Holt and F. Russell, 'Introduction', in D. P. Corbett, Y. Holt and F. Russell (eds.), *The geographies of Englishness* (New Haven and London, 2002), p. xi.

be aestheticised by artists, it was a focus of tourist interest and also of a robustly demotic patriotic sentiment. Local pride in this landscape of mills, warehouses, assertive public buildings and bustling streets – and in the history of that landscape – was mutually supportive of a wider sense of Englishness that encompassed rather than rejected the urban and the industrial. Indeed, the example of Manchester is a particularly good illustration of the extent to which English national identity was importantly rooted in and mediated through local or regional contexts. Thus it was that projects such as Waterhouse's Town Hall were powerful embodiments of locality and history – of civic patriotism – while at the same time also expressive of a wider sense of national identity, and of Manchester's contribution, over time, to the development of that identity.[7] Such a point might similarly be made with reference to the other landscapes discussed in this book. It is also one applicable to quite different cultural preoccupations: one early-twentieth-century example was the craze for historical pageants, which saw communities up and down the country fuse the dramatic re-telling of their histories with that of the wider narrative of the nation.[8] In England as elsewhere in Europe (one thinks particularly of Germany, with its strong *Heimat* culture),[9] the construction of national identities over the course of the long nineteenth century was in a complementary, not antonymous, relationship with local and regional expressions of belonging.

London mattered too, of course. The landscape in and around the metropolis – and specifically that associated with the Thames – was the subject of the final chapter. Long a source of patriotic pride on account of its associations with the capital, cultivated taste and British commercial greatness, the Thames and its banks came to be seen as an inheritance of the people as a whole – a perspective that, in an increasingly democratic age, served further to enhance its nationalistic connotations. Its course from source to sea linked the rural past with the metropolitan present, and so the Thames became a notably powerful

[7] For some perceptive comments in this vein, and with reference to the Manchester Town Hall, see Whyte, 'Building the nation in the town'.
[8] Readman, 'Place of the past'; also Hulme, 'A nation of town criers', and M. Freeman, '"Splendid display; pompous spectacle": Historical pageants in twentieth-century Britain', *Social History*, 38 (2013), 423–55.
[9] Confino, *Nation as a local metaphor*; Applegate, *A nation of provincials*; T. M. Lekan, *Imagining the nation in nature: Landscape preservation and German identity, 1885–1945* (Cambridge, MA, 2004).

symbol of the continuity of national history. Its upstream reaches provided reassurance that touch had not been lost with an older locus of Englishness (one that gave solace to the largely urban-dwelling population of the present), while the vista downstream gave ample evidence of the – admittedly gritty – vitality and prosperity of contemporary England.

The role played by the landscapes of London and Manchester in the construction of national identity provides an important check to the argument that the ideology of Englishness was somehow mired in nostalgia for a wholly green and pleasant land. Urban topographies were integrated into the English national imaginary. But it is further worth emphasising that even 'rural' iterations of Englishness, for all their prizing of the historical associations attaching to place, were not necessarily indicative of a culturally (or politically) conservative sensibility. Cultural engagement with the rural – whatever its ideological complexion – can be seen as an integral part of the modern condition, something that increases in intensity as a society becomes more urbanised, more industrial. Thus it is that preoccupation with the English countryside and its associations with the past – and with the long continuities of national history – was an important means by which English men and women came to terms with the pace of contemporary change. Visions of the rural – and, for that matter, visions of the past – stood in complementary and accommodative relation to modernity; they were not antithetical to it. And for all that these visions involved myth-making and idealisation they had real-world significance for people at the time, being an important support of a coherent sense of national identity. As with the content of nationalistic discourse more generally, it is misleading to see them as 'invented traditions', as fabricated rewritings and manipulations of the past on the part of elites. These visions had various origins, and were generated for various purposes, but they had real meaning for individual English men and women, and this cultural agency was a function of their congruence with normative, pre-existing understandings of the nation and its history.[10]

---

[10] For a recent critique of the 'invention of tradition' paradigm and a discussion of its effects on historical writing, see Vandrei, *Queen Boudica and historical culture*. The work of Anthony D. Smith is particularly eloquent on the problems with the 'invention of tradition'

The popular currency of such ideas of landscape and nation was one expression of a newly popular sense of Englishness – that is to say, an Englishness that was inclusive of ordinary people, and took cognisance of their stake in the national domain. In the context of political democratisation, landscapes were increasingly valued – and increasingly of national significance – because they were understood to belong to the whole people. This is not to suggest that aristocratic landscapes were utterly disdained by nineteenth-century English culture, but it is to emphasise the strength of the shift away from what the art historian Elizabeth Helsinger has called the 'landscape of property', hitherto dominant in the more socially exclusive cultural life of the eighteenth century.[11] As we saw, this shift can be tracked with reference to changing attitudes to the landscapes of the Lake District and the upper Thames Valley, admiration for gentlemanly 'improvements' to the landscape falling out of favour as time passed. It is also apparent in the preservationist focus on footpaths, commons and other open spaces, the National Trust showing scant interest in country houses before 1914.[12] More generally, it can be tracked in artistic and tourist preferences, the open country and the rustic

paradigm as applied to nationalistic discourse. As he wrote some time ago, 'does nationalism write its history as it pleases, or is it also constrained by tradition and the "past" which it records? ... There are, of course, straightforward bits of pure invention – in the sense of fabrication – as in all periods of history ... But in most cases, the mythologies elaborated by nationalists have not been fabrications, but recombinations of traditional, perhaps unanalysed, motifs and myths taken from epics, chronicles, documents of the period, and material artefacts': A. D. Smith, *The ethnic origins of nations* (Oxford, 1986), pp. 177–8. See also Smith, *Myths*; Miller, *On nationality*, esp. pp. 35–6; and, with reference to the English case in particular, Readman, 'Place of the past'. Moreover, even if we do regard nationalist mythologies as fabrications, their cultural currency makes them as 'real' as any other set of ideas. We do not have to be card-carrying post-modernists to see the merit of the view that 'Representations, images, knowledges, fantasies are ... highly concrete stuff, not to be regarded as merely reflective or distortive of the world (though mirroring or distortion may be their declared aim), but as constitutive, as what the world is made of, really': D. Matless, 'An occasion for geography: Landscape, representation, and Foucault's corpus', *Environment and Planning D: Society and Space*, 10 (1992), 41–56 (p. 44).

[11] E. K. Helsinger, 'Land and national representation in Britain', in M. Rosenthal, C. Payne, S. Wilcox et al. (eds.), *Prospects for the nation: Recent essays in British landscape 1750–1880* (New Haven and London, 1997), p. 19.

[12] Only one country house, Barrington Court in Somerset, was acquired by the Trust before 1914, and it proved difficult to raise funds for the purchase: National Trust, *Annual Report* (1905–6), pp. 7, 56.

vernacular proving, as time passed, more popular than the mansions of the elite. To give just one example here, in his *Tourists' guide to Derbyshire* (1887), the Revd J. Charles Cox was very complimentary about Chatsworth Park, noting the pleasing variety of scenery. But, like the late-nineteenth-century visitors to the Thames-side Nuneham Courtenay discussed in Chapter 6, he was not so keen on the house and its gardens. The 'great mass of buildings' was, he felt, 'very much out of place. A palace of this description can never harmonize with the nature of this scenery ... The whole character of the building, with its adjuncts, gardens, and grounds, is essentially formal, square, and artificial.'[13]

We should not exaggerate the cultural significance of what one commentator, writing of the art of Constable and others, called 'humble and unpretentious' English landscapes, an England 'not of the Court, but of the people'.[14] Right up to 1914, the aristocracy retained a significant hold over English politics and society.[15] But its grip was slipping, and the patriotic discourses associated with many of the landscapes discussed in this book provide evidence of its slackening hold.[16] In part because of their demotic character – their focus on the people of England – these discourses may also provide evidence of the construction, over the course of the long nineteenth century, of a distinctively English cultural nationalism. It is often assumed that cultural nationalism – and indeed nationalism gener- ally – has not had much of a presence in England. While English patriotism certainly existed, nationalism was something for other peoples and places – something that could be found in rich and rank profusion in continental Europe (and, latterly, in colonial and post- colonial contexts), as well as closer to home on the 'Celtic Fringes' of Britain. There remains, as Robert Colls and Philip Dodd noted in

---

[13] Revd J. C. Cox, *Tourists' guide to Derbyshire*, 3rd edn (London, 1887), p. 94.

[14] Dick, *Cottage homes of England*, p. 264.

[15] D. Cannadine, *The decline and fall of the British aristocracy* (New Haven, 1992); A. Adonis, *Making aristocracy work: The peerage and the political system in Britain, 1884–1914* (Oxford, 1993).

[16] For evidence of this slipping grip in a cultural context, see Mandler, *Fall and rise of the stately home*. For a case study of the late-nineteenth-century failure of a cer- tain kind of aristocratic politics, see P. Readman, 'Conservatives and the politics of land: Lord Winchilsea's National Agricultural Union, 1893–1901', *English Historical Review*, 121 (2006), 25–69.

2014, 'a reticence to discuss the English as a nationalistic people at all'.[17] But it is an error to show such reticence; in nationalism as in other things, England was less exceptional than is often supposed. In an unfinished essay, Raphael Samuel suggested that it was possible to identify 'an *English* ethnic revival, a movement ... which celebrated the English not as a race of achievers or of conquerors ... but as a *folk*', and that came to fruition in the late Victorian and Edwardian periods.[18] Samuel had in mind such developments as the rediscovery of local customs and traditions, the folk-song and dance revival, the garden city and Arts and Crafts movements, and the cottage aesthetic popularised by the paintings of Allingham and others. But his observation can be extended to apply to the wider field of engagement with landscape discussed in this book. In the context of increasingly assertive expressions of national identity – not least in the other three nations of the United Kingdom – the storied ground of England, from Northumberland to Manchester to the New Forest, attained a newly potent patriotic significance. Of course, in contrast to its counterparts elsewhere, English cultural nationalism was not linked to any focused movement of popular mobilisation. To invoke Michael Billig, it was 'banal'; unlike in Ireland, say, it was not typically associated with political or national grievances.[19] But insofar as cultural nationalism by definition aims at 'the moral regeneration of the national community rather than the achievement of an autonomous state',[20] there is some merit in understanding the language of landscape and nation traced by this book in such terms. As we have seen, it was a language in which the past played an especially significant role. Yet, in common with expressions of cultural nationalism elsewhere, 'this invocation of the past ... must be seen in a positive light' – positive in the sense of being directed towards the present and future – since 'the cultural nationalist seeks not to "regress" into an arcadia but rather to inspire his community to ever higher stages

---

[17] Colls and Dodd, *Englishness*, preface, p. xi.

[18] Samuel, *Island stories*, p. 64 (emphases in original).

[19] Billig, *Banal nationalism*. For the example of Ireland, see J. Hutchinson, *The dynamics of cultural nationalism: The Gaelic Revival and the creation of the Irish nation-state* (London, 1987).

[20] Hutchinson, *Dynamics of cultural nationalism*, p. 9; also his more recent general survey, 'Cultural nationalism', in J. Breuilly (ed.), *The Oxford handbook of the history of nationalism* (Oxford, 2013), pp. 75–94.

of development'.[21] As reflected in and stimulated by engagement with valued landscapes both urban and rural, English cultural nationalism went with the grain of modernity, integrating the contemporary with the traditional, the past with the present.[22] In this respect, at least before 1914, it was remarkably successful.

[21] Hutchinson, *Dynamics of cultural nationalism*.
[22] Cf. *ibid.*, esp. Chapter 1.

SELECT BIBLIOGRAPHY

Space does not permit the inclusion of a full bibliography of all the works cited in this book. The items detailed here include many that have proved especially useful as sources of information, insight and inspiration. But it is by no means an exhaustive list, and so far as secondary sources go, the inclusion (or exclusion) of any given work should not be taken as implying a particular value judgement on my part. In the main, my research has relied on published material, but I have also used some archival sources. For details of these, and of the other sources on which this book draws, please see the footnote references to each chapter.

Primary Sources

Official Publications

British Parliamentary Papers
Hansard's Parliamentary Debates

Periodicals

Art Journal
A Beautiful World
Blackwood's Edinburgh Magazine
Bow Bells
Builder
Climbers' Club Journal
Contemporary Review
Cornhill Magazine
Country Life

Dover Observer
Economist
Edinburgh Review
English Lakes Visitor and Keswick Guardian
Fortnightly Review
Gentleman's Magazine
History of the Berwickshire Naturalists' Club
Independent Review
Lock to Lock Times
London Society
Macmillan's Magazine
Magazine of Art
Manchester Faces and Places
Manchester Guardian
Monthly Chronicle of North-Country Lore and Legend
National Review
Nature Notes
Nineteenth Century
North of England Magazine
Northern Counties Magazine
Pall Mall Gazette
Punch
Saga-Book of the Viking Club
Saturday Magazine
Saturday Review
Spectator
The Times
Westminster Review

Books and articles

Aiken, J., *England delineated; or, A geographical description of every county in England and Wales*, 2nd edn (London, 1790)

Allison, J., *Allison's northern tourist's guide to the Lakes*, 7th edn (Penrith, 1837)

Andrews, C. B. (ed.), *The Torrington diaries: Containing the tours through England and Wales of the Hon. John Byng (later fifth viscount Torrington) between the years 1781 and 1794*, 4 vols (London, 1934–8)

Aston, J., *The Manchester guide: A brief historical description of the towns of Manchester and Salford, the public buildings, and the charitable and literary institutions* (Manchester, 1804)

[Axon, W. E. A.], *Guide to the new town hall* (Manchester, [1878])

Baddeley, M. J. B., *Black's shilling guide to the English Lakes*, 20th edn (London, 1896)

   The thorough guide to the English Lake District, 1st edn (London, 1880)

Baedeker, K., *Great Britain* (Leipzig and London, 1887)

Bates, C. J., *The border holds of Northumberland*, Vol. 1 (Newcastle-upon-Tyne, 1891)

Belloc, H., *The historic Thames* (Exeter, 1988 [1907])

Black's guide to Kent (Edinburgh, 1878)

Black's guide to Manchester and Salford (Edinburgh, 1868)

Bradley, A. G., *The romance of Northumberland* (London, 1908)

Bradshaw, G., *Bradshaw's hand-book to the manufacturing districts of Great Britain* (London, [1854])

Brayley, E. W., J. Britton, T. Maiden, J. Harris, B. Crosby *et al.*, *The beauties of England and Wales*, 18 vols. (London, 1801–15)

Bullock, T. A., *Bradshaw's illustrated guide to Manchester and surrounding districts* (Manchester, 1857)

Burke, E., *A philosophical enquiry into the origin of our ideas of the sublime and beautiful* (Oxford, 1990 [2nd edn, London, 1759 (1757)])

Catt, G. R., *The pictorial history of Manchester* (London [?1845])

Chignell, R., *The life and paintings of Vicat Cole, R.A.*, 3 vols. (London, 1898)

Cobbett, W., *Rural rides*, ed. I. Dyck (Harmondsworth, 2001 [1830])

Collingwood, W. G., *The Lake counties*, 1st edn (London, 1902)

[Combe, W.], *An history of the principal rivers of Great Britain*, 2 vols. (London, 1794)

Cook, C. H., *Thames rights and Thames wrongs: A disclosure* (London, 1894)

Cornish's stranger's guide to Liverpool and Manchester (London, 1838)

Creighton, M., *The story of some English shires* (London, 1897)

Darbyshire, A., *A booke of olde Manchester and Salford* (Manchester, 1887)

Defoe, D., *A tour thro' the whole island of Great Britain*, 2 vols. (London, 1968 [1724–6])

Dibdin, C., *Observations on a tour through almost the whole of England*, 2 vols. (London, 1801)

Dick, S., *The cottage homes of England: Drawn by Helen Allingham and described by Stewart Dick* (London, 1909)

Dickens, C., *Dickens's dictionary of the Thames* (Oxford, 1972 [London, 1893])

Duffield, H. G., *The stranger's guide to Manchester* (Swinton, 1984 [Manchester, 1850])

Ferguson, R., *The northmen in Cumberland and Westmoreland* (London, 1856)

Gaskell, E., *North and south* (Harmondsworth, 1970 [1854–5])

Gilpin, W., *Observations on the coasts of Hampshire, Sussex, and Kent, relative chiefly to picturesque beauty: Made in the summer of the year 1774* (London, 1804)

    Observations, relative chiefly to picturesque beauty, made in the year 1772, on several parts of England: Particularly the mountains, and lakes of Cumberland, and Westmoreland, 2 vols. (London, 1786)

    Remarks on forest scenery, and other woodland views (relative chiefly to picturesque beauty) illustrated by the scenes of New-Forest in Hampshire, 3 vols. (London, 1791)

Graham, P. A., *Highways and byways in Northumbria* (London, 1920)

Gray, T., *A supplement to the tour through Great-Britain, containing a catalogue of the antiquities, houses, parks, plantations, scenes, and situations, in England and Wales* (London, 1787)

Grindon, L. H., *Manchester walks and wild-flowers* (London and Manchester, [1859])

Hare, A. J. C., *The story of two noble lives*, 3 vols. (London, 1893)

Harper, C. G., *The Kentish coast* (London, 1914)

Head, G., *A home tour through the manufacturing districts of England in the summer of 1835* (London, 1836)

Heath, F. G., *Our English woodlands* (London, 1878)

Heywood, A., *Heywood's pictorial guide to Manchester and companion to the Art Treasures Exhibition* (Manchester, 1857)

Heywood, J., *John Heywood's illustrated guide to Dover* (London [1894])

Hill, O., 'Natural beauty as a national asset', *Nineteenth Century*, 58 (December 1905), 935–41

Octavia Hill's letters to fellow workers, 1872–1911, ed. R. Whelan (London, 2005)

Hodgson, J., *A history of Northumberland* (Newcastle-upon-Tyne, 1820–58)

Howitt, W., *Visits to remarkable places* (London, 1840)

Huish, M. B., *Happy England as painted by Helen Allingham* (London, 1903)

Hunter, R., 'Places of interest and things of beauty', *Nineteenth Century*, 43 (April 1898), 570–89

    The preservation of places of interest or beauty (Manchester, 1907)

Hutchinson, H. G., *The New Forest* (London, 1904)

Hutchinson, W., *A view of Northumberland*, 2 vols. (Newcastle-upon-Tyne, 1778)

Ireland, S., *Picturesque views on the river Thames from its source in Glocestershire to the Nore*, 2 vols. (London, 1792)

Jenkinson, H. I., *Jenkinson's practical guide to the English Lake District* (London, 1872)

    Jenkinson's practical guide to the English Lake District, 4th edn (London, 1879)

Jerome, J. K., *Three men in a boat* (London, 2004 [1889])

Kay, J. P., *The moral and physical condition of the working classes employed in the cotton manufacture in Manchester*, 2nd edn (London, 1832)

Knight, R. P., *The landscape, a didactic poem … Addressed to Uvedale Price, Esq.*, 2nd edn (London, 1793)

Krause, A. S., *A pictorial history of the Thames* (London, 1889)

Lascelles, G., *Thirty-five years in the New Forest* (London, 1915)

Leslie, G. D., *Our river* (London, 1888)

Measom, G., *The official illustrated guide to the North-Western Railway … Including descriptions of the most important manufactories in the large towns on the line* (London, 1859)

Menpes, M. and G. E. Mitton, *The Thames* (London, 1906)

Mudie, R., *Hampshire: Its past and present condition and future prospects*, 3 vols. (Winchester, [1838])

National Trust, *Annual reports*

Neville, H. M., *Under a border tower: Sketches and memories of Ford Castle, Northumberland* (Newcastle-upon-Tyne, 1896)

The new Manchester guide (Manchester, 1815)

Nicholls, T., *The steam-boat companion* (London, 1823)

Ogden, J., *A description of Manchester* (Manchester, 1783)

Ousby, I. (ed.), *James Plumptre's Britain: The journals of a tourist in the 1790s* (London, 1992)

Pearson's gossipy guide to the Thames from source to sea (London, [1902])

Pennell, J. and E. R. Pennell, *The stream of pleasure: A month on the Thames* (London, 1891)

Price, U., *An essay on the picturesque* (London, 1794)

Pyne, W. H., *Lancashire illustrated, in a series of views* (London, 1829–31)

Radcliffe, A., *A journey made in the summer of 1794, through Holland and the western frontier of Germany, with a return down the Rhine: To which are added observations during a tour to the lakes of Lancashire, Westmoreland, and Cumberland*, 2 vols., 2nd edn (London, 1795)

Rawlinson, W. G., *The engraved work of J. M. W. Turner*, 2 vols. (London, 1908)

Rawnsley, H. D., *By fell and dale at the English Lakes* (Glasgow, 1911)

'Footpath preservation: A national need', *Contemporary Review*, 50 (September 1886), 373–86

Round the Lake country (Glasgow, 1909)

Reach, A. B. [Angus Bethune], *London on the Thames*, 2 vols. (London, [1848])

[Redding, C.], *An illustrated itinerary of the county of Lancaster* (London, 1842)

Rogers, W. H., *Guide to the New Forest*, 5th edn (Southampton, [1894])

Ruskin, J., *Library edition of the works of John Ruskin*, ed. E. T. Cook and A. Wedderburn, 39 vols. (London, 1903–12)

Salter, J. H. and J. A. Salter, *Salter's guide to the Thames,* 13th edn (Oxford, 1910)

Scott, W., *Marmion: A tale of Flodden Field* (Edinburgh, 1808)
   Minstrelsy of the Scottish border, 3 vols. (Kelso, 1802–3)

Shaw, W. A., *Manchester old and new,* 3 vols. (London, 1894)

Shaw Lefevre, G. [Lord Eversley], *English commons and forests: The story of the battle during the last thirty years for public rights over the commons and forests of England and Wales* (London, 1894)

Skrine, H., *A general account of all the rivers of note in Great Britain* (London, 1801)

Taunt, H. W., *A new map (illustrated with eighty photographs) of the river Thames … taken during the summer of 1871* (Oxford, 1872)

Tomlinson, W., *The pictorial record of the Royal Jubilee Exhibition, Manchester, 1887* (Manchester, 1887)

Tomlinson, W. W., *Comprehensive guide to the county of Northumberland,* 10th edn (London, 1923 [1889])

Vincent, J. E., *The story of the Thames* (London, 1909)

Walker, A. [Adam], *Remarks made in a tour from London to the Lakes of Westmoreland and Cumberland, in the summer of 1791* (London, 1792)

Warner, R., *A tour through the northern counties of England, and the borders of Scotland,* 2 vols. (Bath, 1802)

West, T., *A guide to the Lakes in Cumberland, Westmorland and Lancashire* (London, 1778)

Westall, W. and S. Owen, *Picturesque tour of the River Thames* (London, 1828)

Wise, J. R., *The New Forest: Its history and its scenery,* 4th edn (London, 1883 [1863])

Wordsworth, W., *A description of the scenery of the lakes in the north of England,* 3rd edn (London, 1822)

Wyllie, W. L. and G. Allen, *The tidal Thames: Catalogue of the drawings of Mr W. L. Wyllie exhibited at the Fine Art Society 148 New Bond Street with introductory chapter by Mr Grant Allen* (London, 1884)
   The tidal Thames with twenty full-page photogravure plates (London, 1892)

Secondary Sources

Andrews, M., *The search for the picturesque: Landscape aesthetics and tourism in Britain, 1760–1800* (Aldershot, 1989)

Archer, J. H. G. (ed.), *Art and architecture in Victorian Manchester* (Manchester, 1985)

Baigent, E. and B. Cowell (eds.), *'Nobler imaginings and mightier struggles': Octavia Hill, social activism and the remaking of British society* (London, 2016)

Bate, J., *Romantic ecology: Wordsworth and the environmental tradition* (London, 1991)

Behrman, C. F., *Victorian myths of the sea* (Athens, OH, 1977)

Bolland, R. R., *Victorians on the Thames* (Tunbridge Wells, 1974)

Brace, C., 'Finding England everywhere: Regional identity and the construction of national identity, 1890–1940', *Ecumene*, 6 (1998), 90–109

'Looking back: The Cotswolds and English national identity, *c.* 1890–1950', *Journal of Historical Geography*, 25 (1999), 502–16

Brett, D., *The construction of heritage* (Cork, 1996)

Briggs, A., *Victorian cities*, 2nd edn (Harmondsworth, 1968 [1963])

Burstall, P., *The golden age of the Thames* (Newton Abbot, 1981)

Cannadine, D, *The decline and fall of the British aristocracy* (New Haven and London, 1992)

Colley, L., *Britons: Forging the nation, 1707–1837*, 2nd edn (New Haven and London, 2009 [1994])

Colls, R., *Identity of England* (Oxford, 2002)

(ed.), *Northumbria: History and identity 547–2000* (Chichester, 2007)

Colls, R. and P. Dodd (eds.), *Englishness: Politics and culture 1880–1920*, 2nd edn (London, 2014 [1986])

Cosgrove, D. and S. Daniels (eds.), *The iconography of landscape: Essays on the symbolic representation, design, and use of past environments* (Cambridge, 1988)

Crook, J. M., 'Northumbrian Gothick', *Journal of the Royal Society of Arts*, 121 (April 1973), 271–83

Daniels, S., *Fields of vision: Landscape imagery and national identity in England and the United States* (Cambridge, 1994)

Daunton, M. and B. Rieger (eds.), *Meanings of modernity: Britain from the late-Victorian era to World War II* (Oxford and New York, 2001)

Dellheim, C., *The face of the past: The preservation of the medieval inheritance in Victorian England* (Cambridge, 1982)

Dennis, R., *Cities in modernity: Representations and productions of metropolitan space, 1840–1930* (Cambridge, 2008)

Hartwell, C., *Manchester* (New Haven and London, 2002)

Hill, D., *Turner in the north: A tour through Derbyshire, Yorkshire, Durham, Northumberland, the Scottish borders, the Lake District, Lancashire and Lincolnshire* (New Haven and London, 1996)

Turner on the Thames: River journeys in the year 1805 (New Haven and London, 1993)

Howard, P., 'Painters' preferred places', *Journal of Historical Geography*, 11 (1985), 138–54

Howard, P. J., 'Changing taste in landscape art: An analysis based on works exhibited at the Royal Academy, 1769–1980, and depictions of Devonshire landscape', Ph.D. dissertation (University of Exeter, 1983)

Hunt, T., *Building Jerusalem: The rise and fall of the Victorian city* (London, 2004)

Joyce, P., *Visions of the people: Industrial England and the question of class, 1840–1914* (Cambridge, 1991)

Kern, S. *The culture of time and space, 1880–1918,* 2nd edn (Cambridge, MA, 2003)

Kidd, A. J., *Manchester: A history* (Lancaster, 2006)

Klingender, F. D., *Art and the Industrial Revolution,* 2nd edn (Chatham, 1968 [1947])

Kumar, K., *The making of English national identity* (Cambridge, 2003)

Layton-Jones, K., *Beyond the metropolis: The changing image of urban Britain, 1780–1880* (Manchester, 2016)

Lees, A., *Cities perceived: Urban society in European and American thought, 1820–1940* (Manchester, 1985)

Lowenthal, D., 'British national identity and the English landscape', *Rural History*, 2 (1991), 205–30

   The past is a foreign country (Cambridge, 2015 [1986])

Luckin, B., *Pollution and control: A social history of the Thames in the nineteenth century* (Bristol, 1986)

Mandler, P., 'Against "Englishness": English culture and the limits to rural nostalgia, 1850–1940', *Transactions of the Royal Historical Society*, 6th series, 7 (1997), 155–75

   The English national character: The history of an idea from Edmund Burke to Tony Blair (New Haven and London, 2006)

   The fall and rise of the stately home (New Haven and London, 1997)

   History and national life (London, 2002)

Marsh, J., *Back to the land: The pastoral impulse in England, from 1880 to 1914* (London, 1982)

Marshall, J. D. and J. K. Walton, *The Lake counties from 1830 to the mid-twentieth century: A study in regional change* (Manchester, 1981)

Massey, D., *Space, place and gender* (Cambridge, 1994)

Meinig, D. W. (ed.), *The interpretation of ordinary landscapes* (Oxford, 1979)

Melman, B., *The culture of history: English uses of the past 1800–1953* (Oxford, 2006)

Moir, E., *The discovery of Britain: The English tourists 1540–1840* (London, 1964)

Nead, L., *Victorian Babylon: People, streets and images in Victorian London* (New Haven and London, 2000)

Påhlsson, C., *The Northumbrian burr: A sociolinguistic study* (Lund, 1972)

Pevsner, N. and I. Richmond, *Northumberland* (New Haven and London, 2002)

Readman, P., *Land and nation in England: Patriotism, national identity and the politics of land, 1880–1914* (Woodbridge, 2008)

  'The place of the past in English culture, *c.* 1890–1914', *Past & Present*, 186 (2005), 147–99

  'Preserving the English landscape, 1870–1914', *Cultural and Social History*, 5 (2008), 197–218

Reed, J., *The border ballads* (Stocksfield, 1991)

Ritvo, H., *The dawn of green: Manchester, Thirlmere, and modern environmentalism* (Chicago, 2009)

Roberts, M. J. D., 'Gladstonian Liberalism and environment protection, 1865–76', *English Historical Review*, 128 (2013), 292–322

Samuel, R., *Theatres of memory*, Vol. I: *Past and present in contemporary culture* (London, 1994)

  Theatres of memory, Vol. II: *Island stories: Unravelling Britain* (London, 1998)

Schneer, J., *The Thames* (New Haven and London, 2005)

Smith, A. D., *The ethnic origins of nations* (Oxford, 1986)

  Myths and memories of the nation (Oxford, 1999)

Spirn, A. W., *The language of landscape* (New Haven and London, 1998)

Stewart, C., *The stones of Manchester* (London, 1956)

Stilgoe, J. R., *What is landscape?* (Cambridge, MA, 2015)

Sweet, R., *The English town, 1680–1840: Government, society and culture* (Harlow, 1999)

Taylor, H., *A claim on the countryside: A history of the British outdoor movement* (London, 1997)

Townend, M., *The Vikings and Victorian Lakeland: The Norse medievalism of W. G. Collingwood and his contemporaries* ([Kendal], 2009)

Tuan, Y.-F., *Space and place* (Minneapolis, 2008 [1977])

Vandrei, M., *Queen Boudica and historical culture in Britain since 1600: An image of truth* (Oxford, 2018)

Victoria and Albert Museum, *The discovery of the Lake District: A northern Arcadia and its uses* (London, 1984)

Wheeler, M. (ed.), *Ruskin and the environment* (Manchester, 1995)

Wiener, M. J., *English culture and the decline of the industrial spirit, 1850–1980* (Cambridge, 1981)

Williams, R., *The country and the city* (London, 1973)

Winter, J., *Secure from rash assault: Sustaining the Victorian environment* (Berkeley, 1999)

INDEX